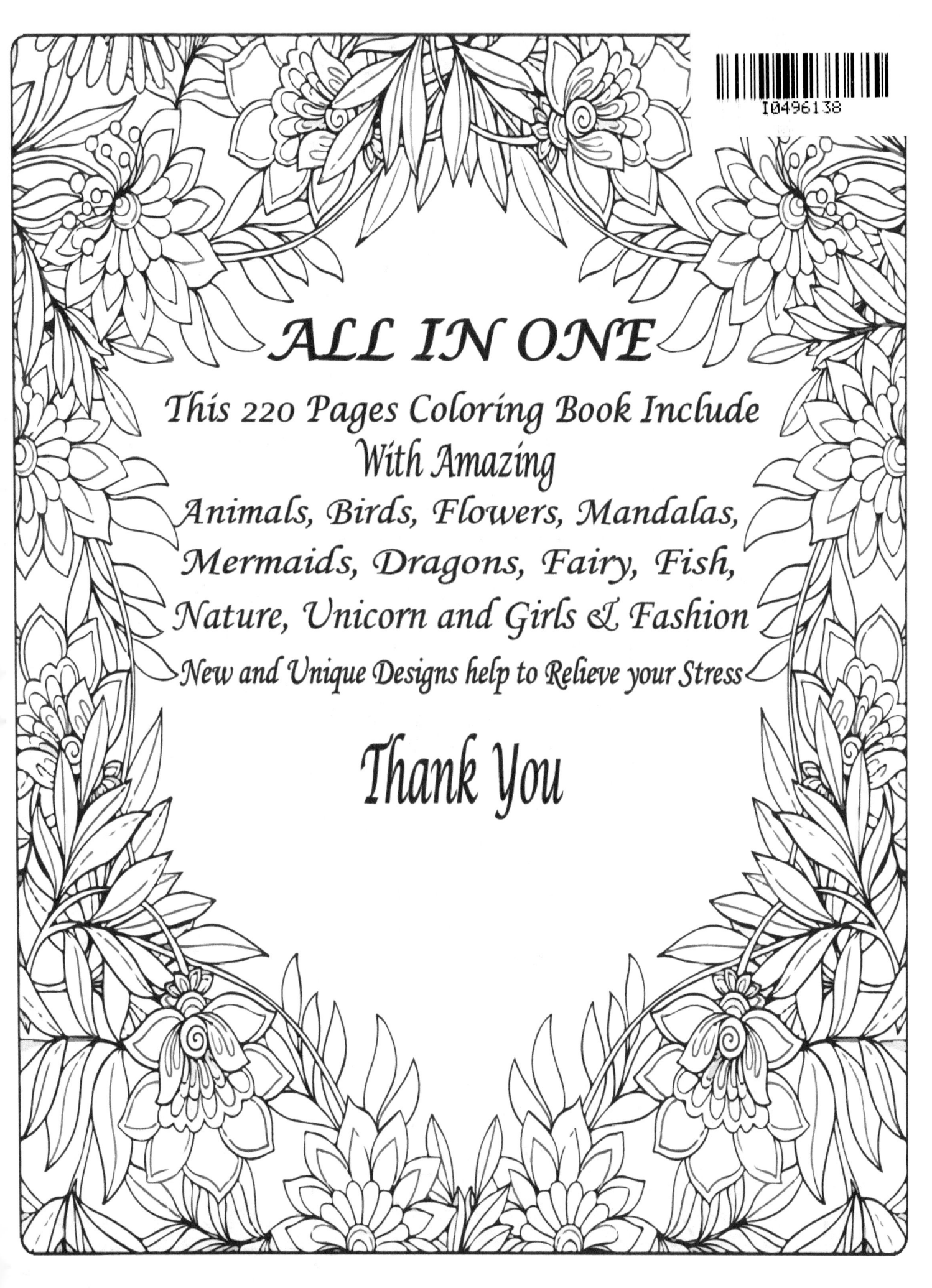

ALL IN ONE

This 220 Pages Coloring Book Include
With Amazing
Animals, Birds, Flowers, Mandalas,
Mermaids, Dragons, Fairy, Fish,
Nature, Unicorn and Girls & Fashion
New and Unique Designs help to Relieve your Stress

Thank You

Sample Design

Bird
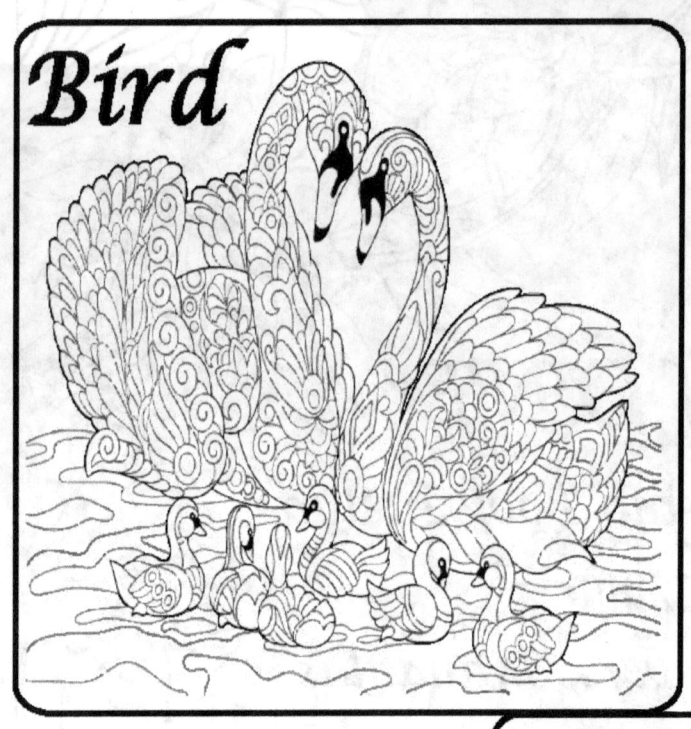

Animal
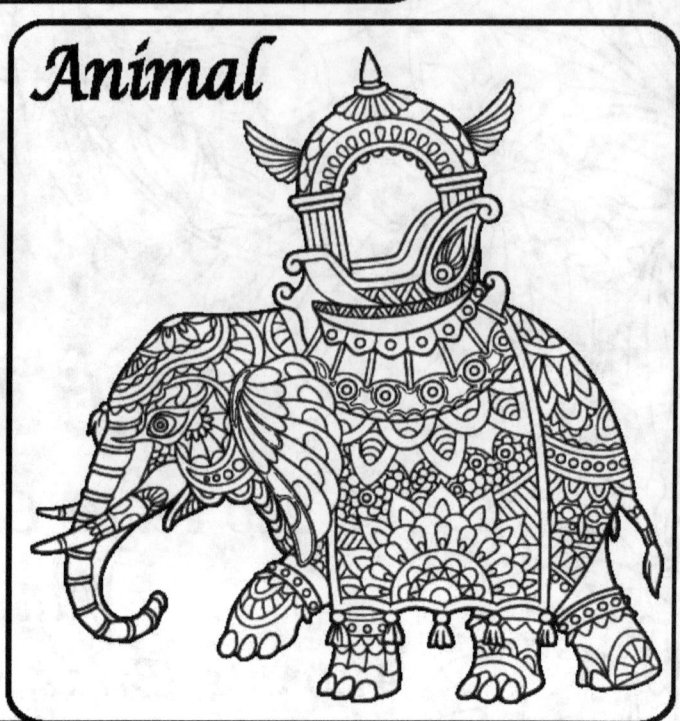

Color Test
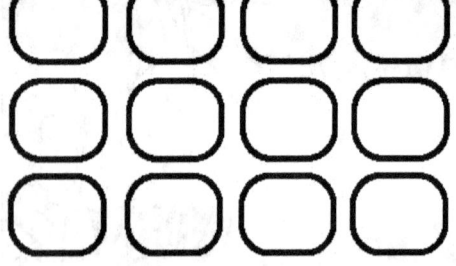

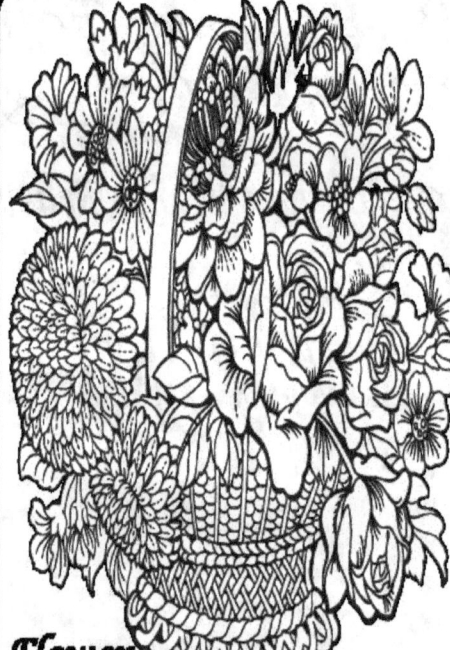
Flower

Color Test
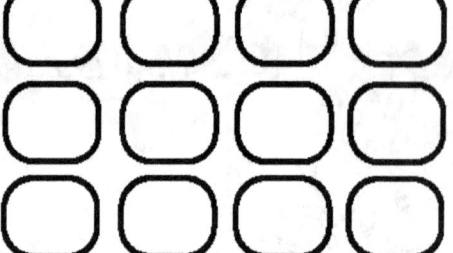

Unicorn
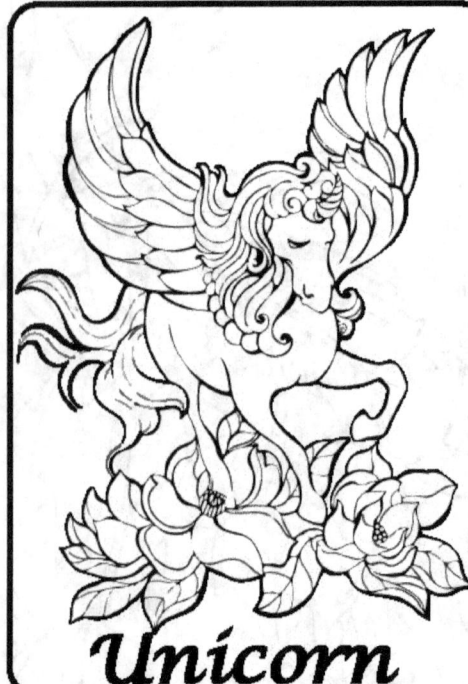

Color Test
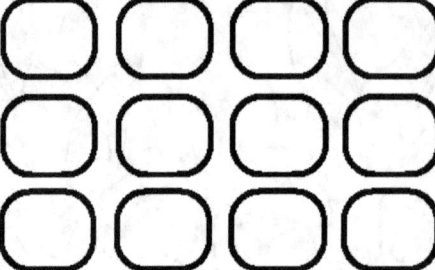

Mandala
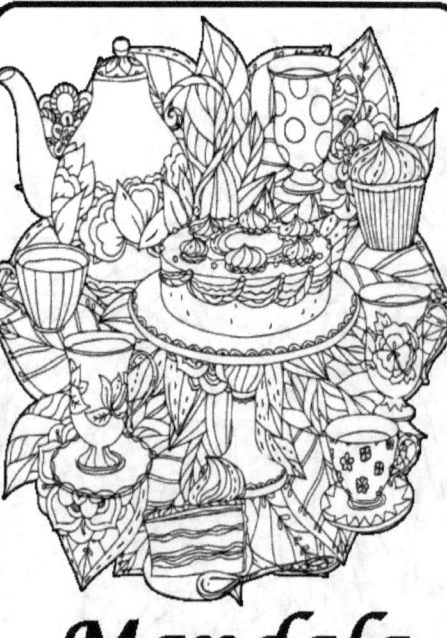

Sample Design

Color Test

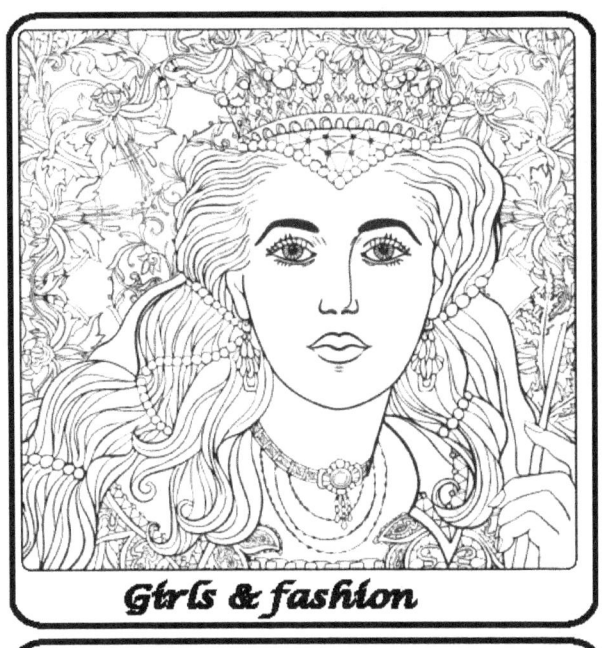
Girls & fashion

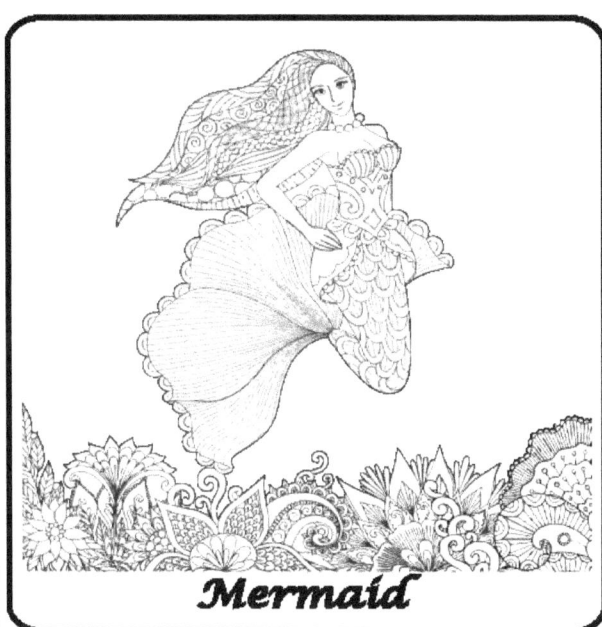
Mermaid

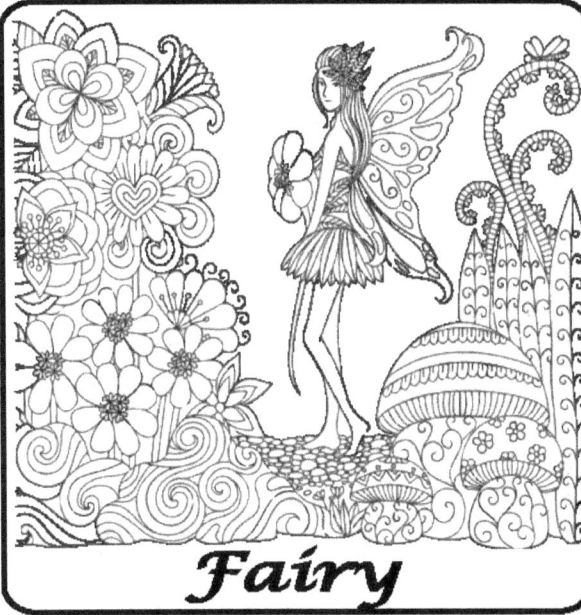
Fairy

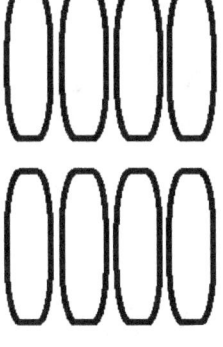

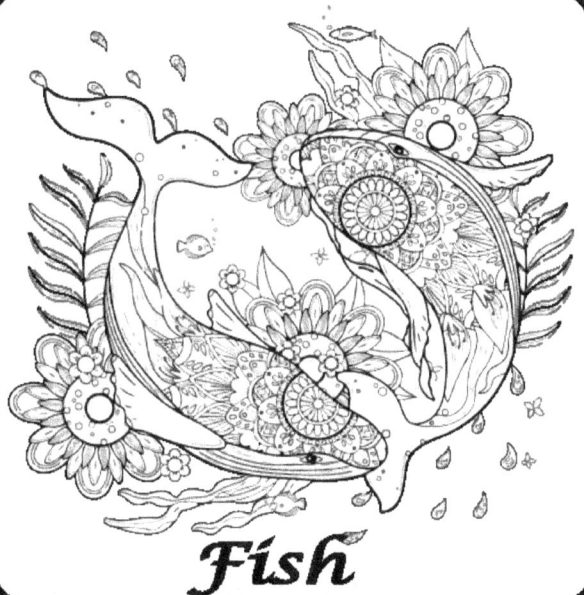
Fish

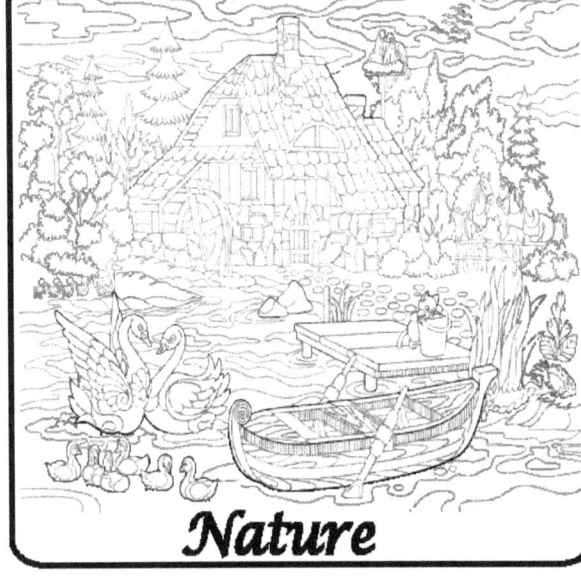
Nature

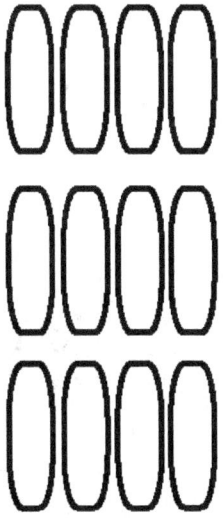

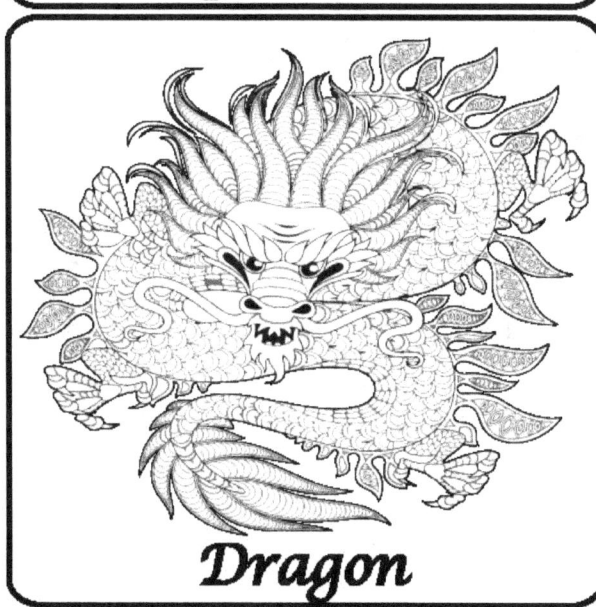
Dragon

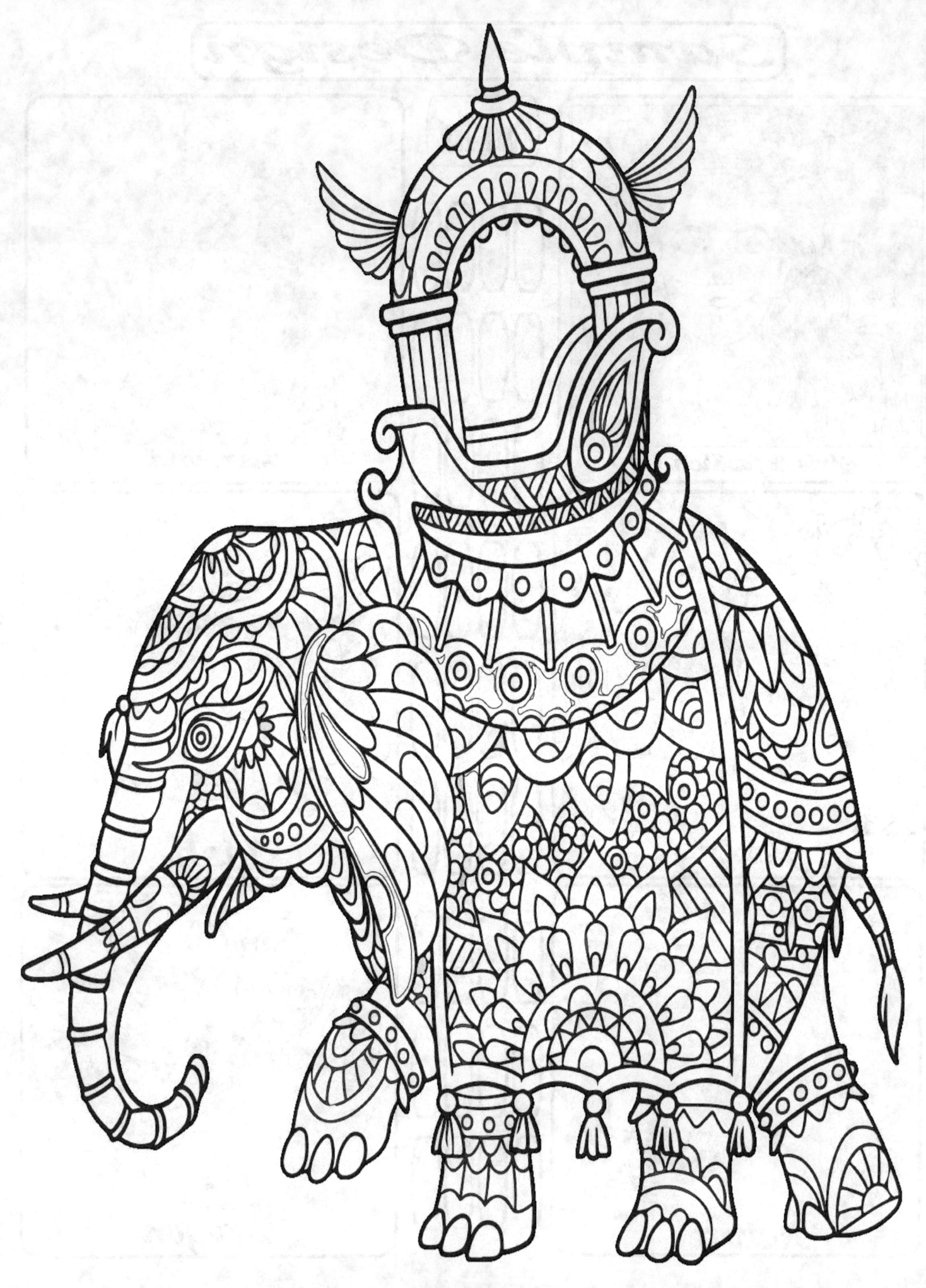

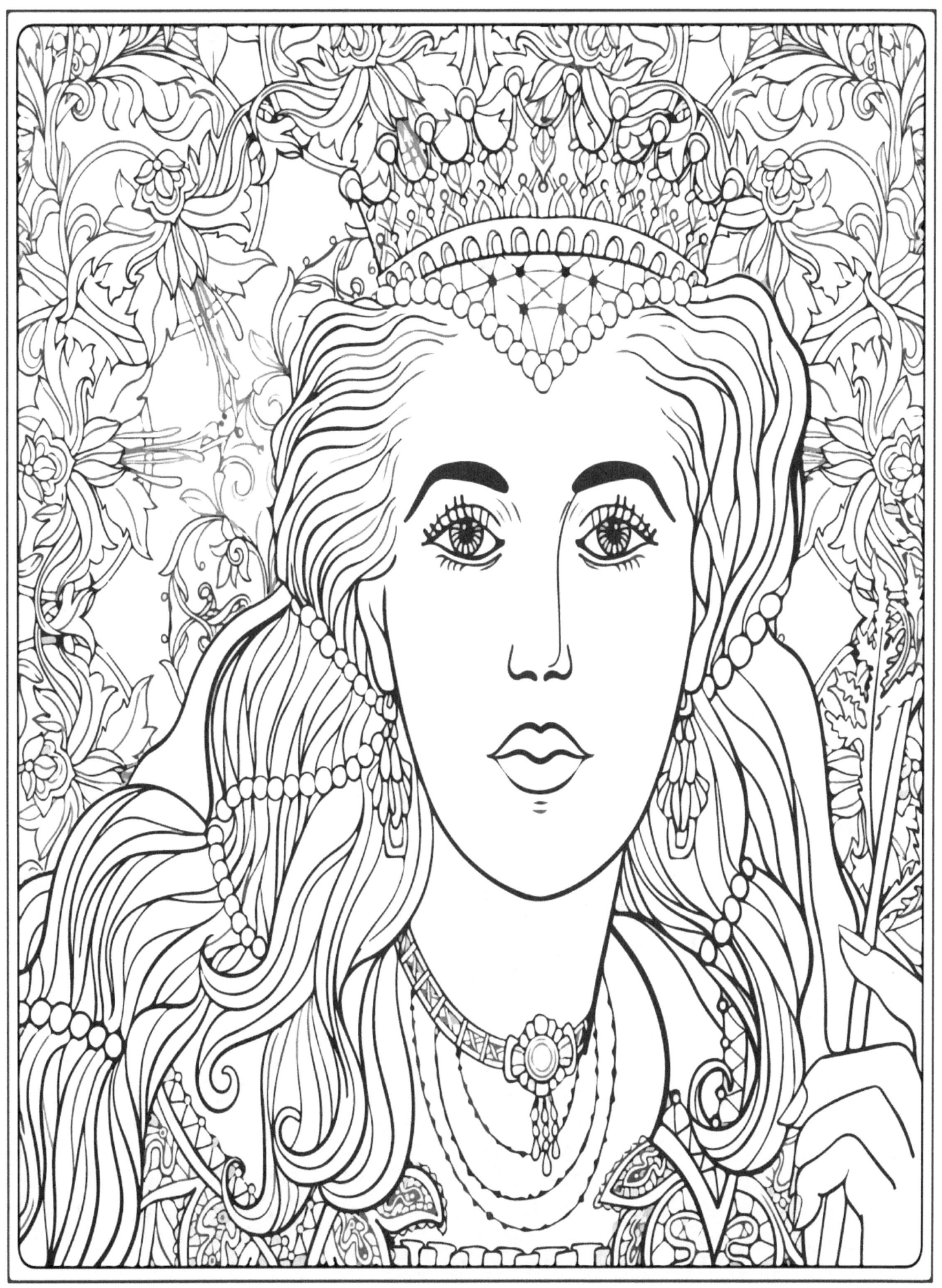

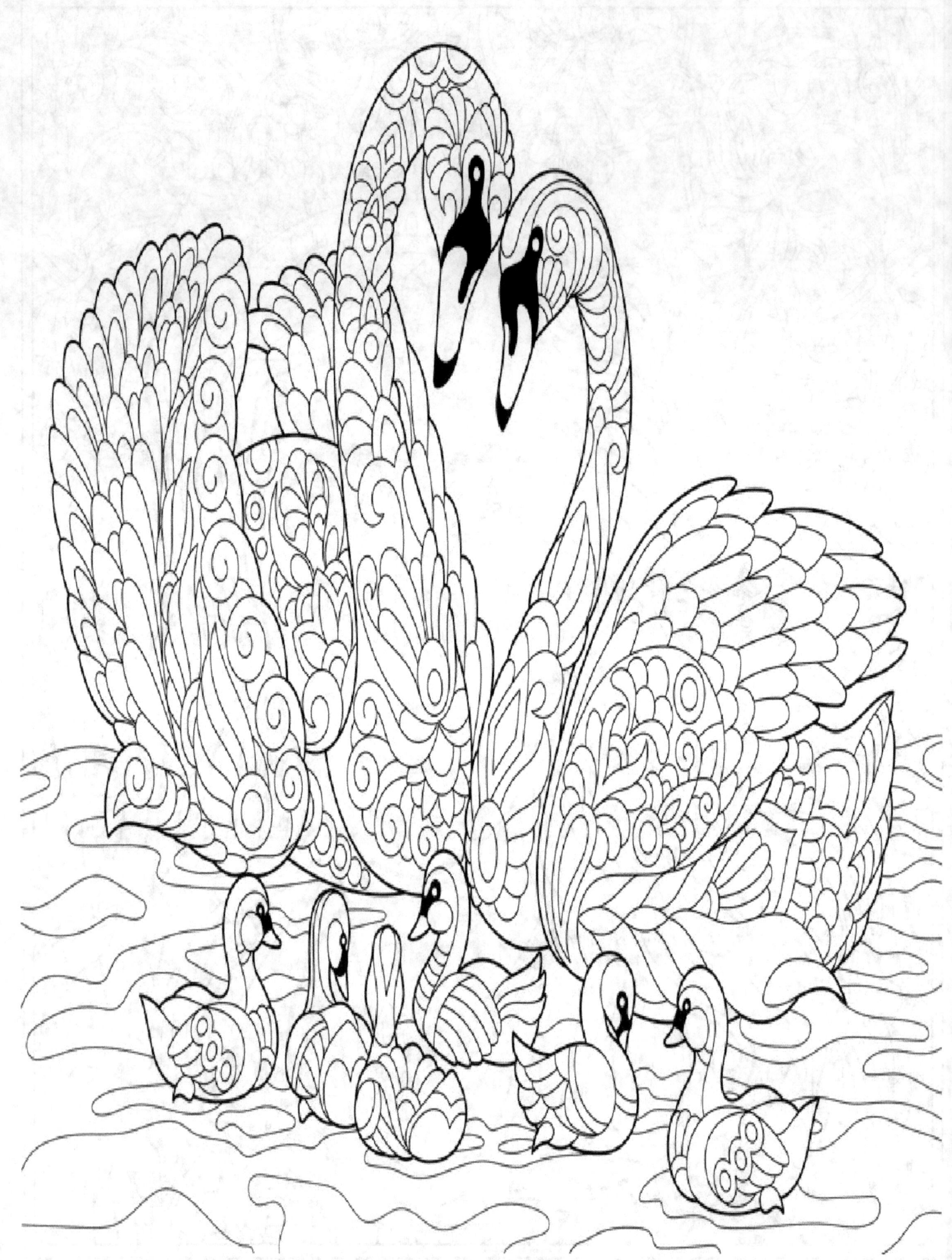

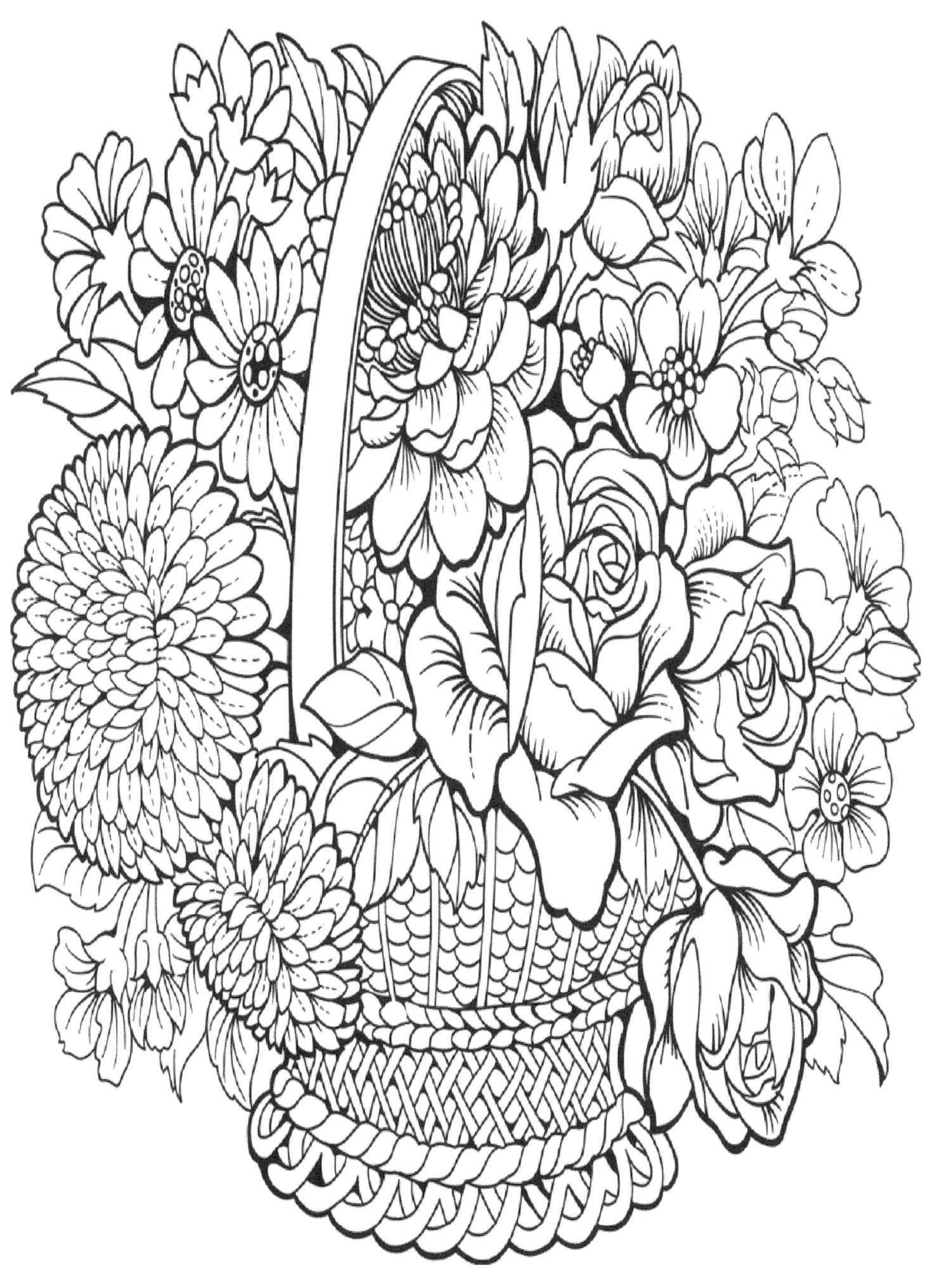

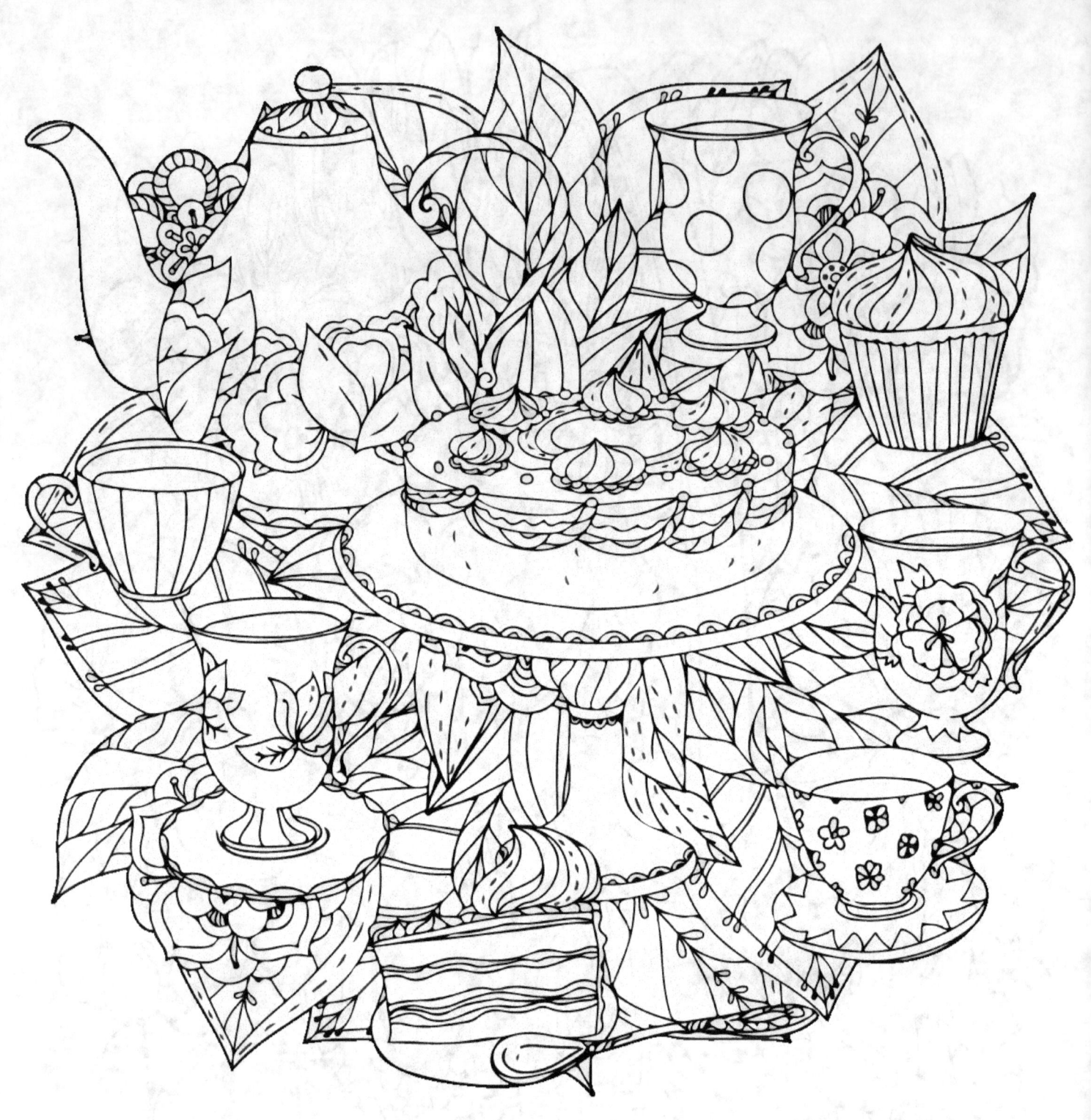

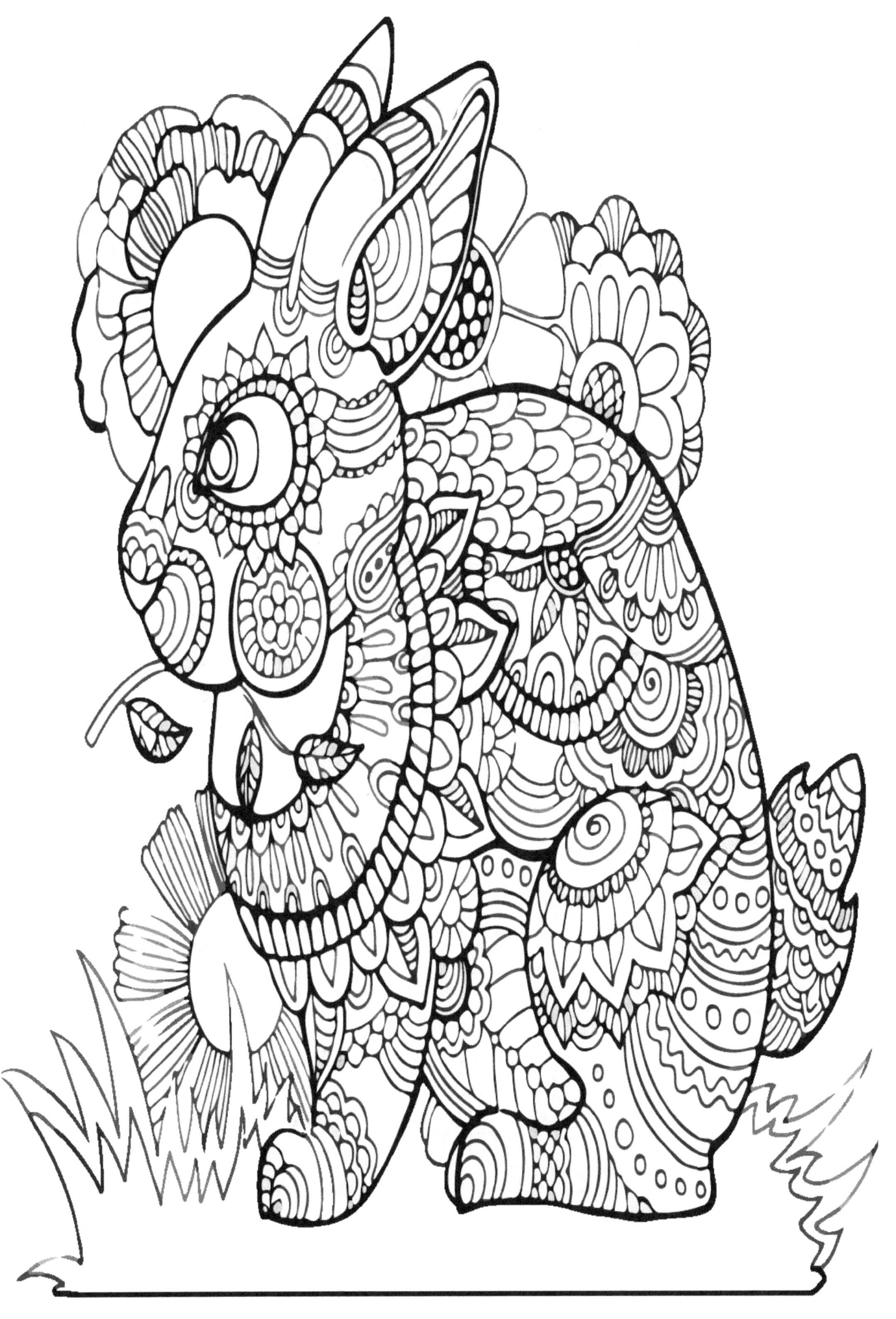

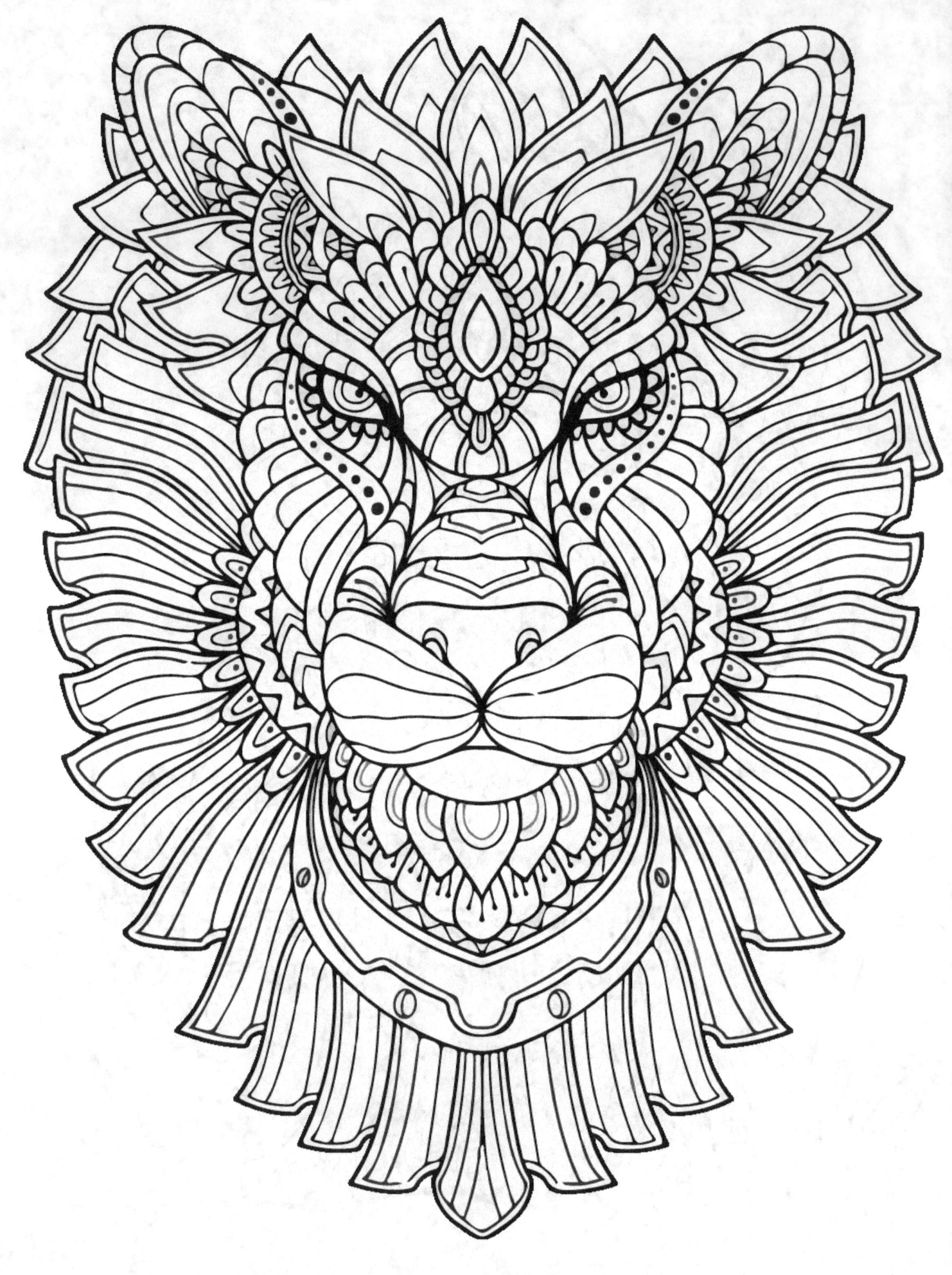

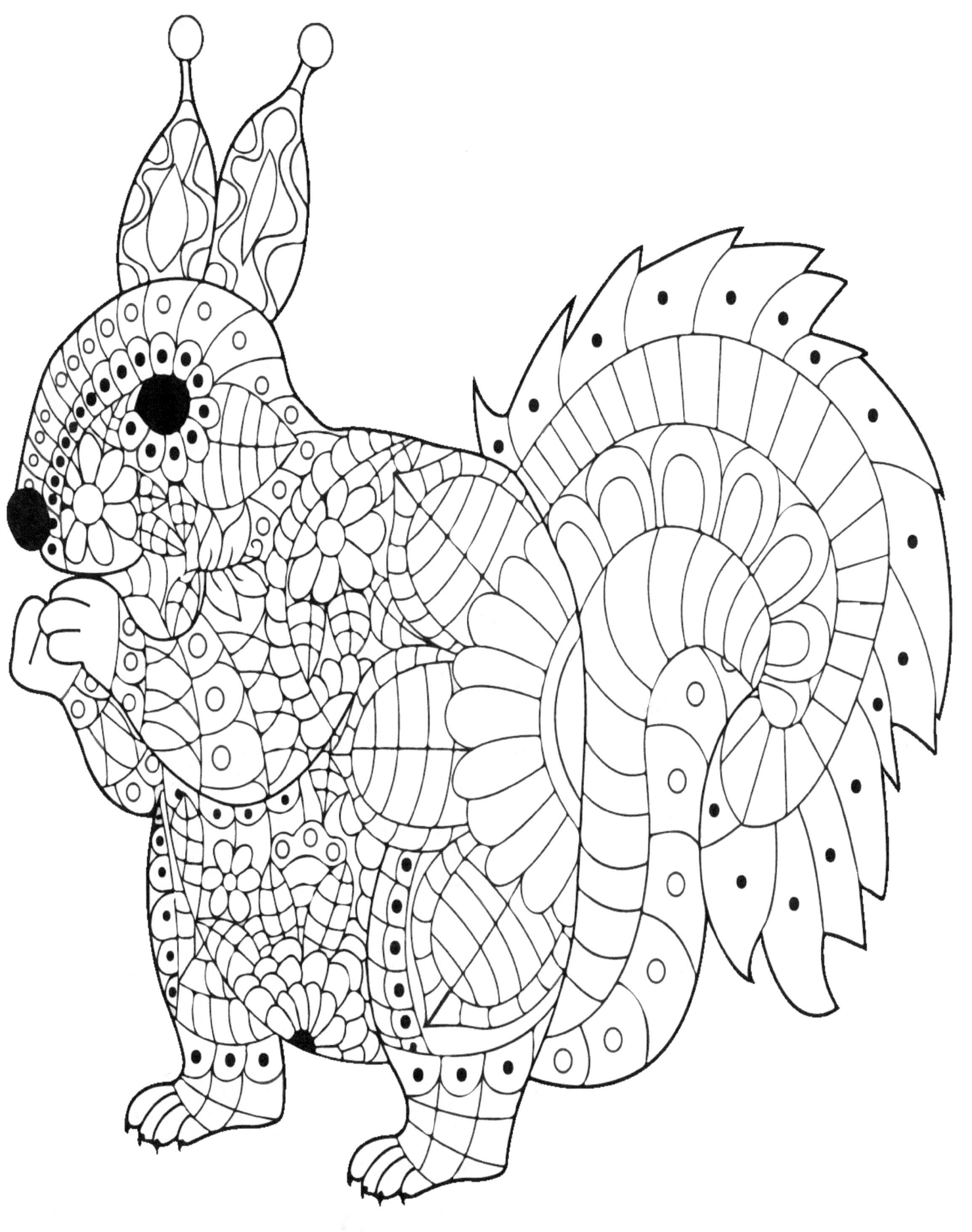

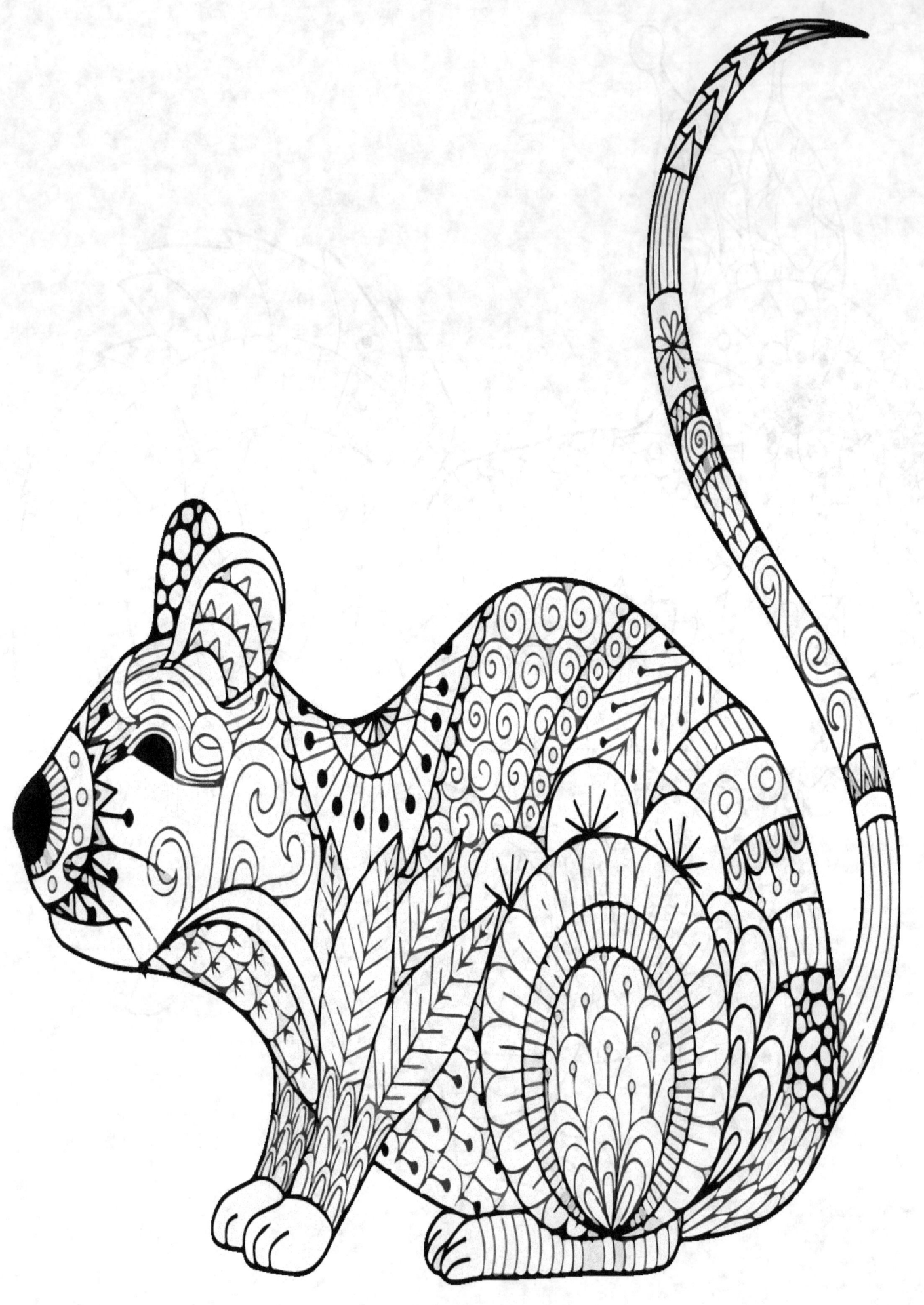

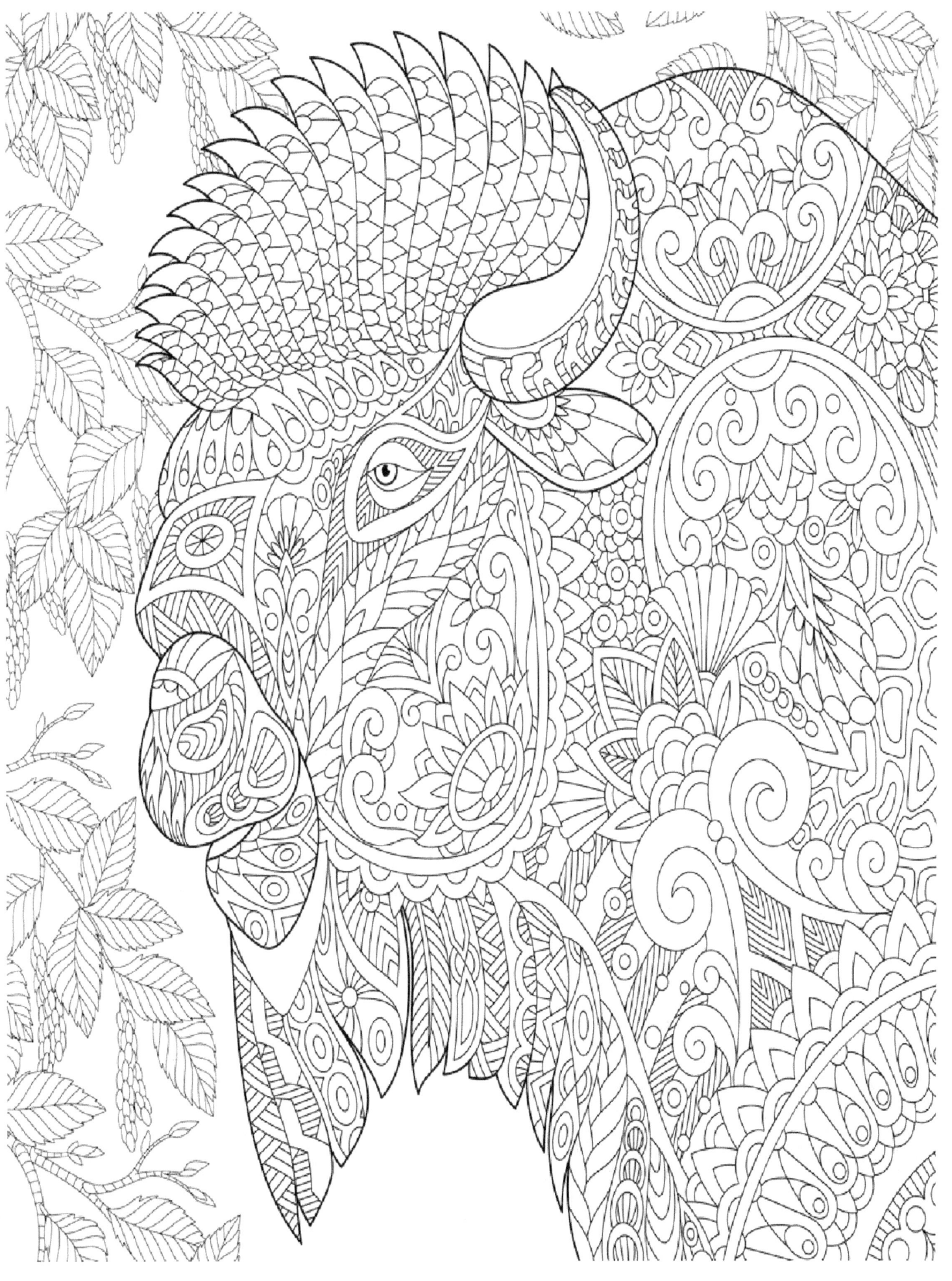

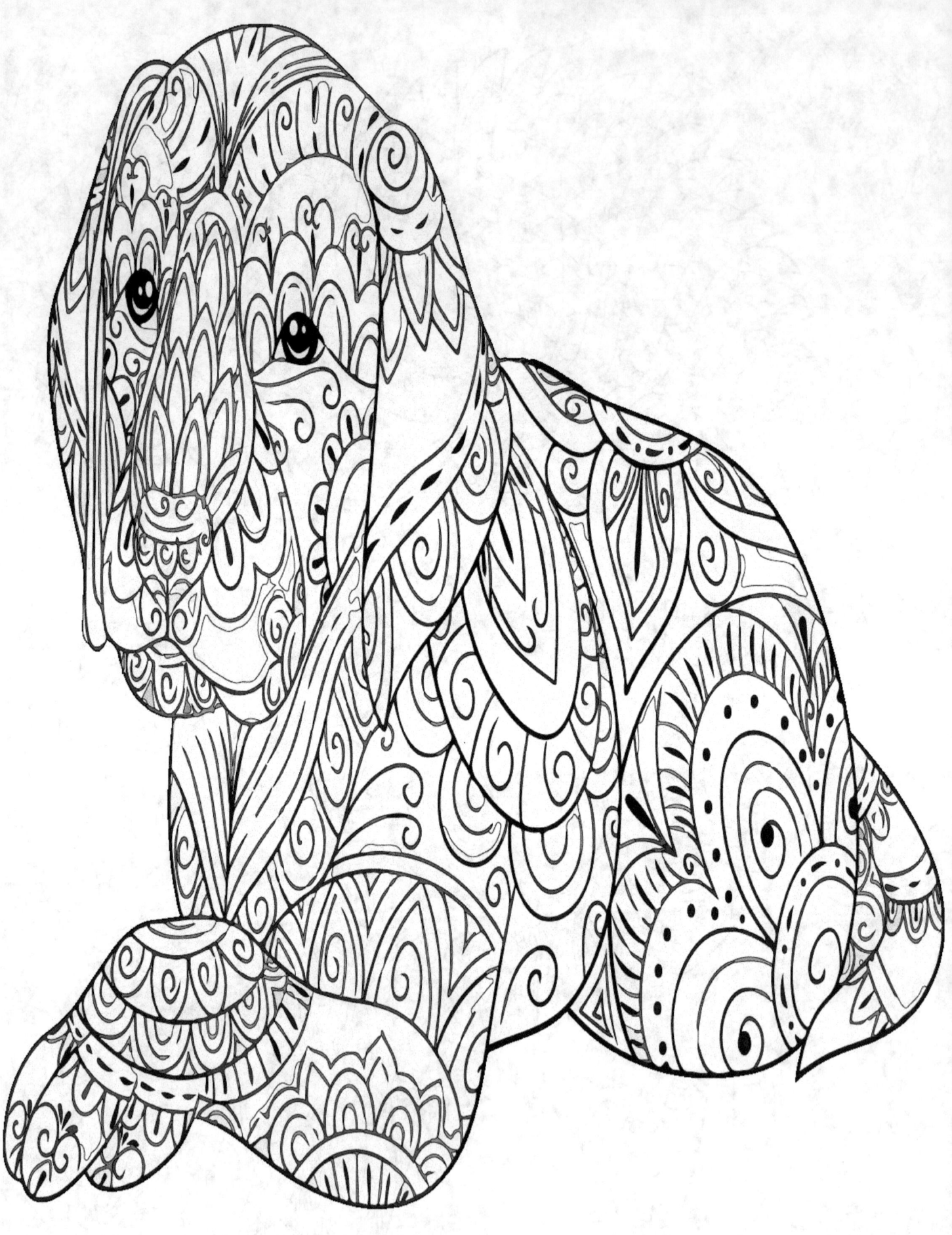

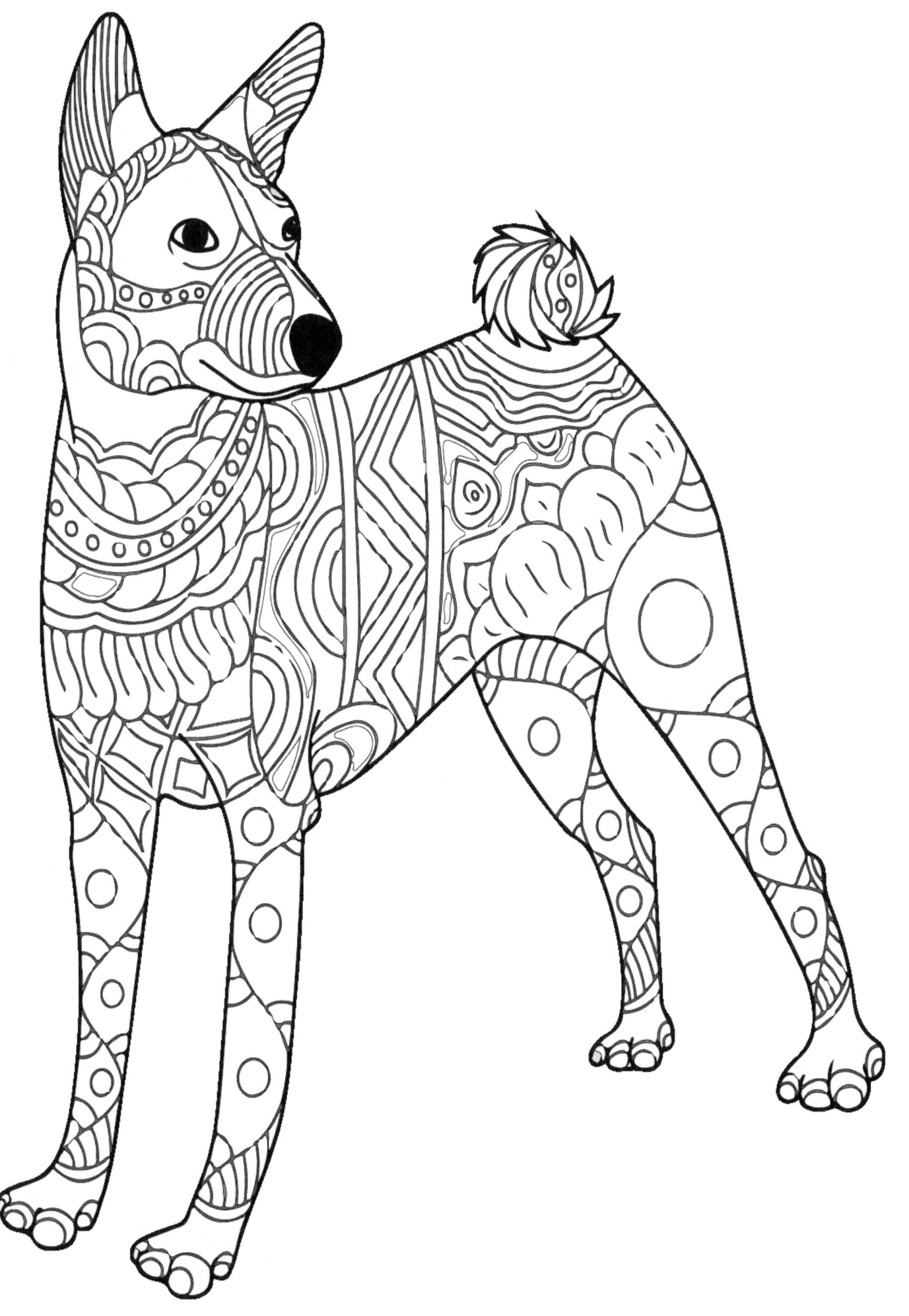

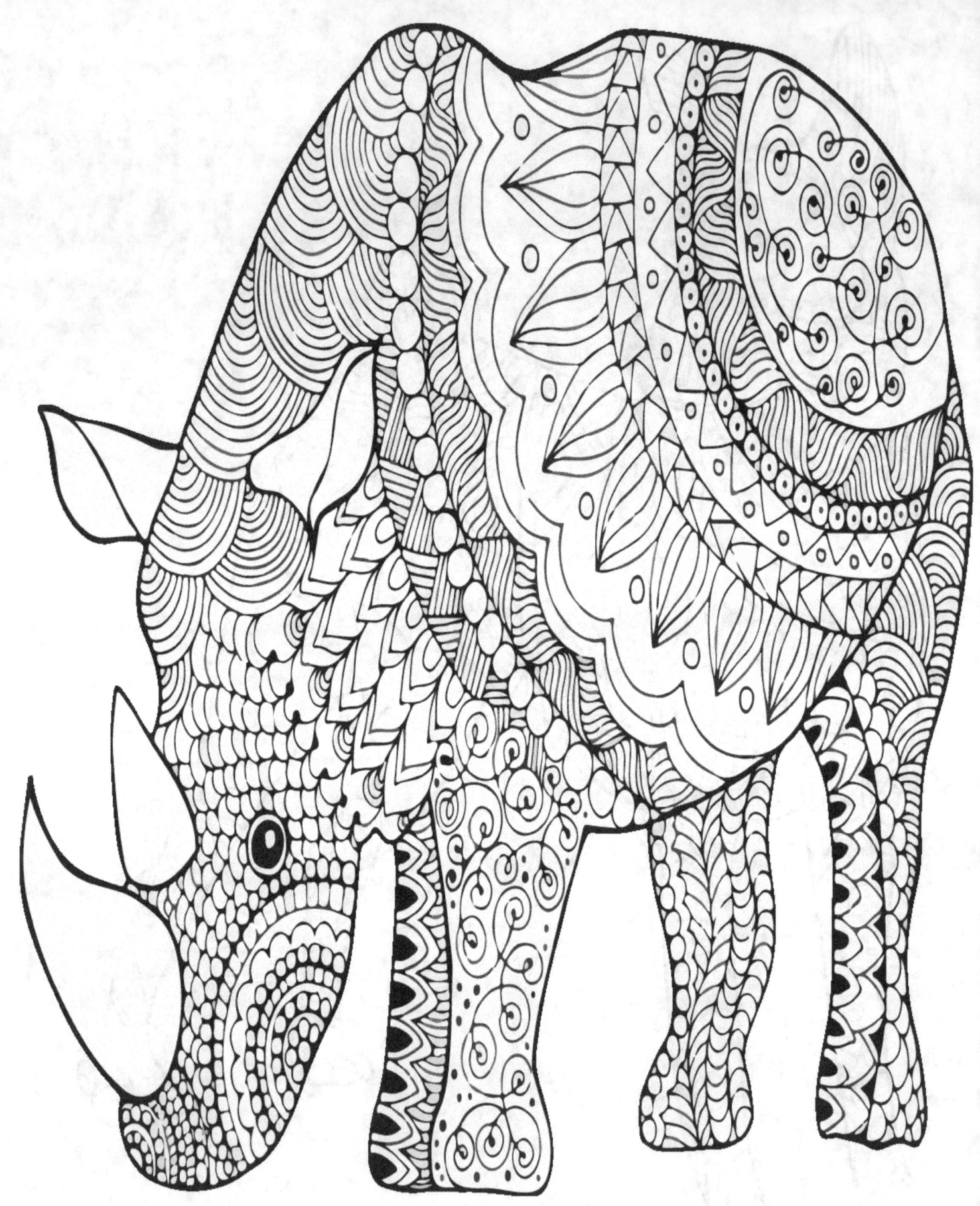

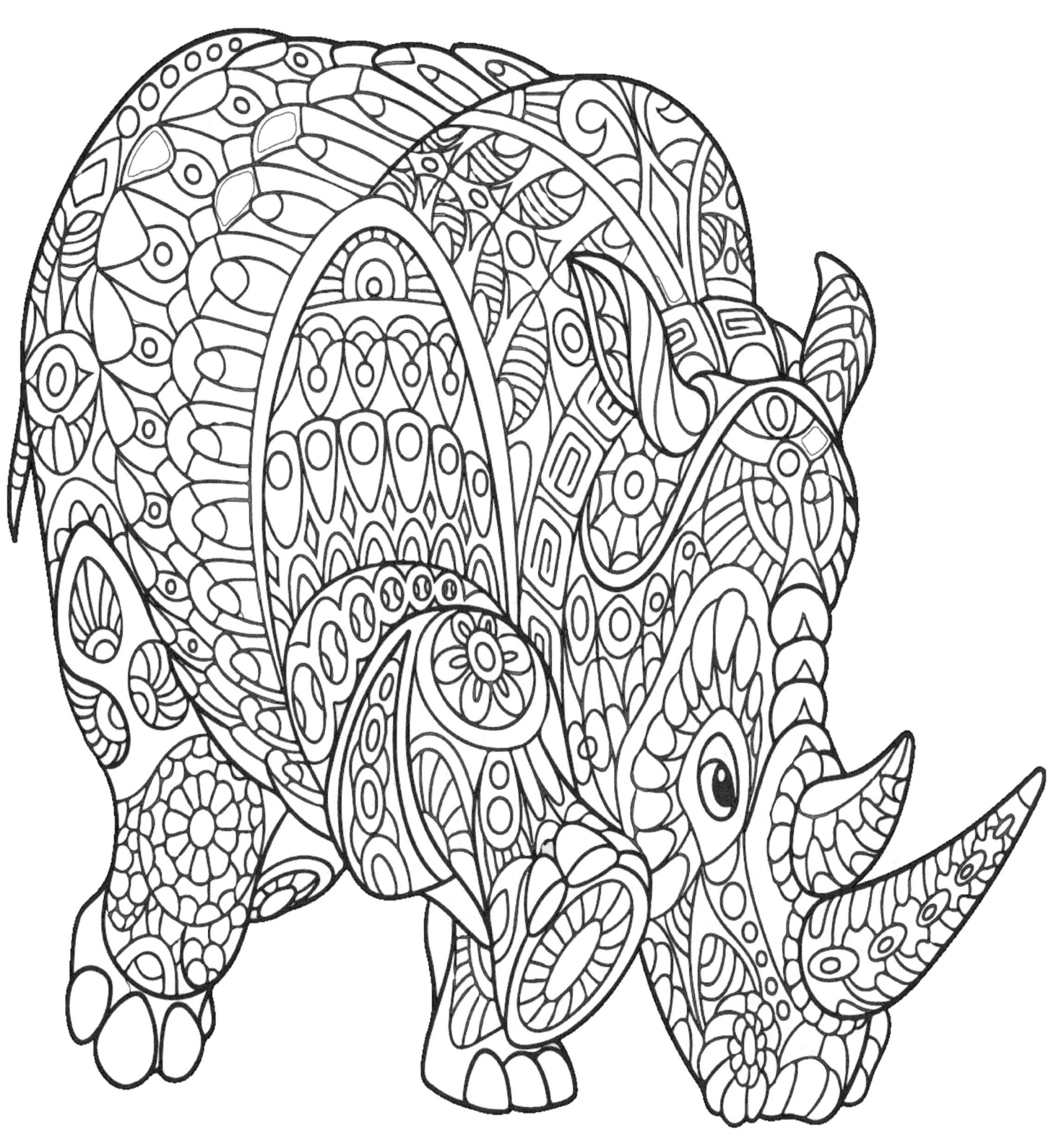

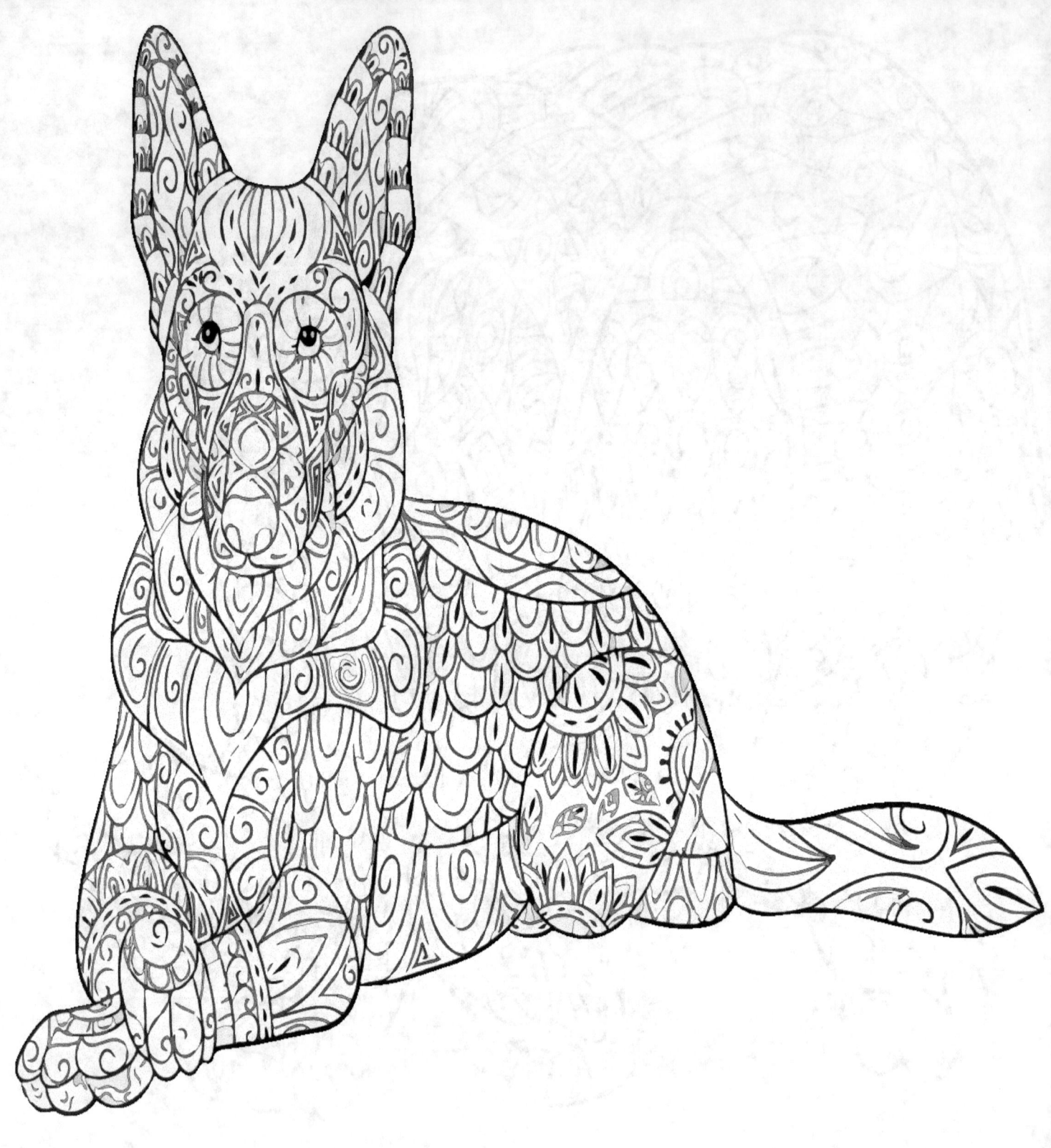

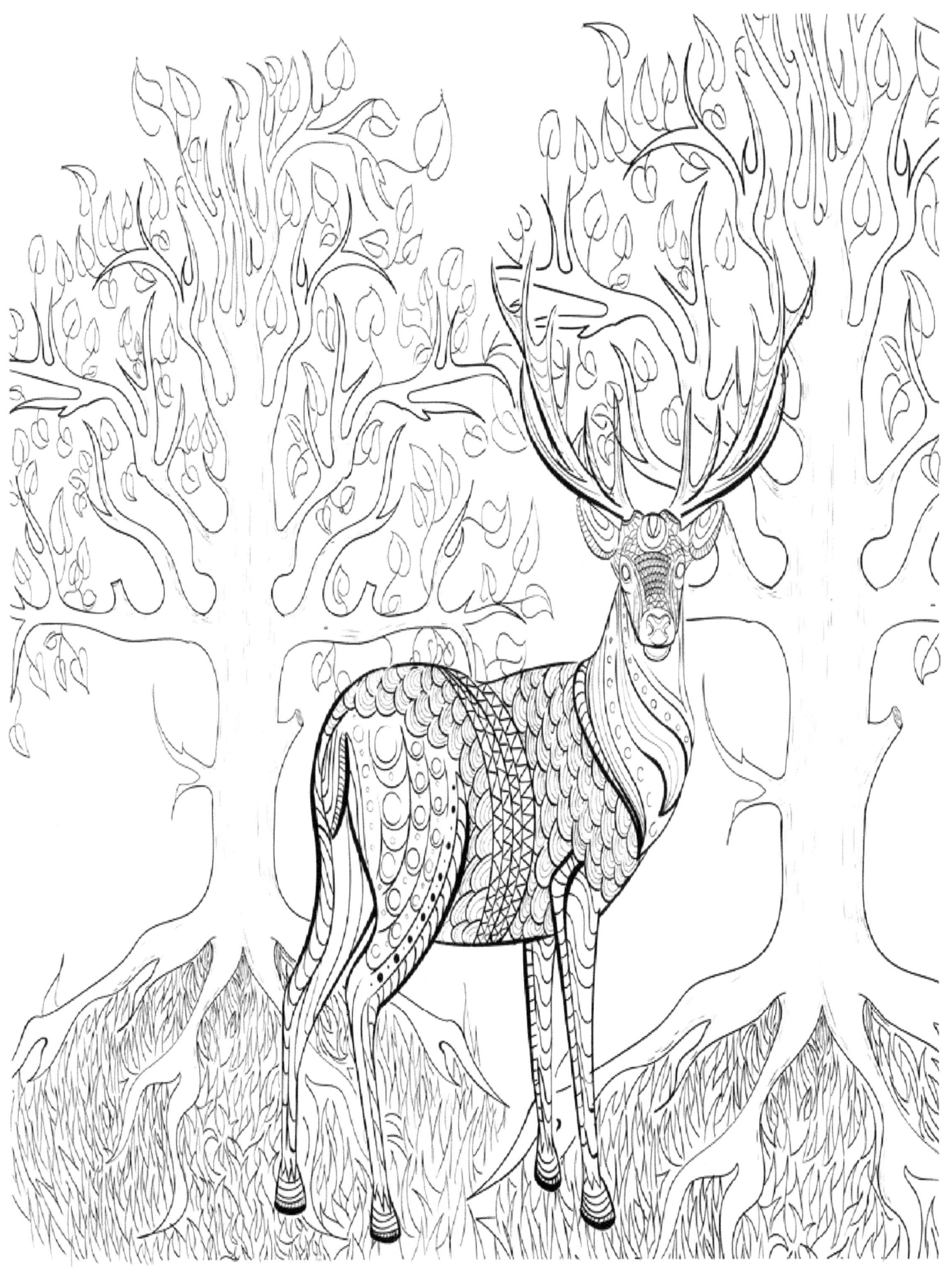

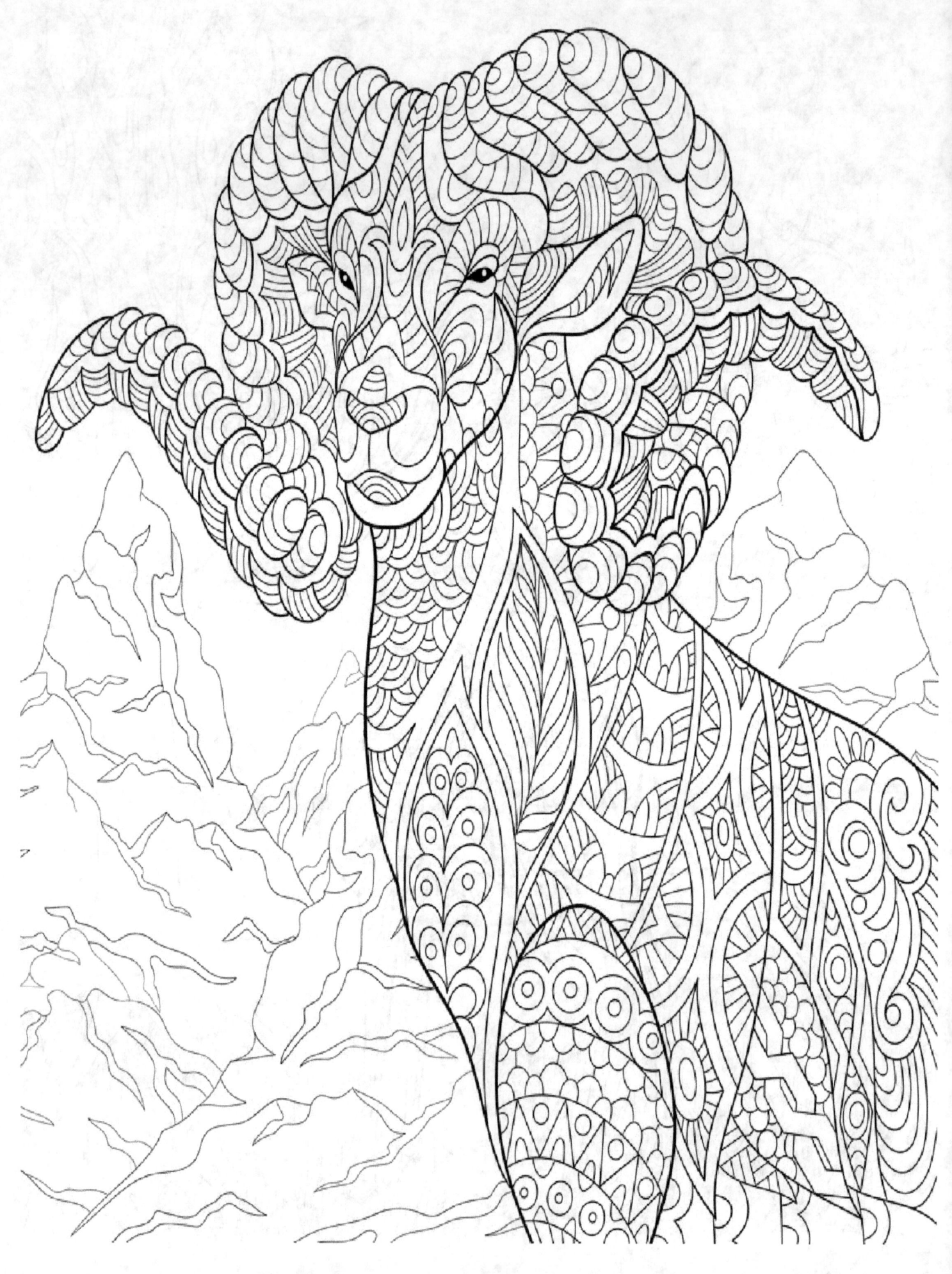

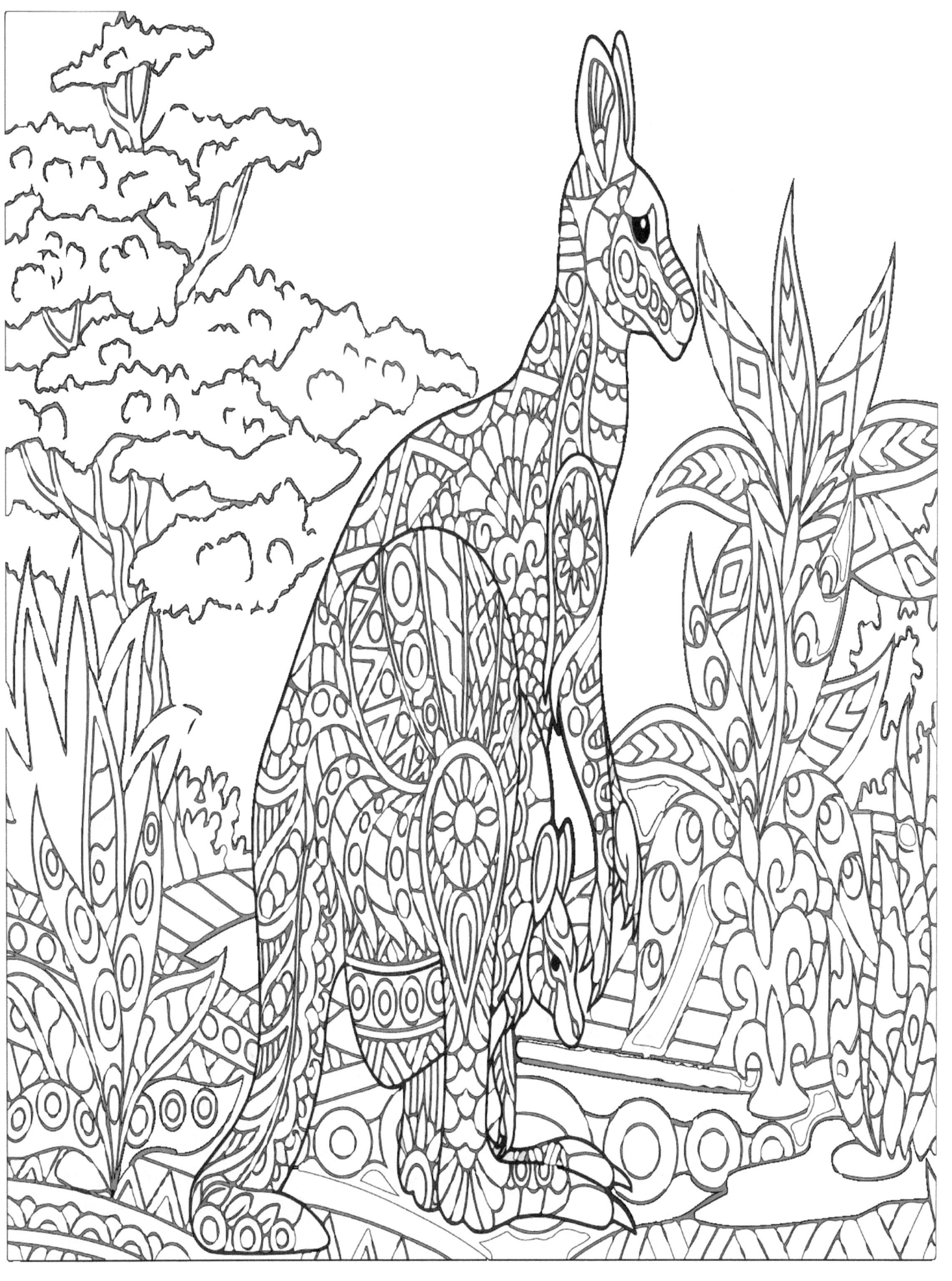

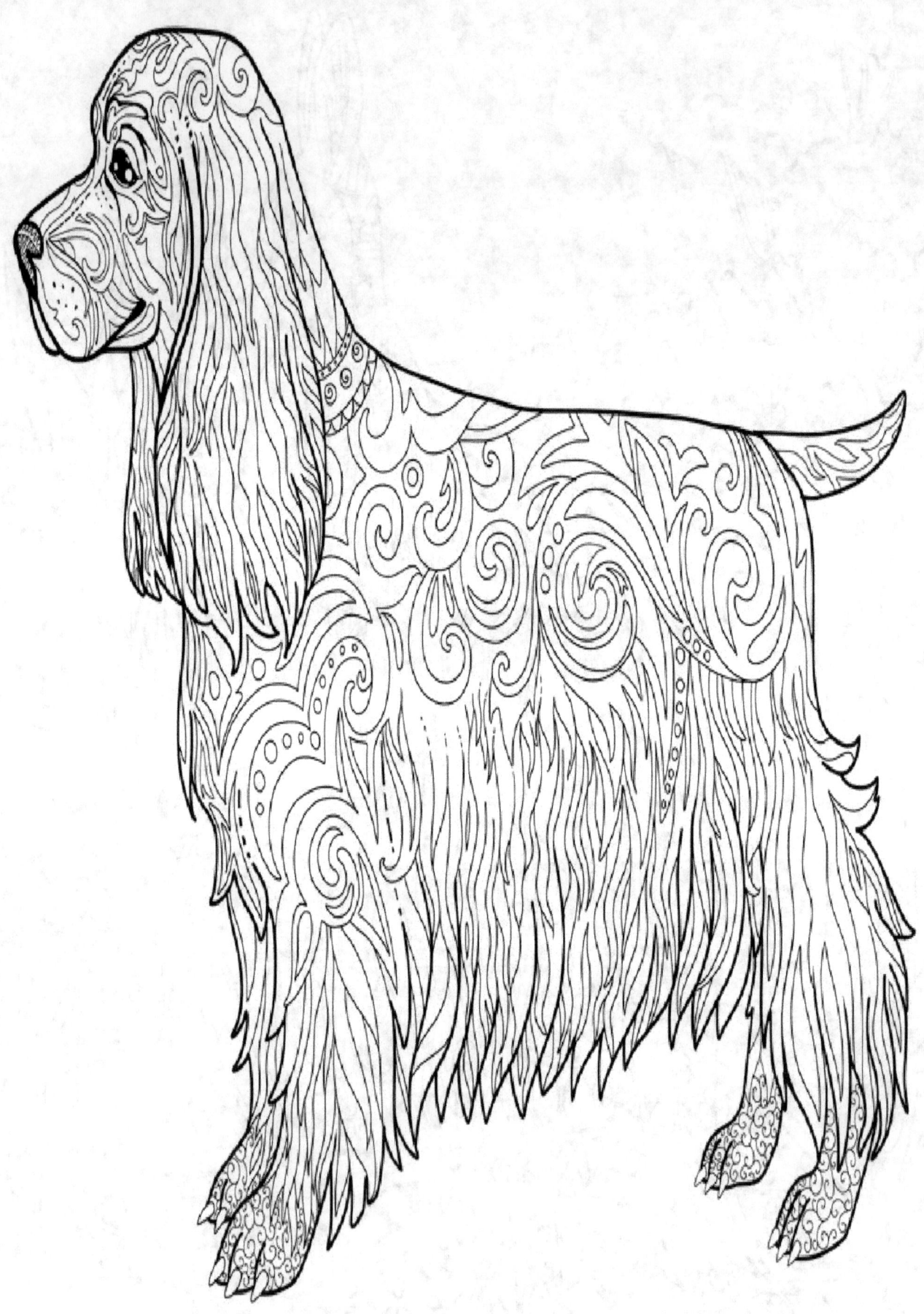

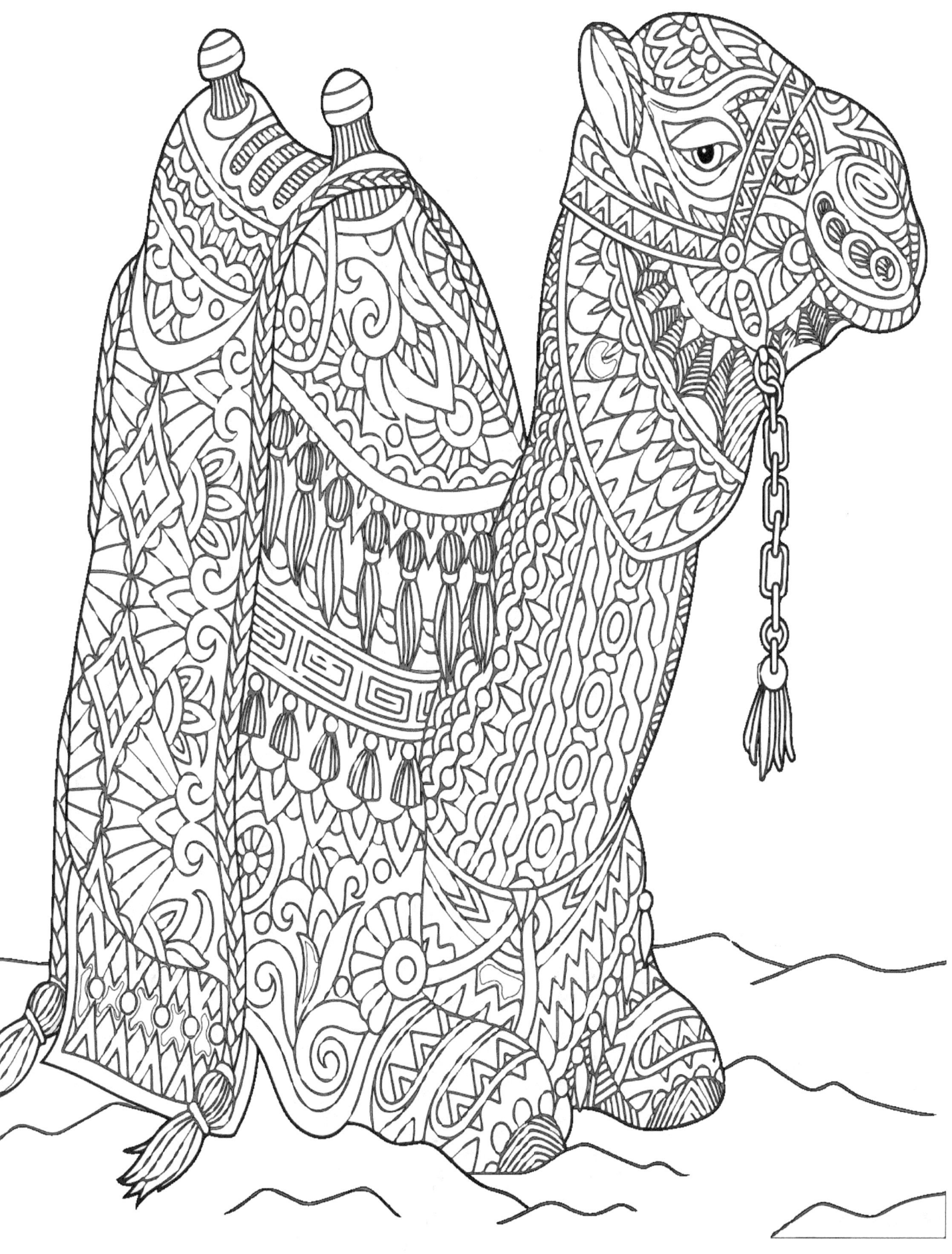

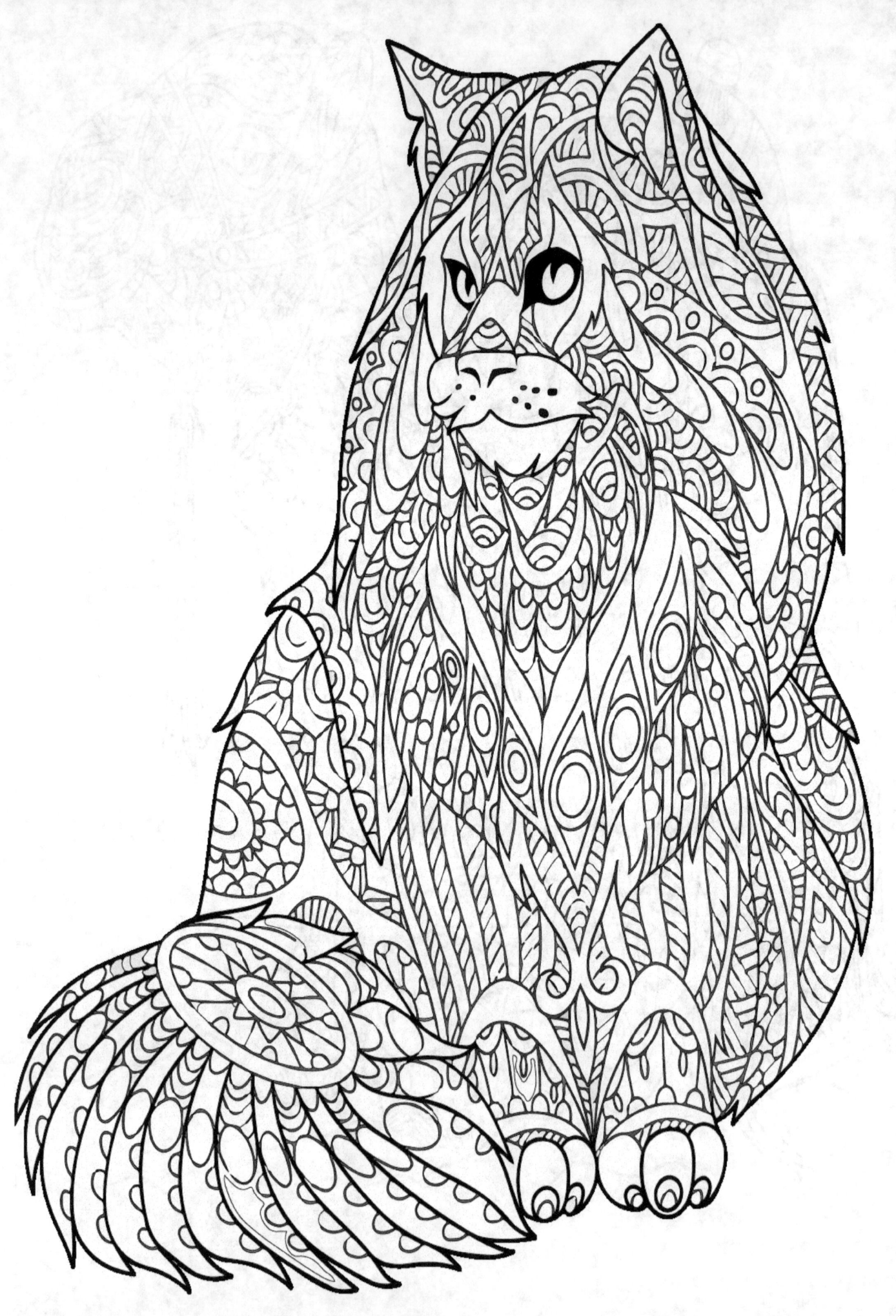

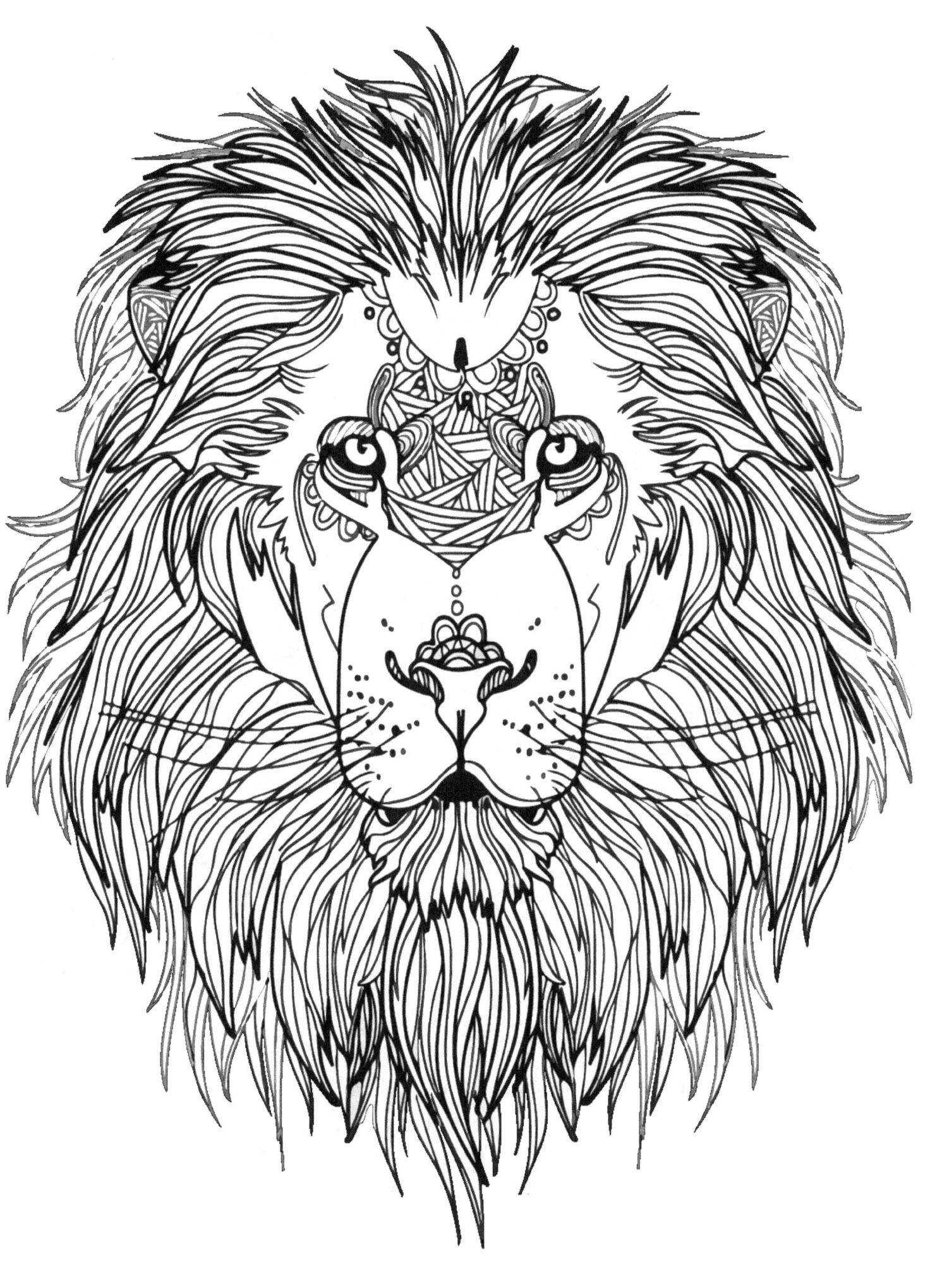

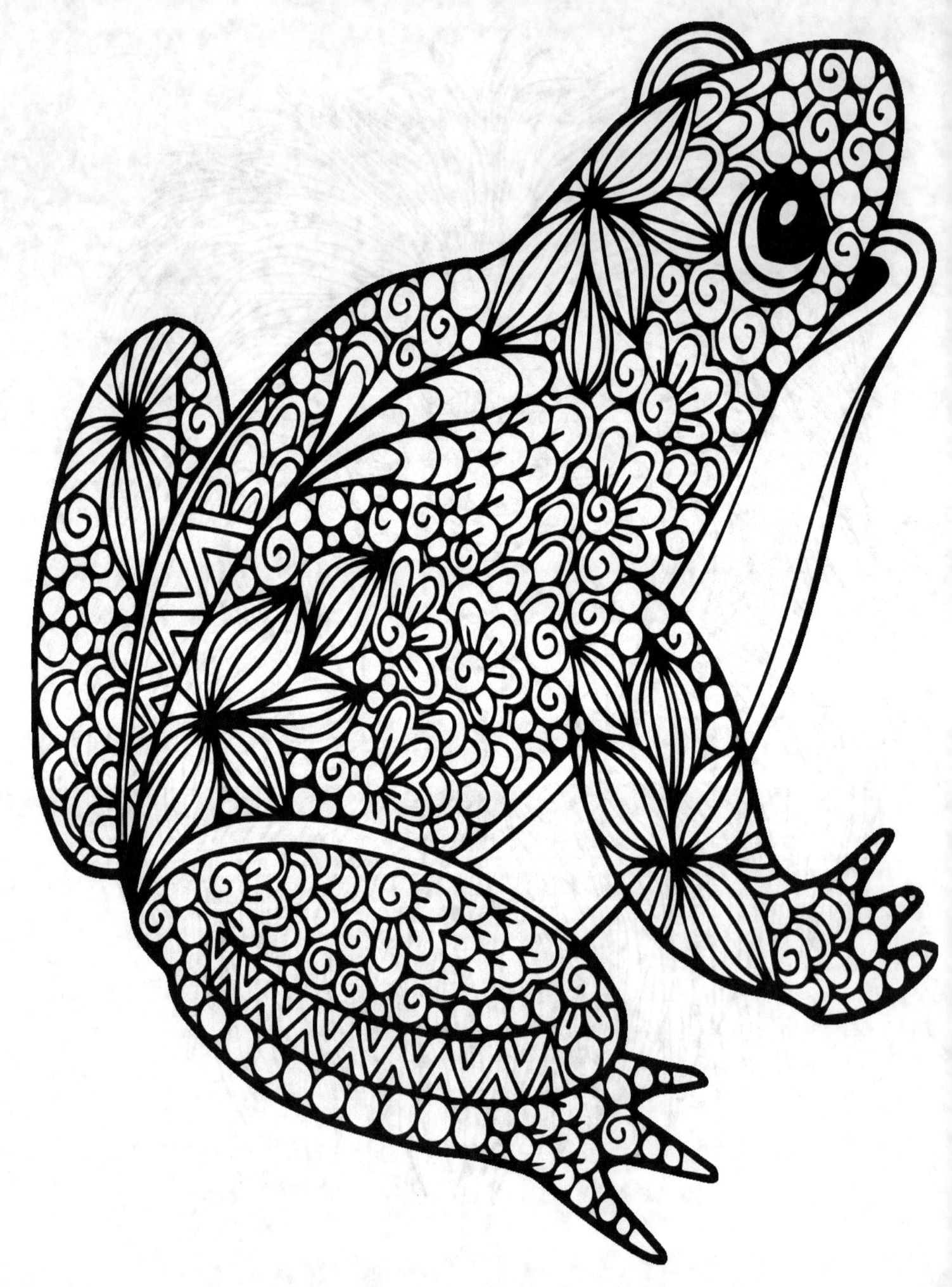

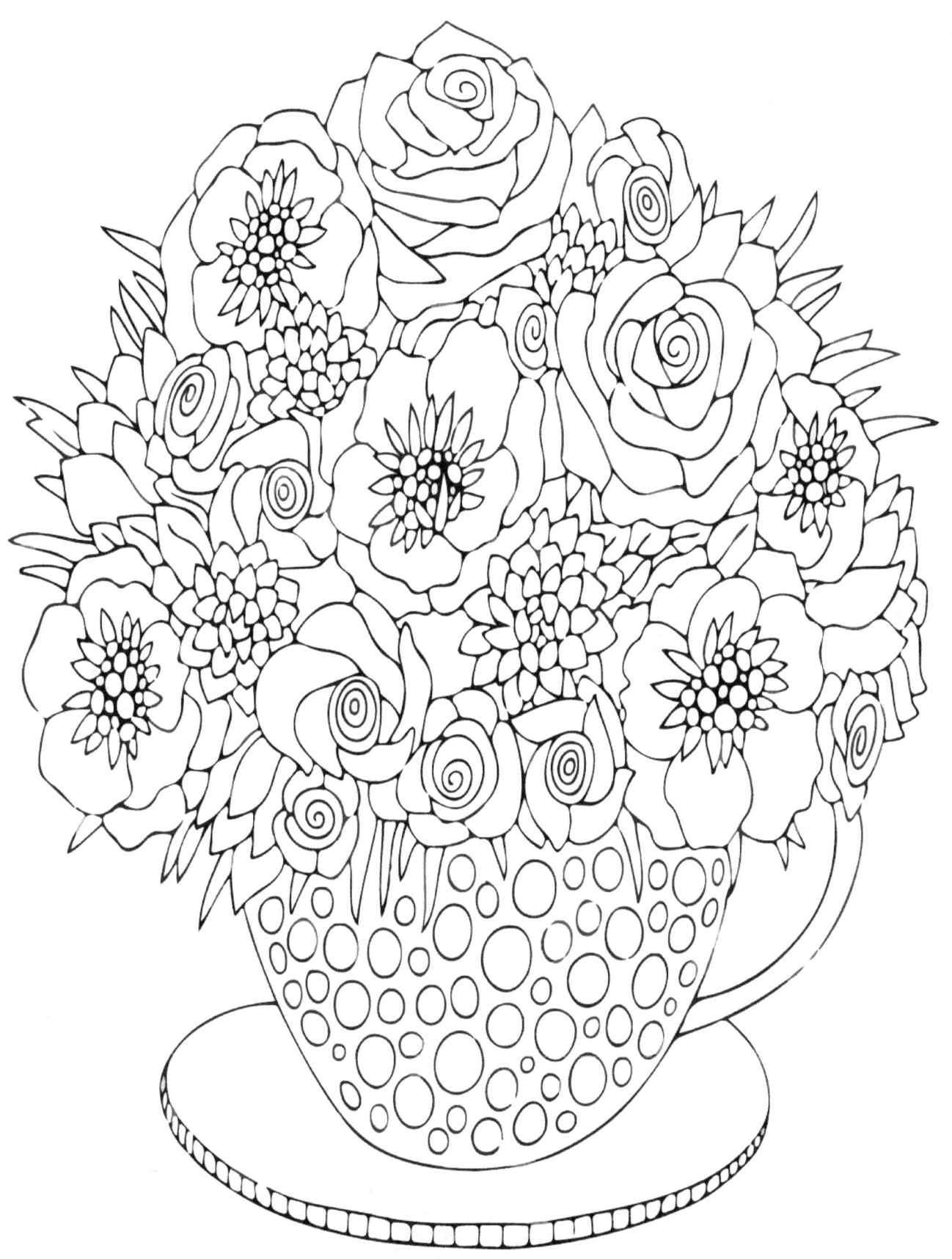

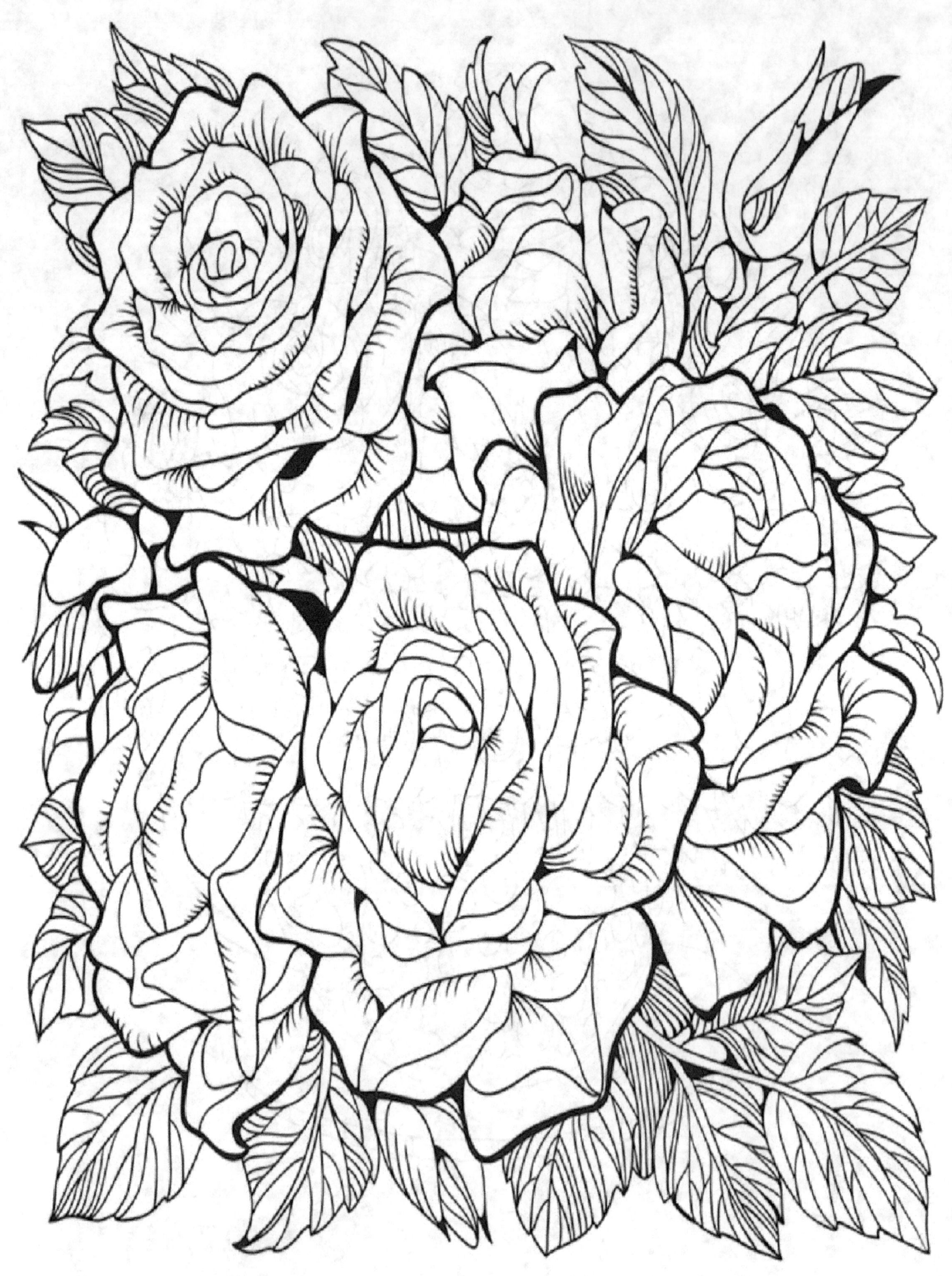

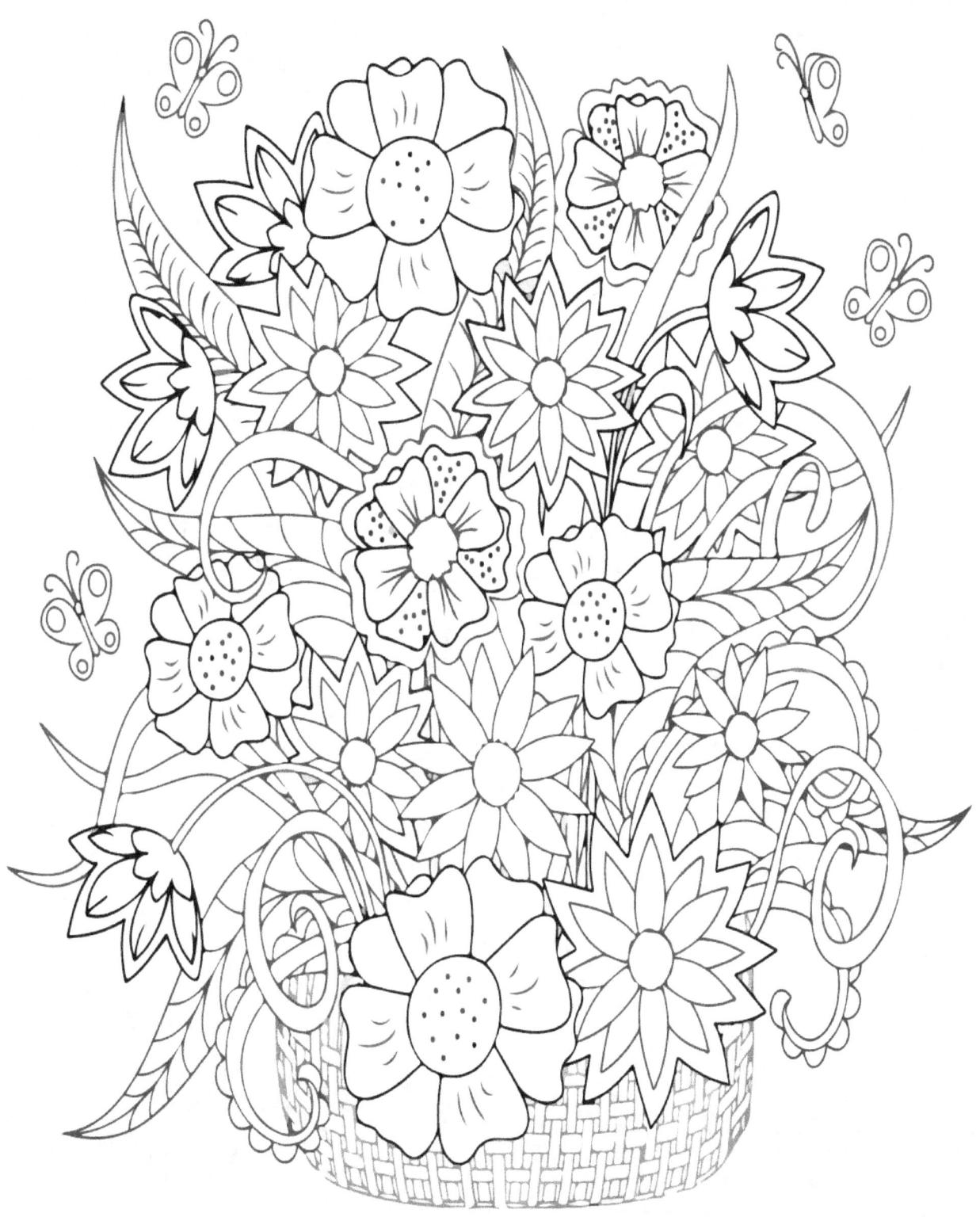

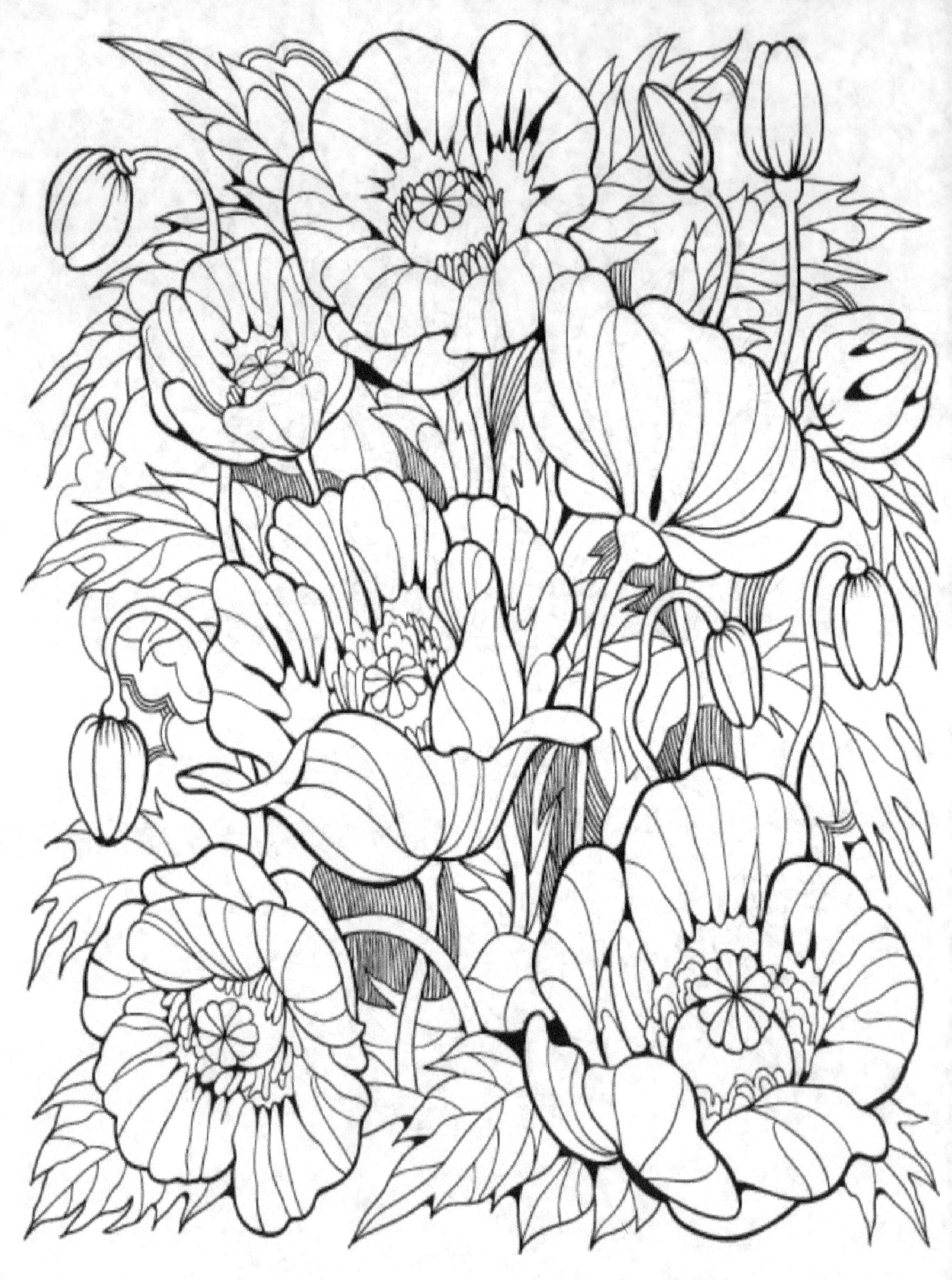

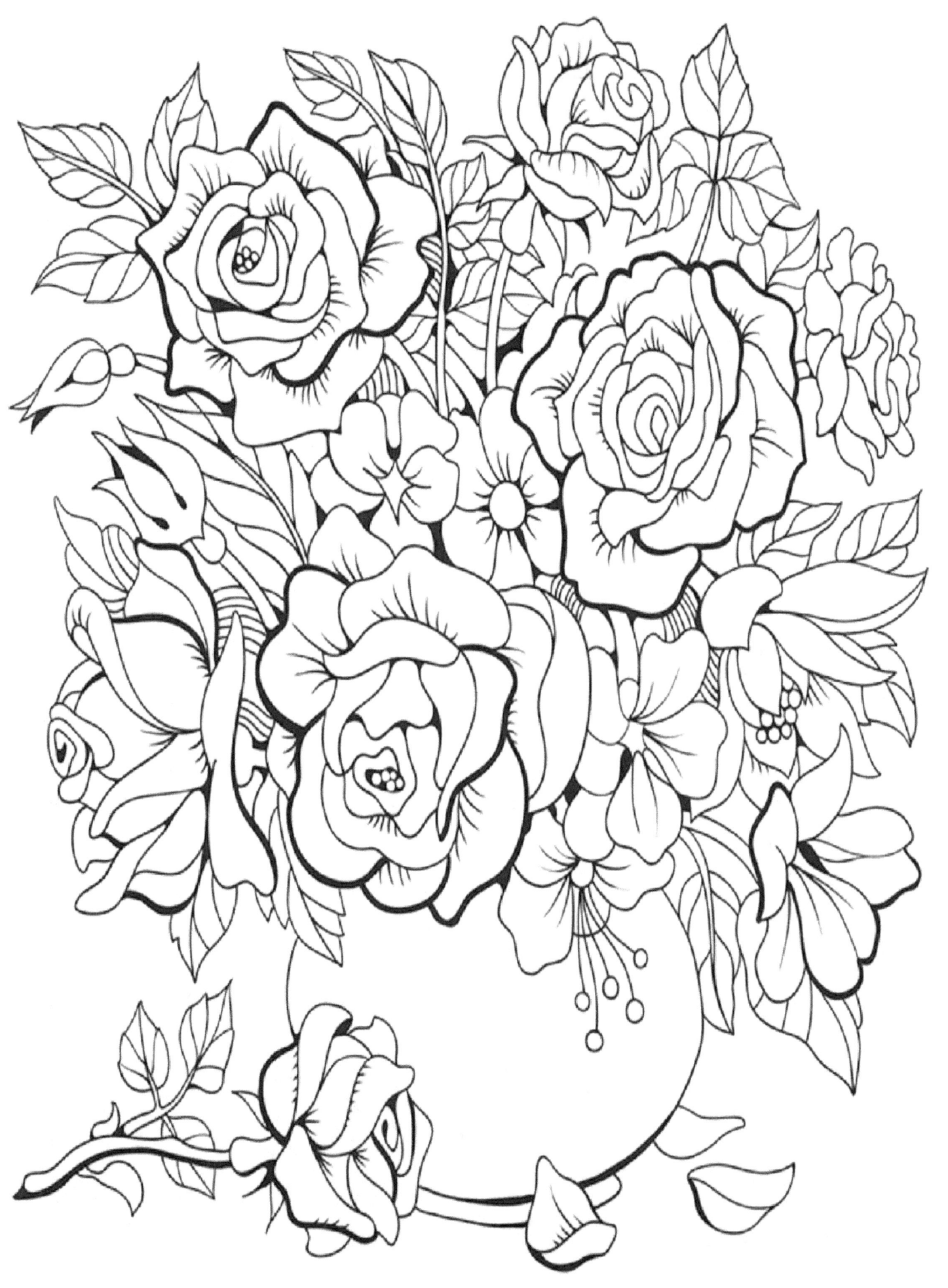

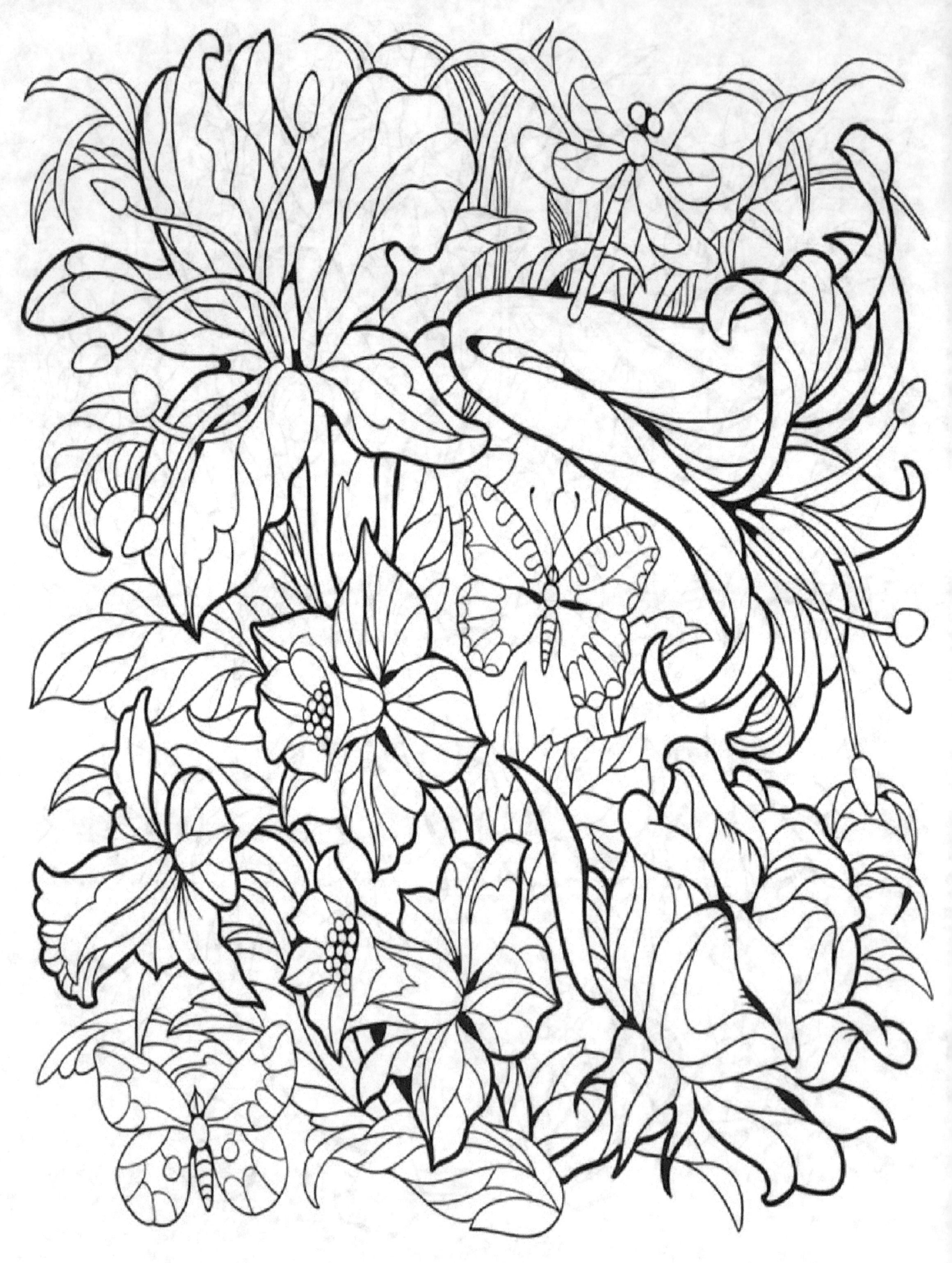

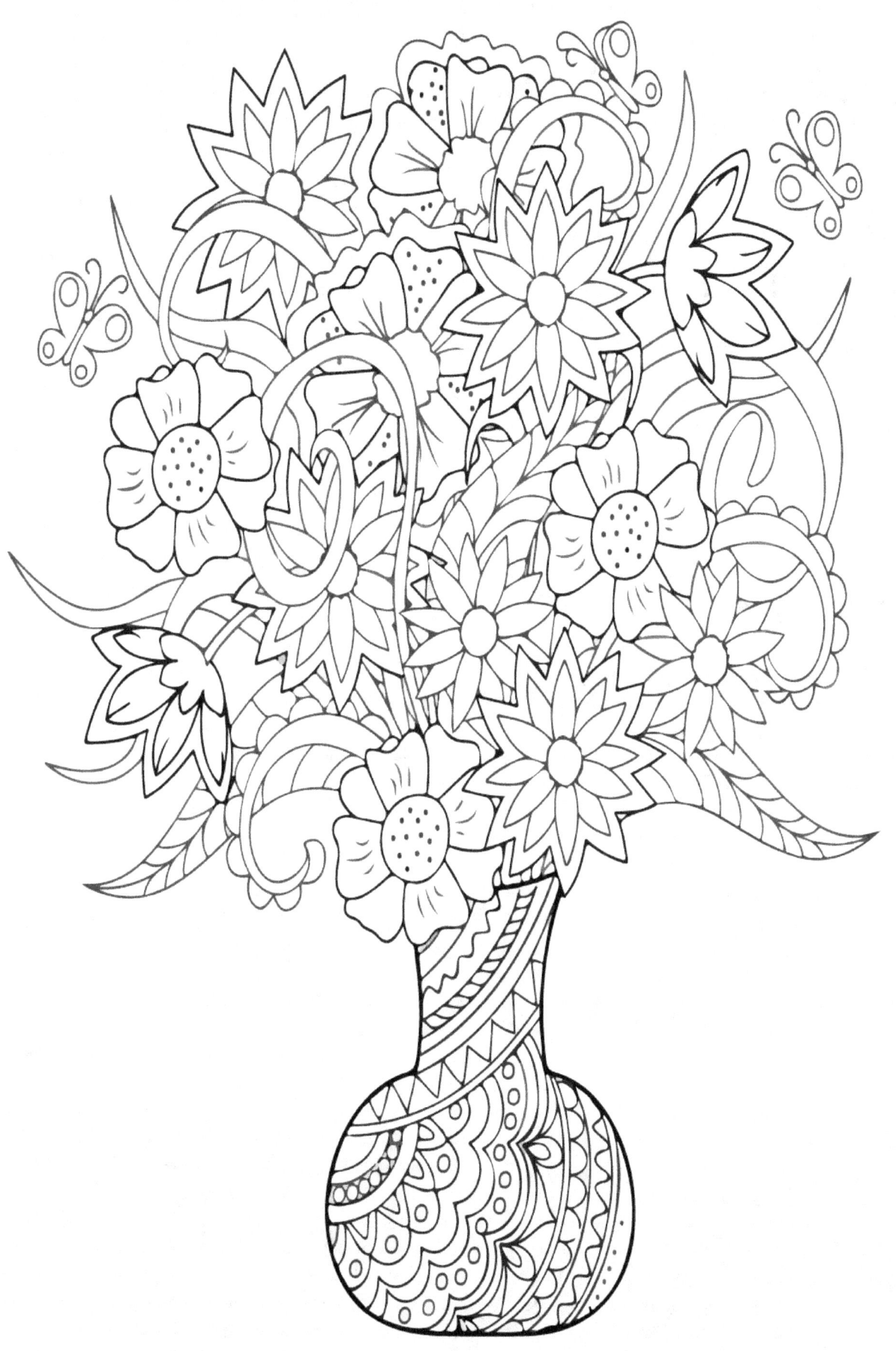

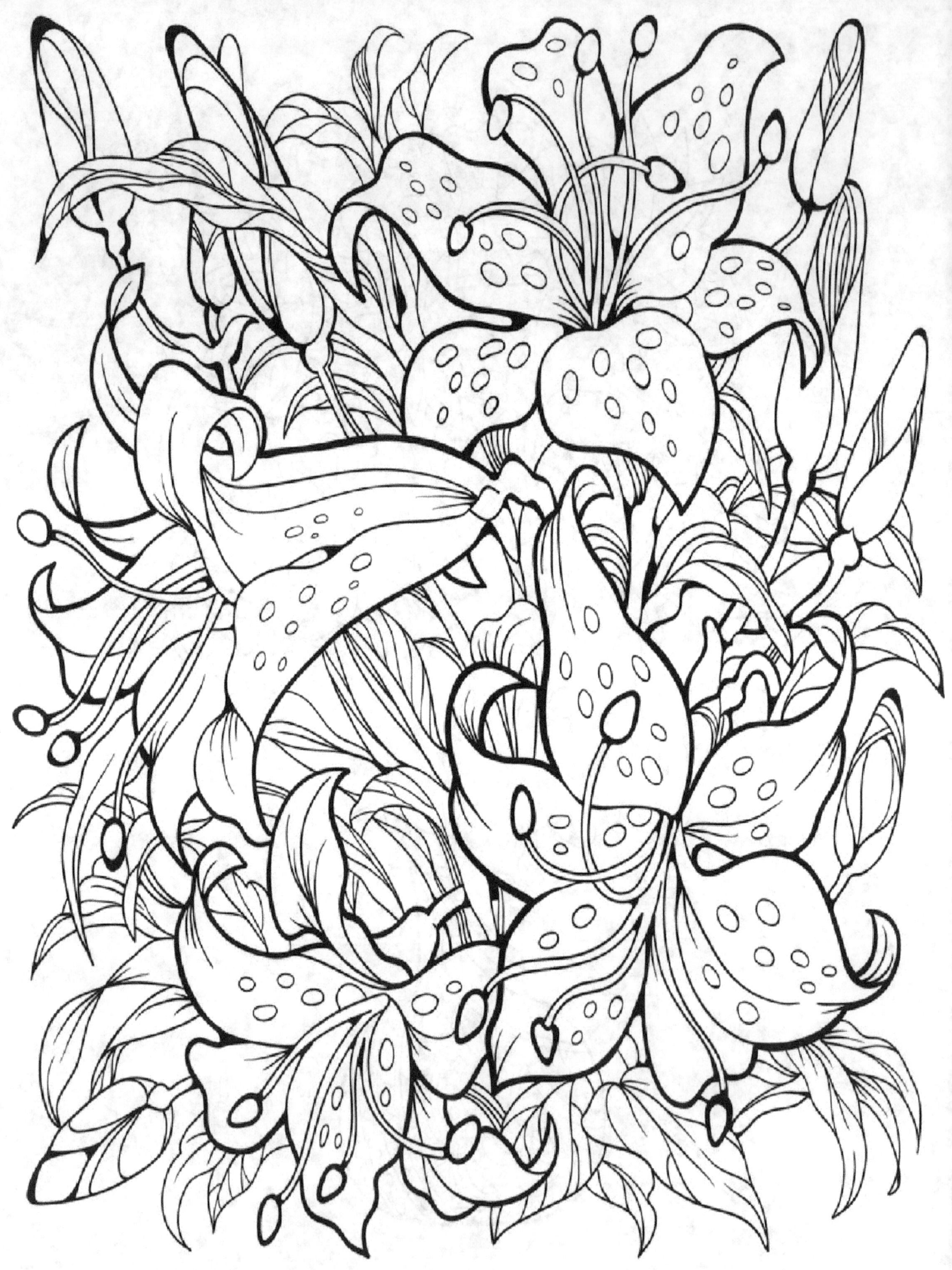

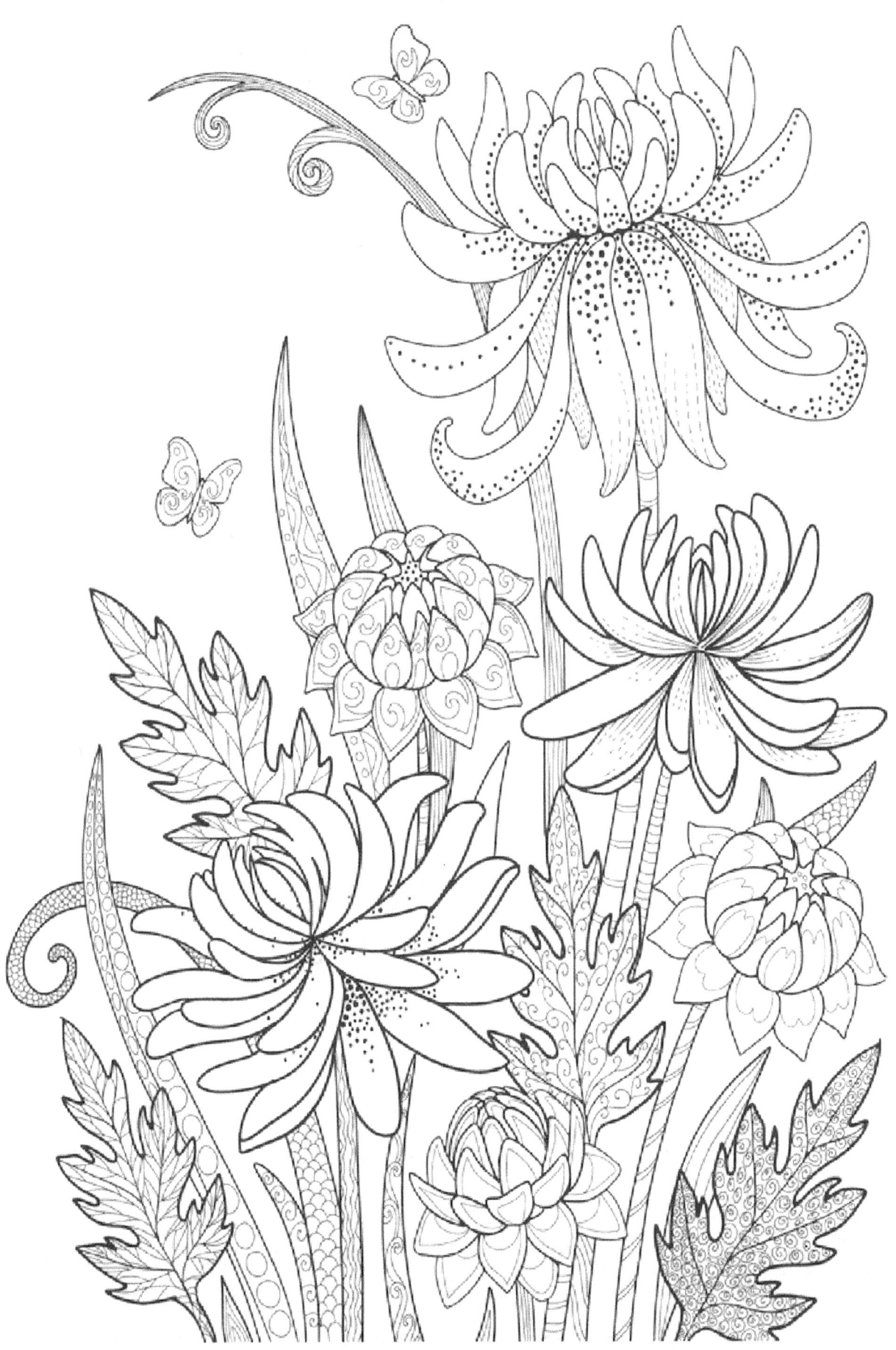

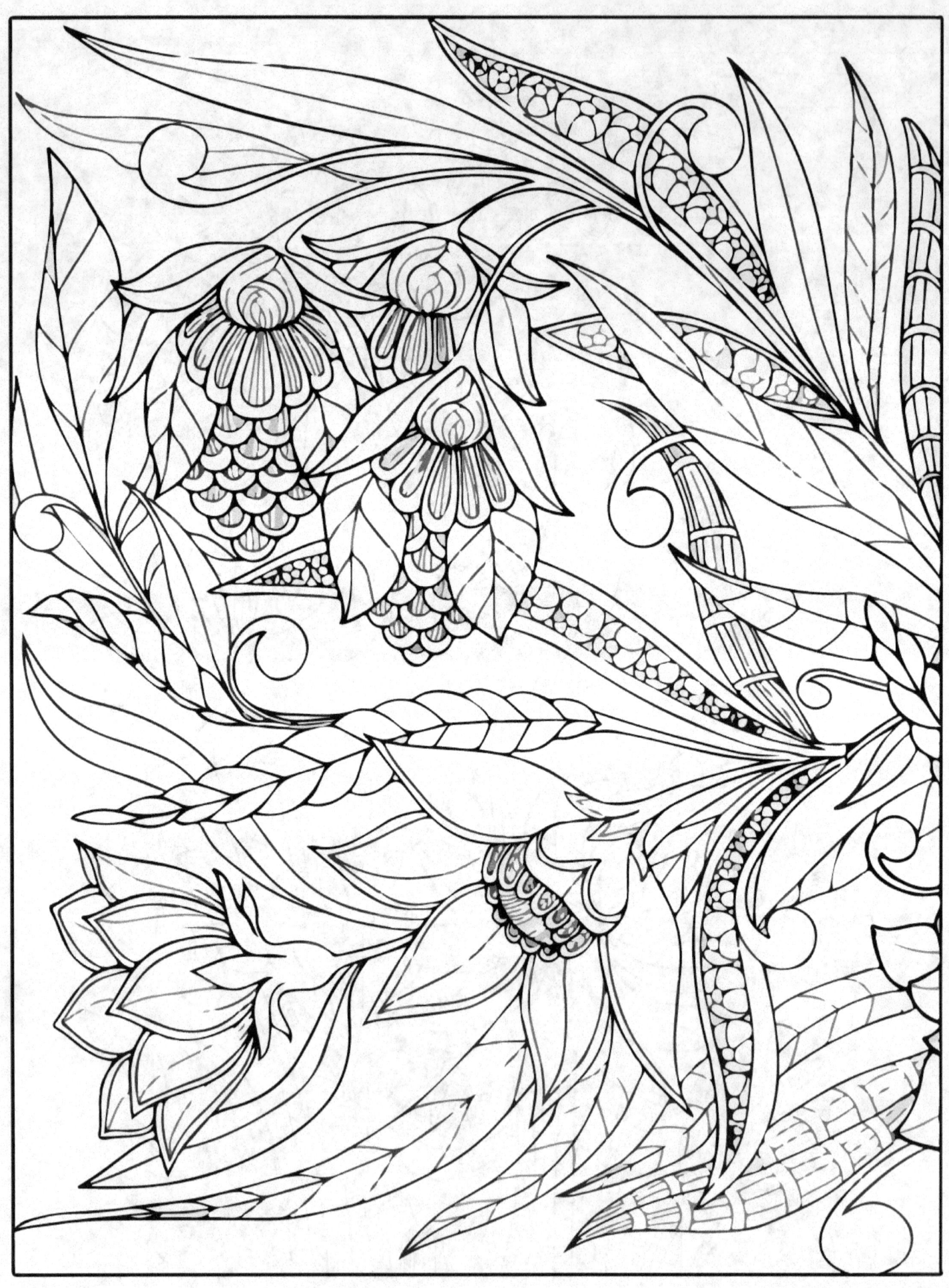

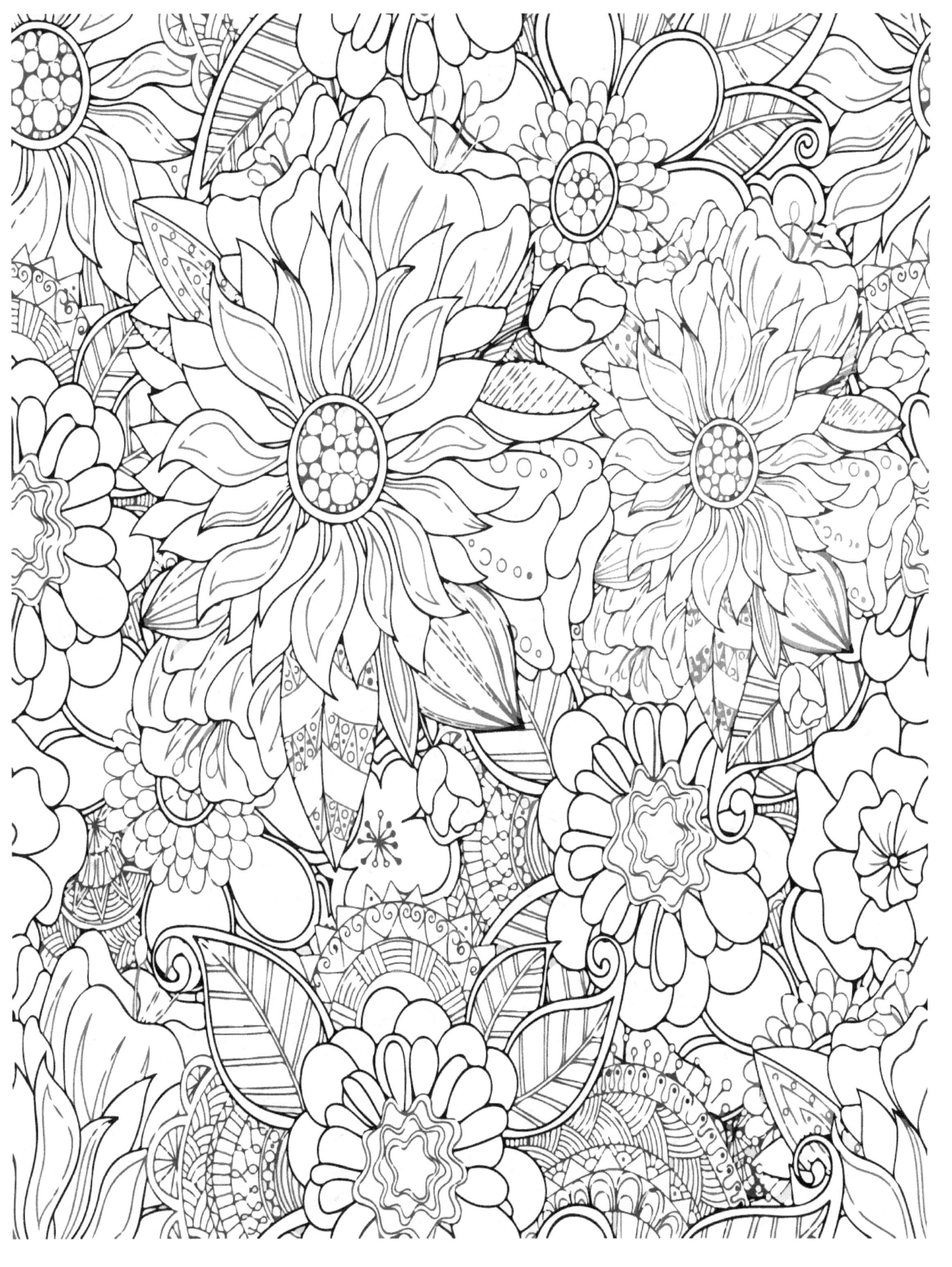

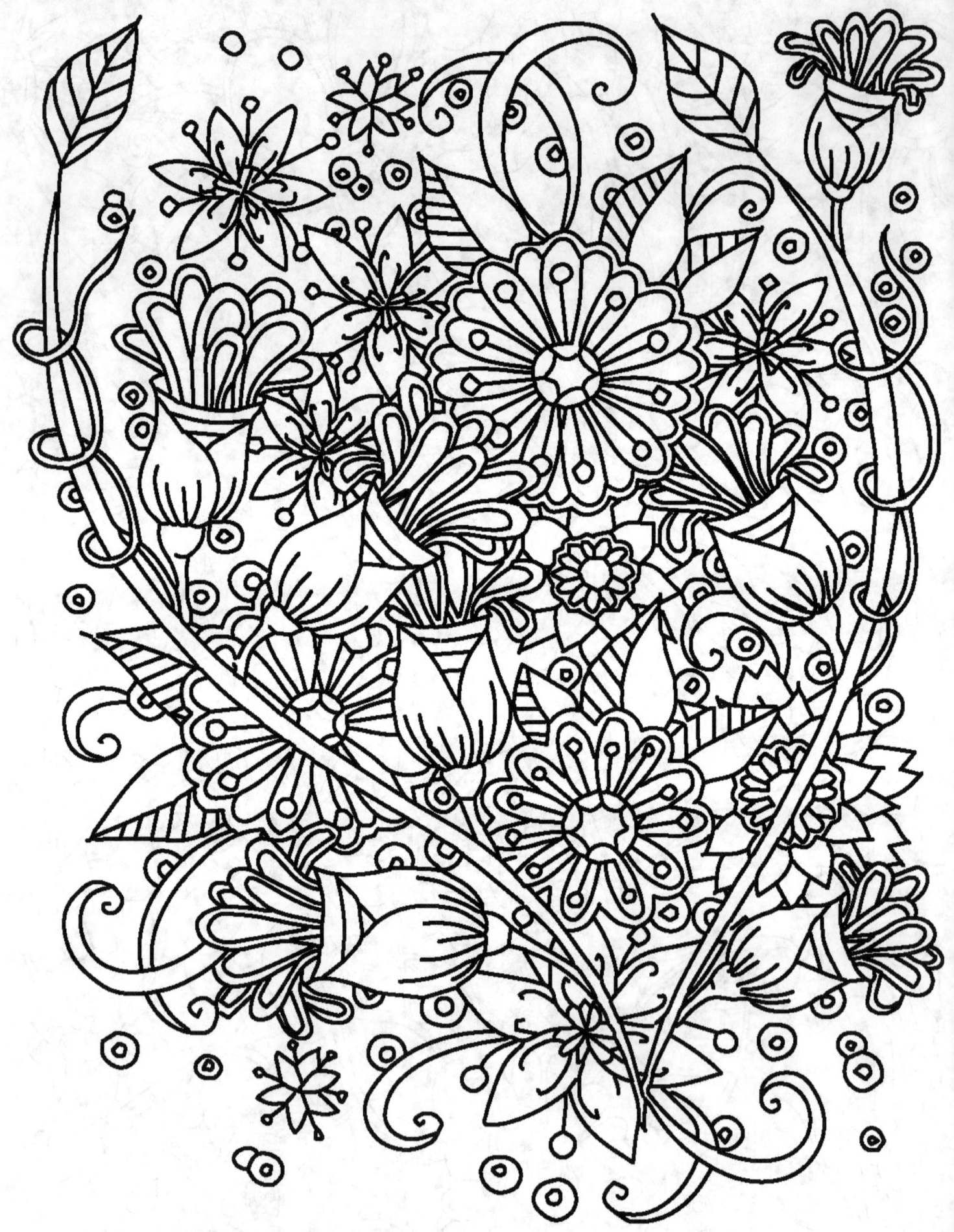

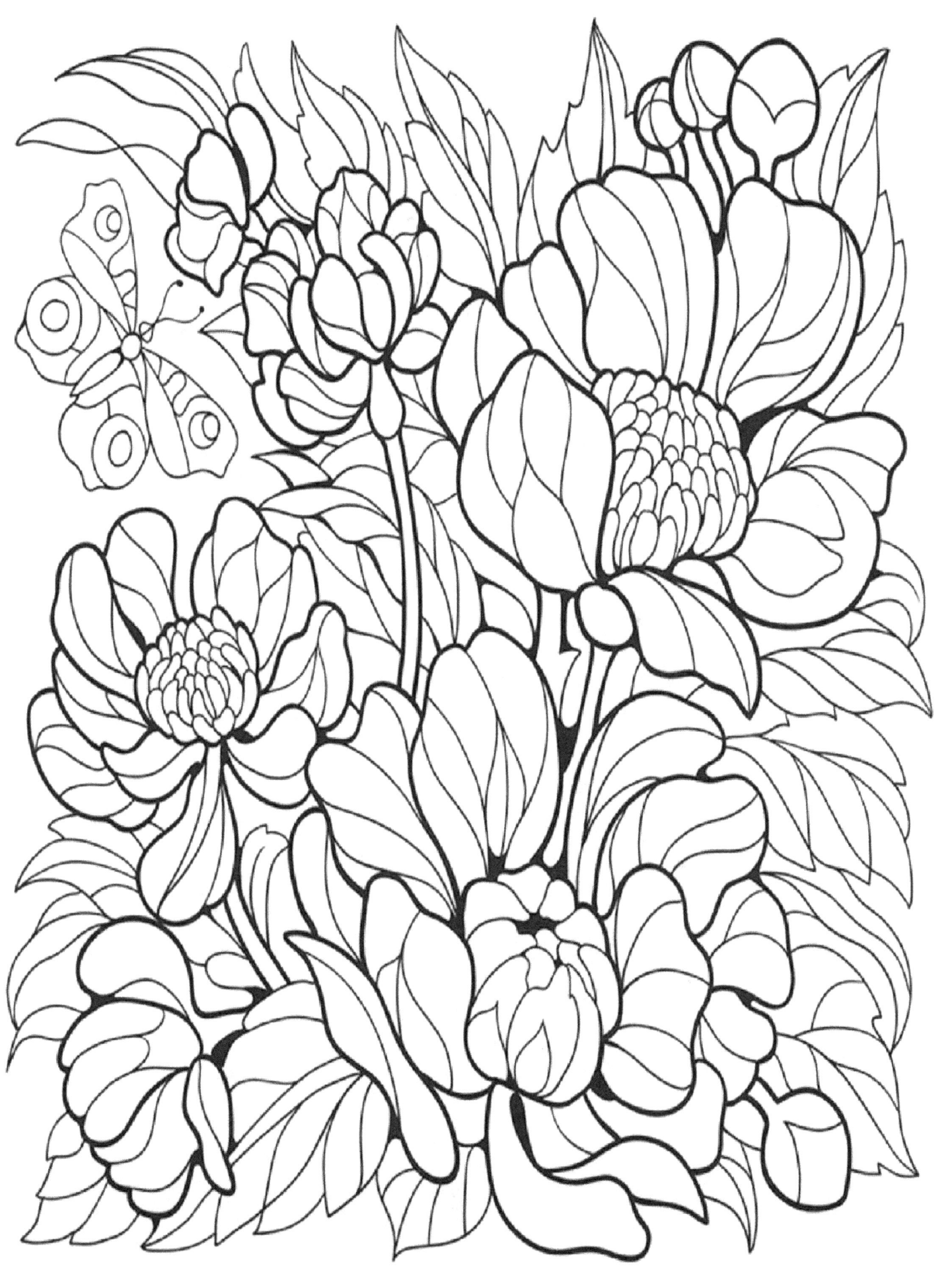

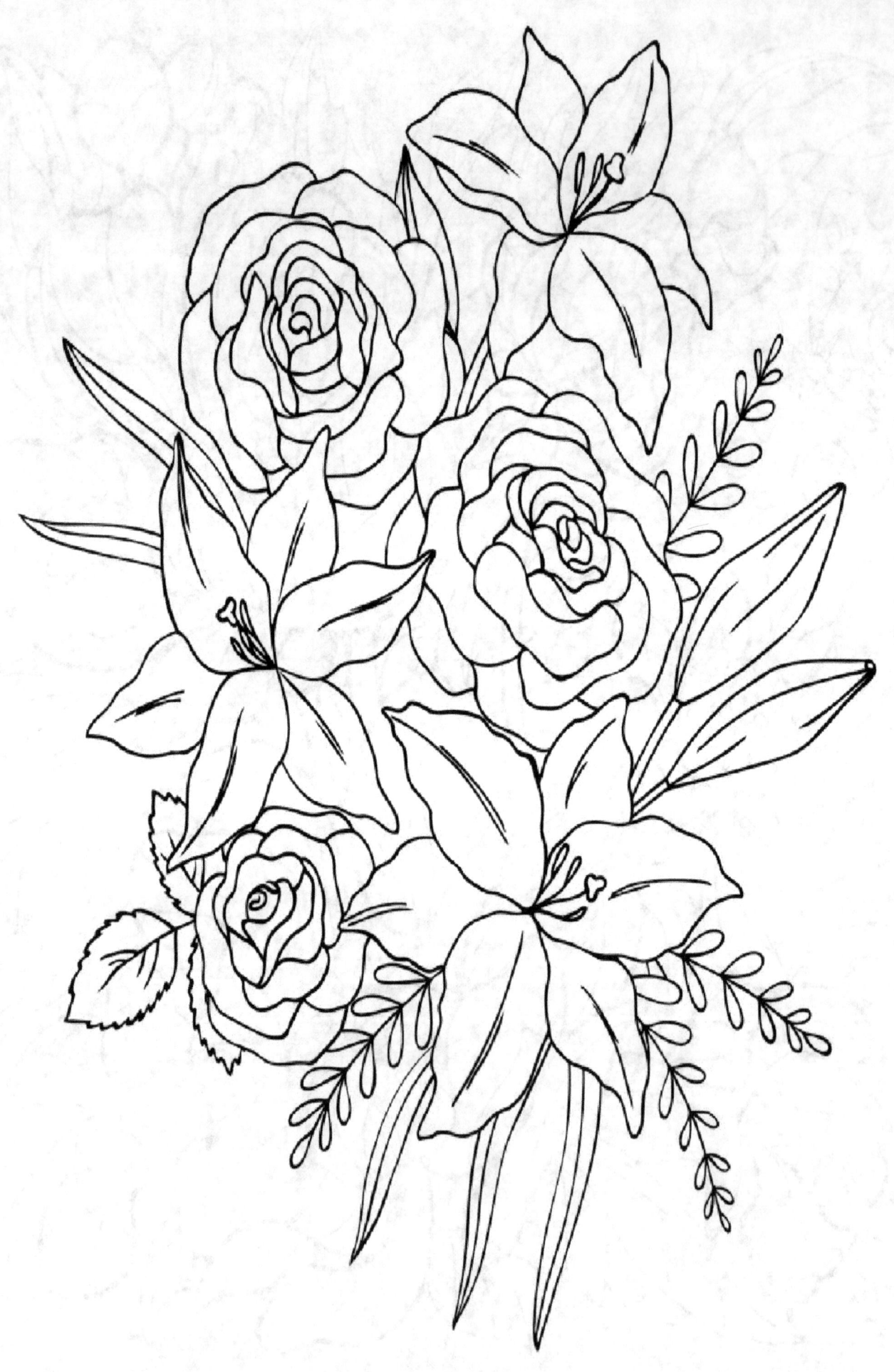

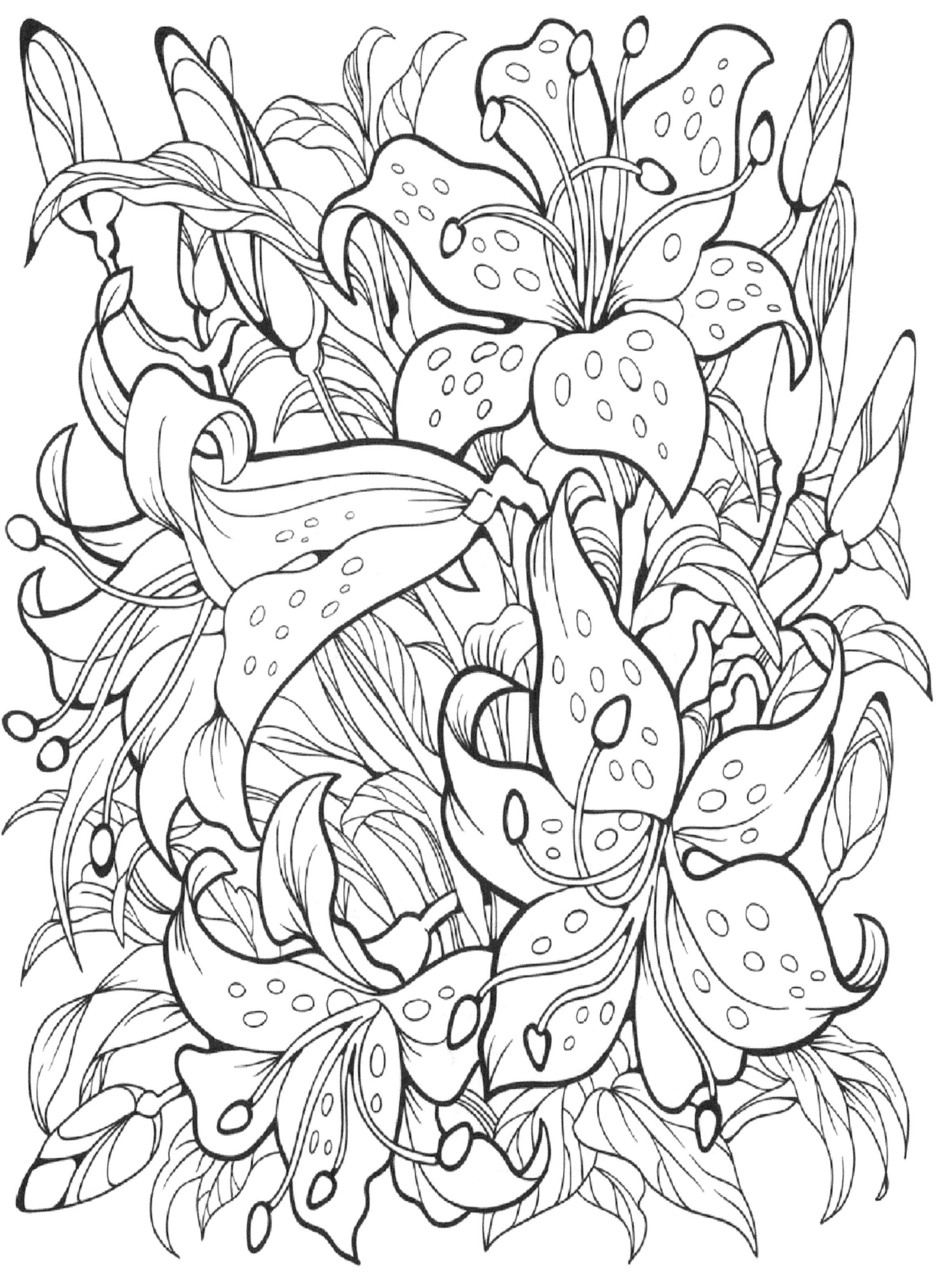

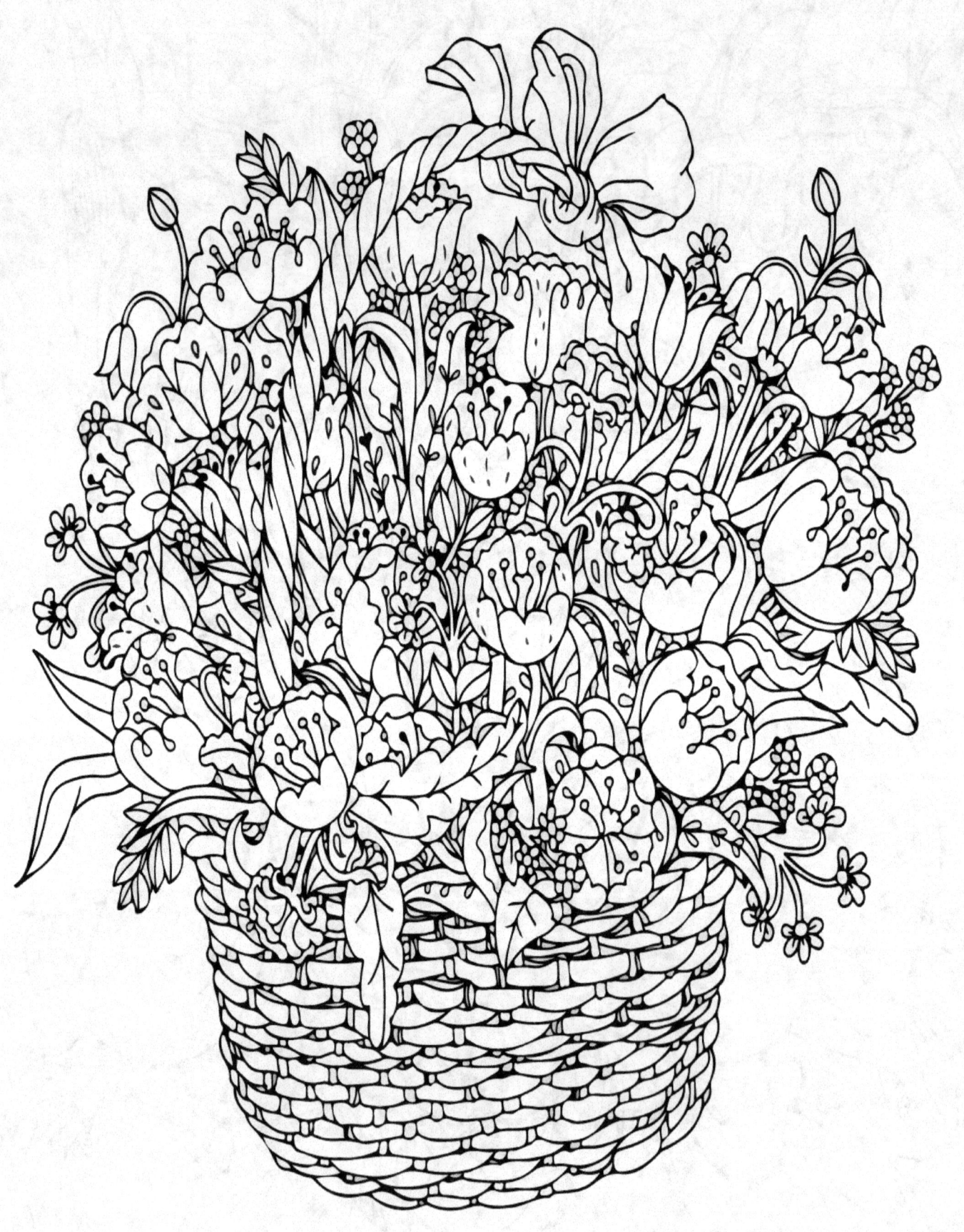

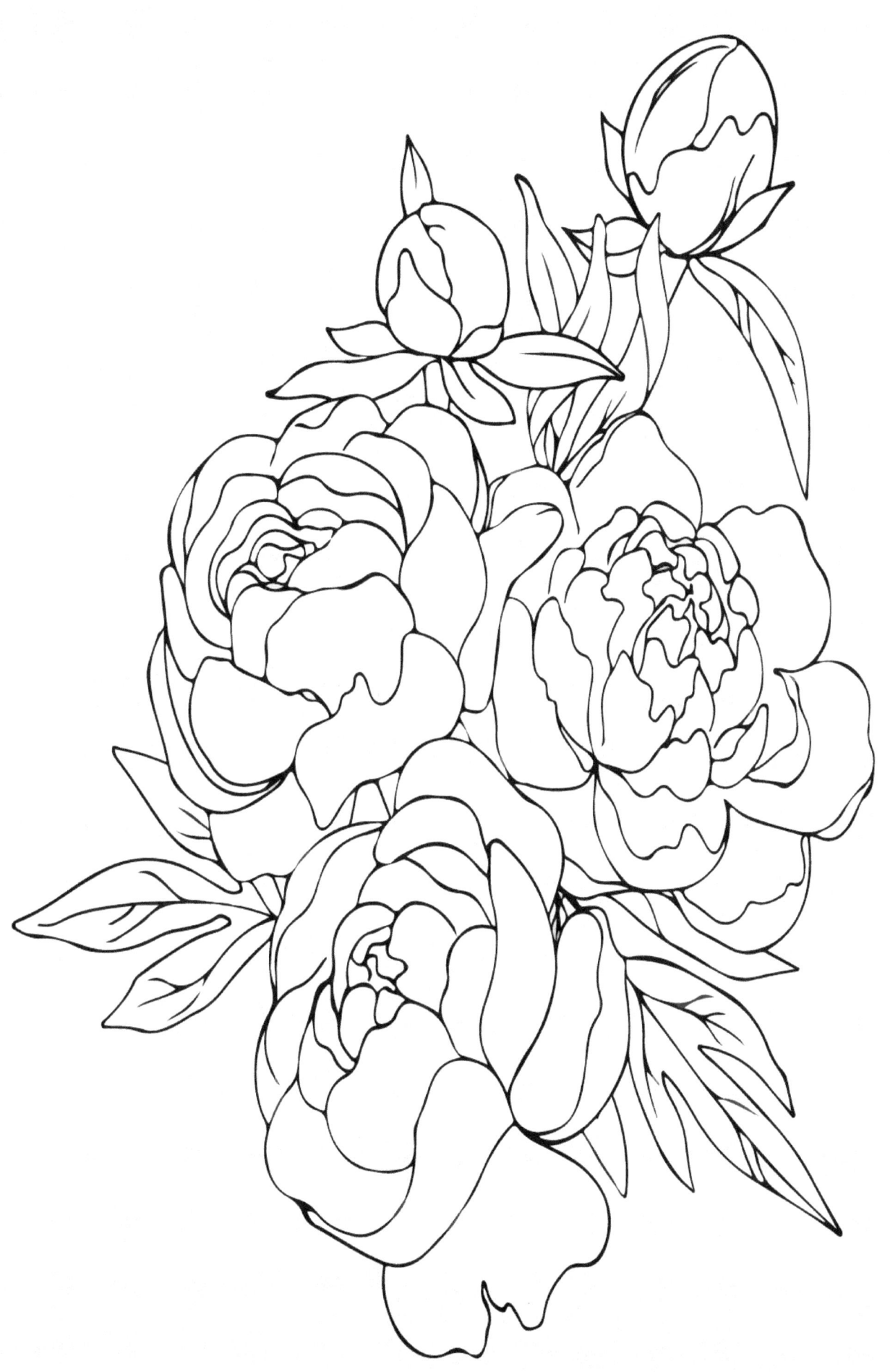

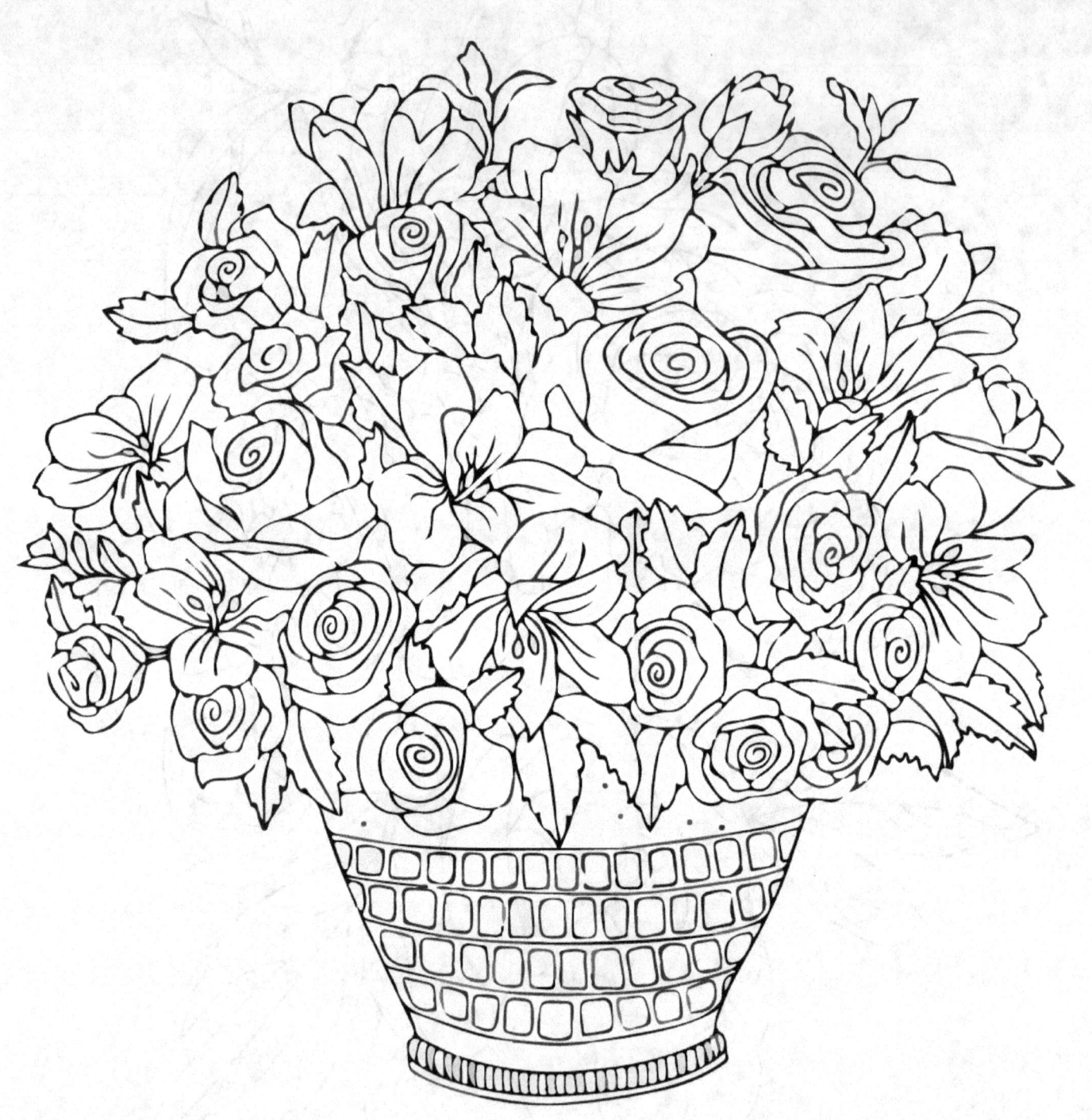

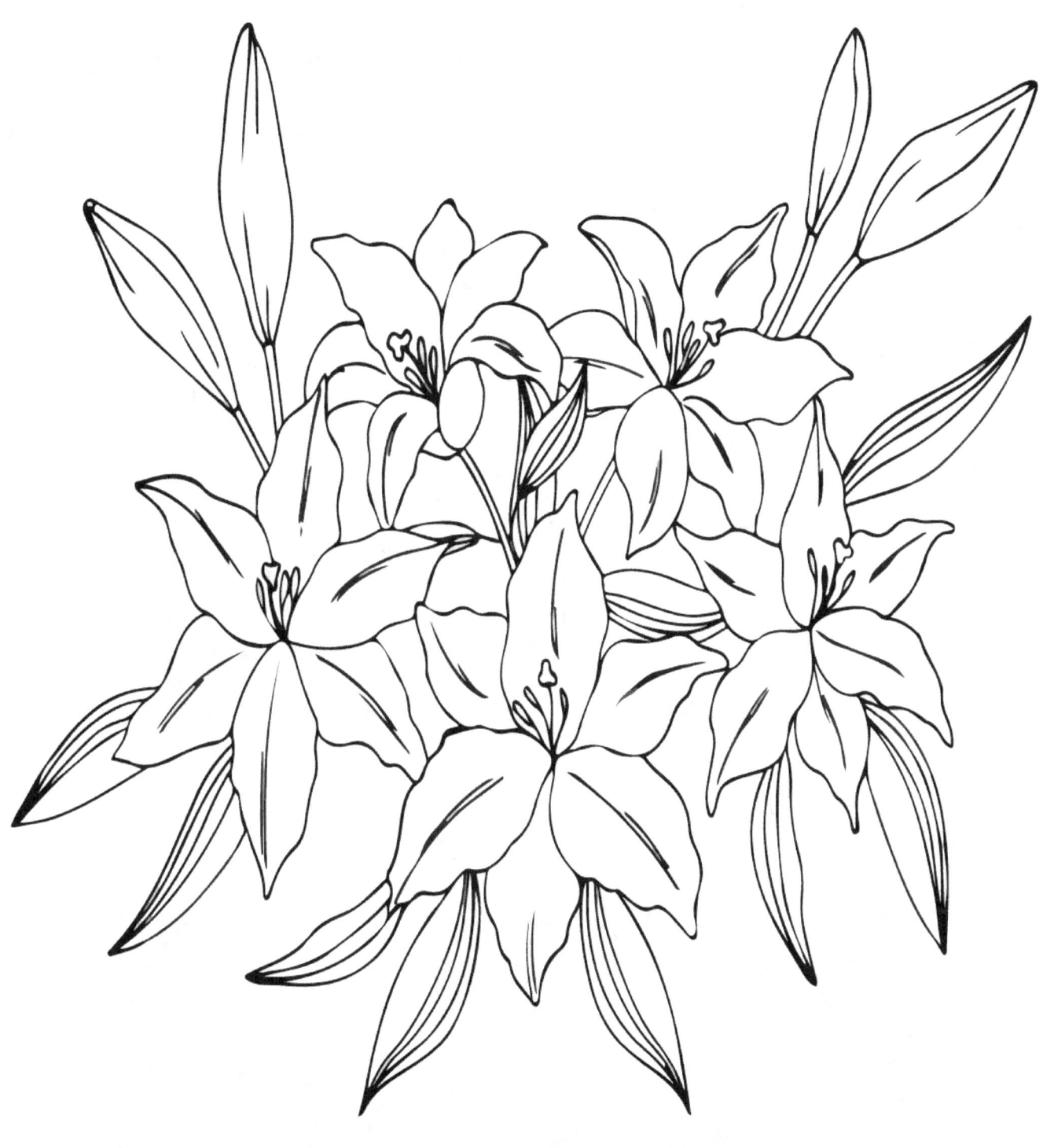

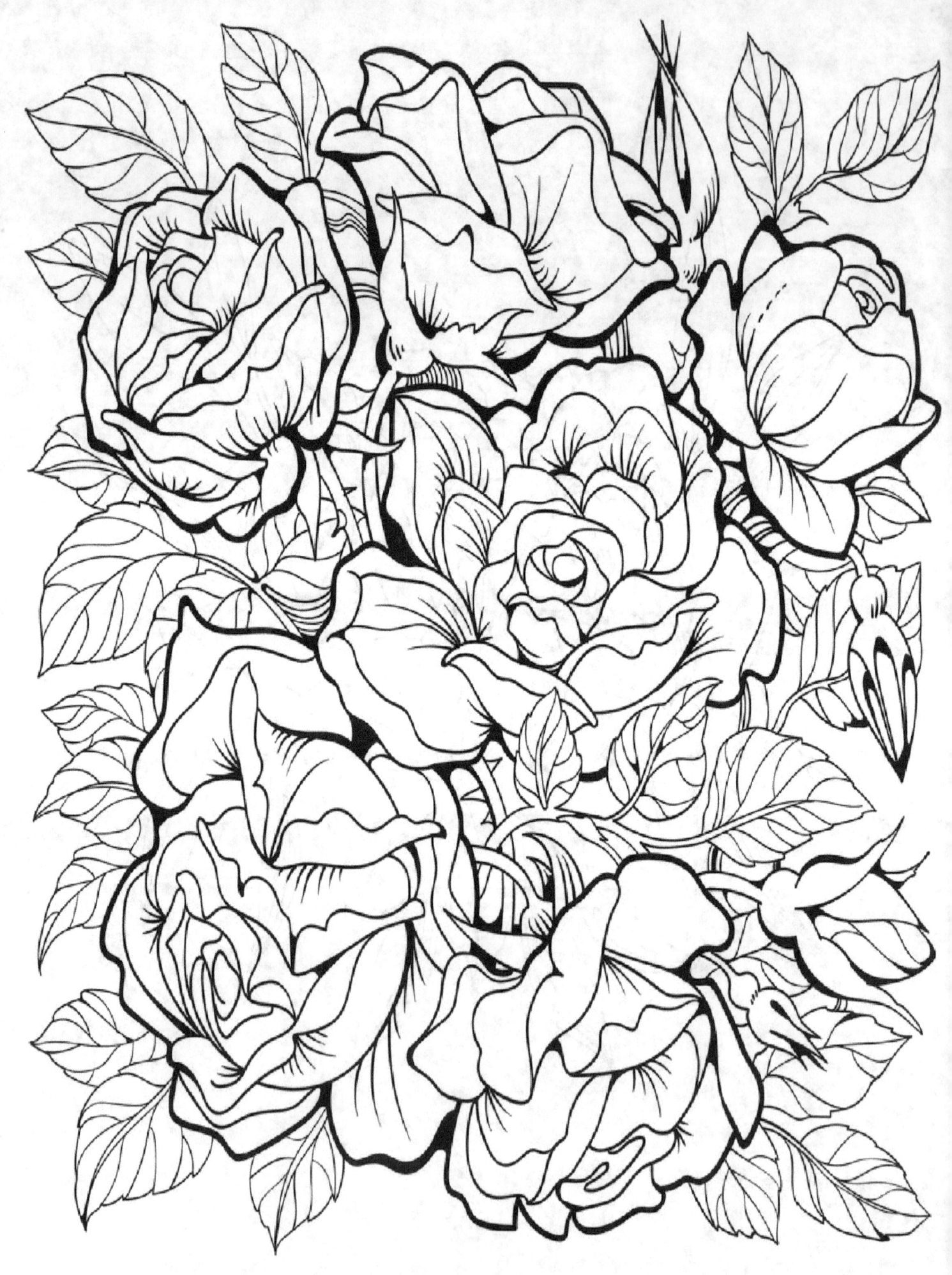

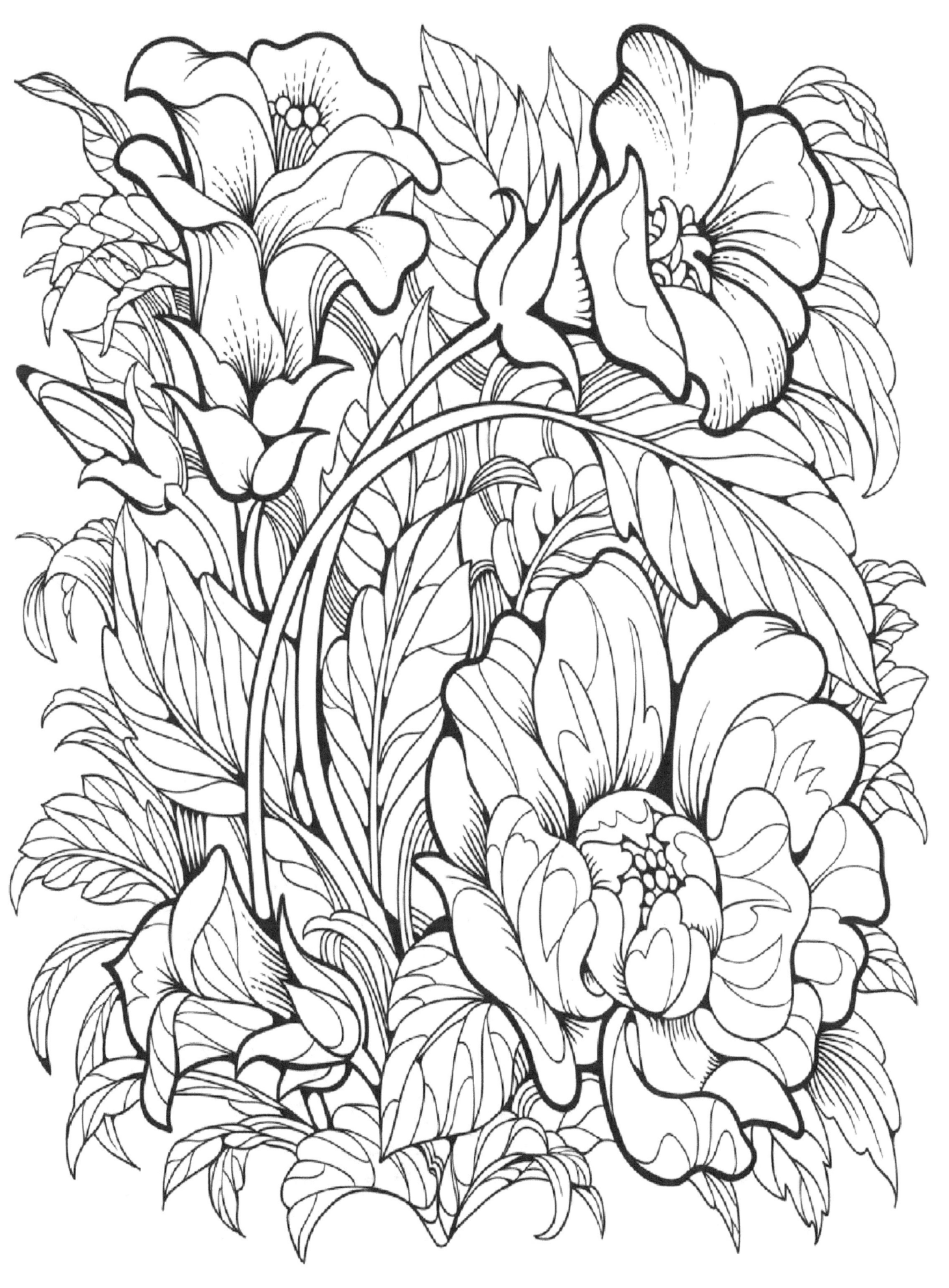

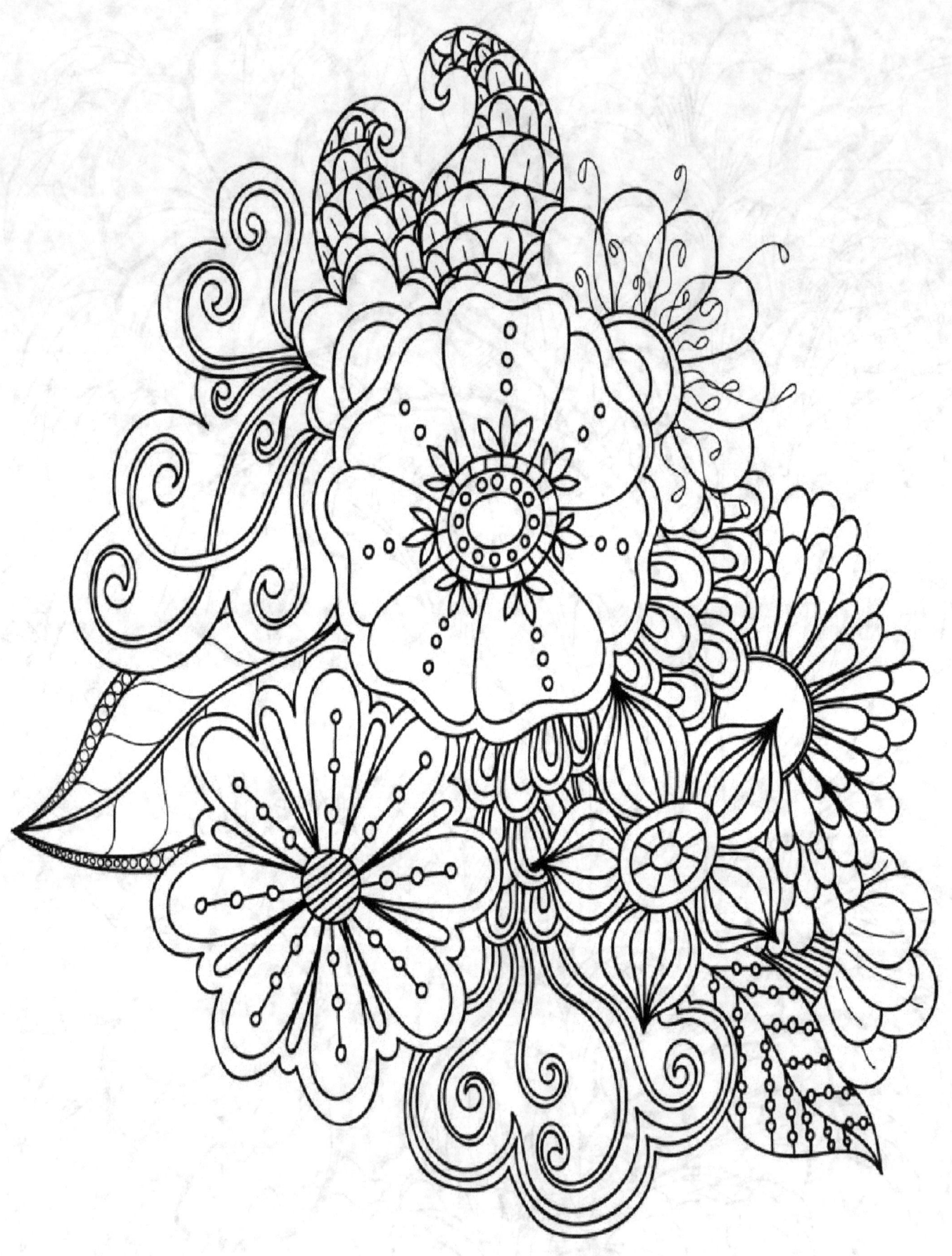

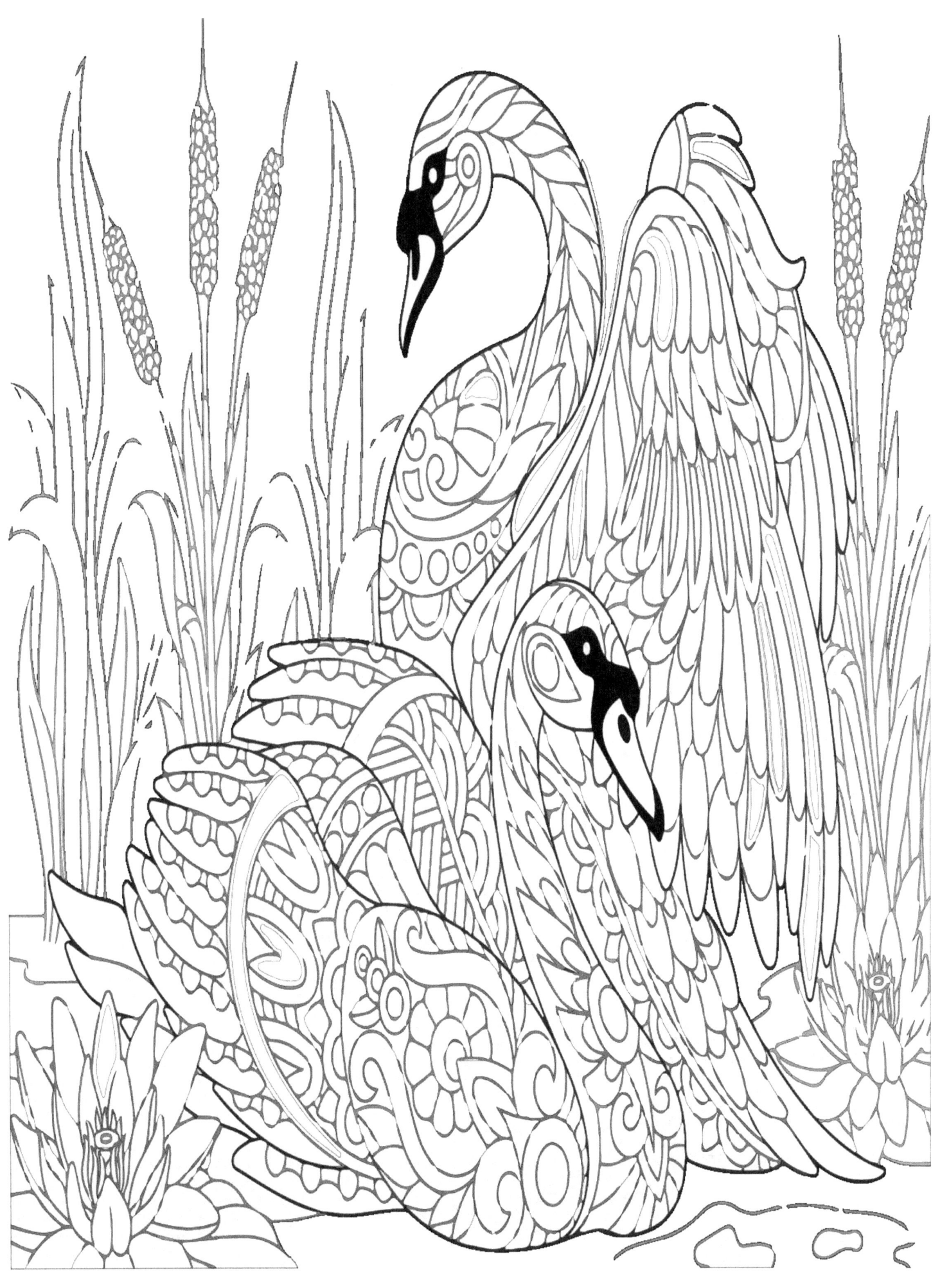

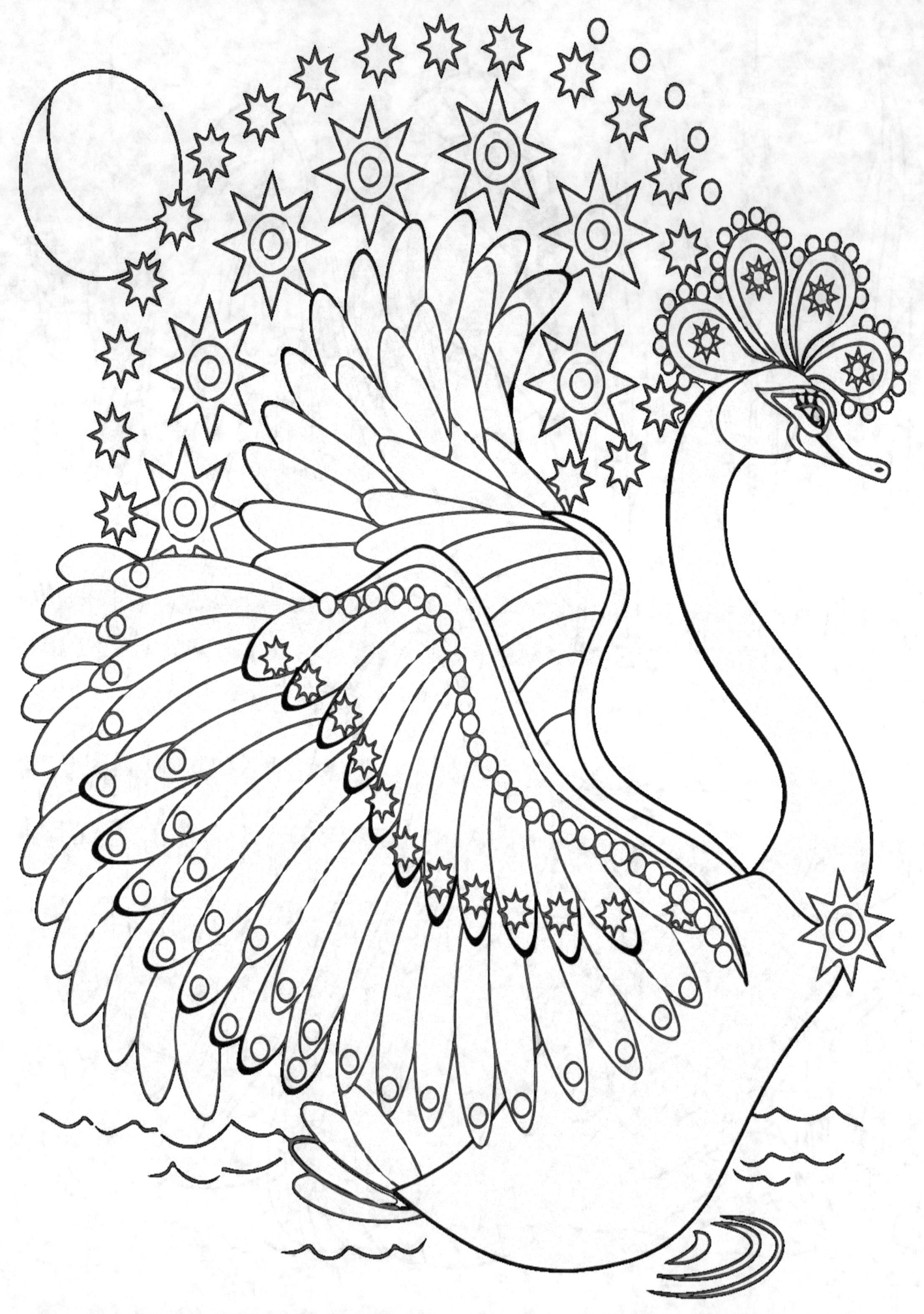

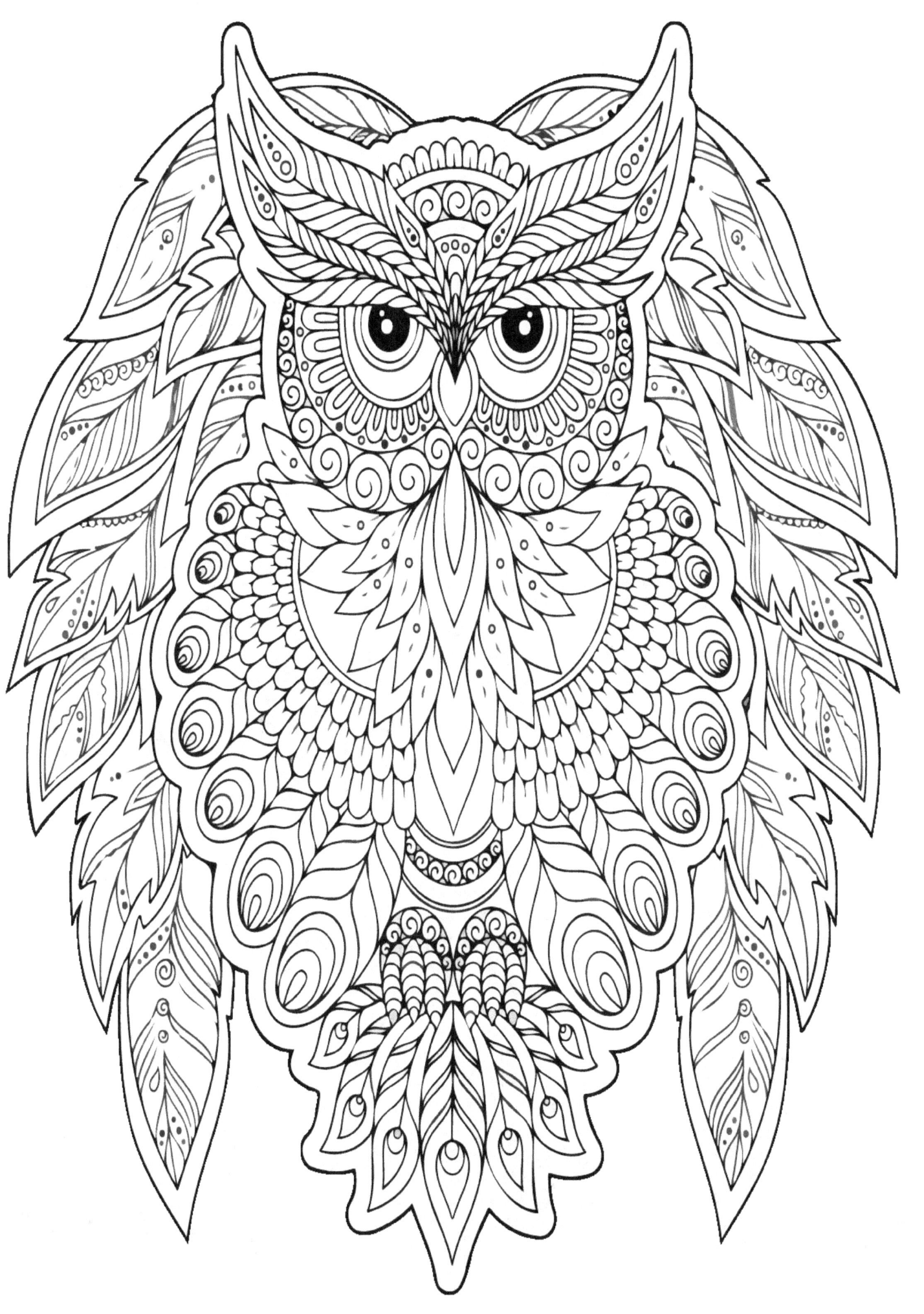

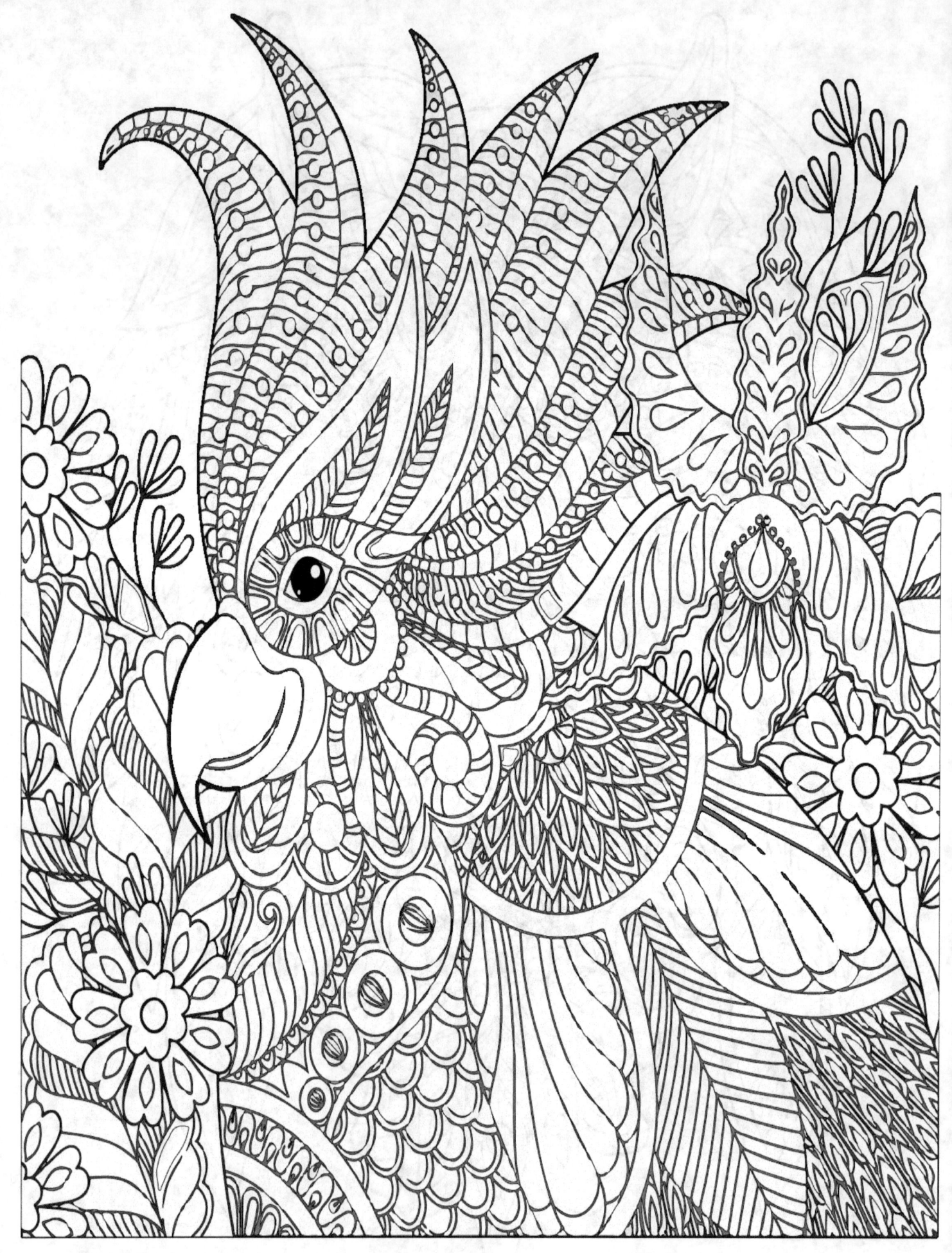

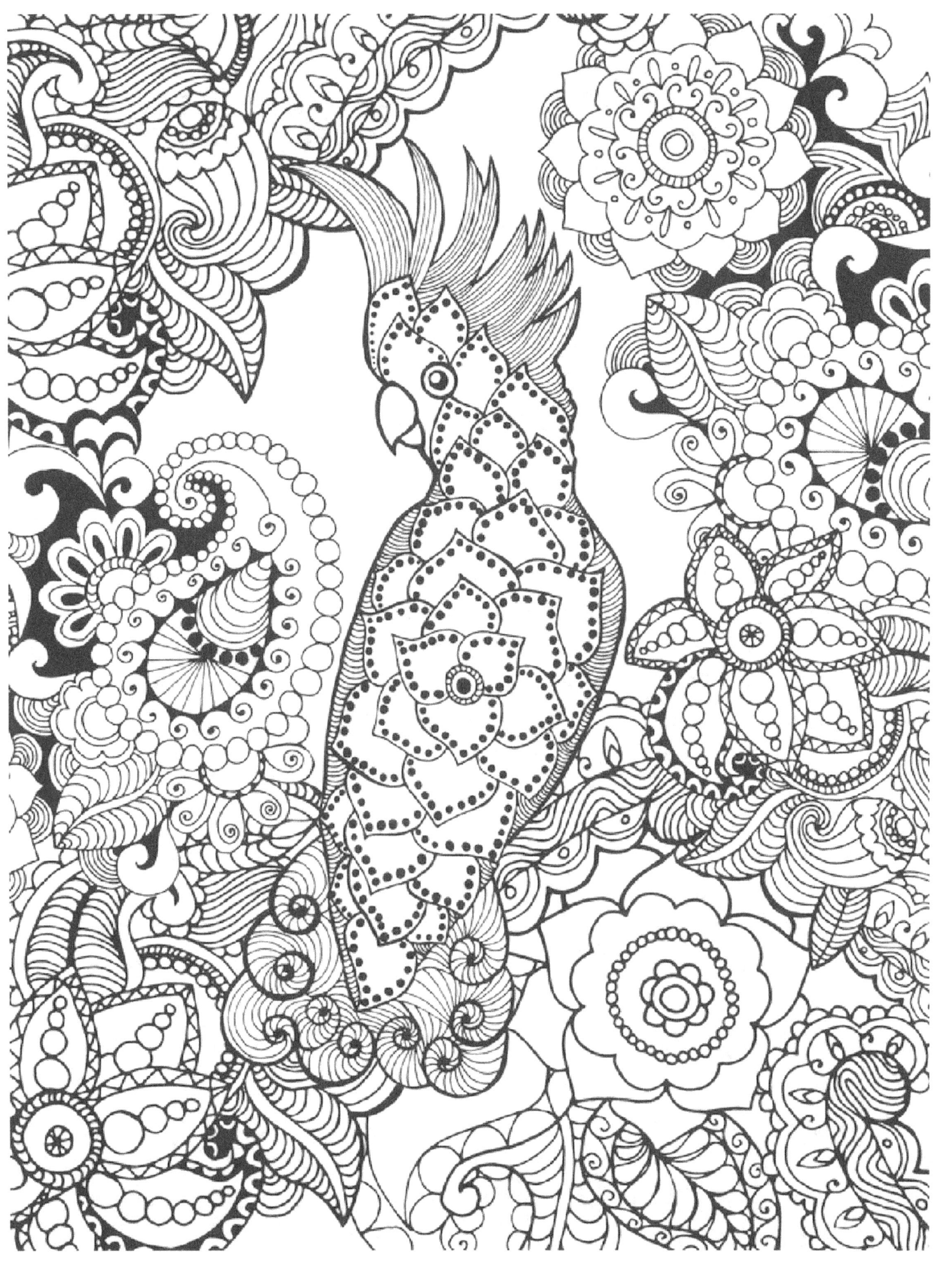

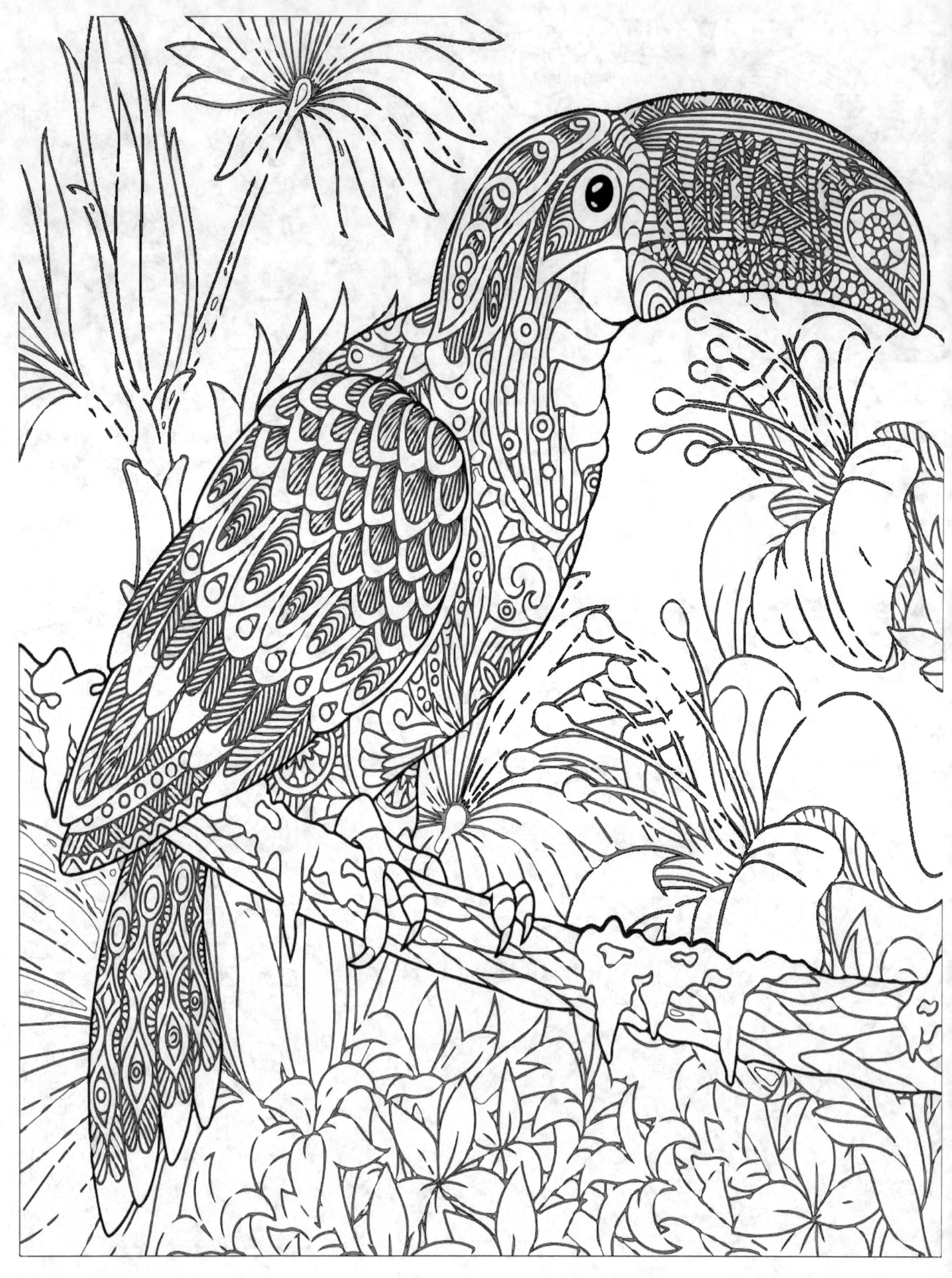

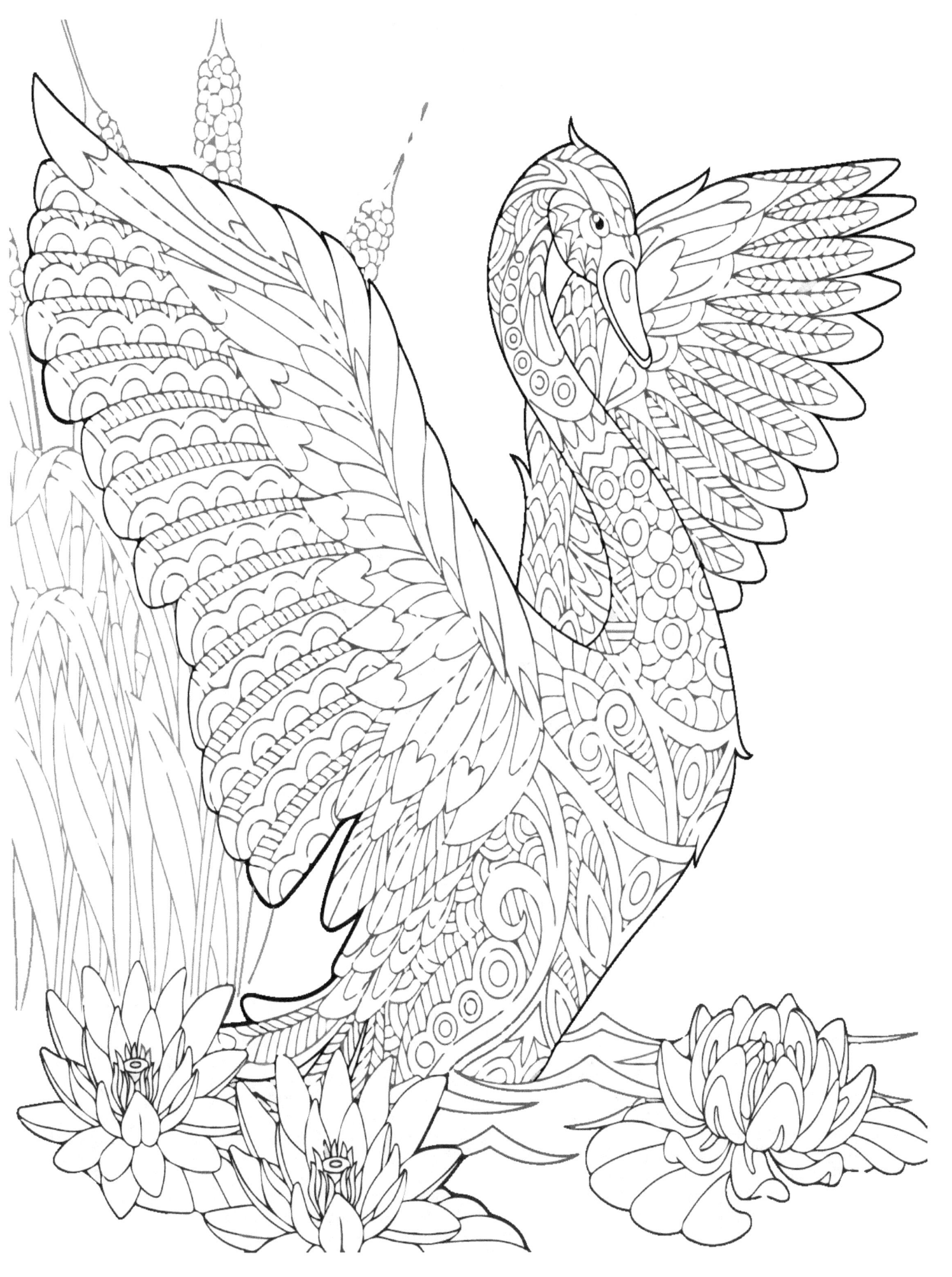

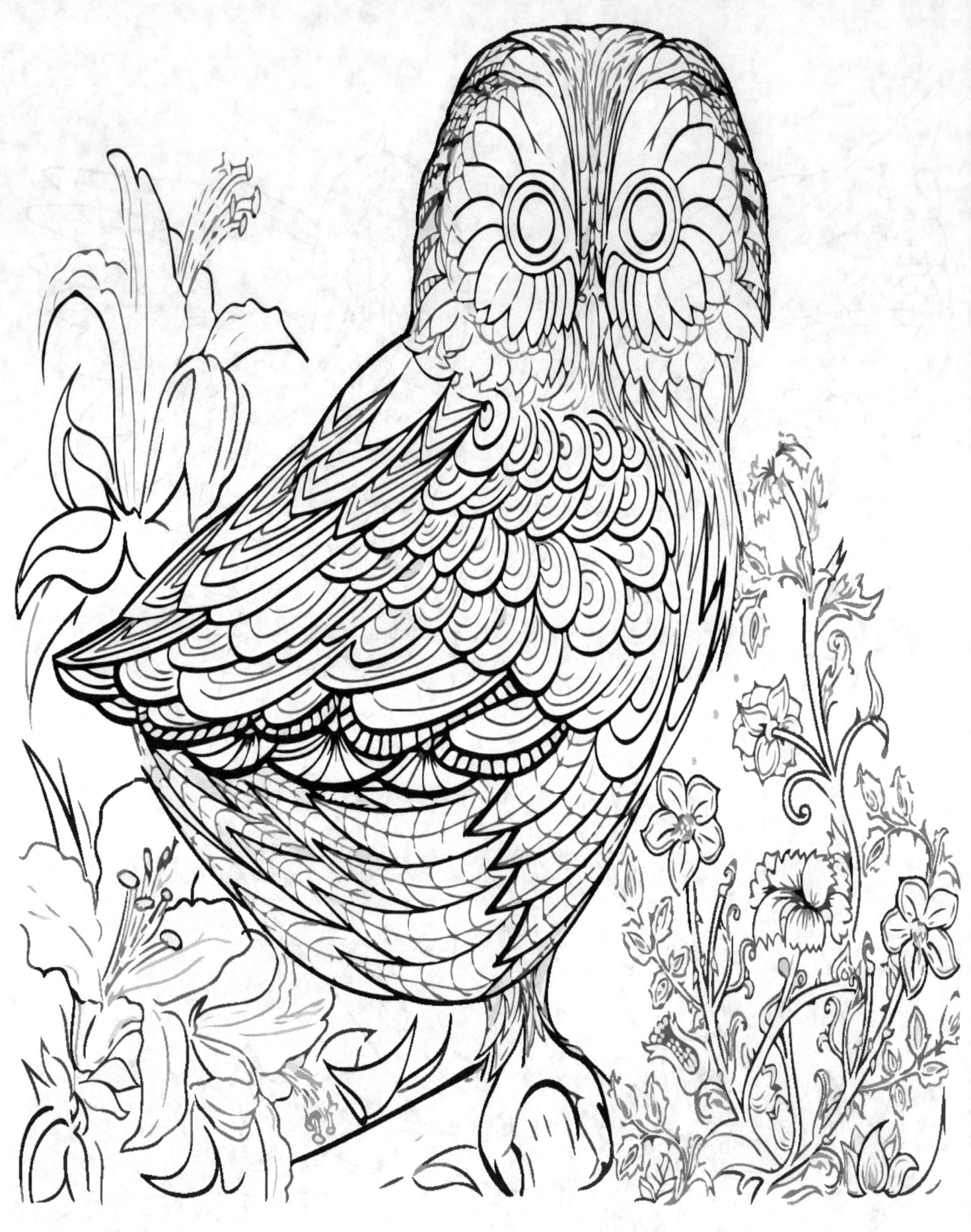

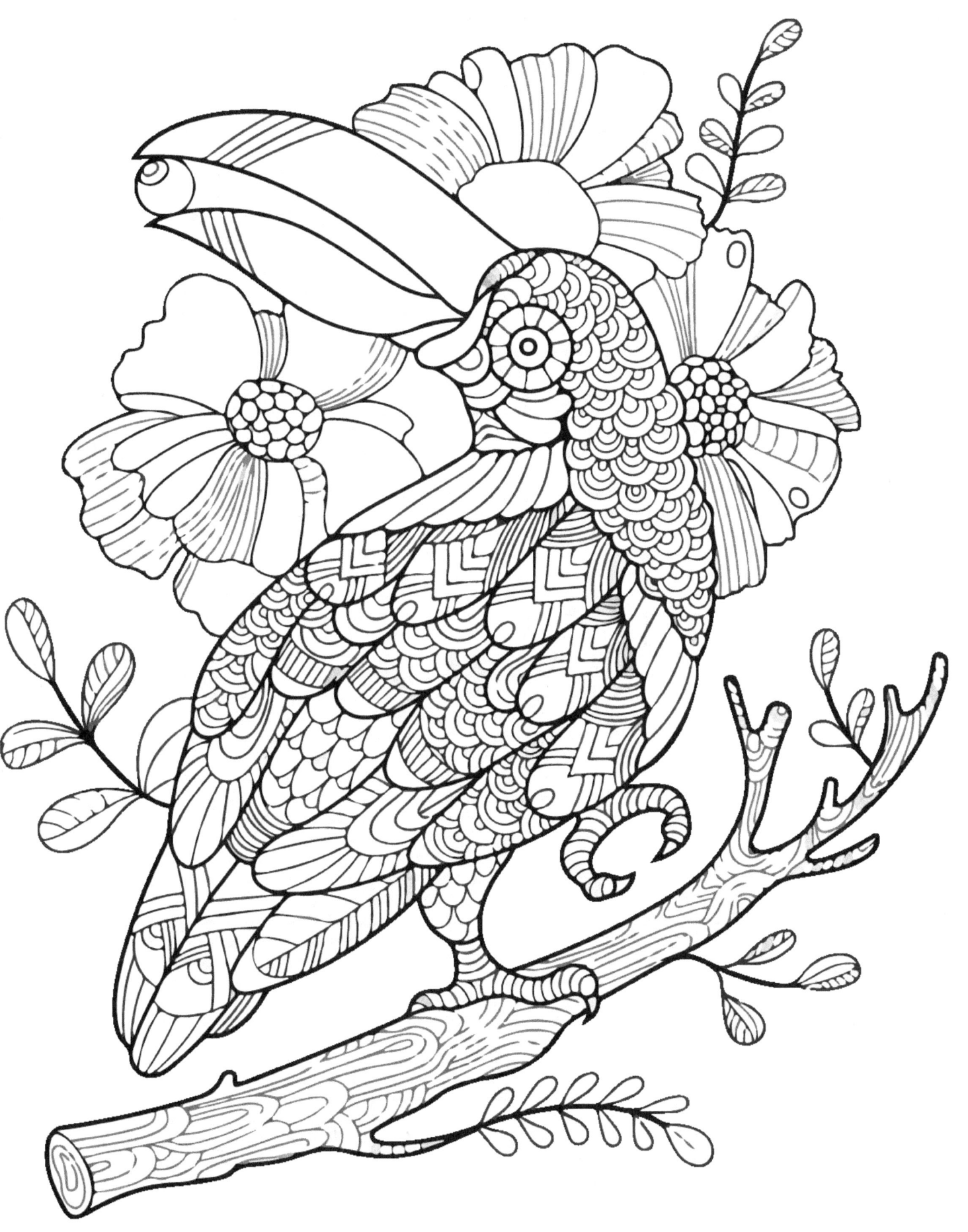

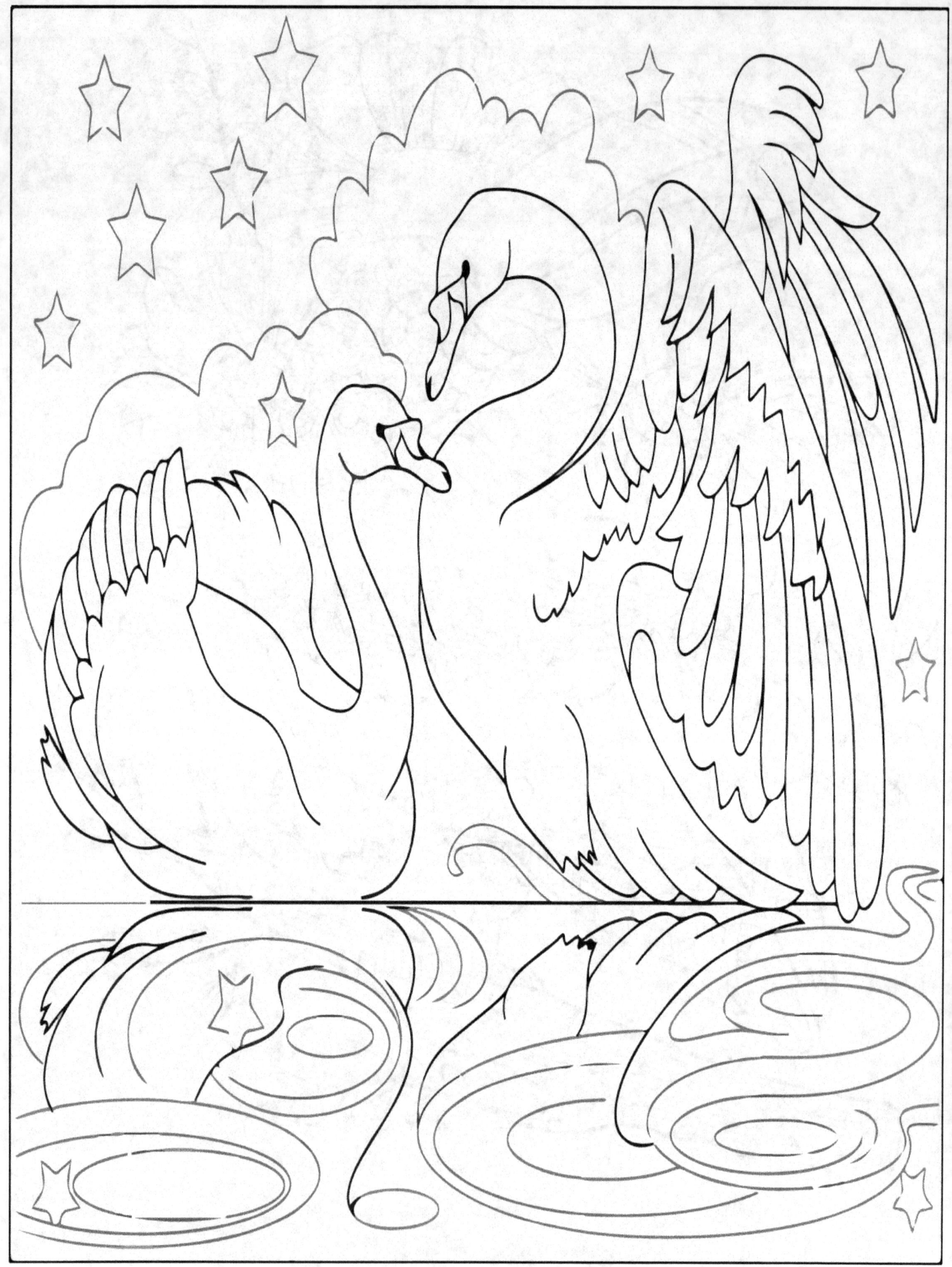

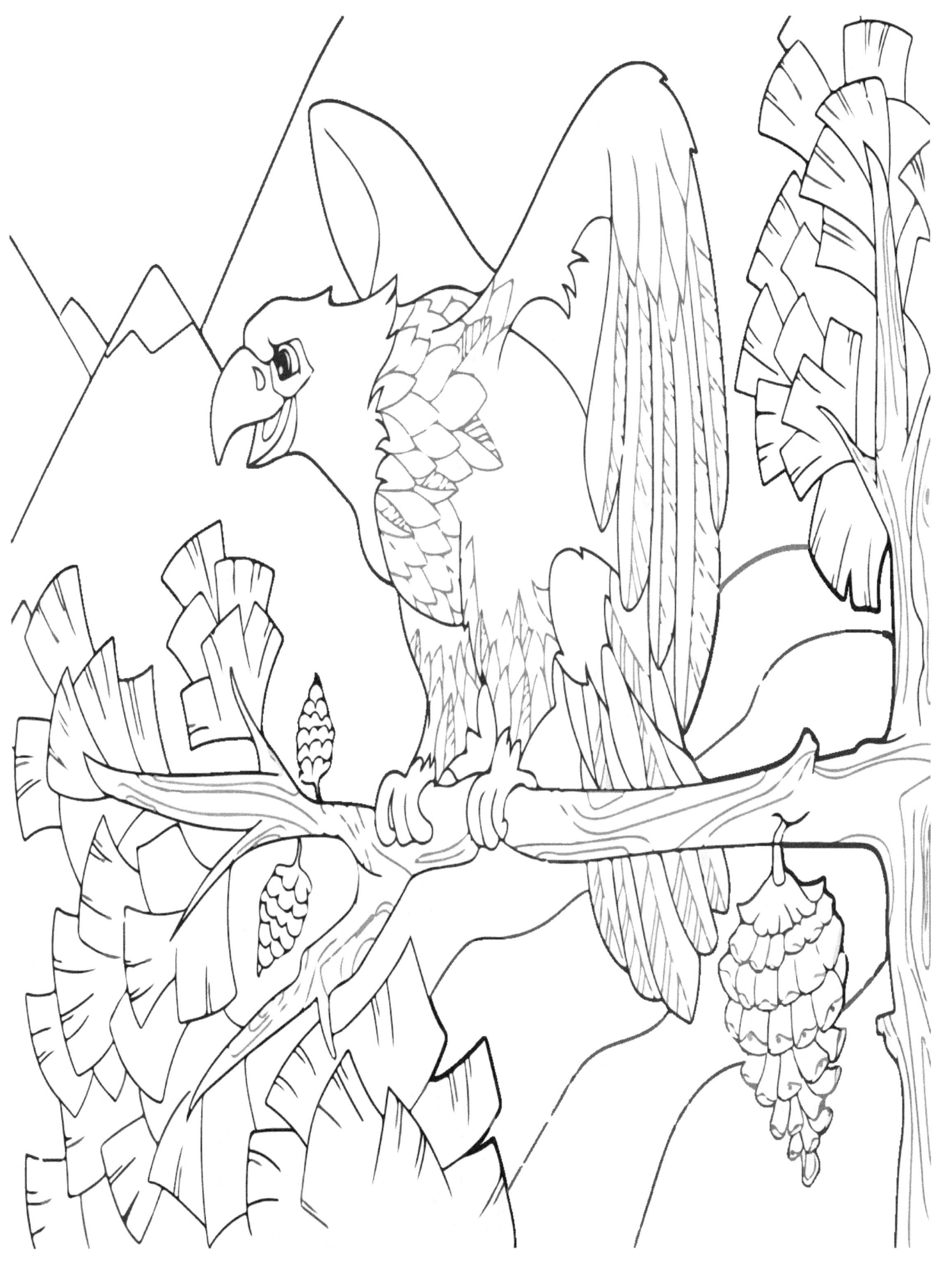

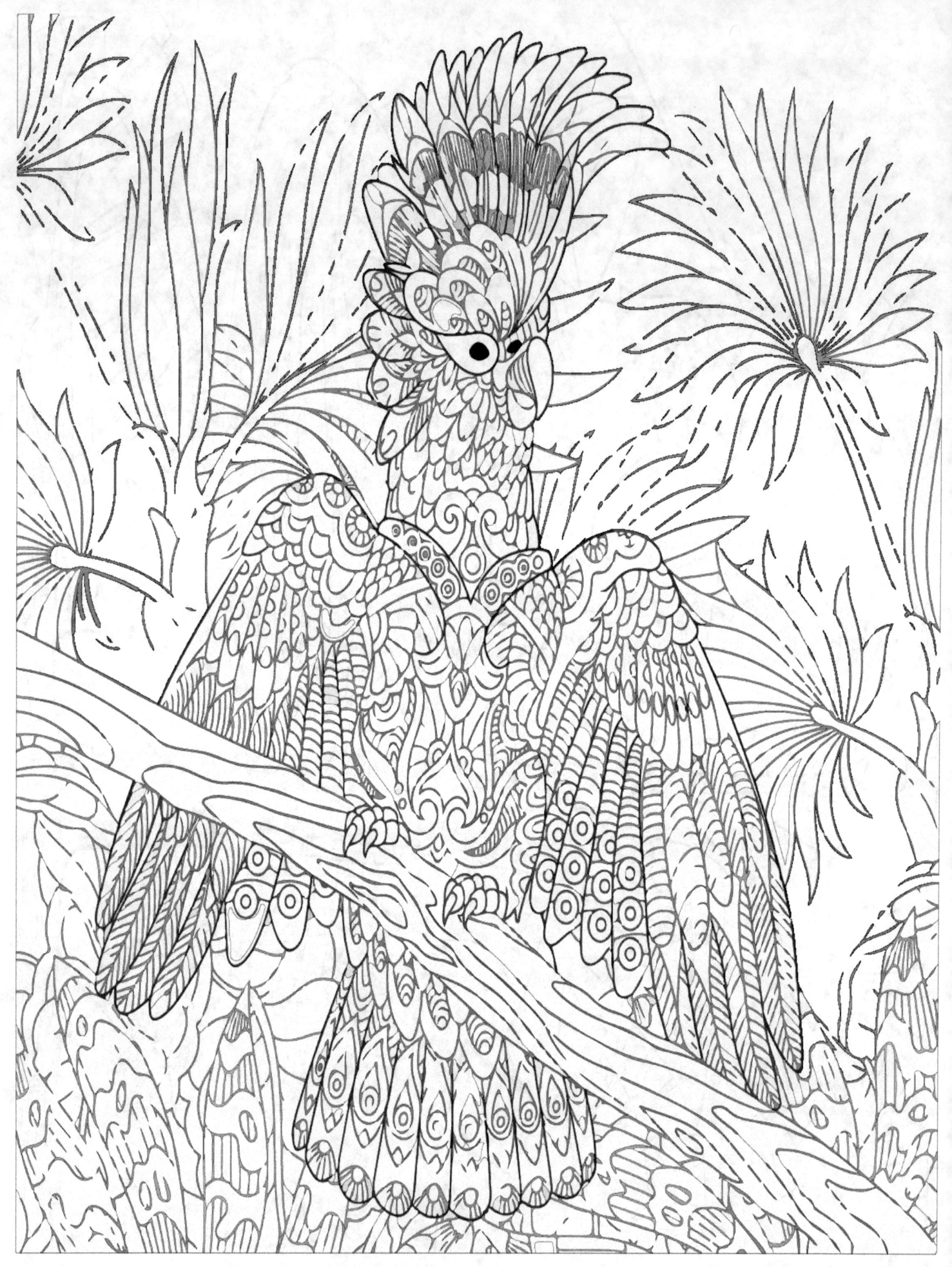

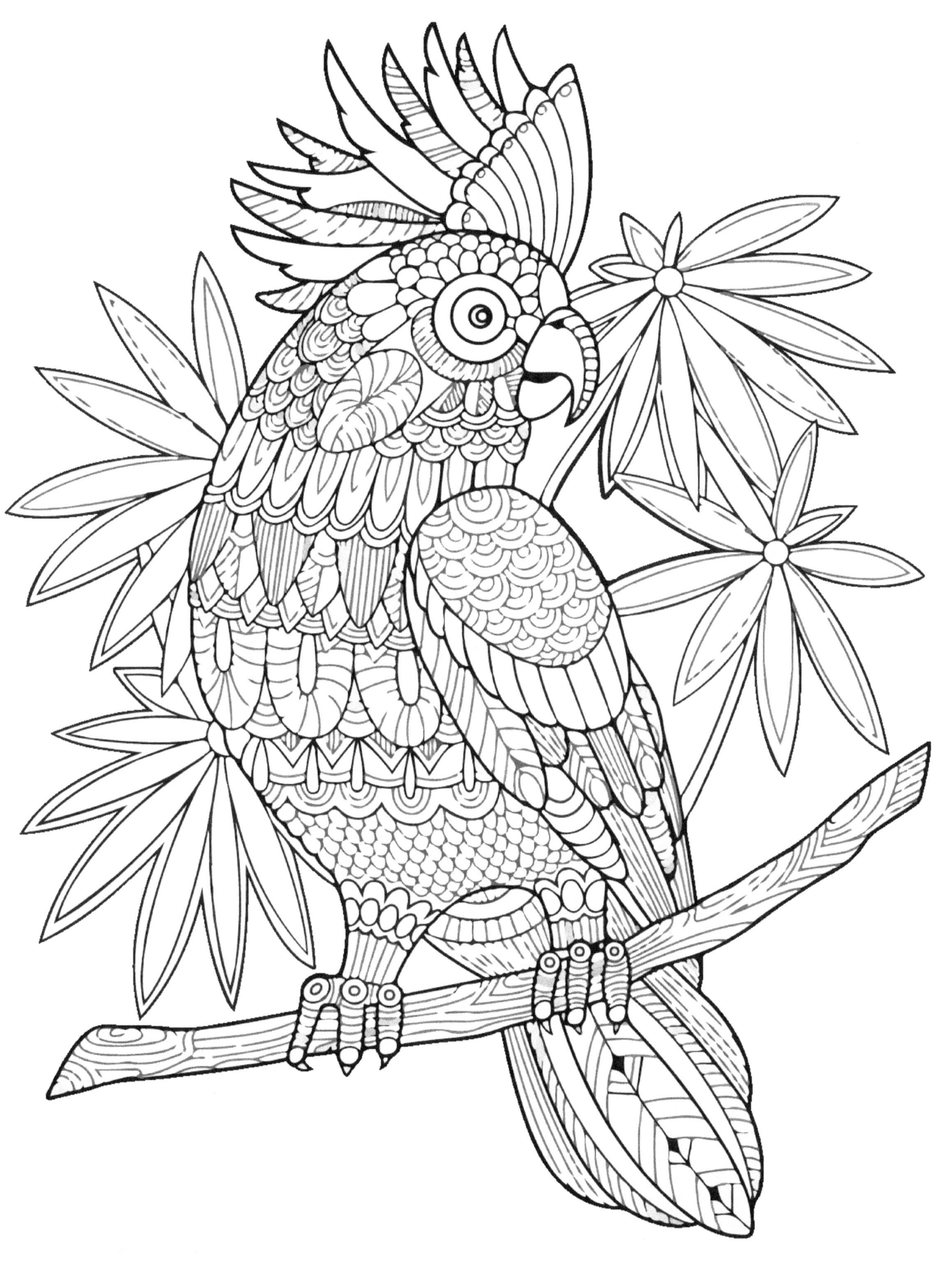

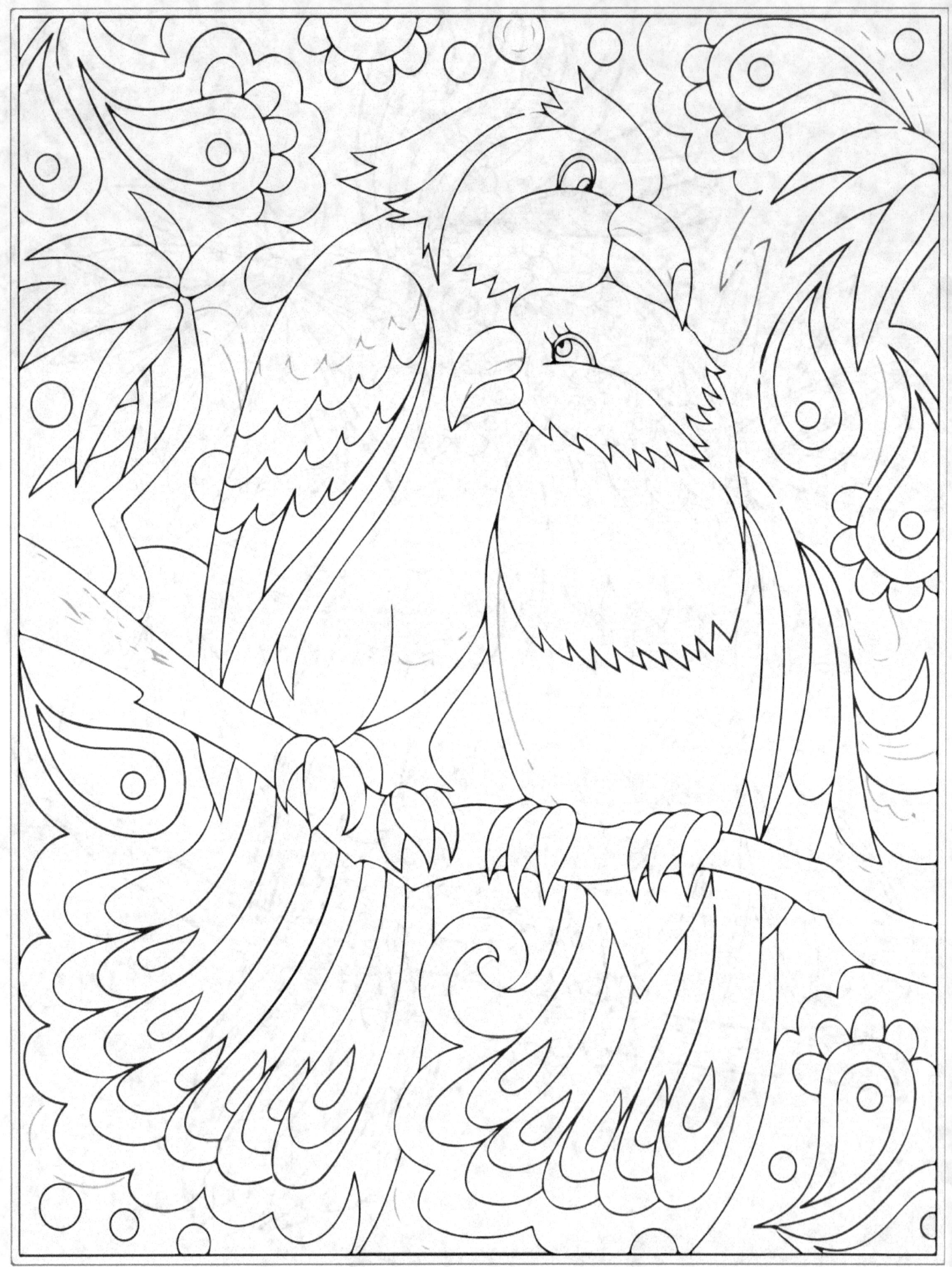

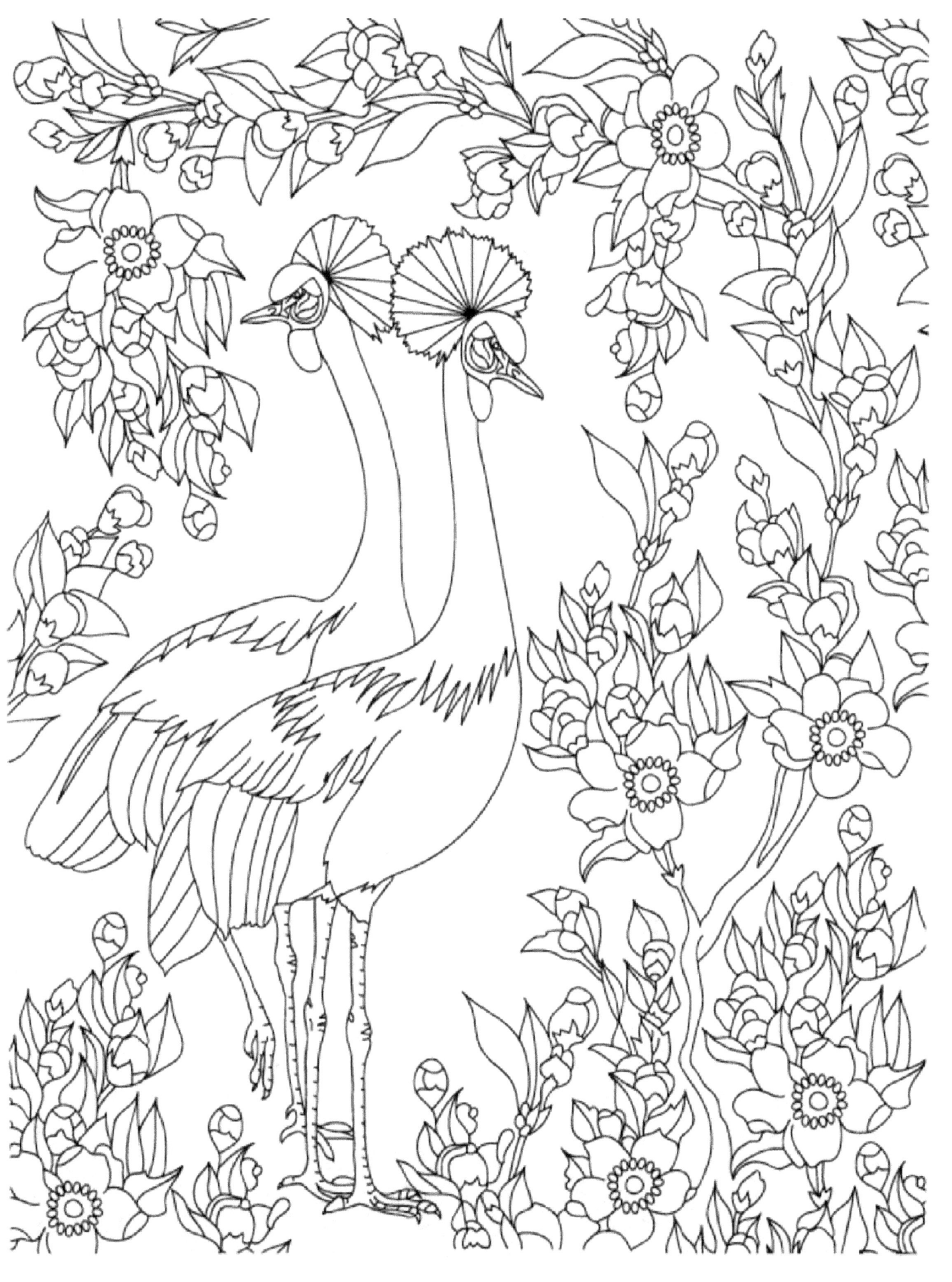

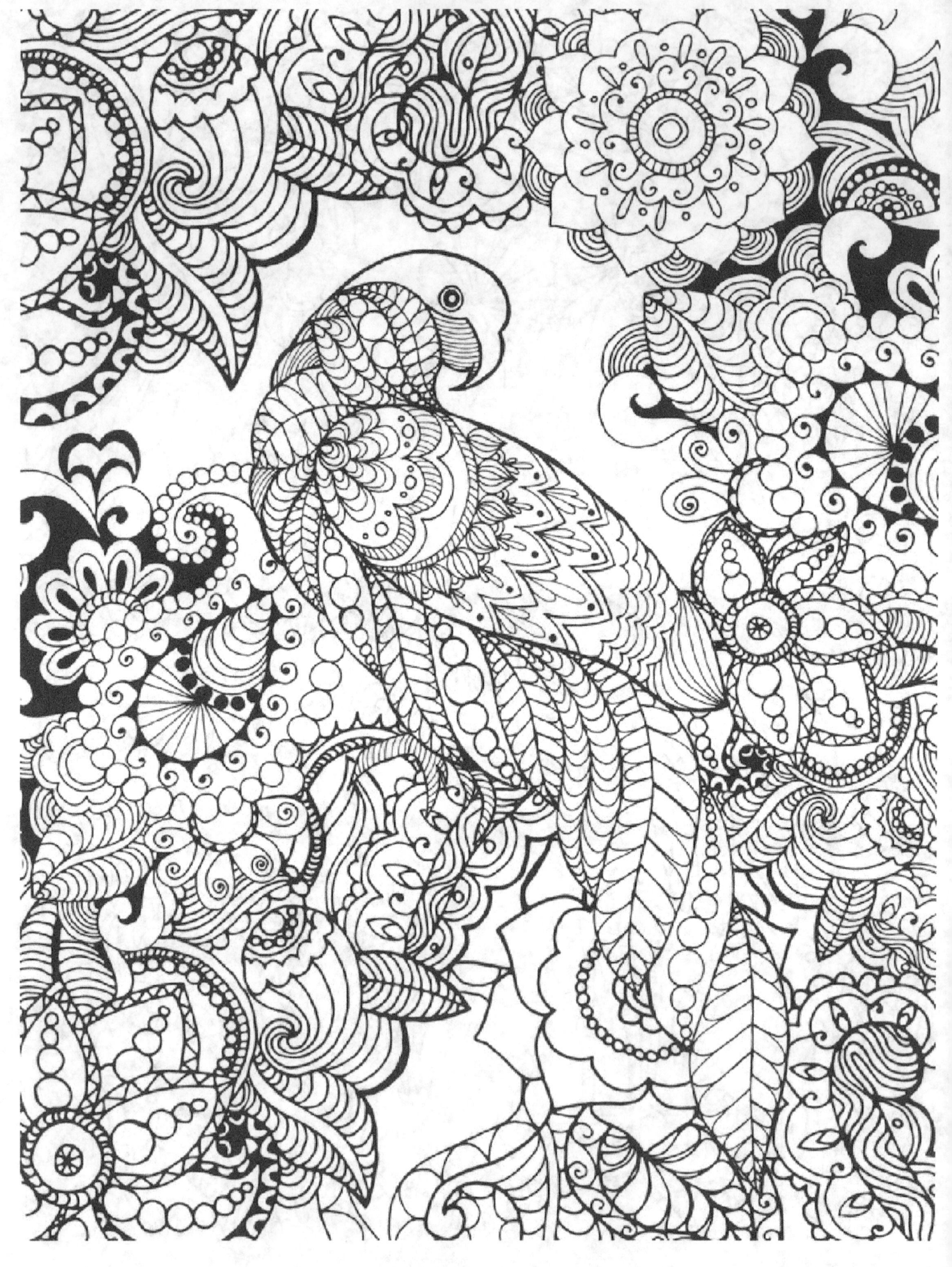

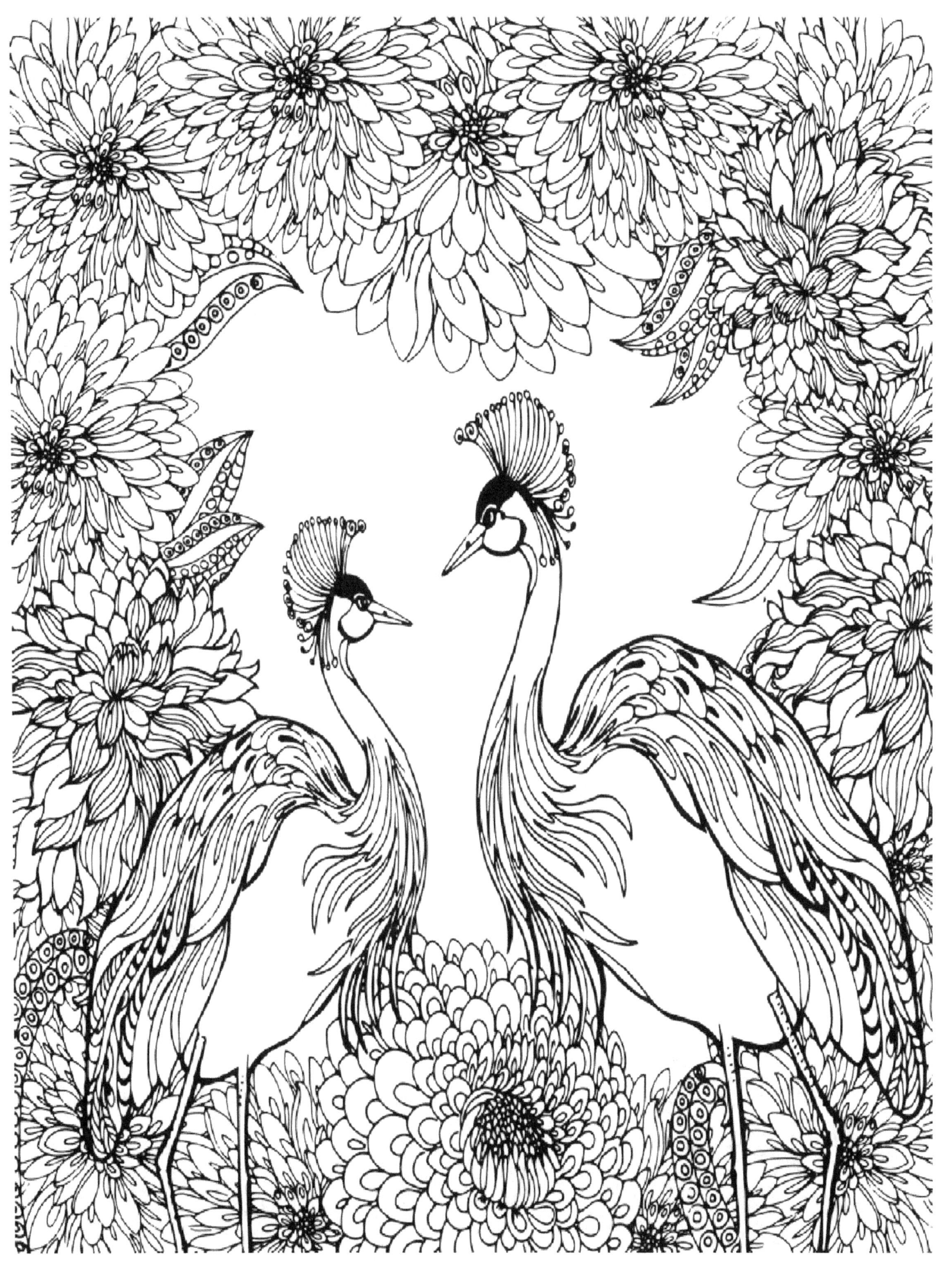

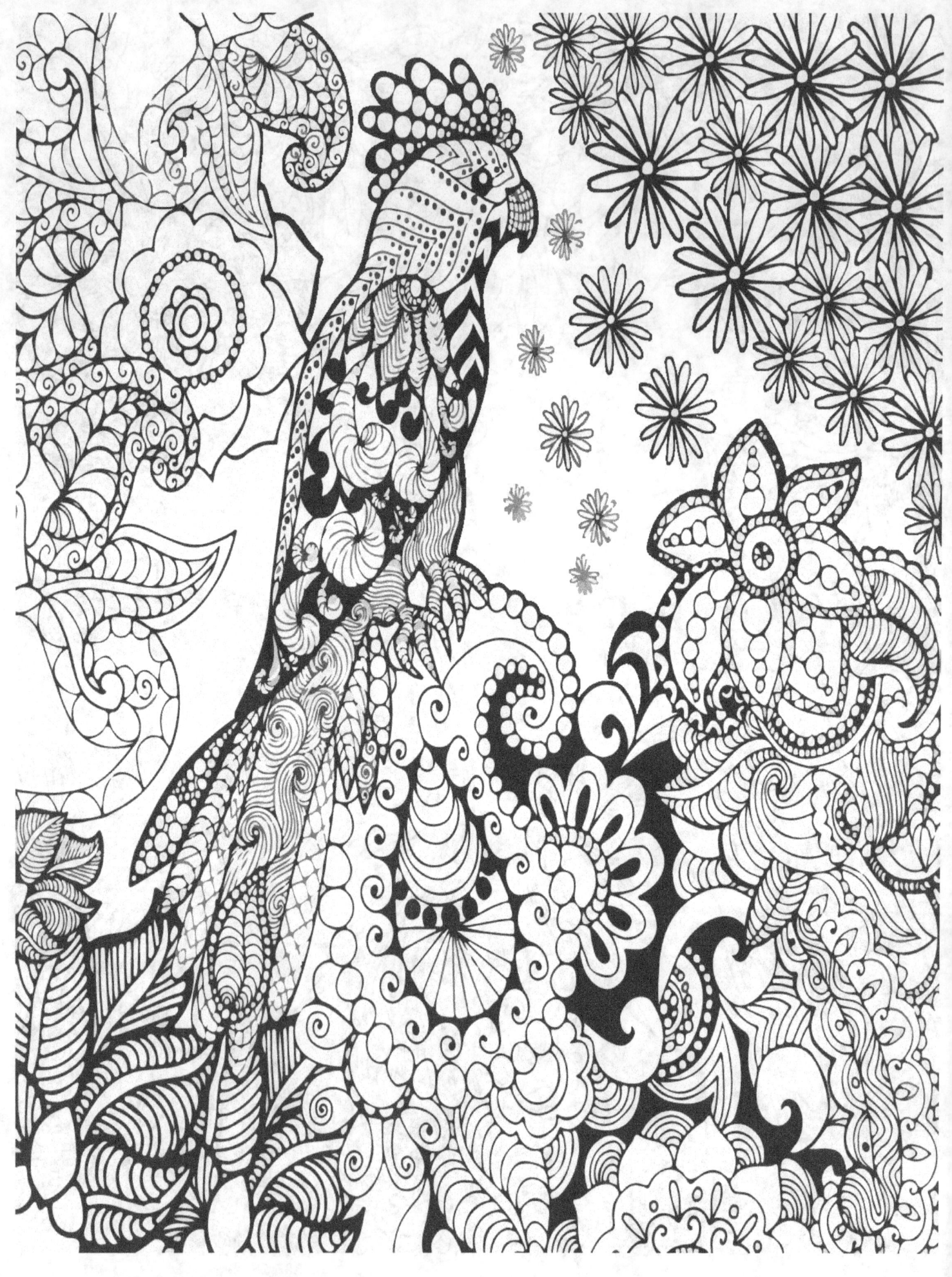

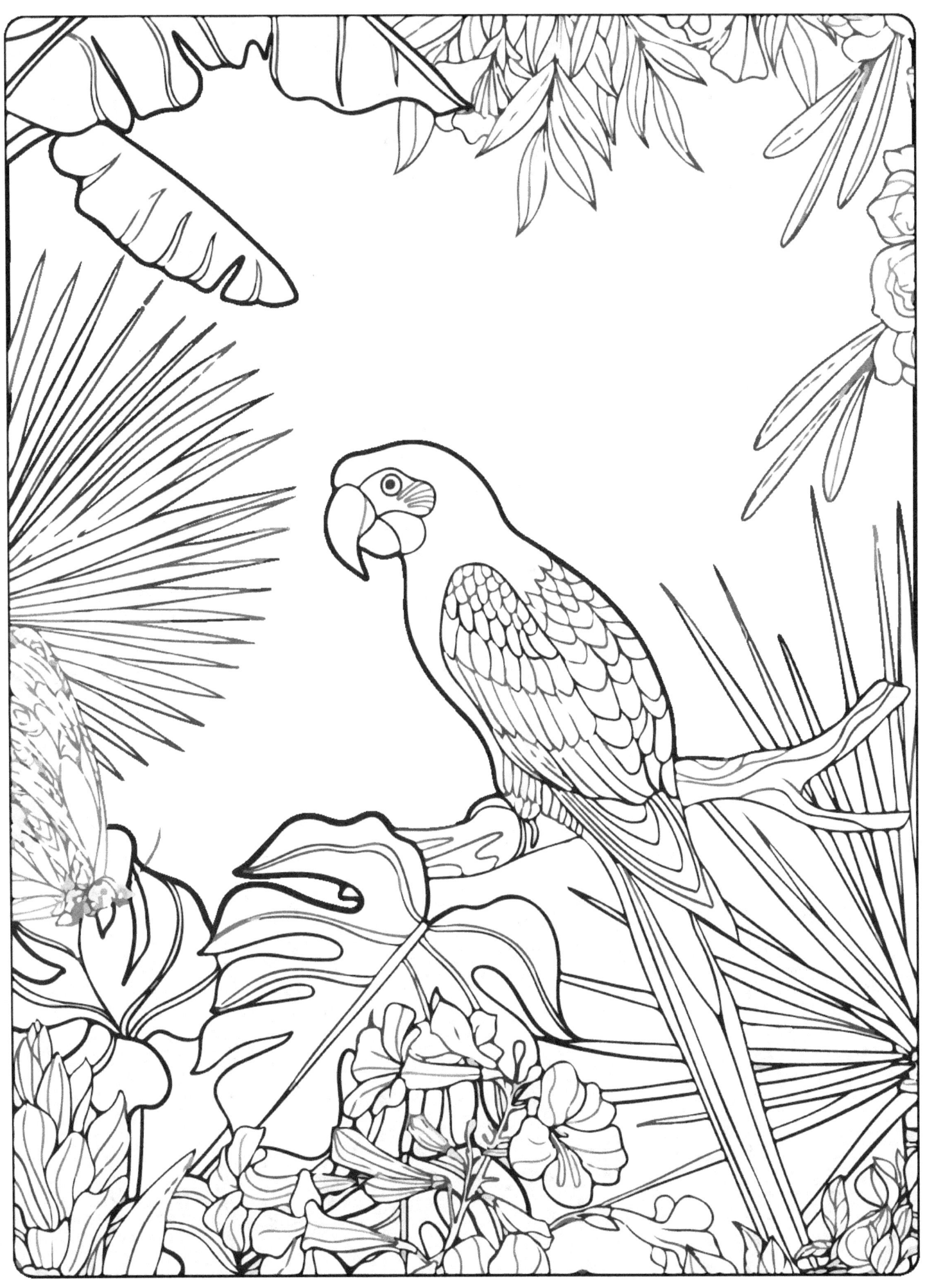

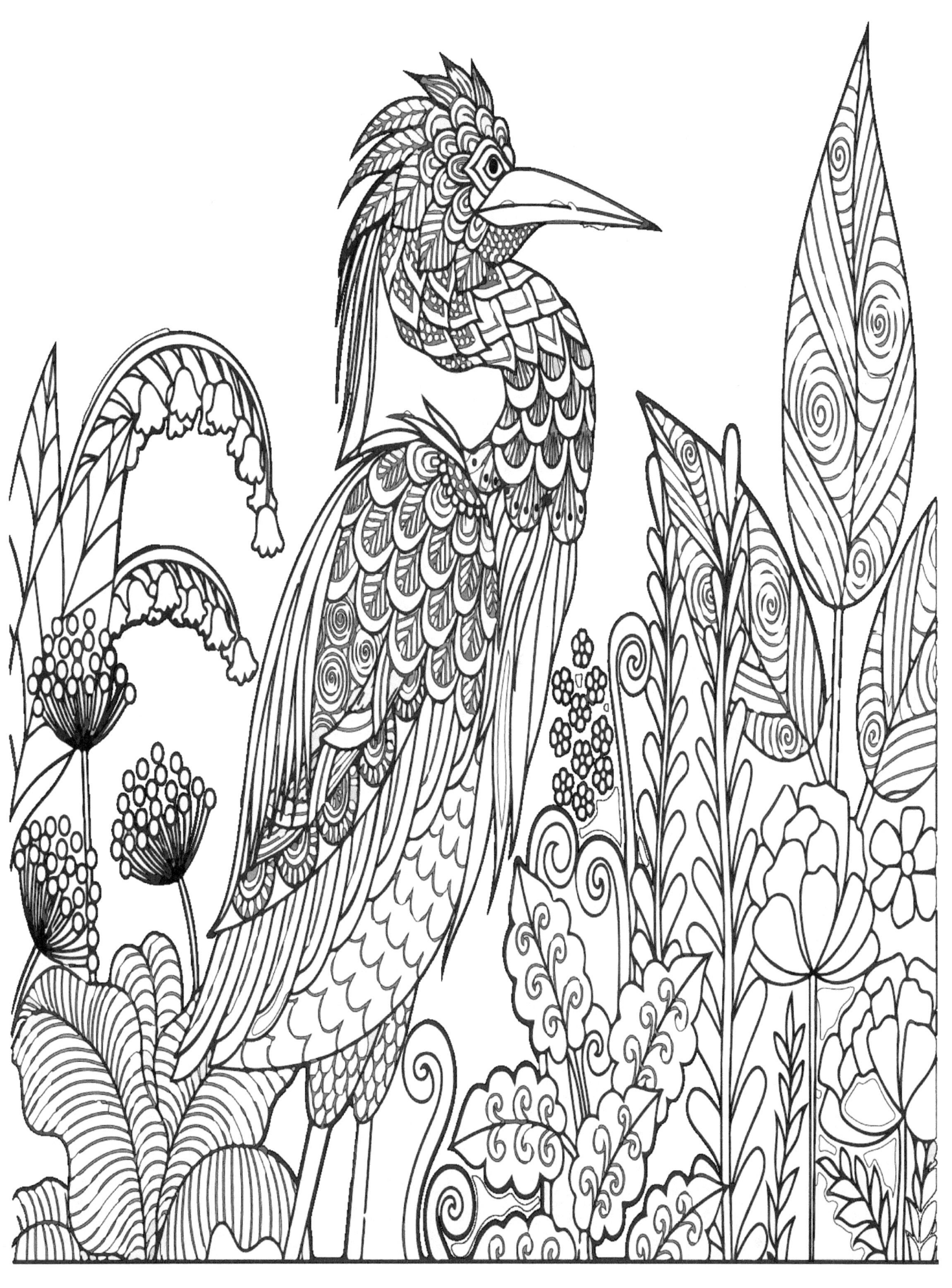

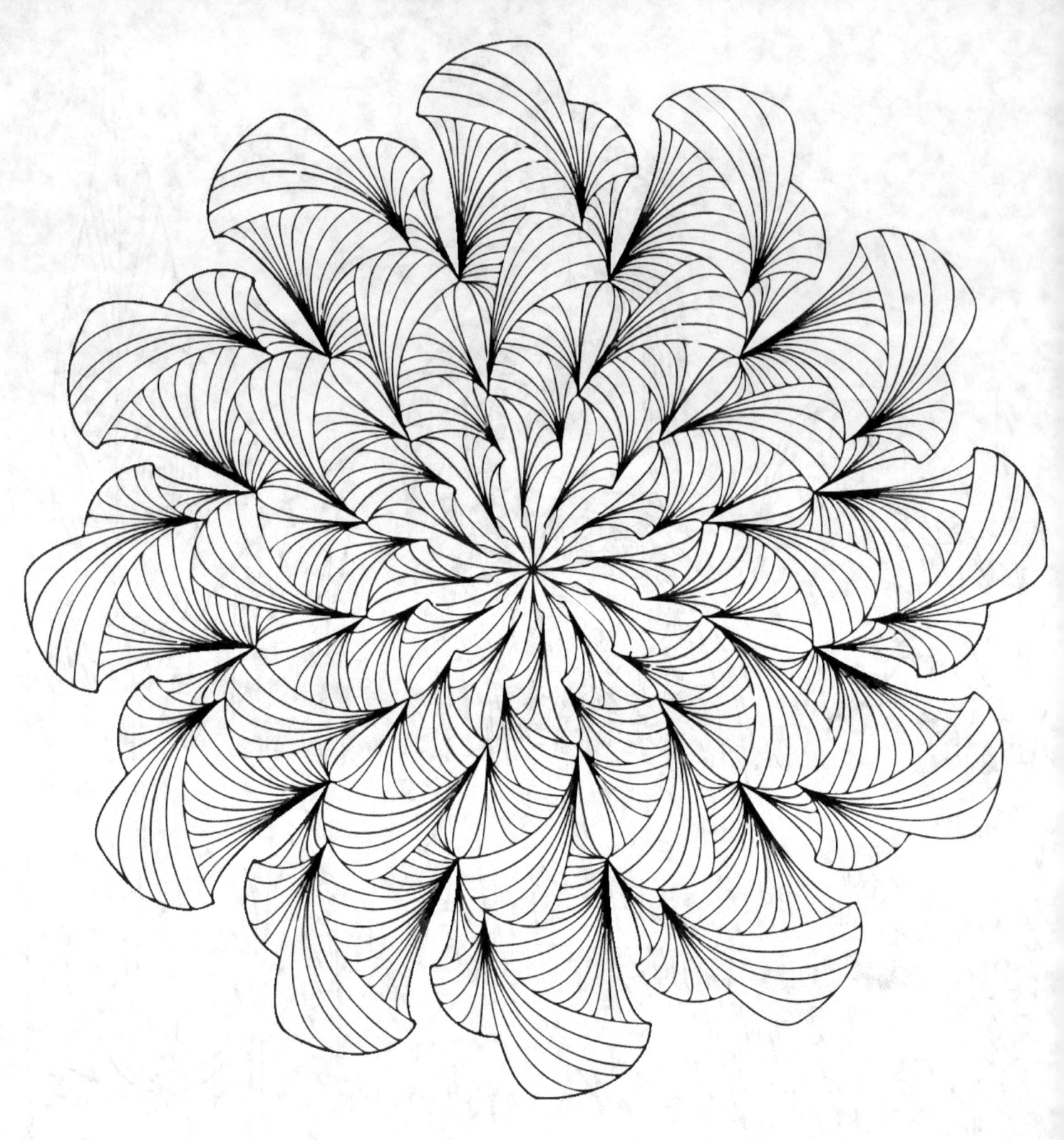

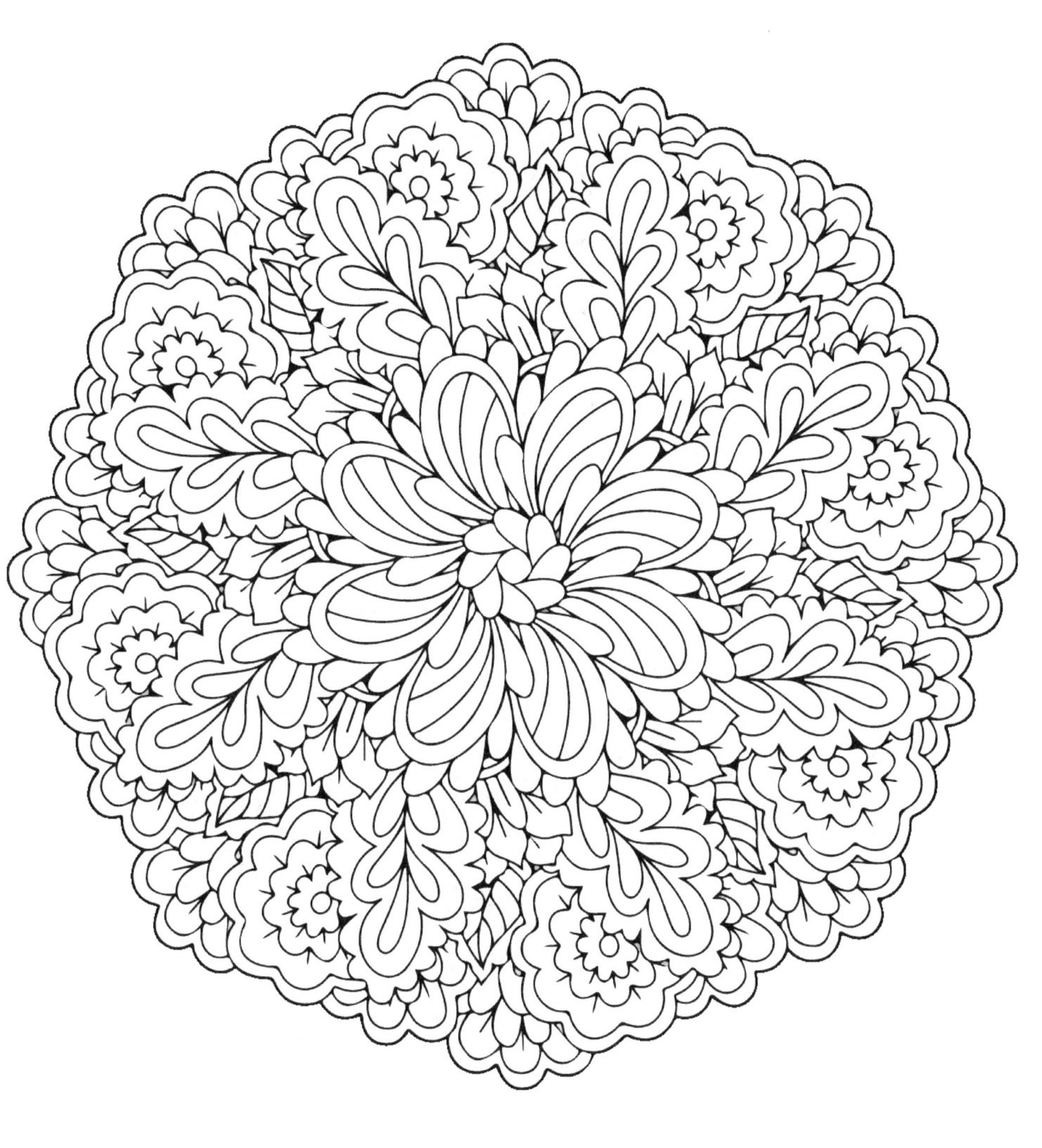

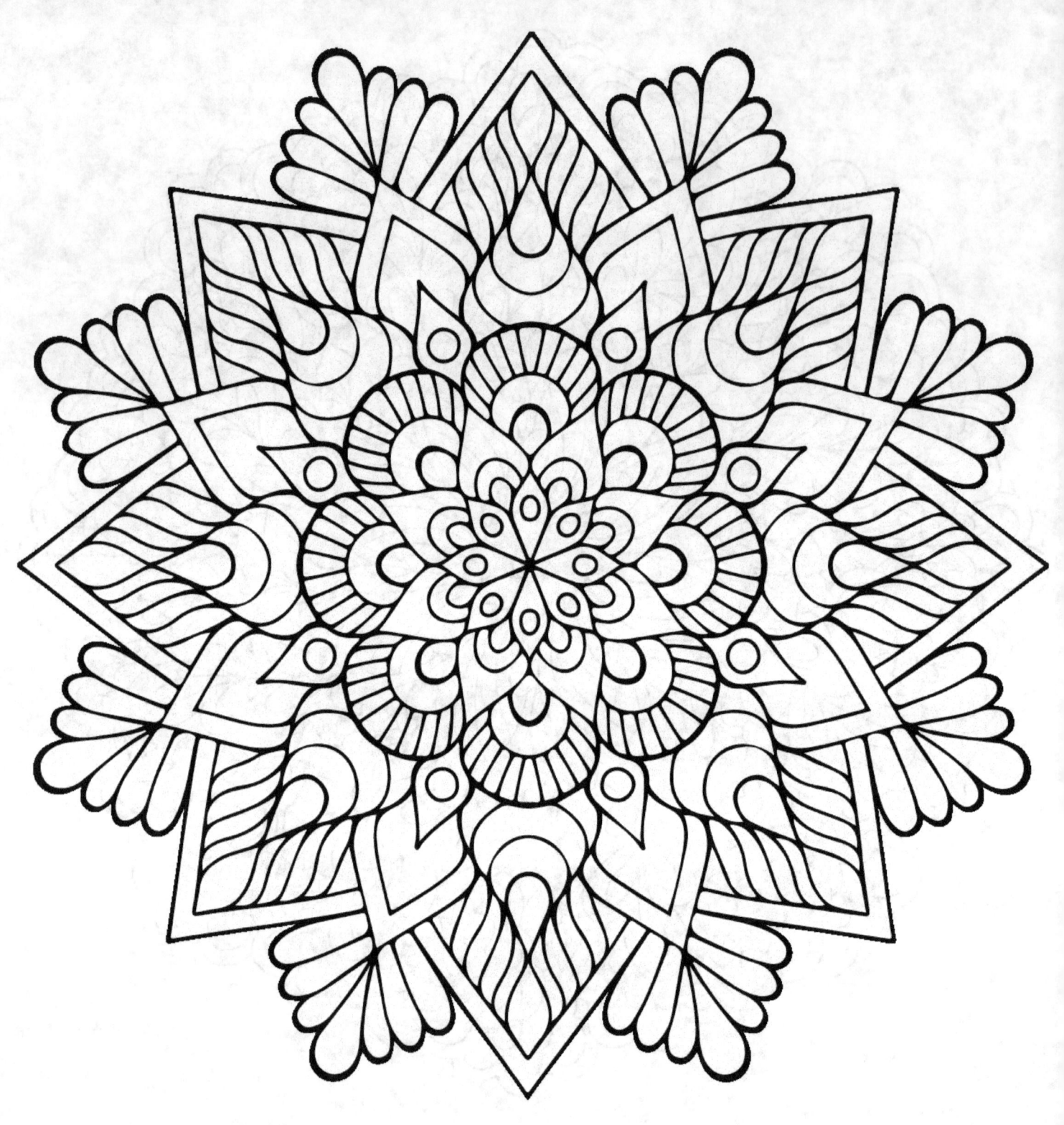

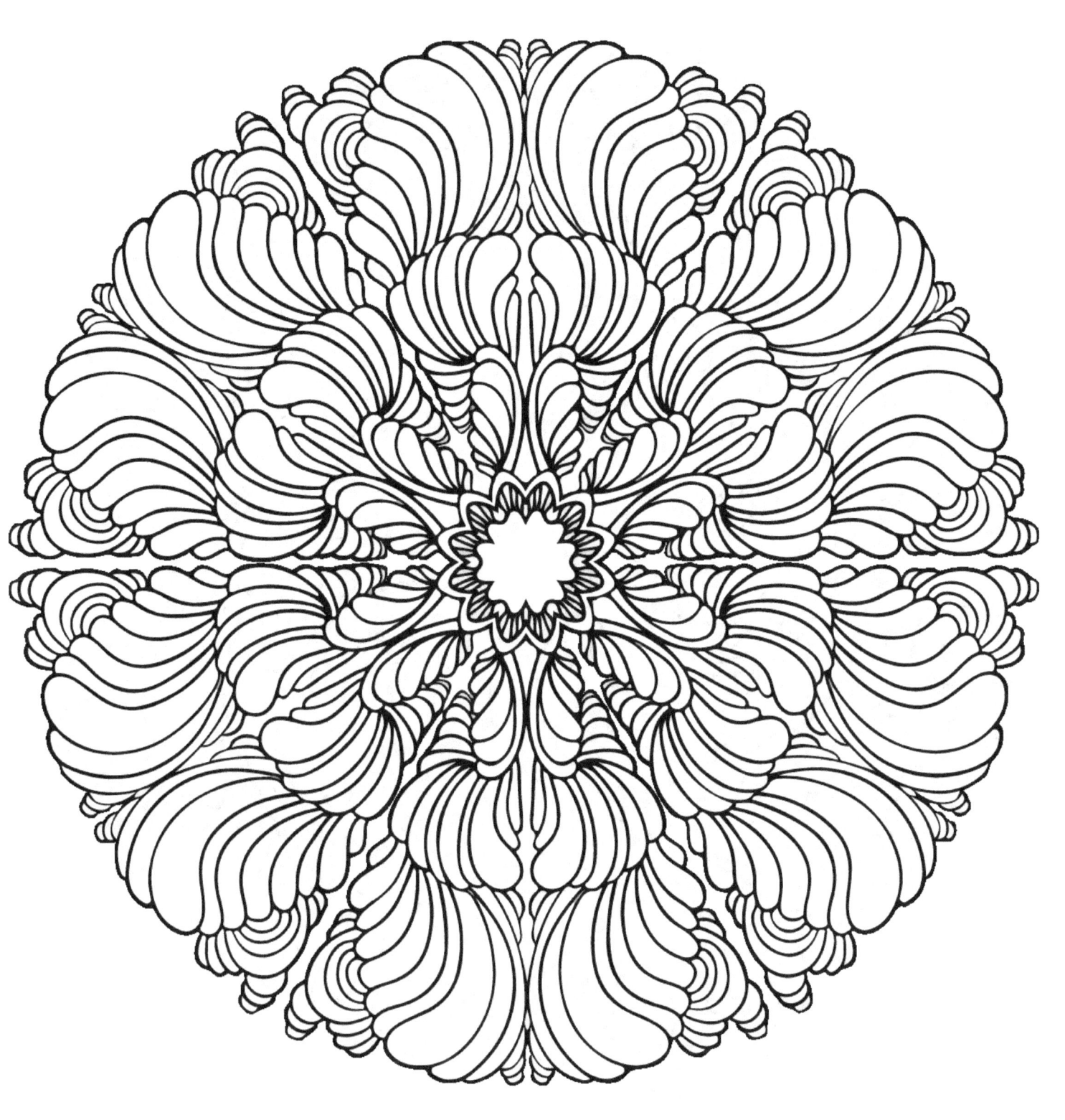

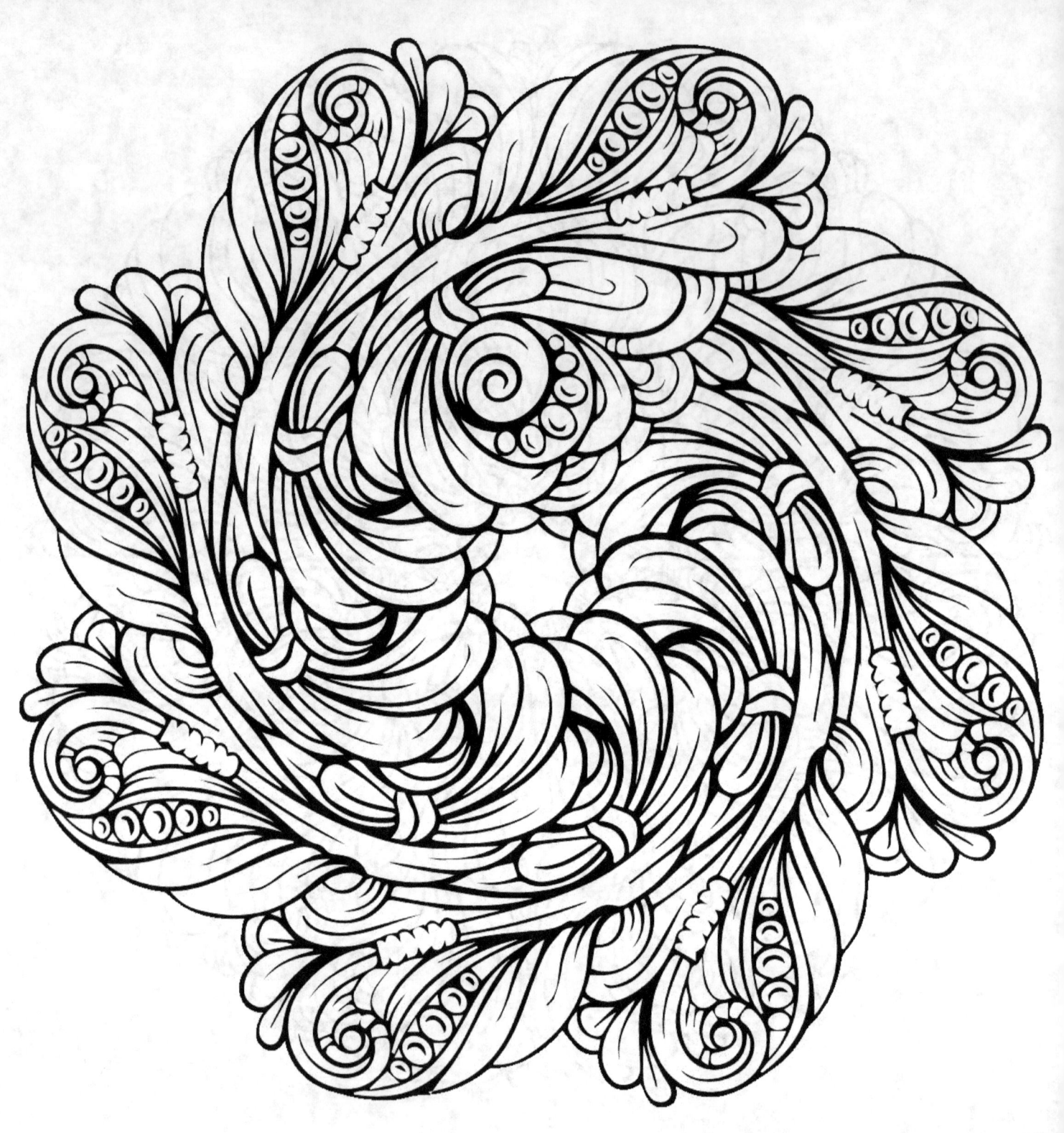

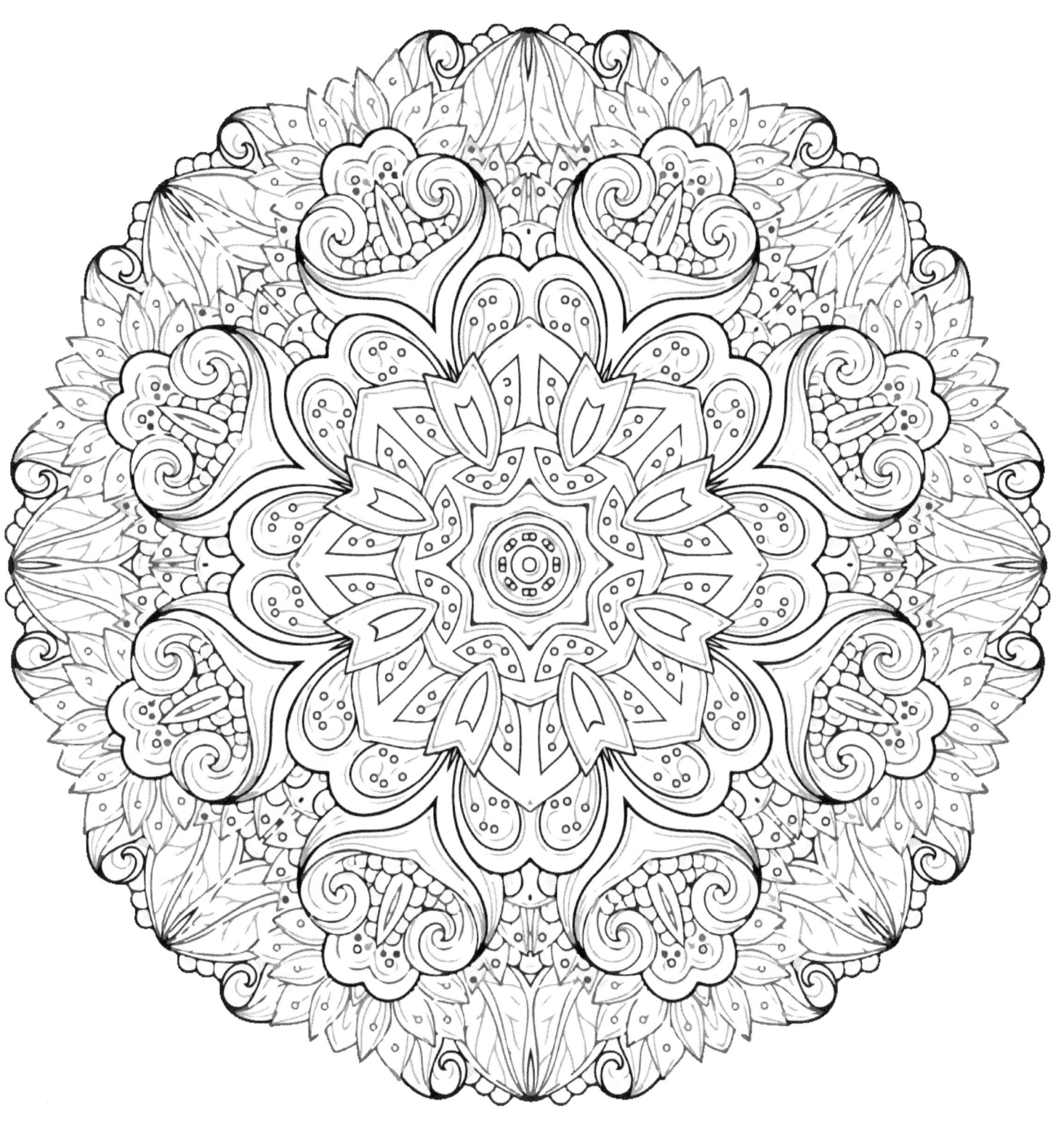

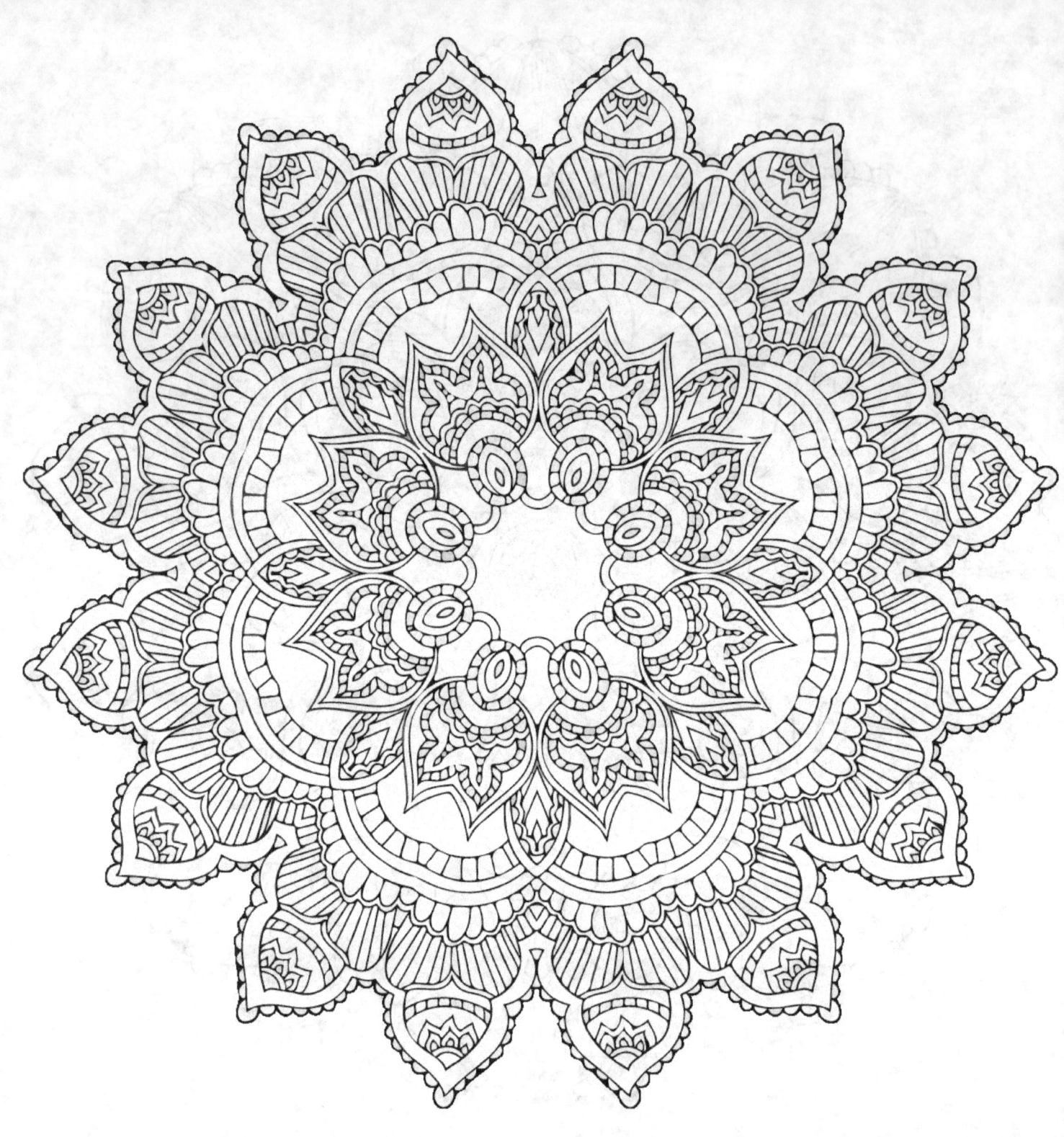

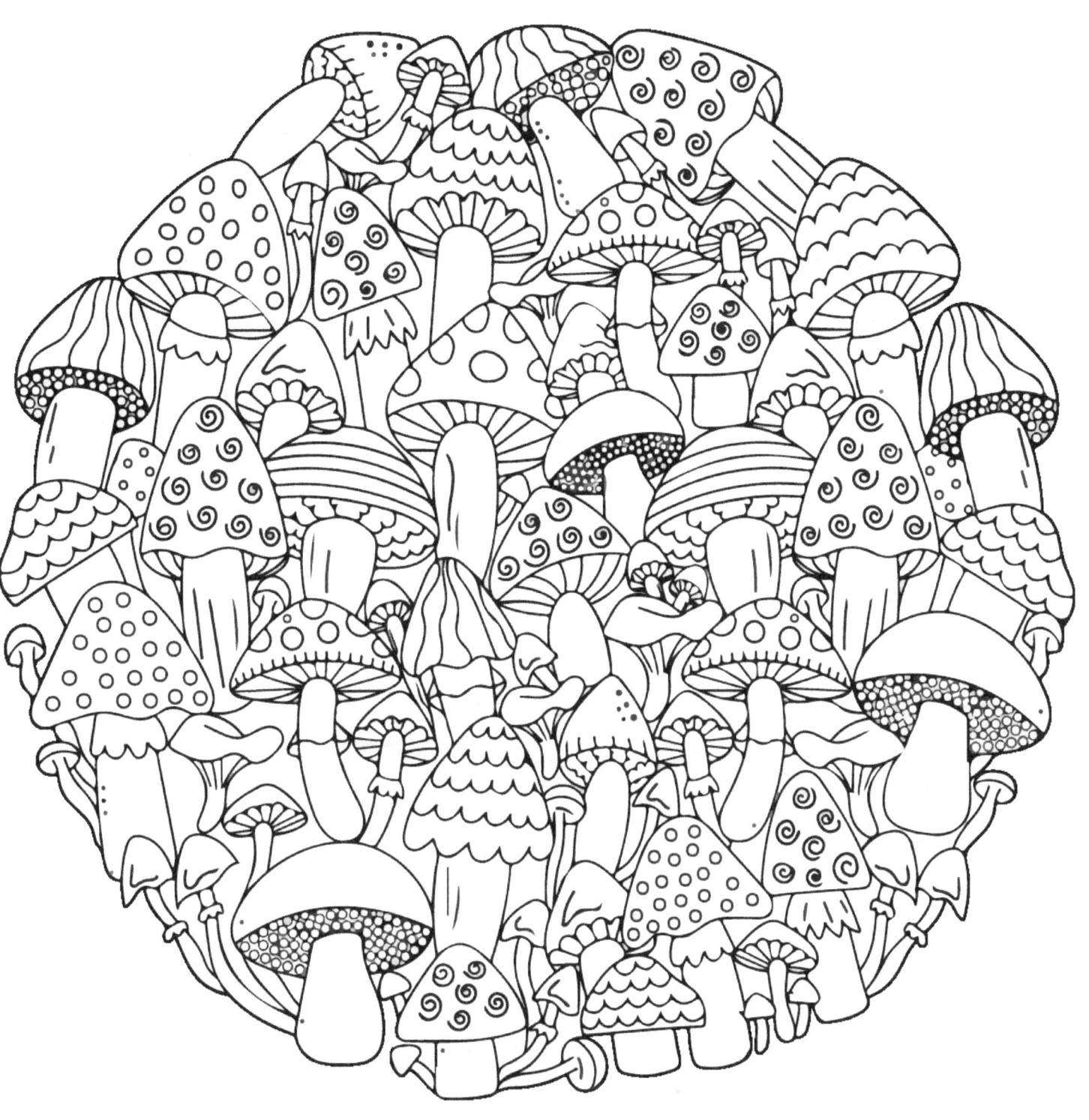

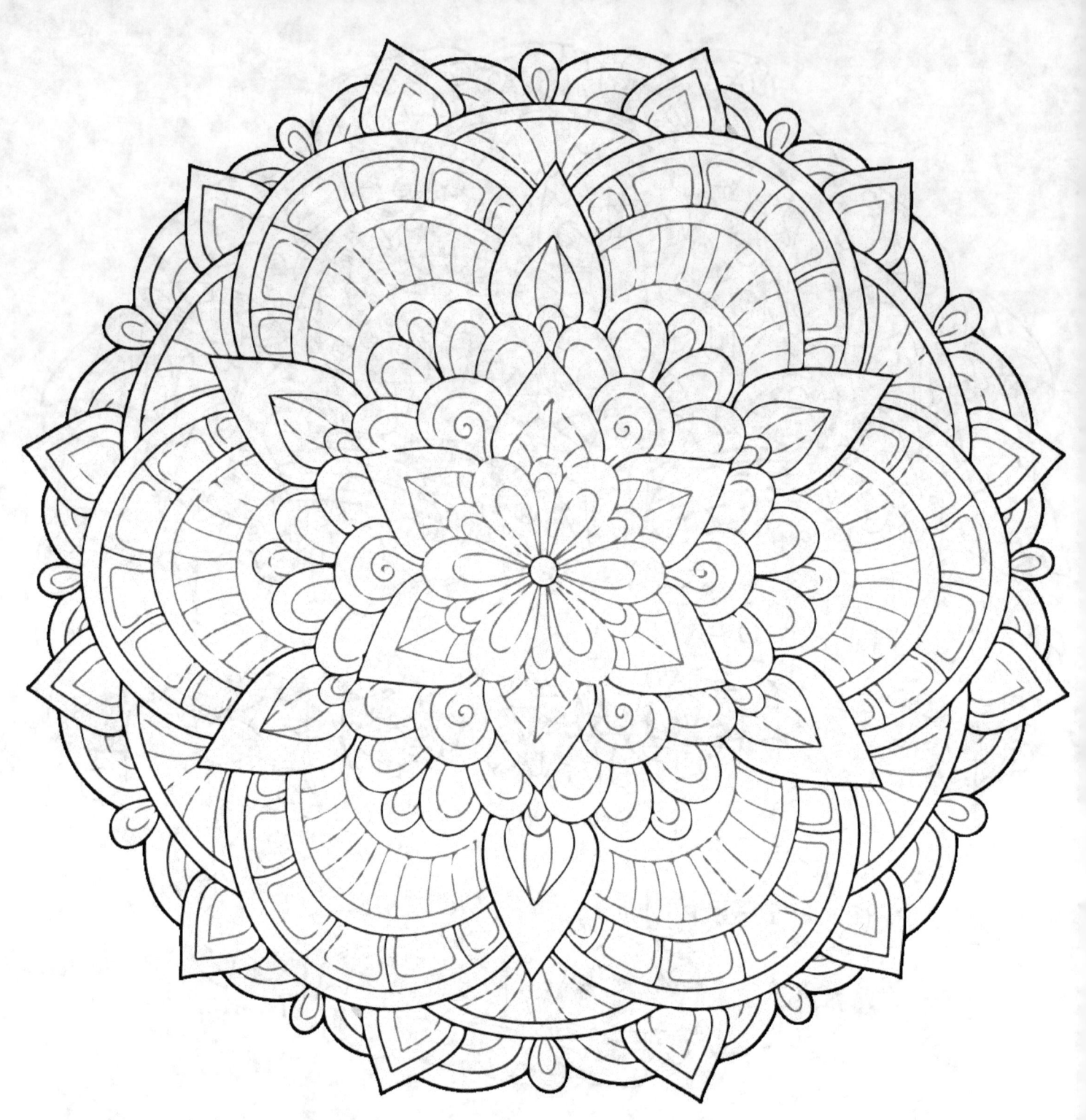

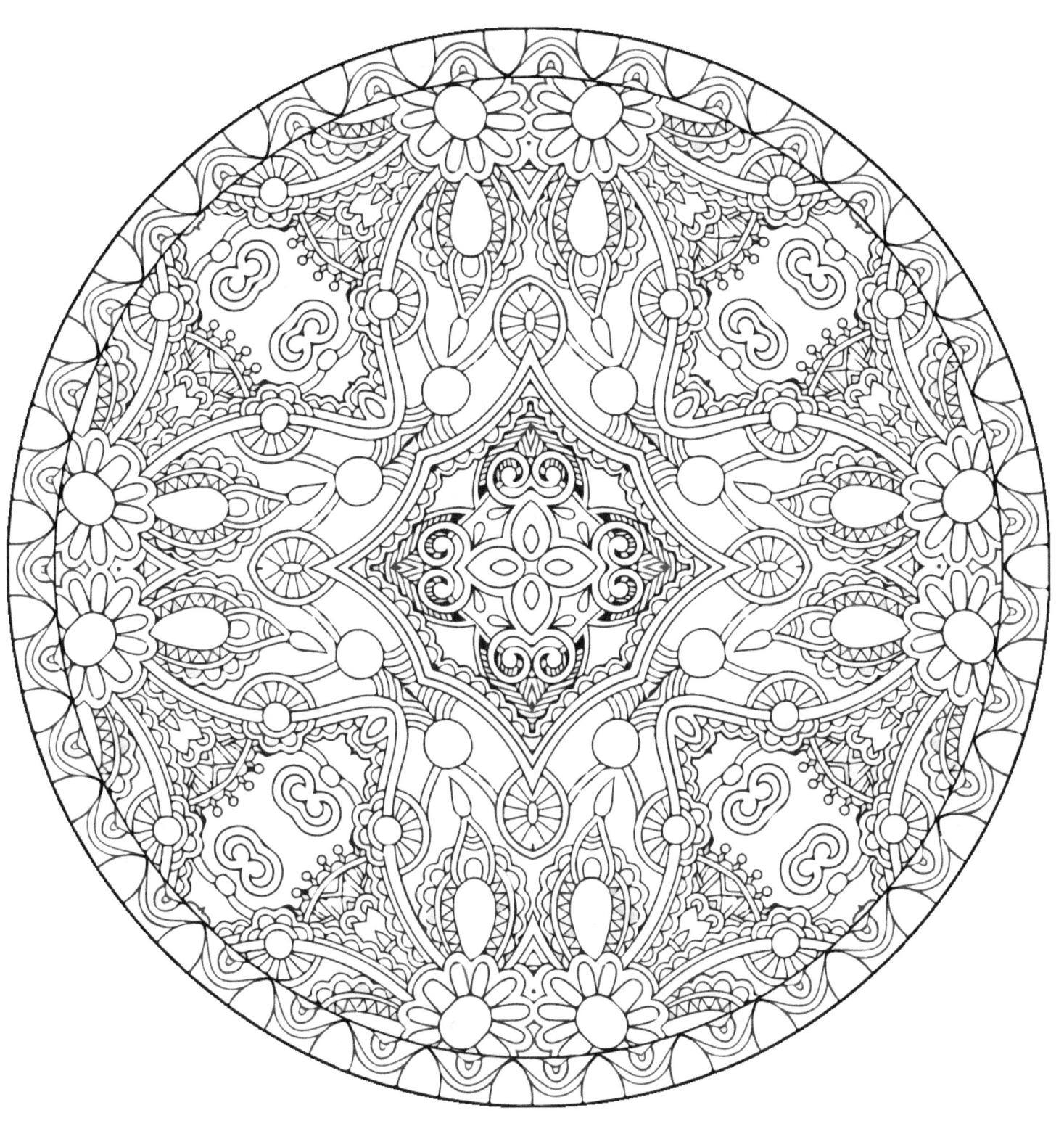

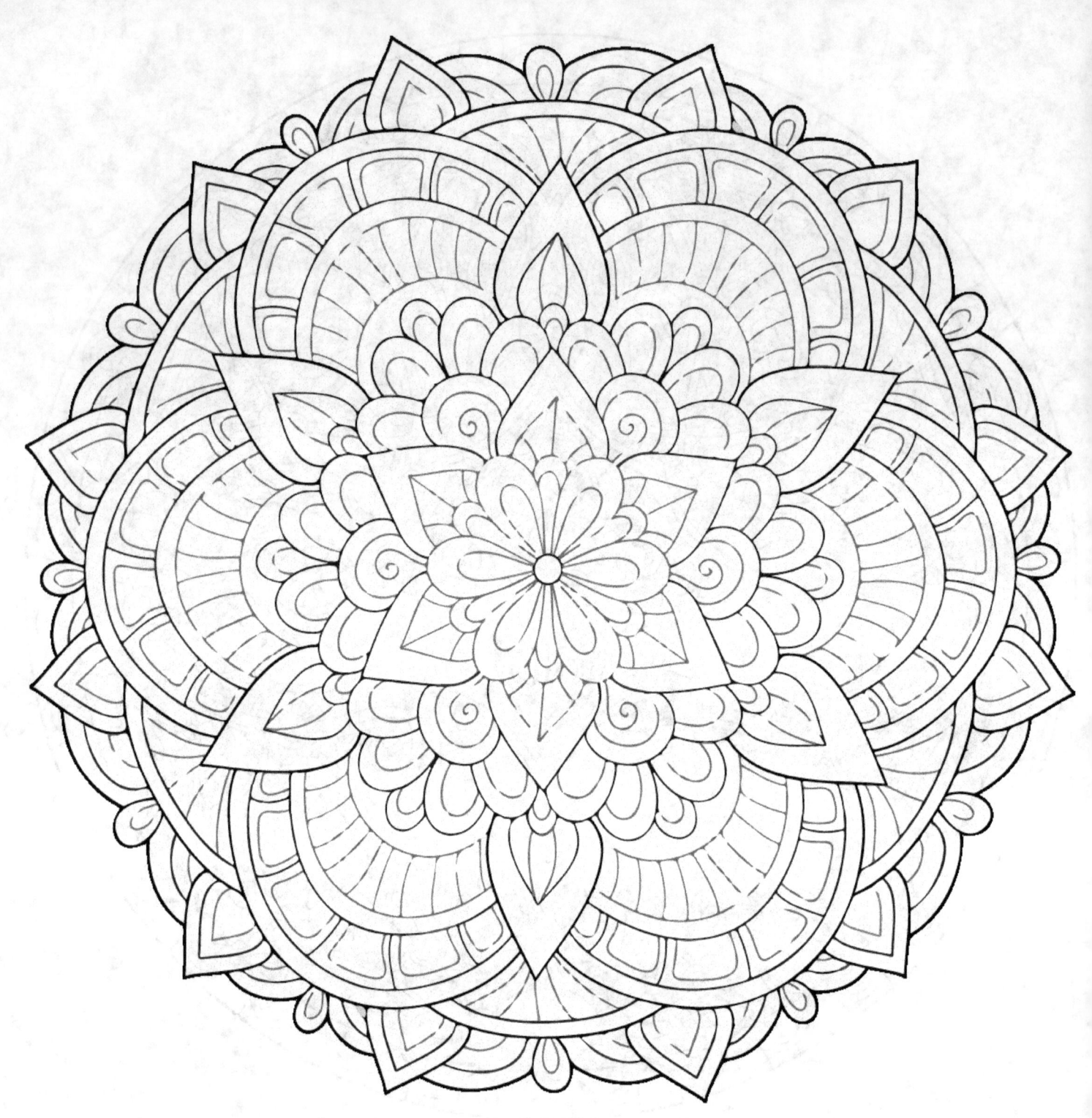

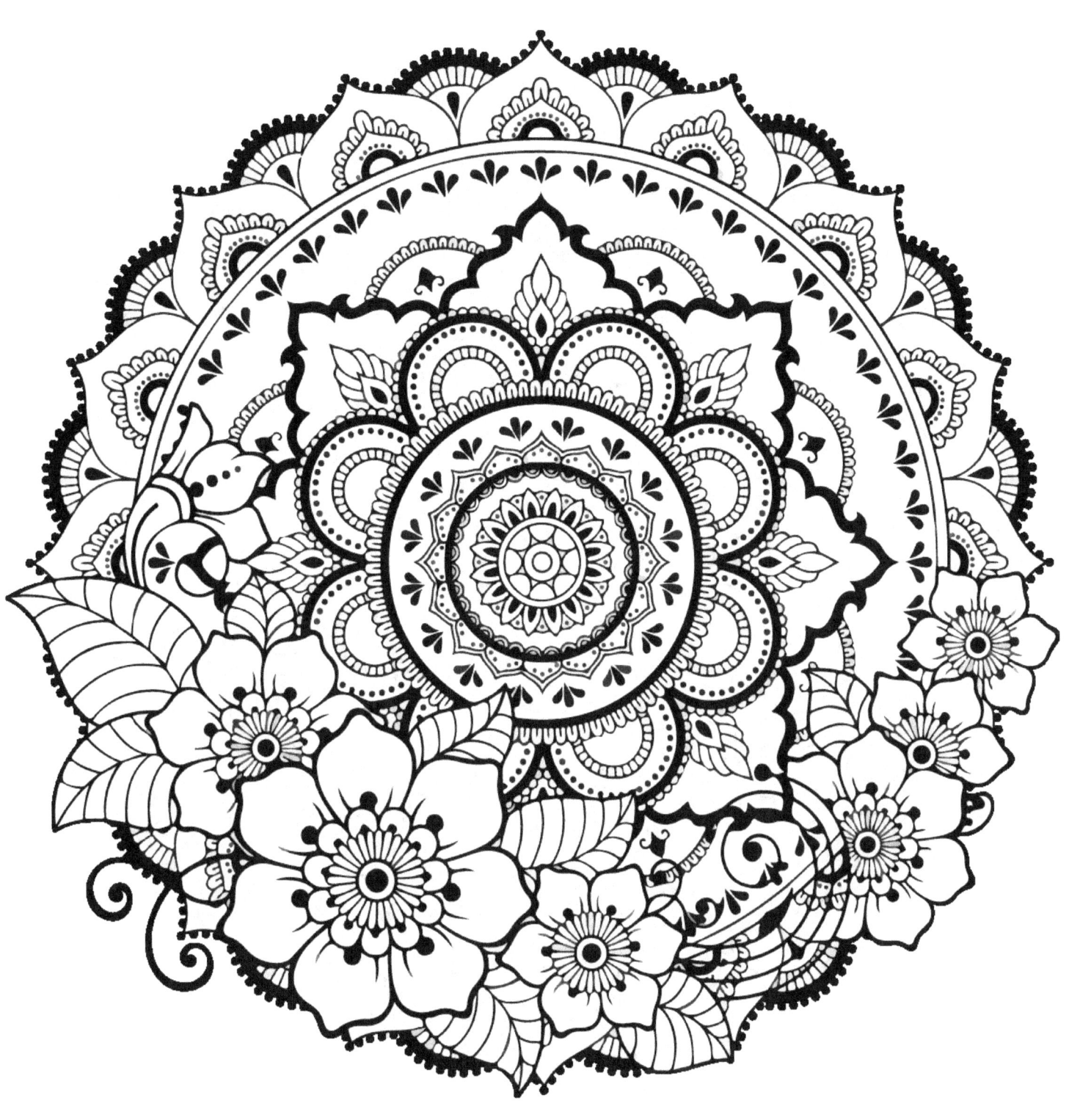

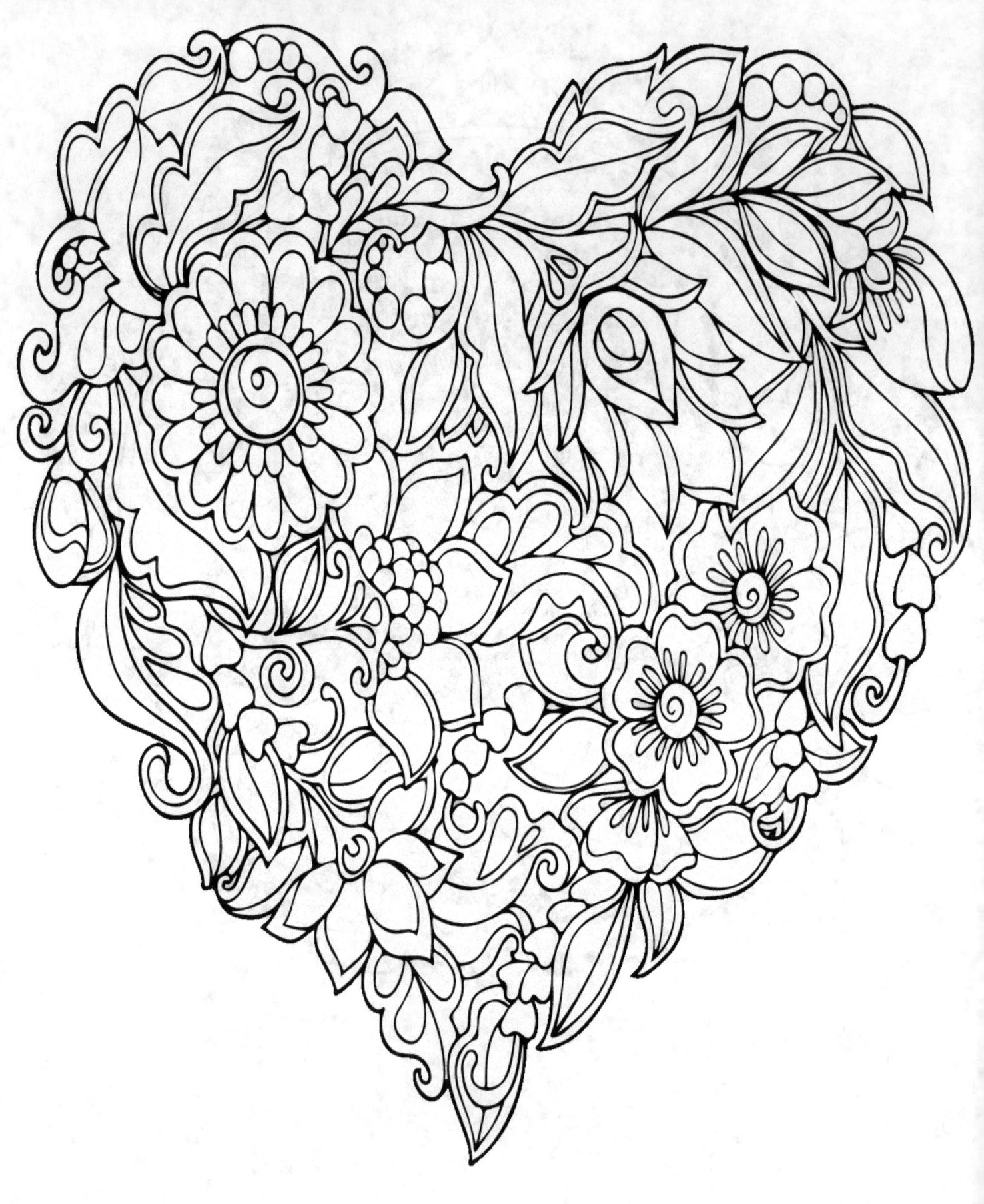

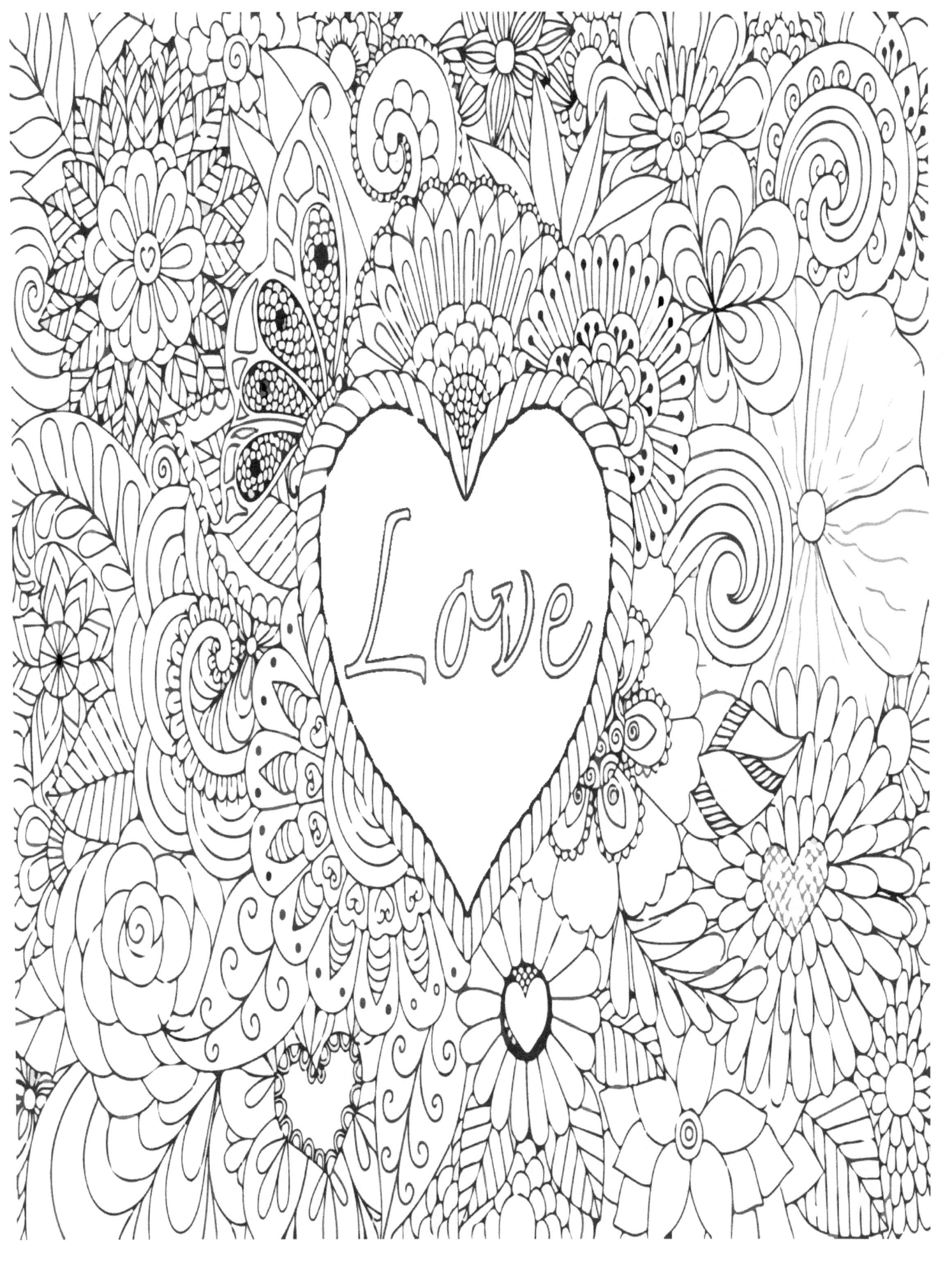

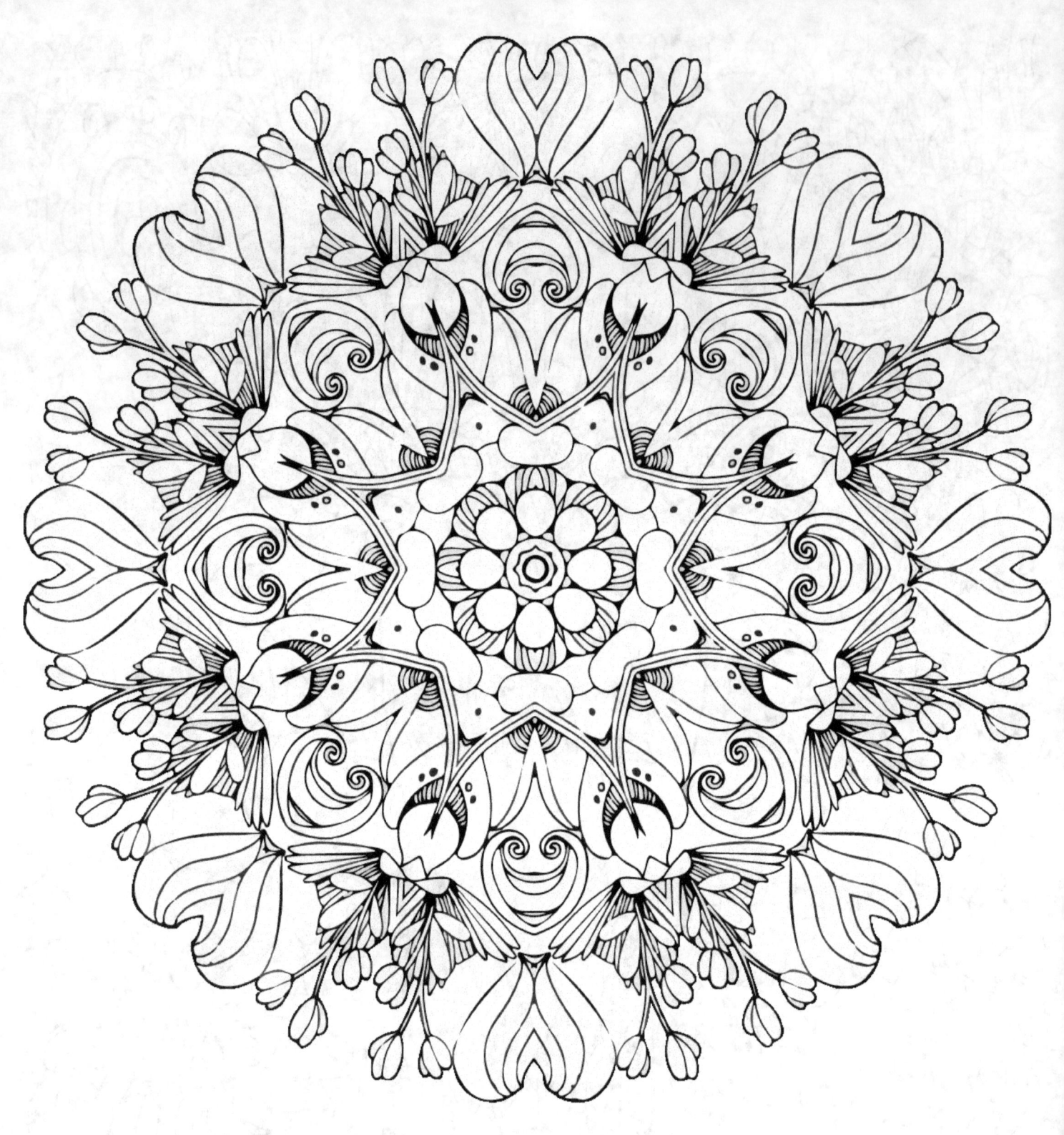

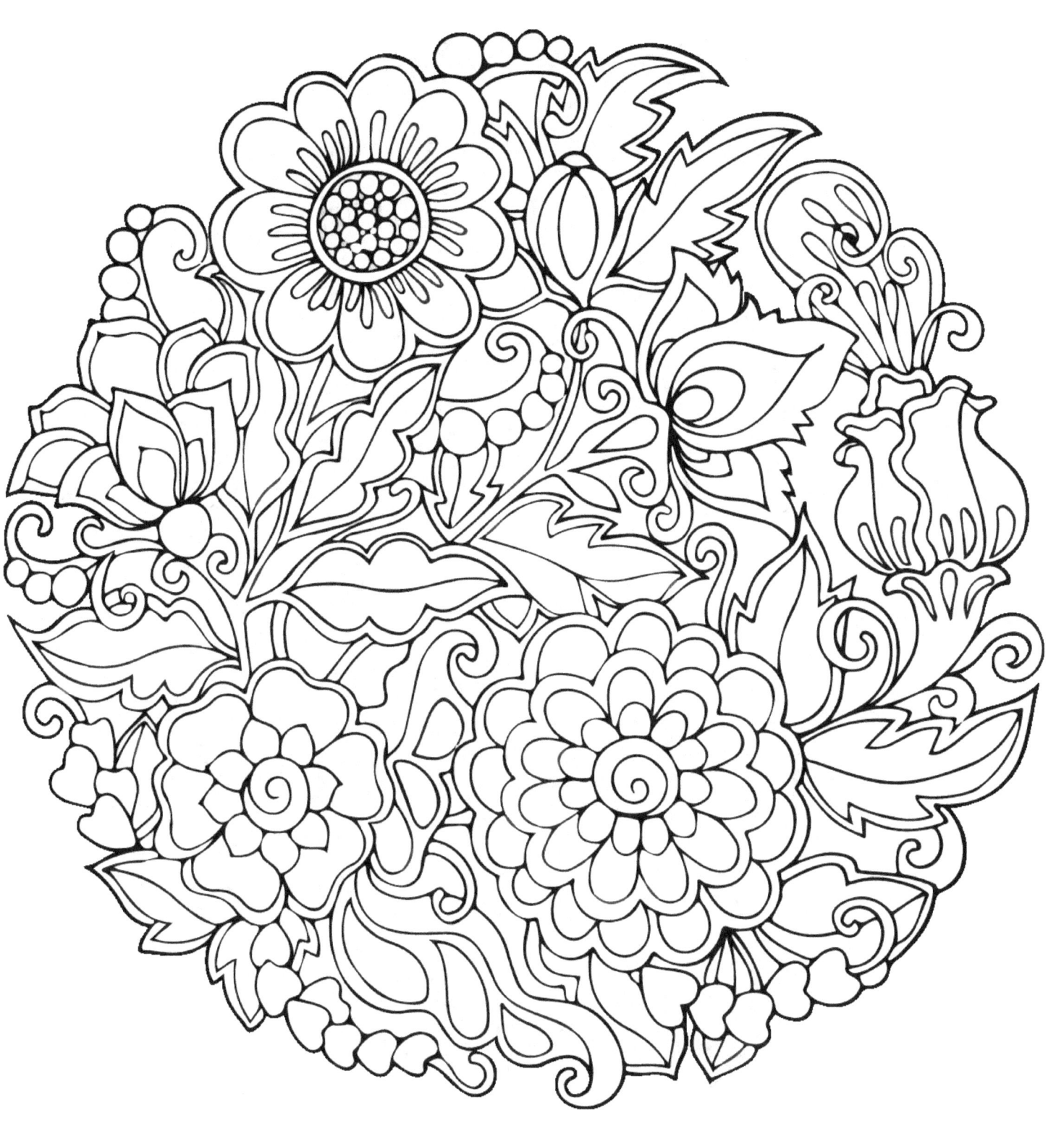

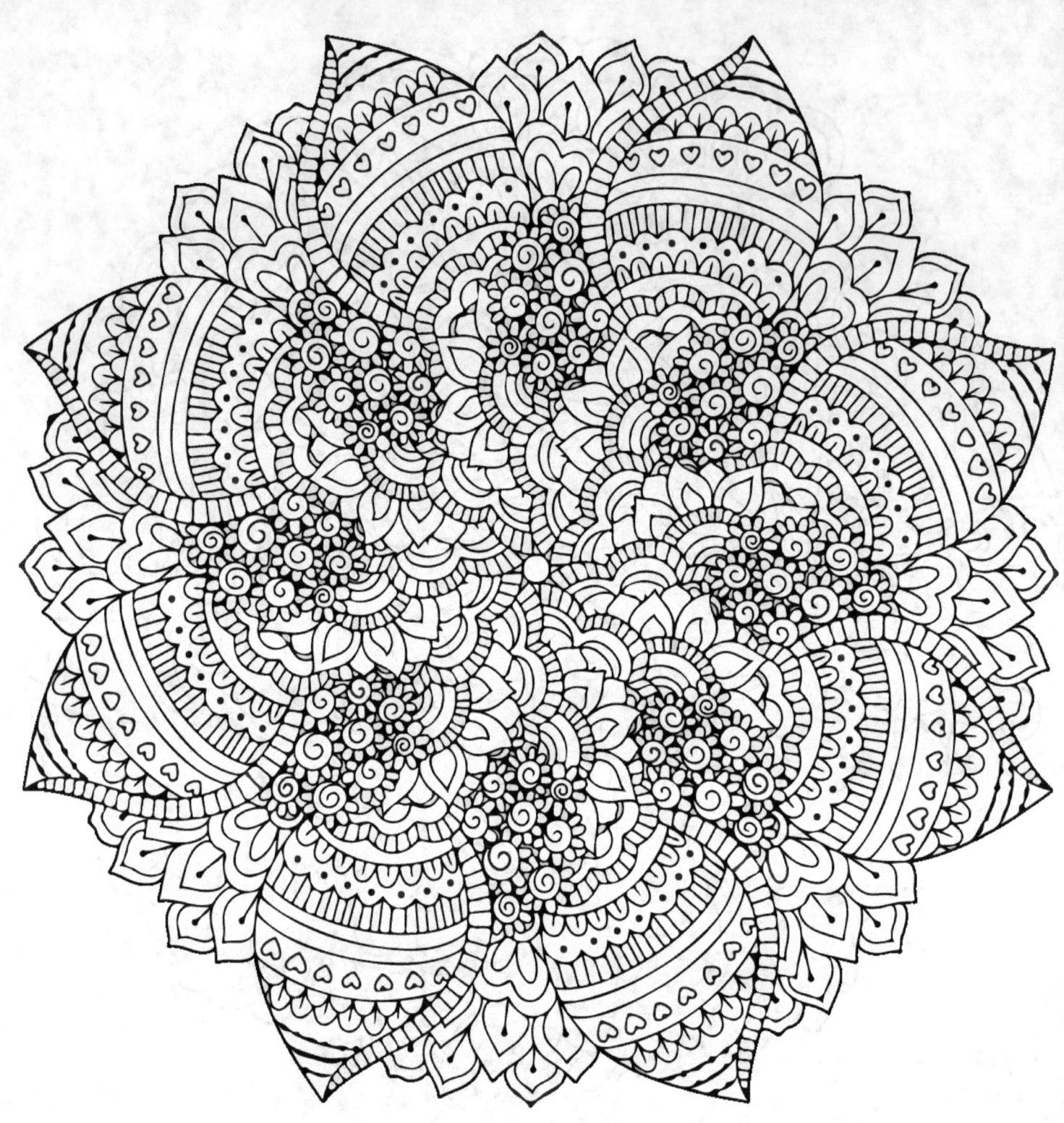

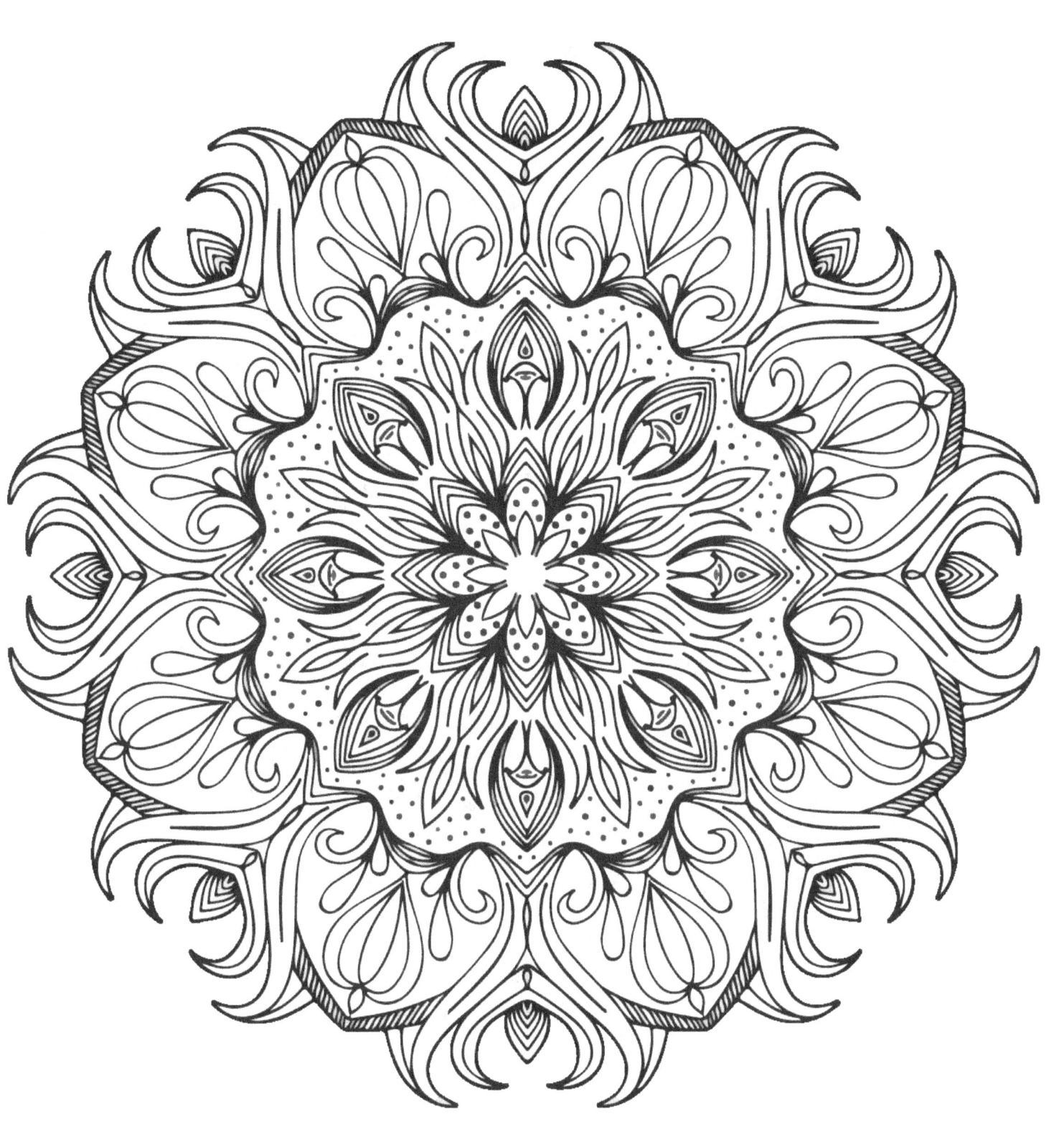

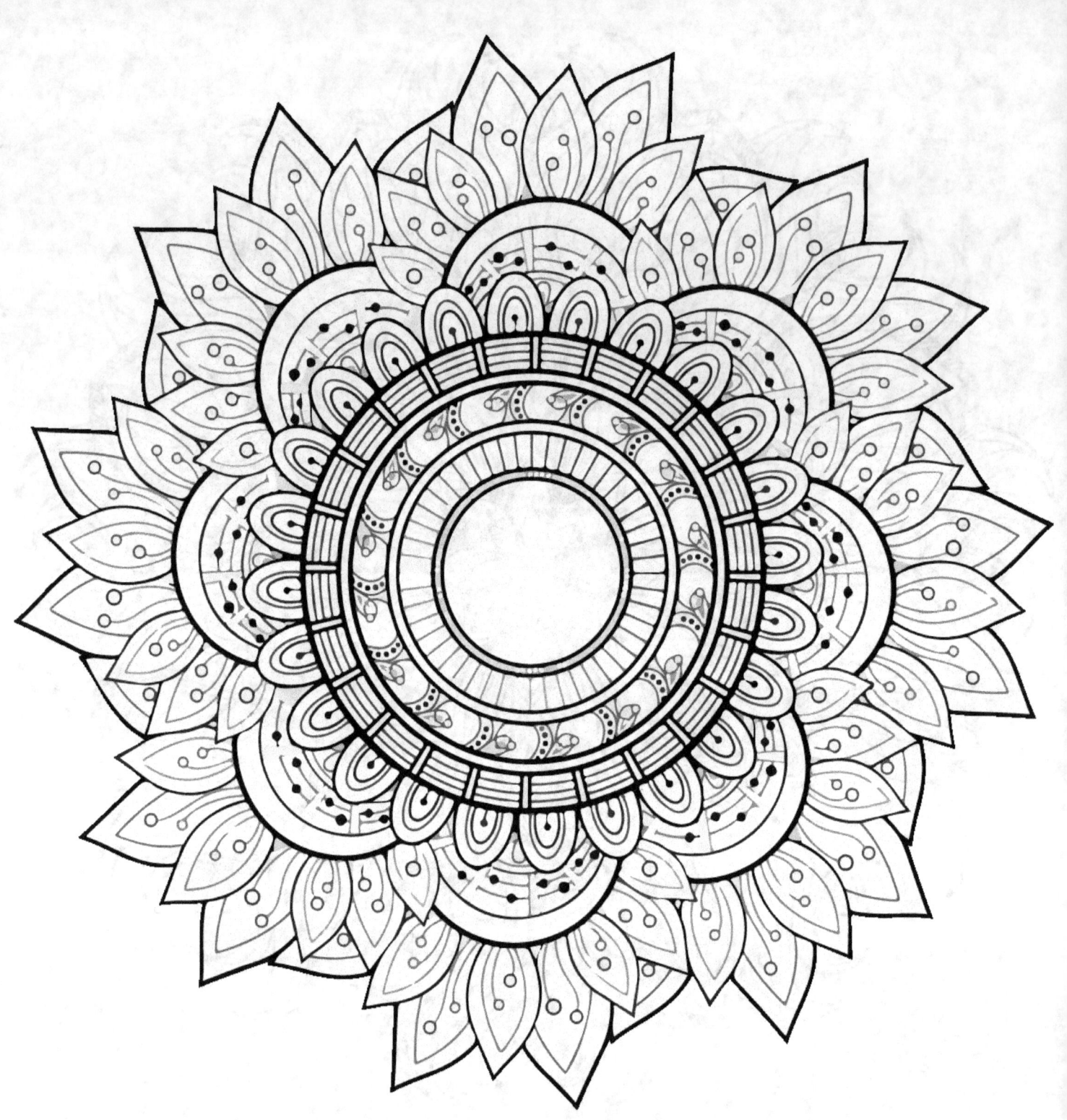

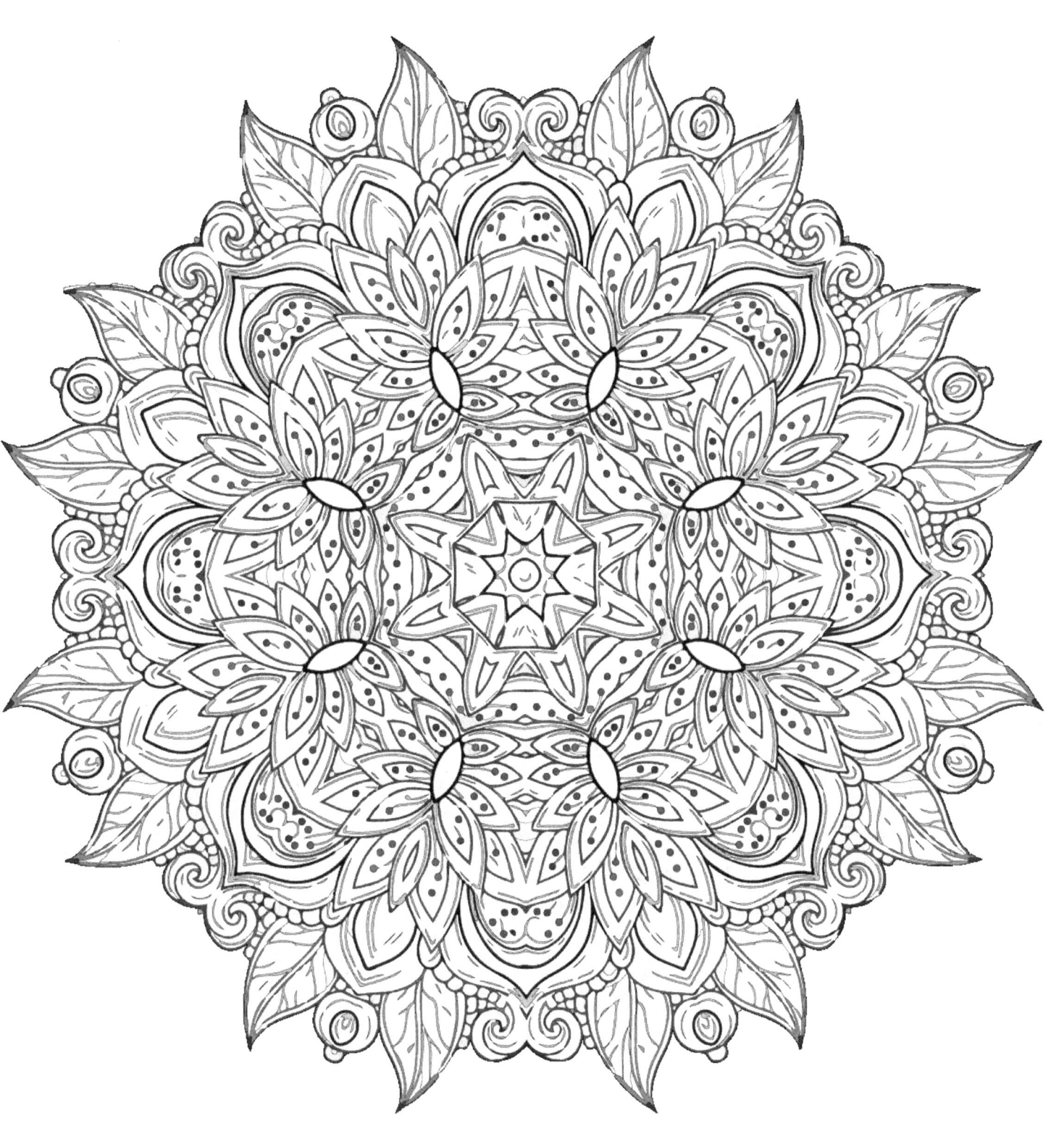

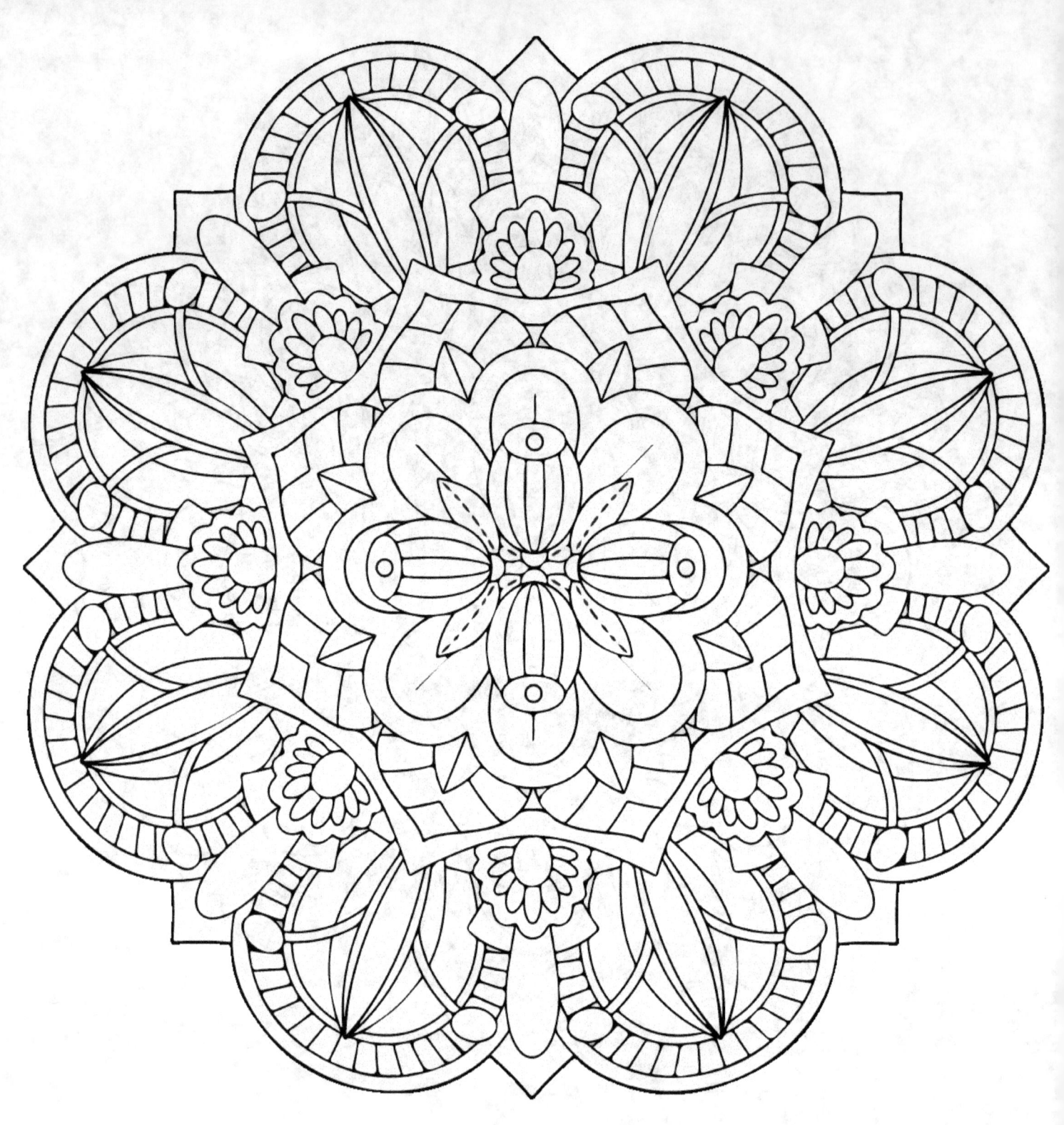

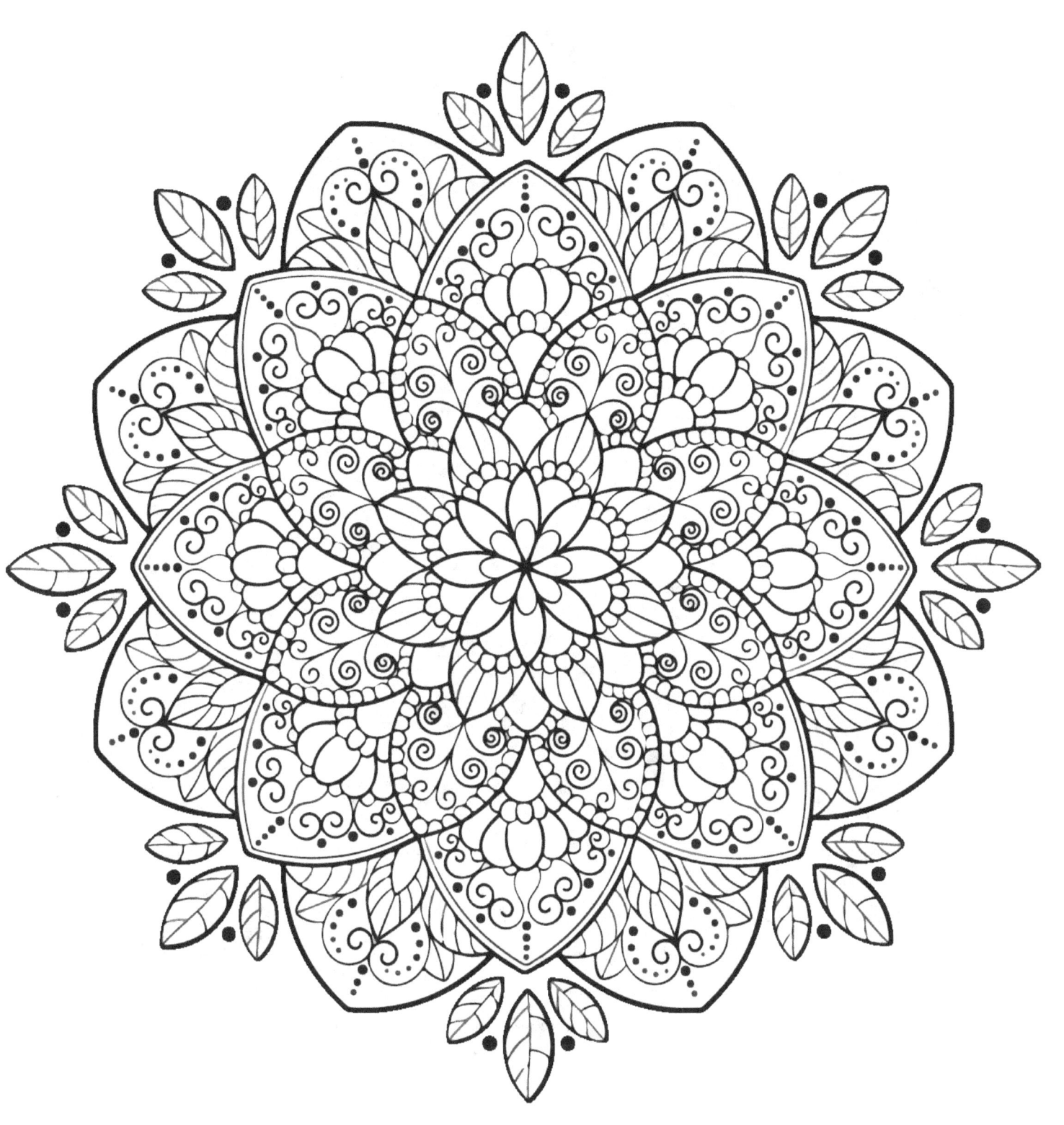

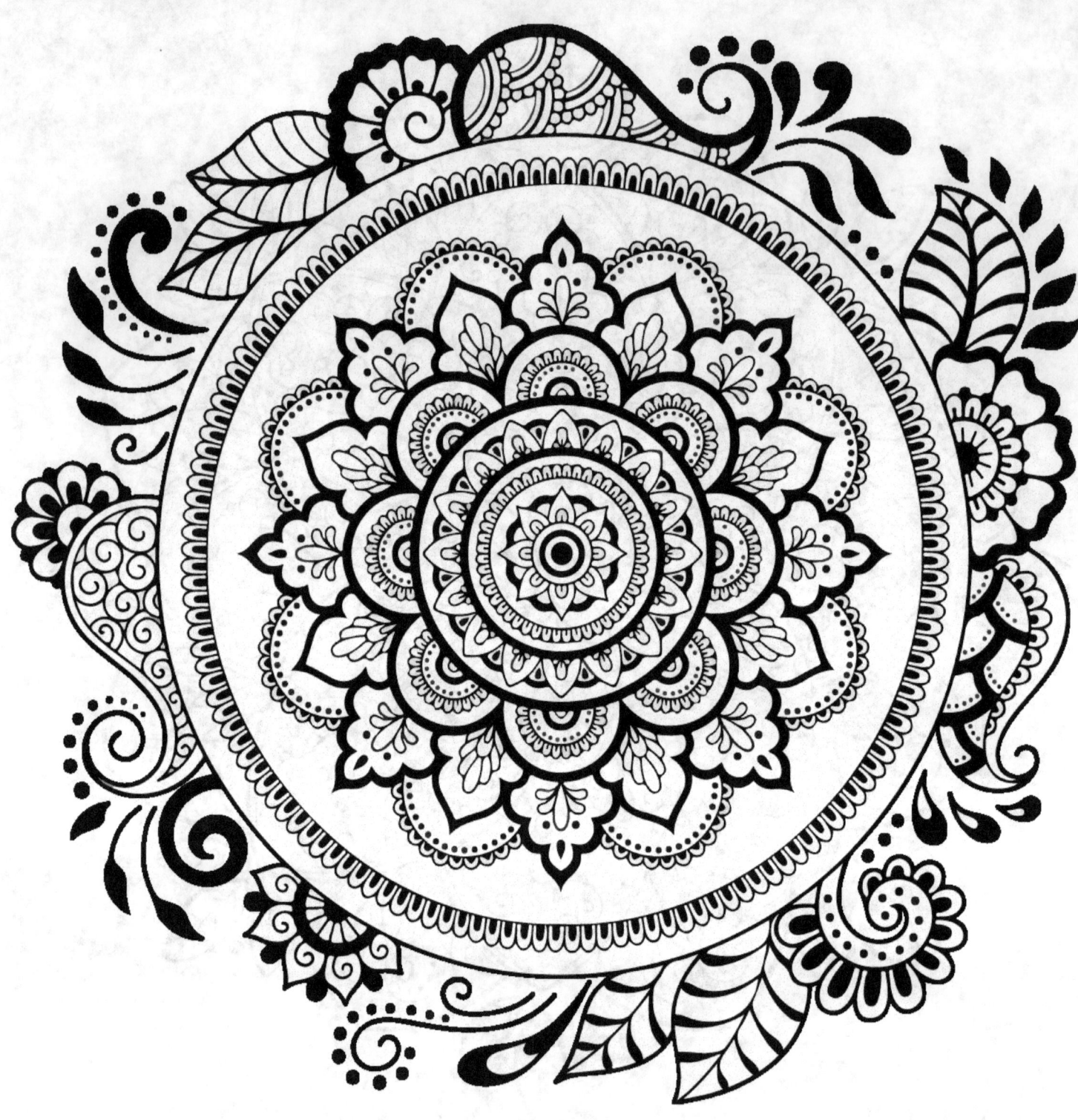

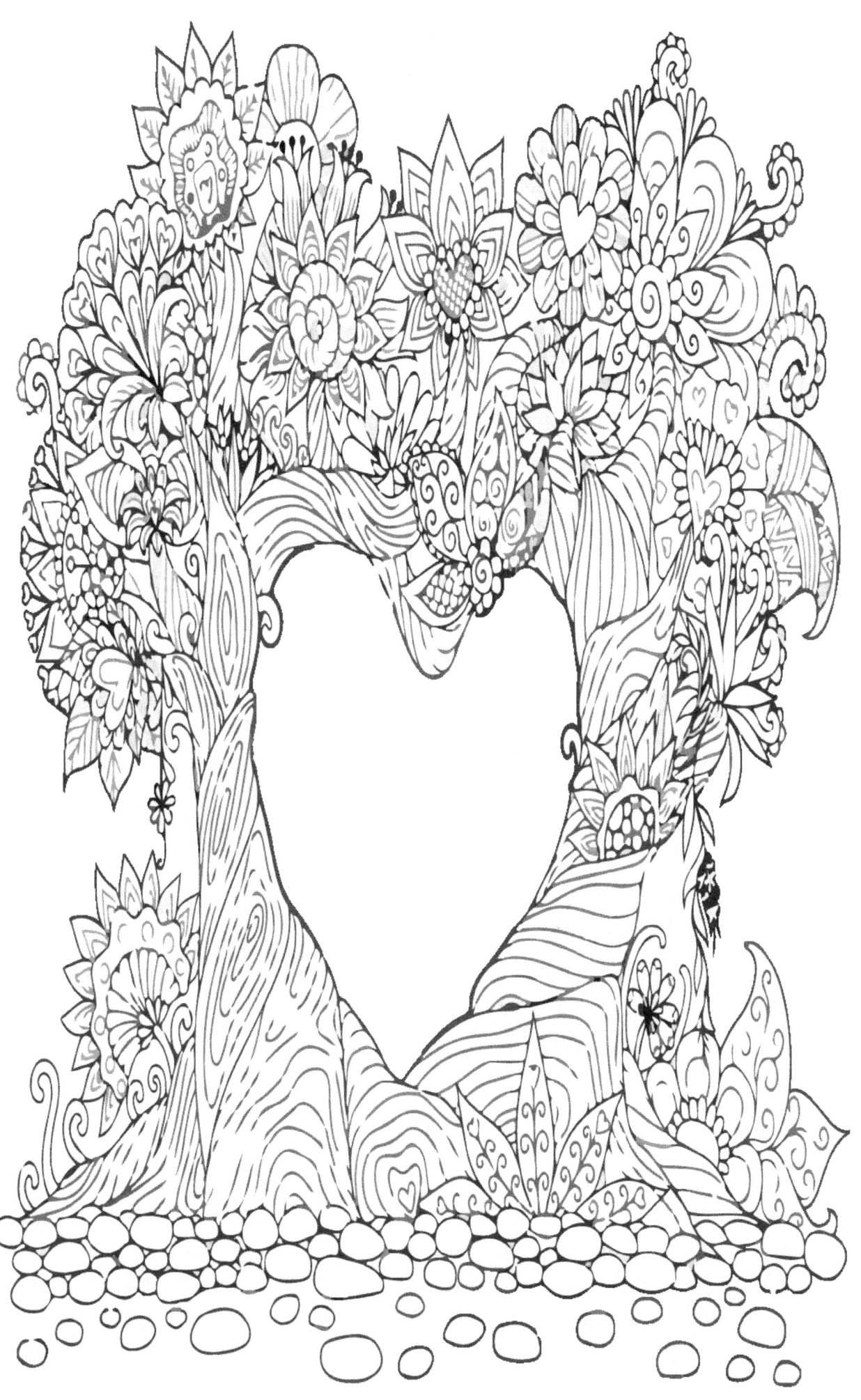

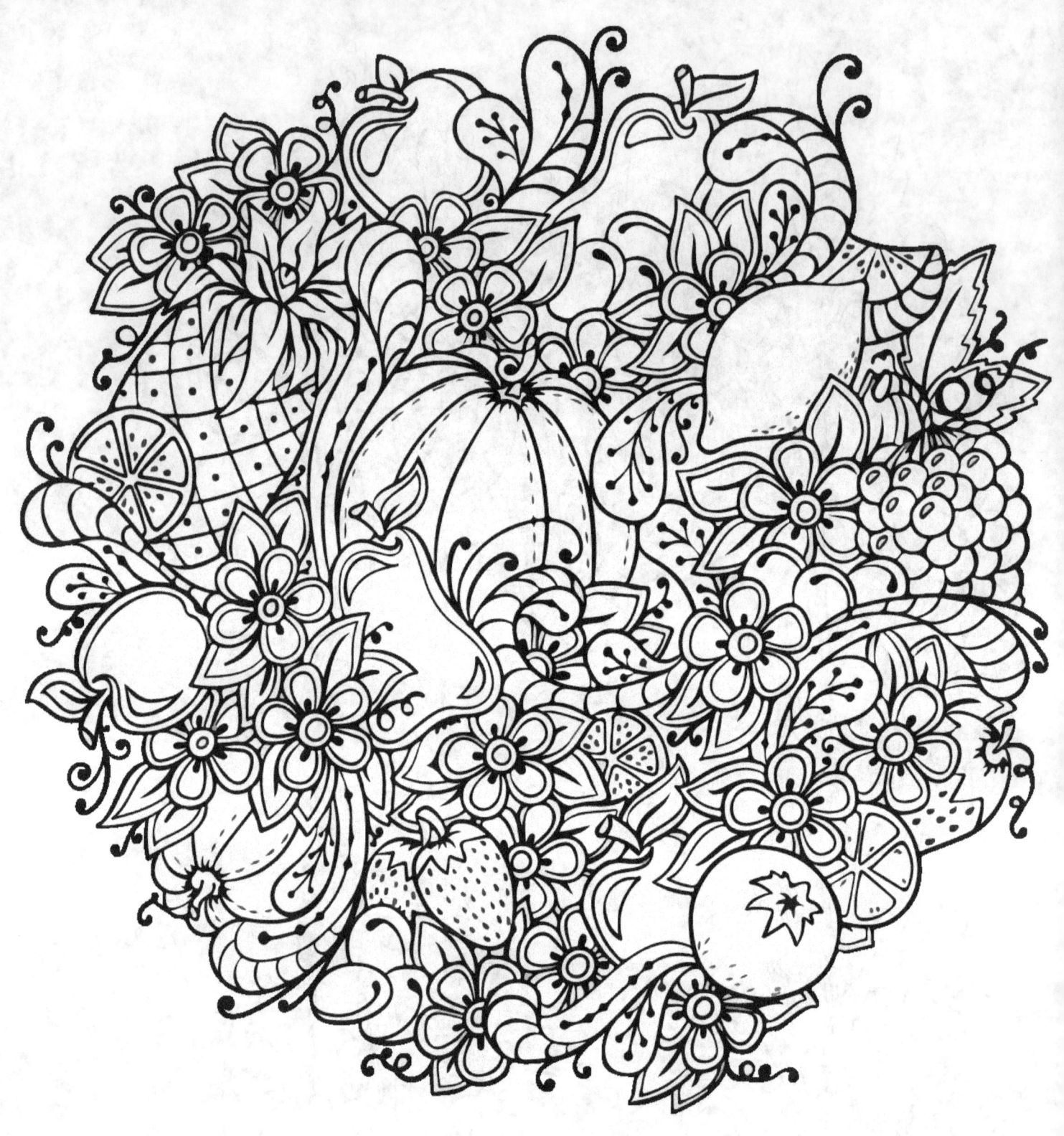

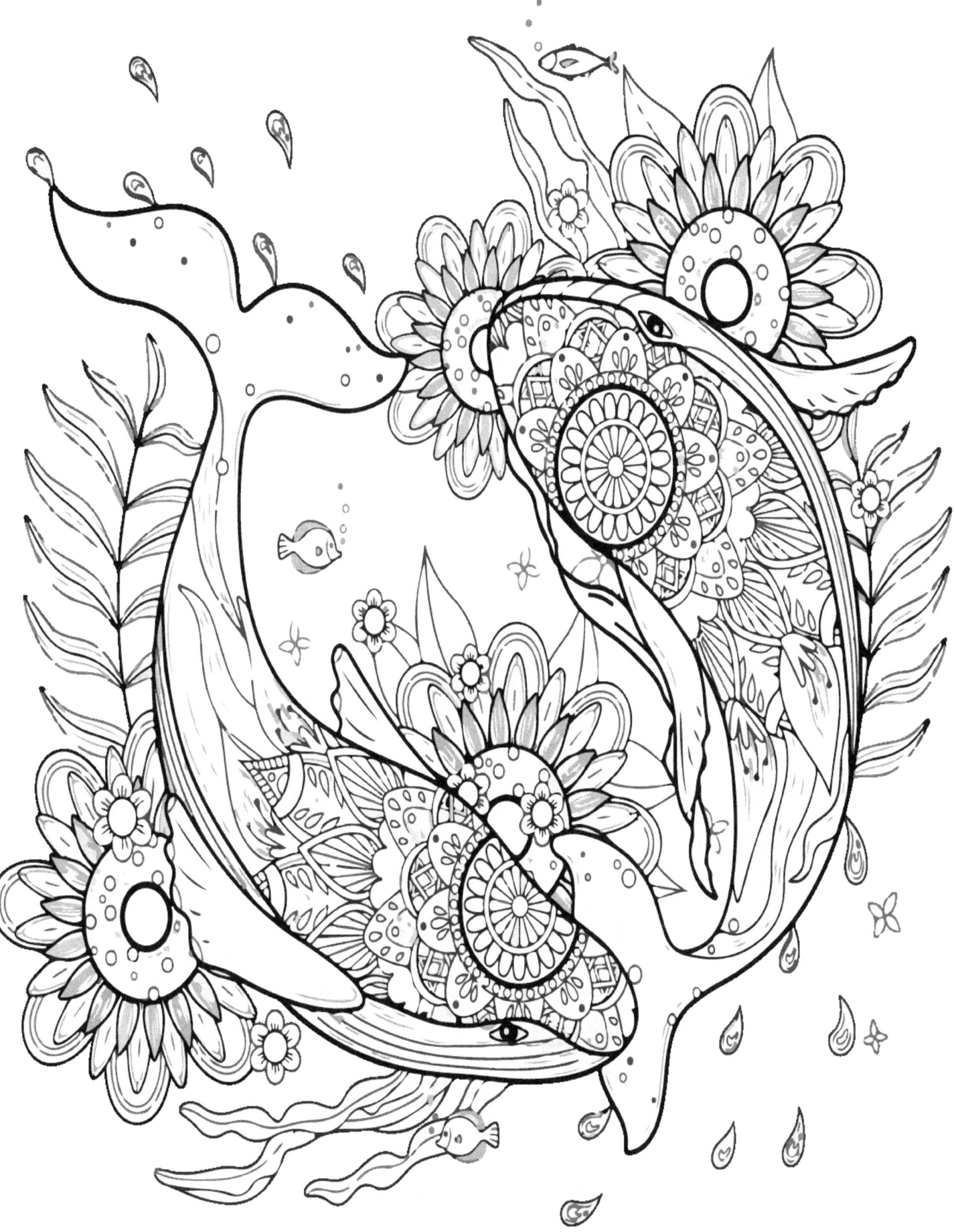

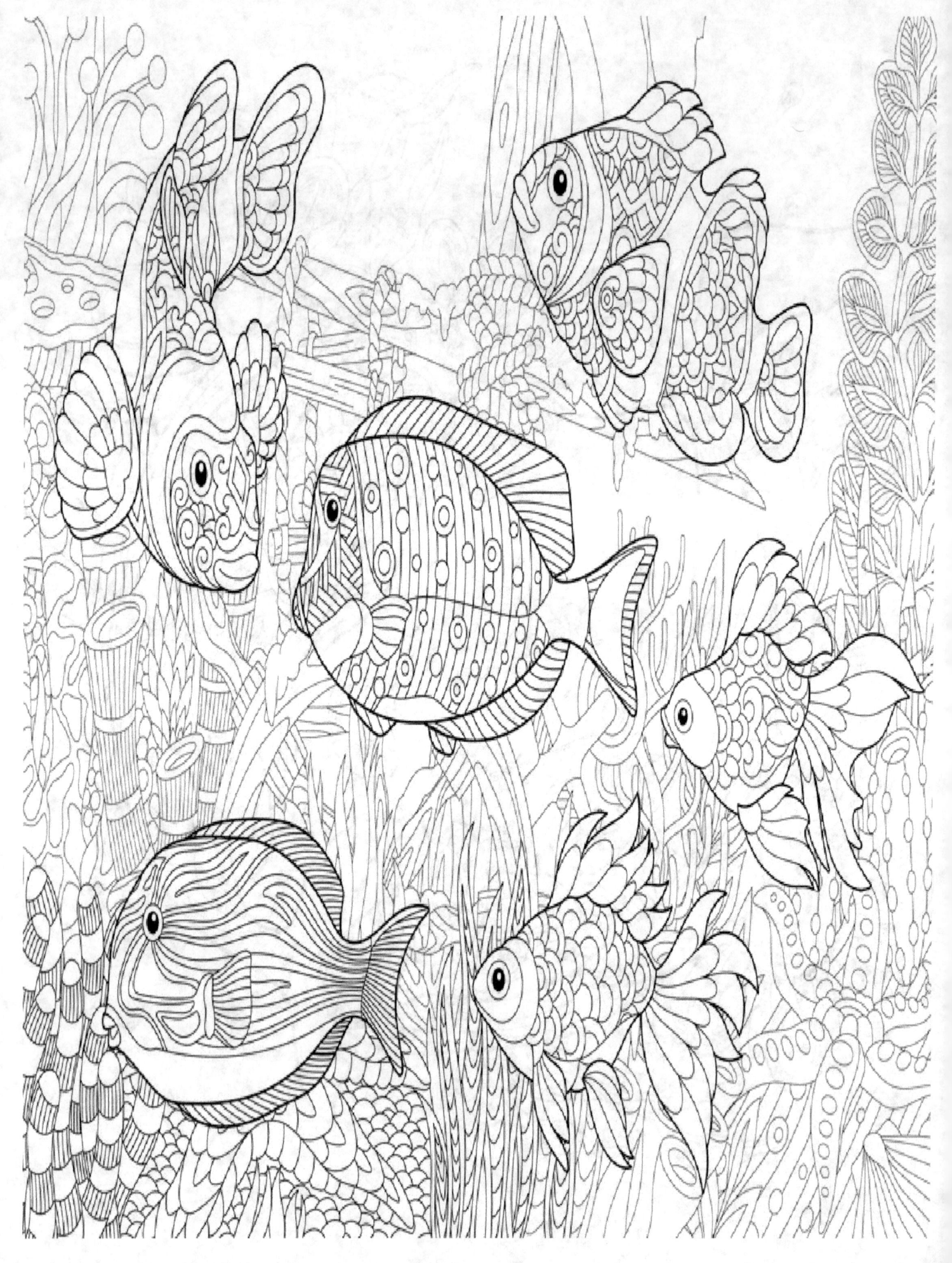

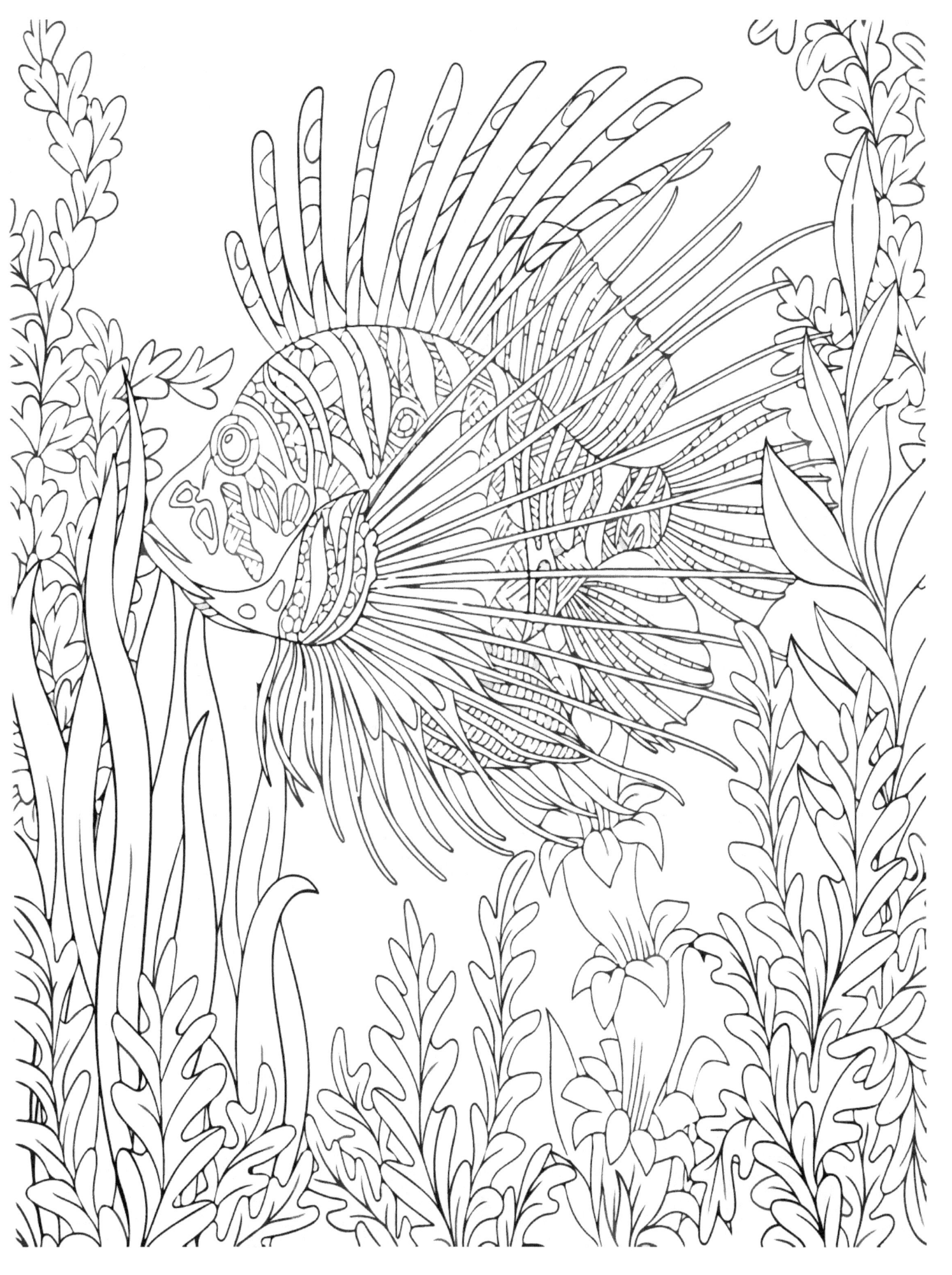

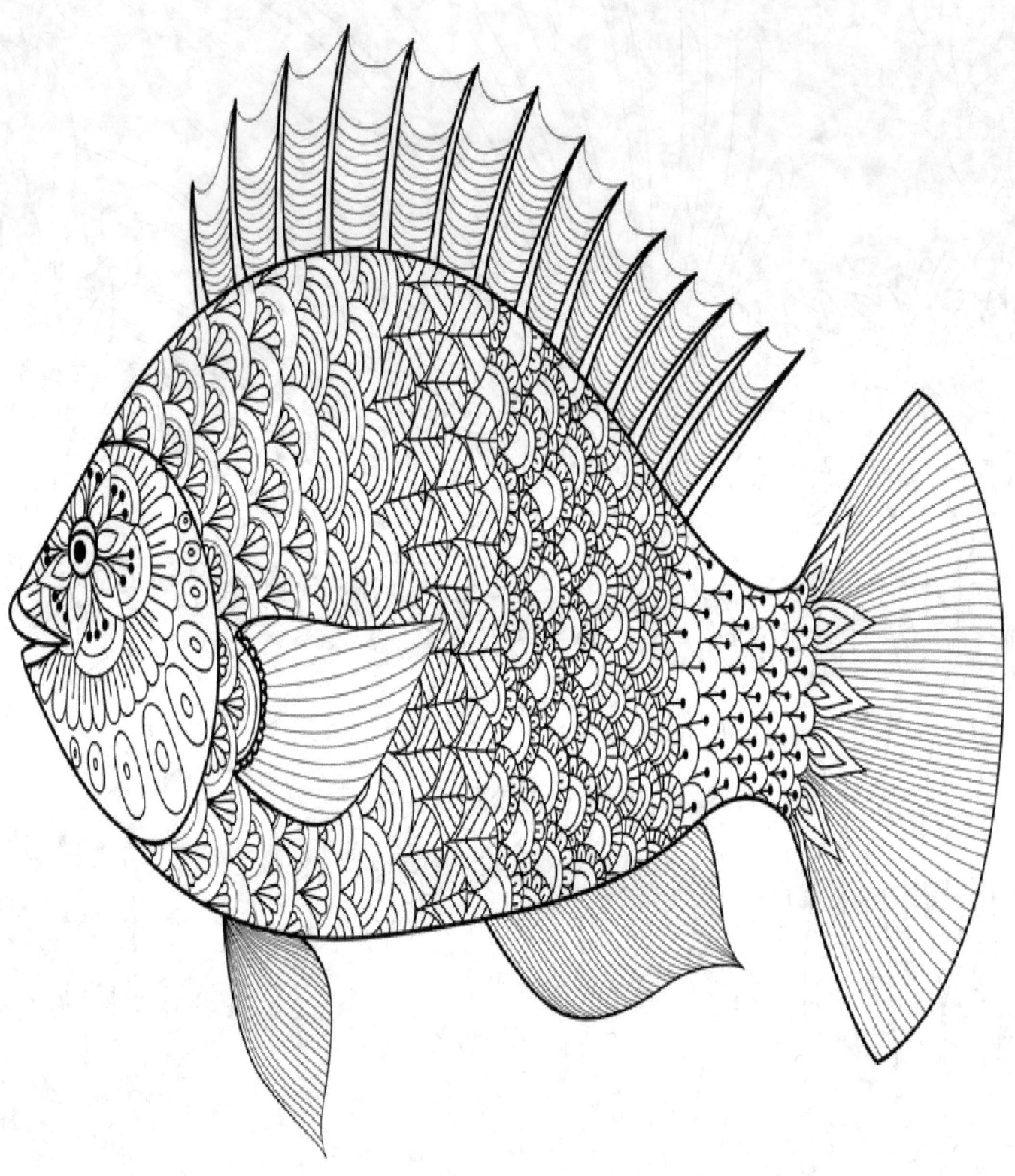

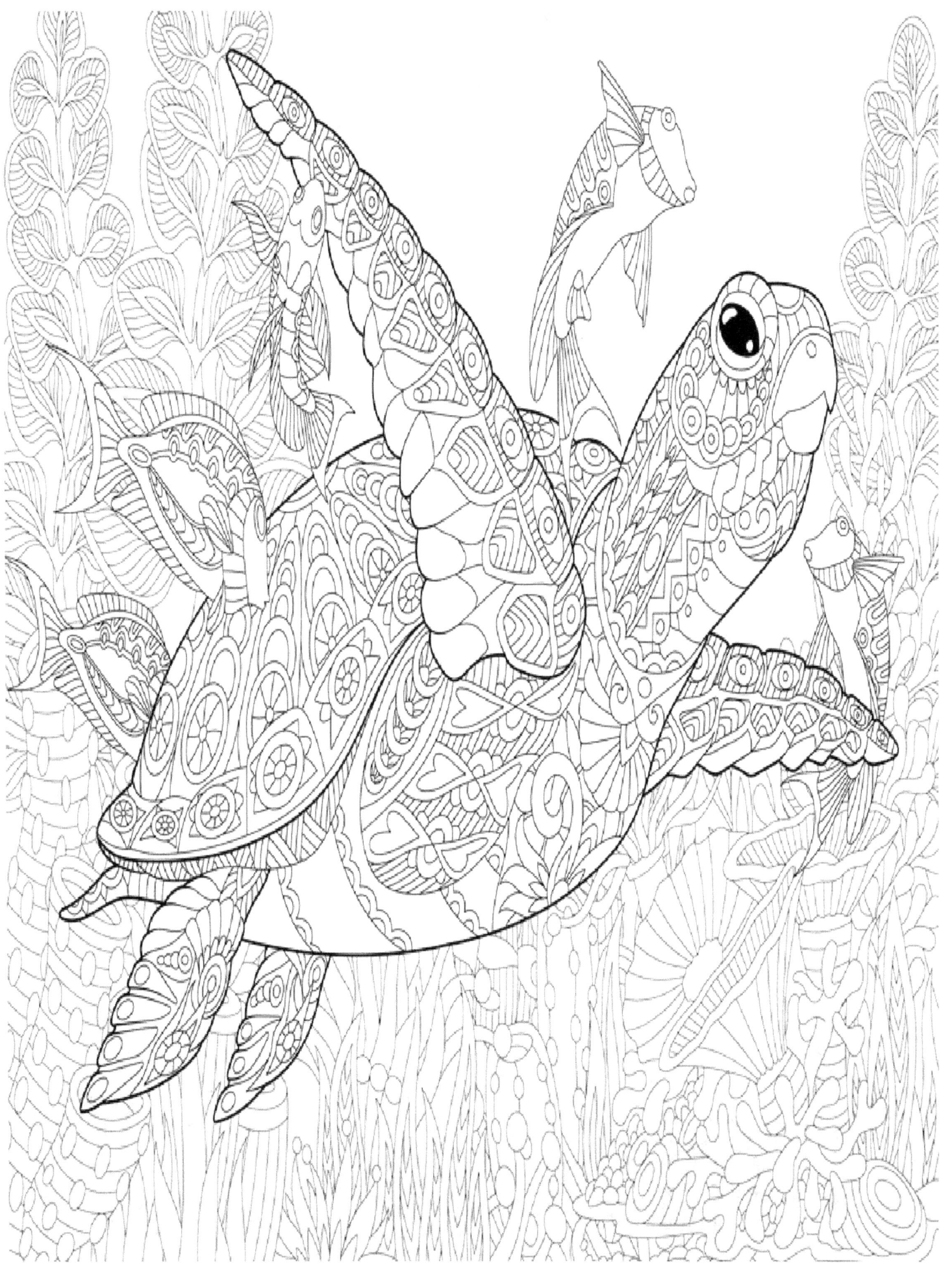

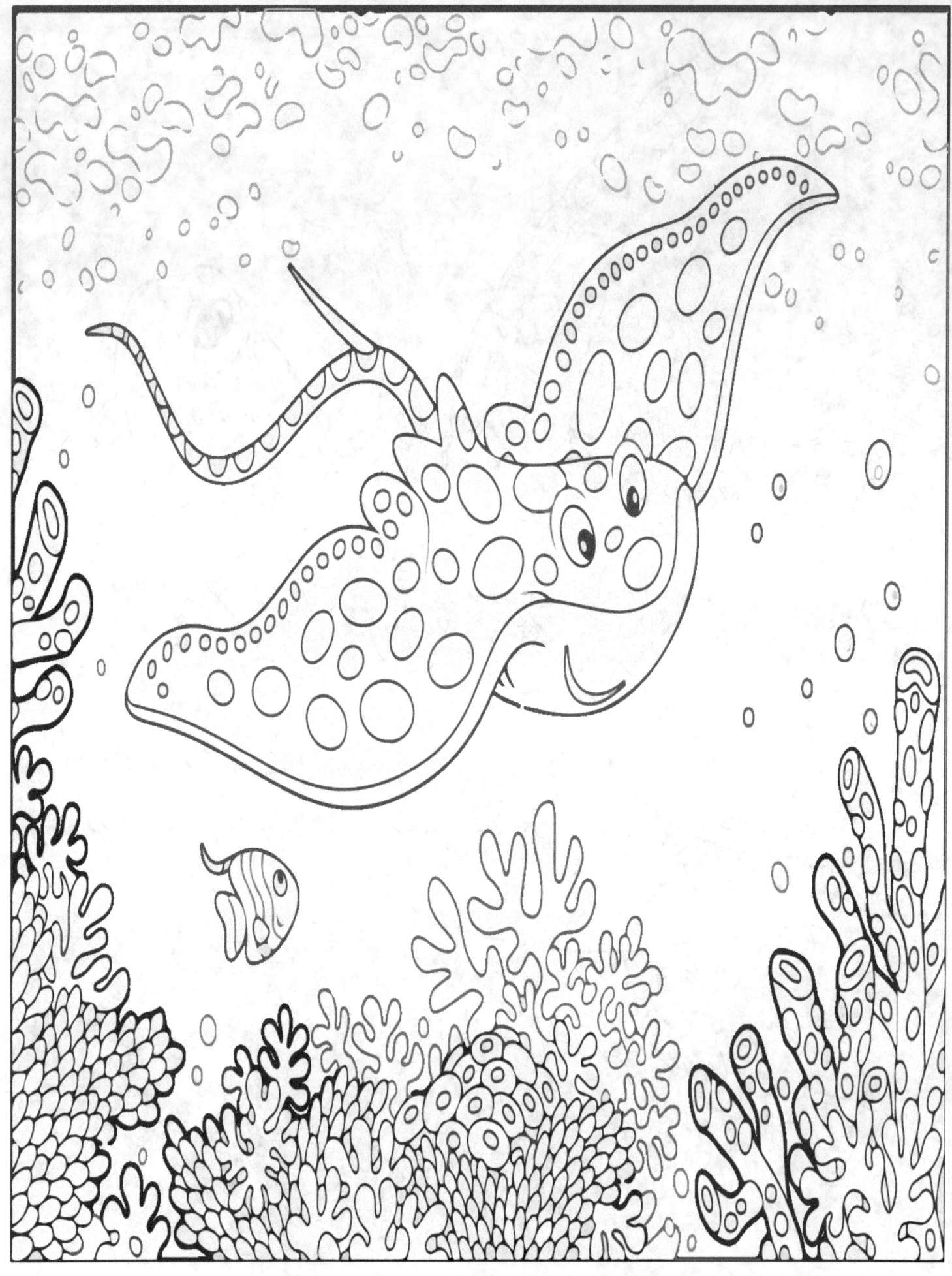

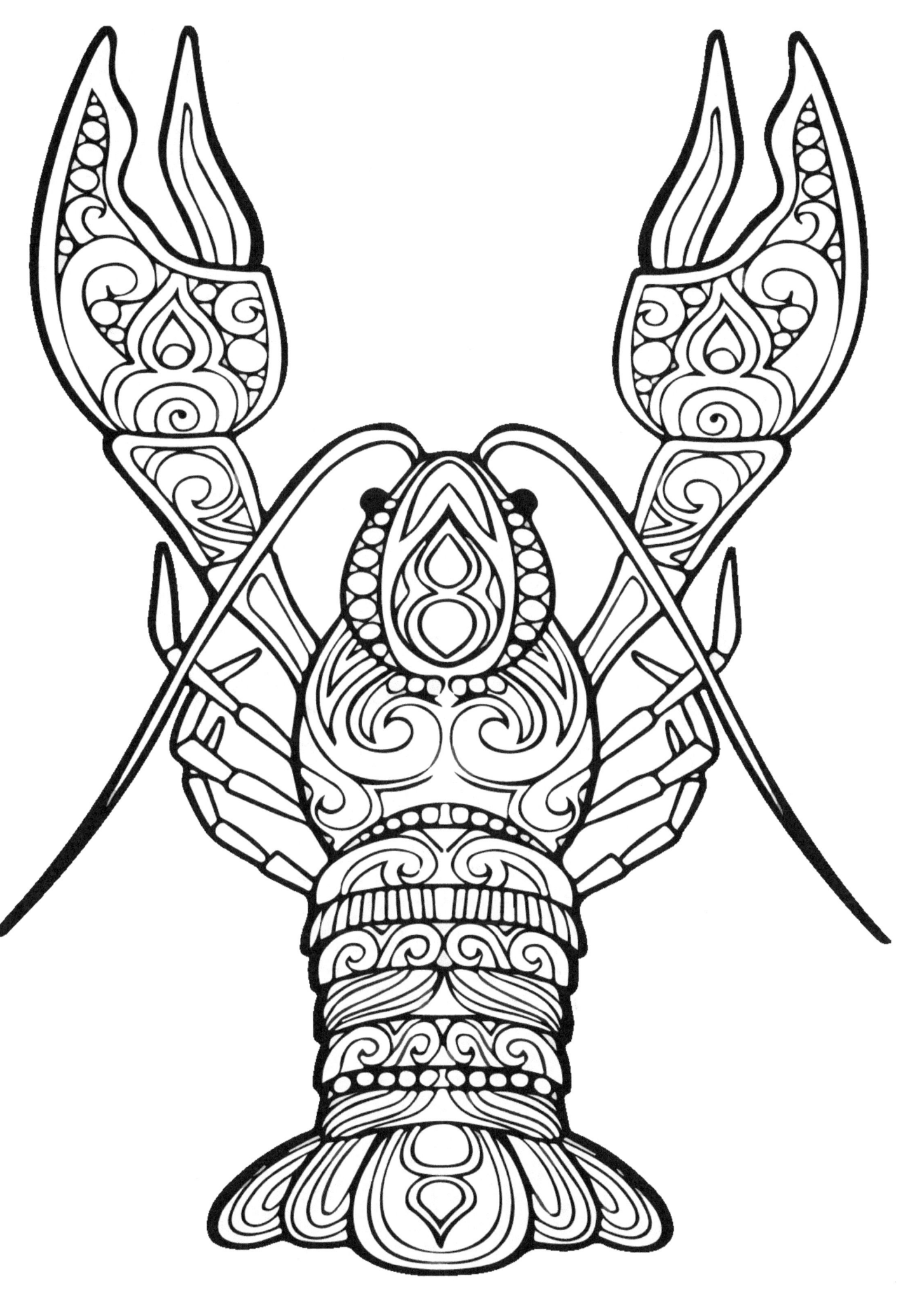

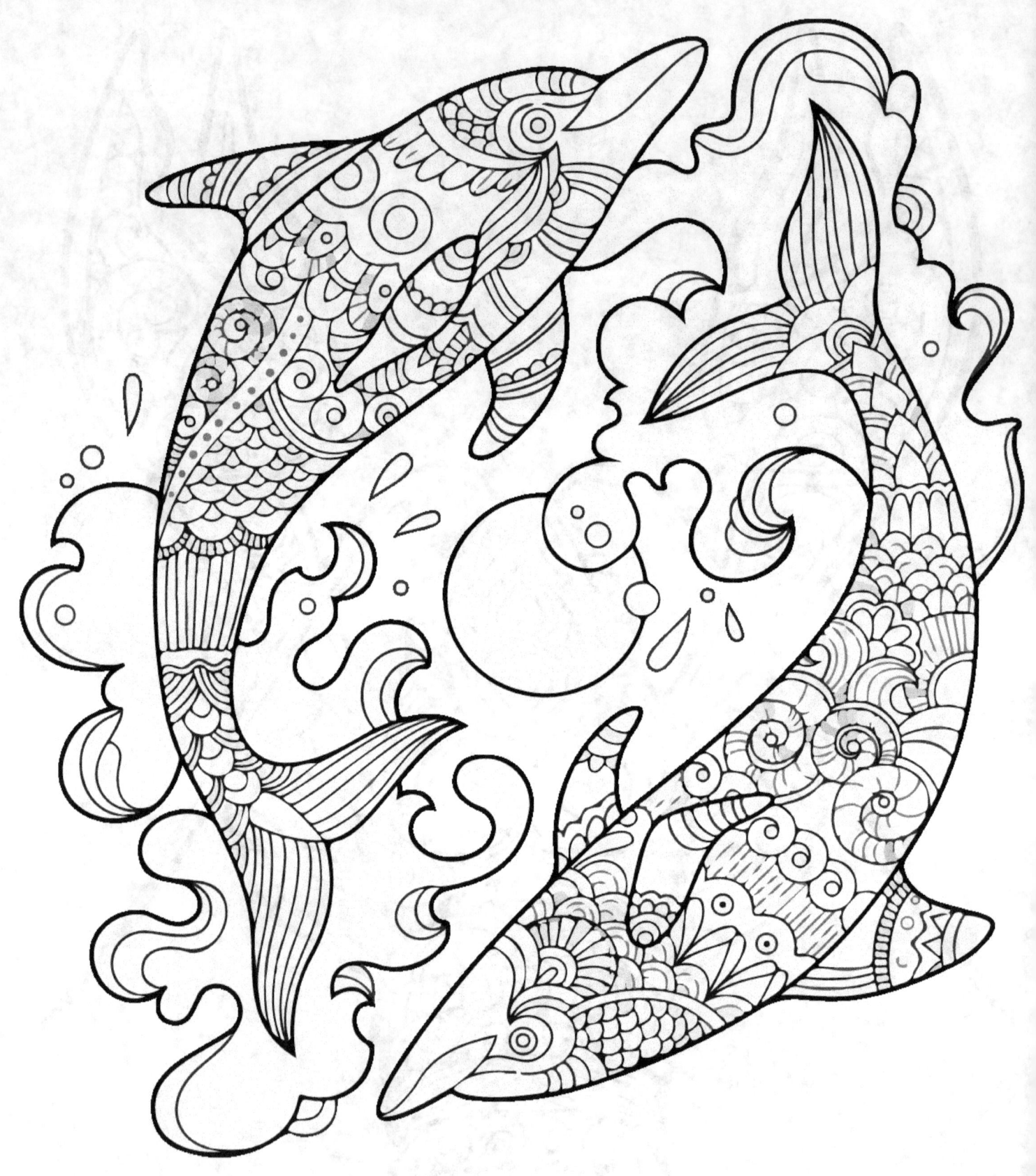

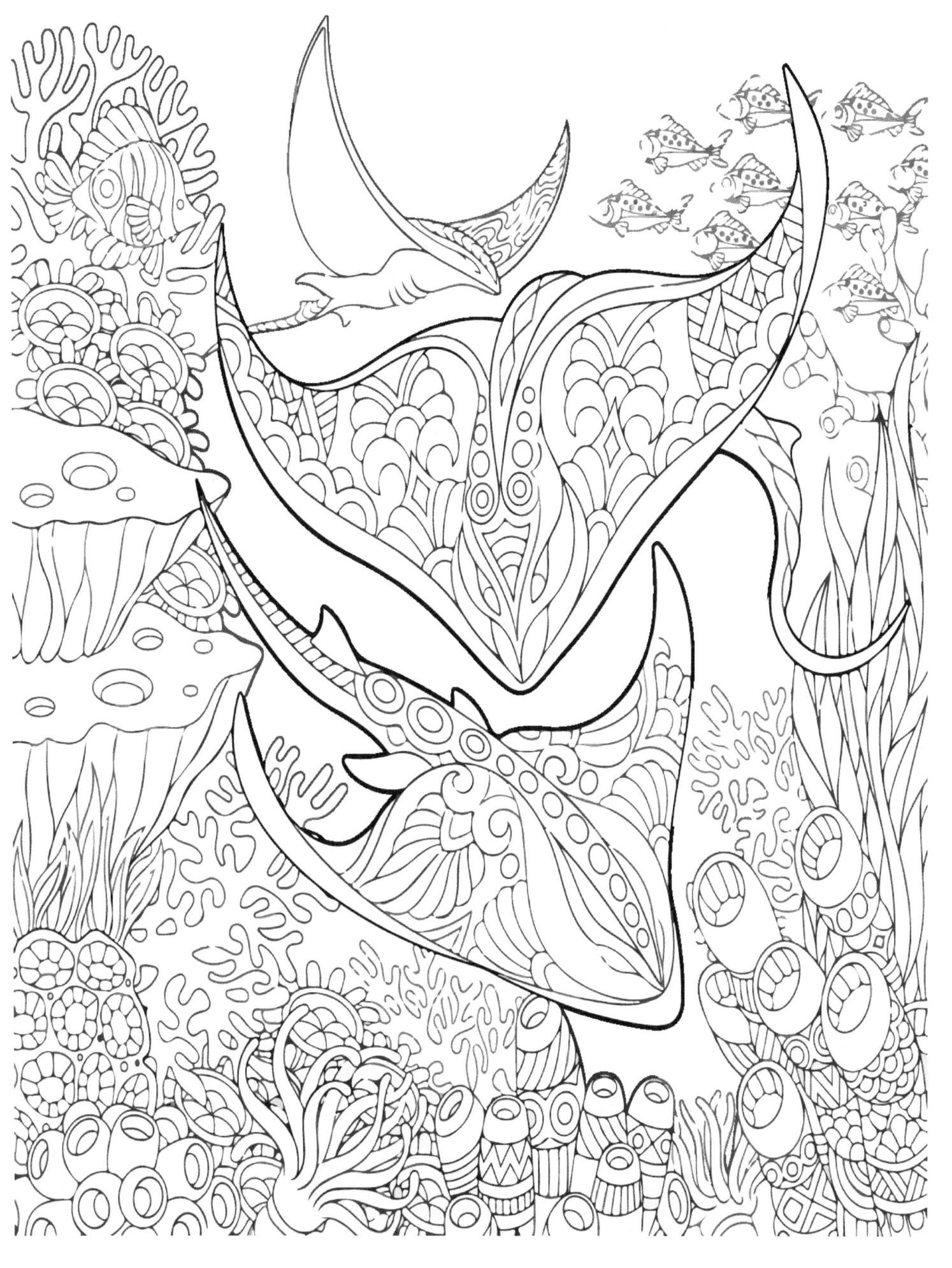

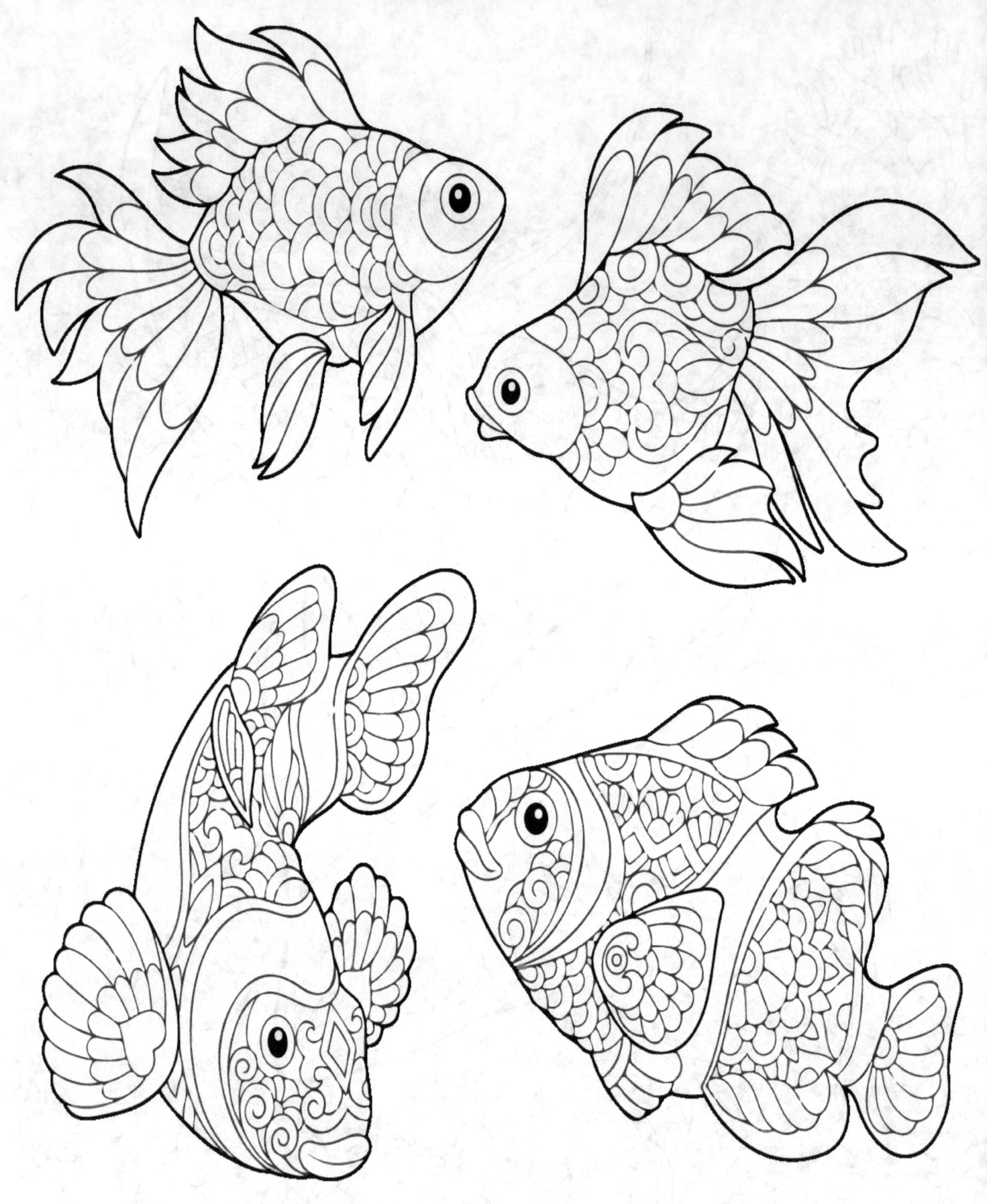

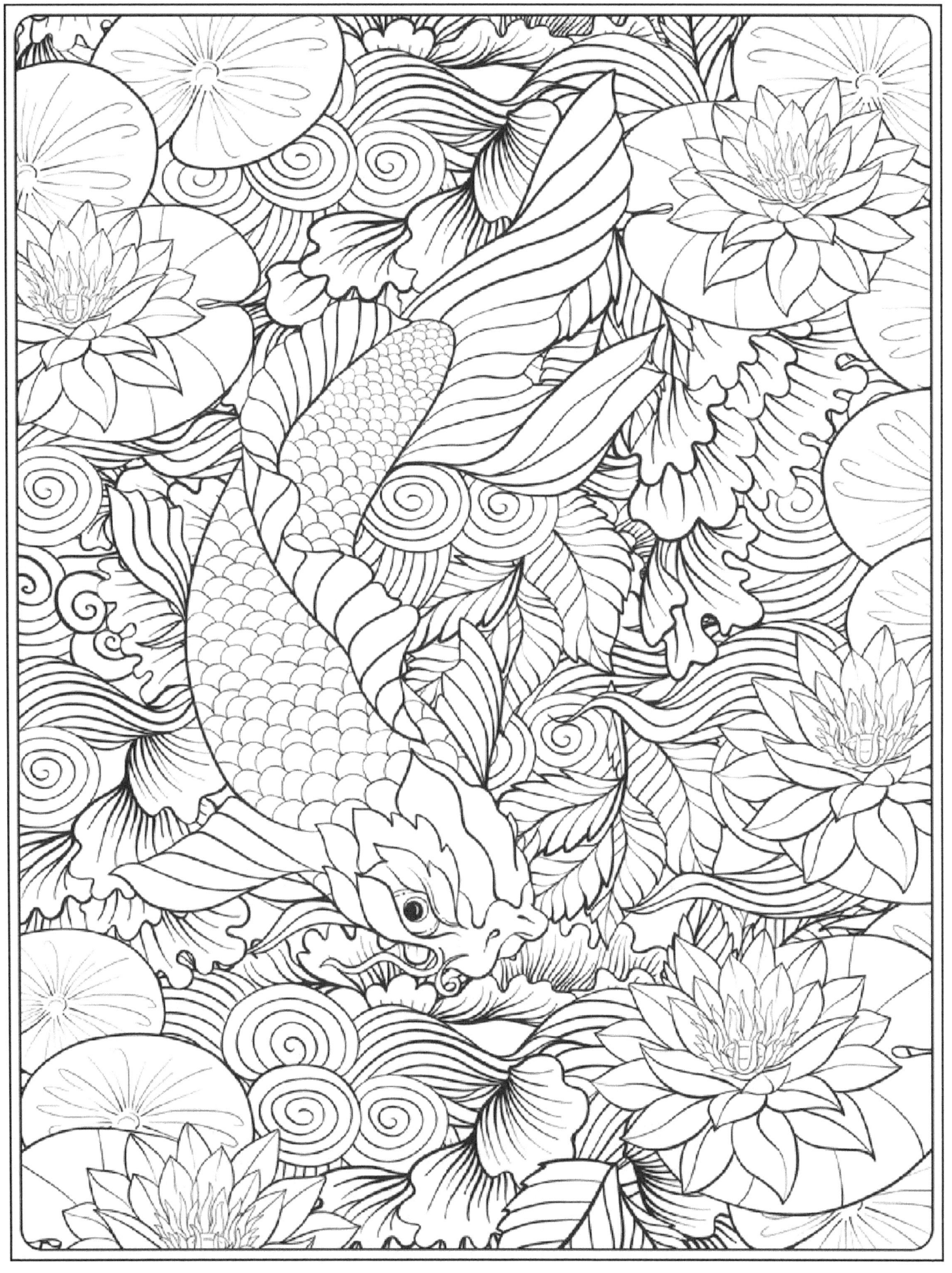

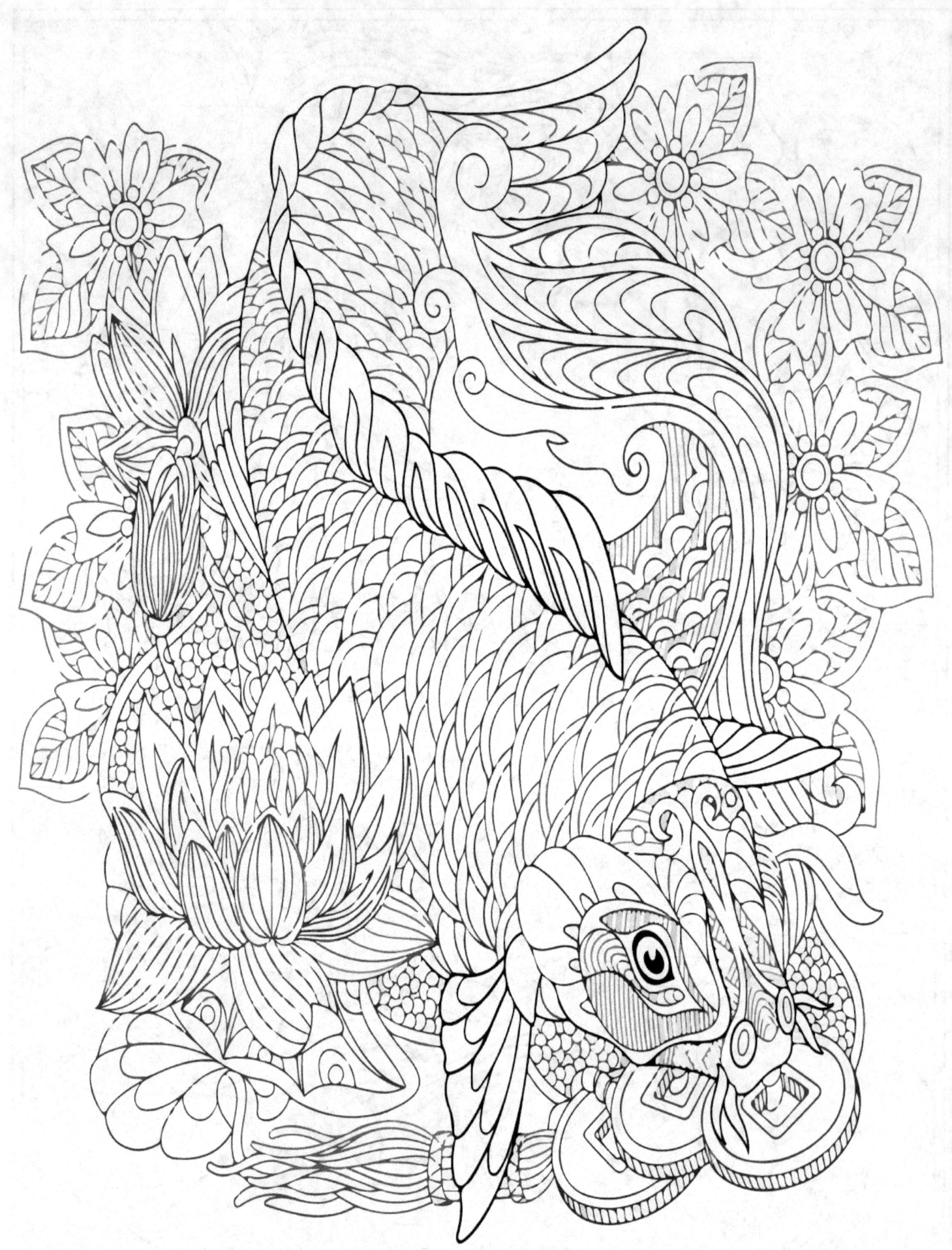

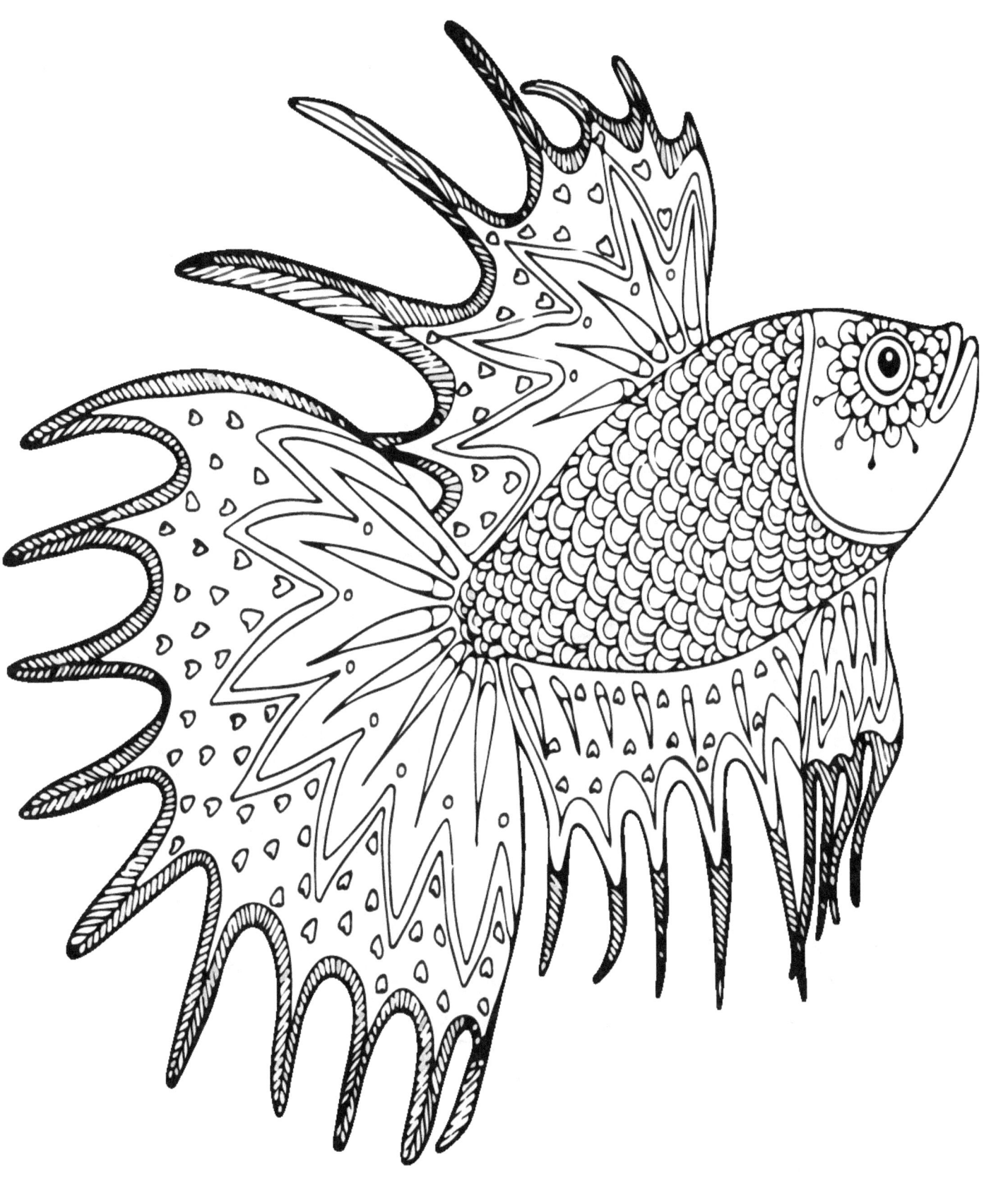

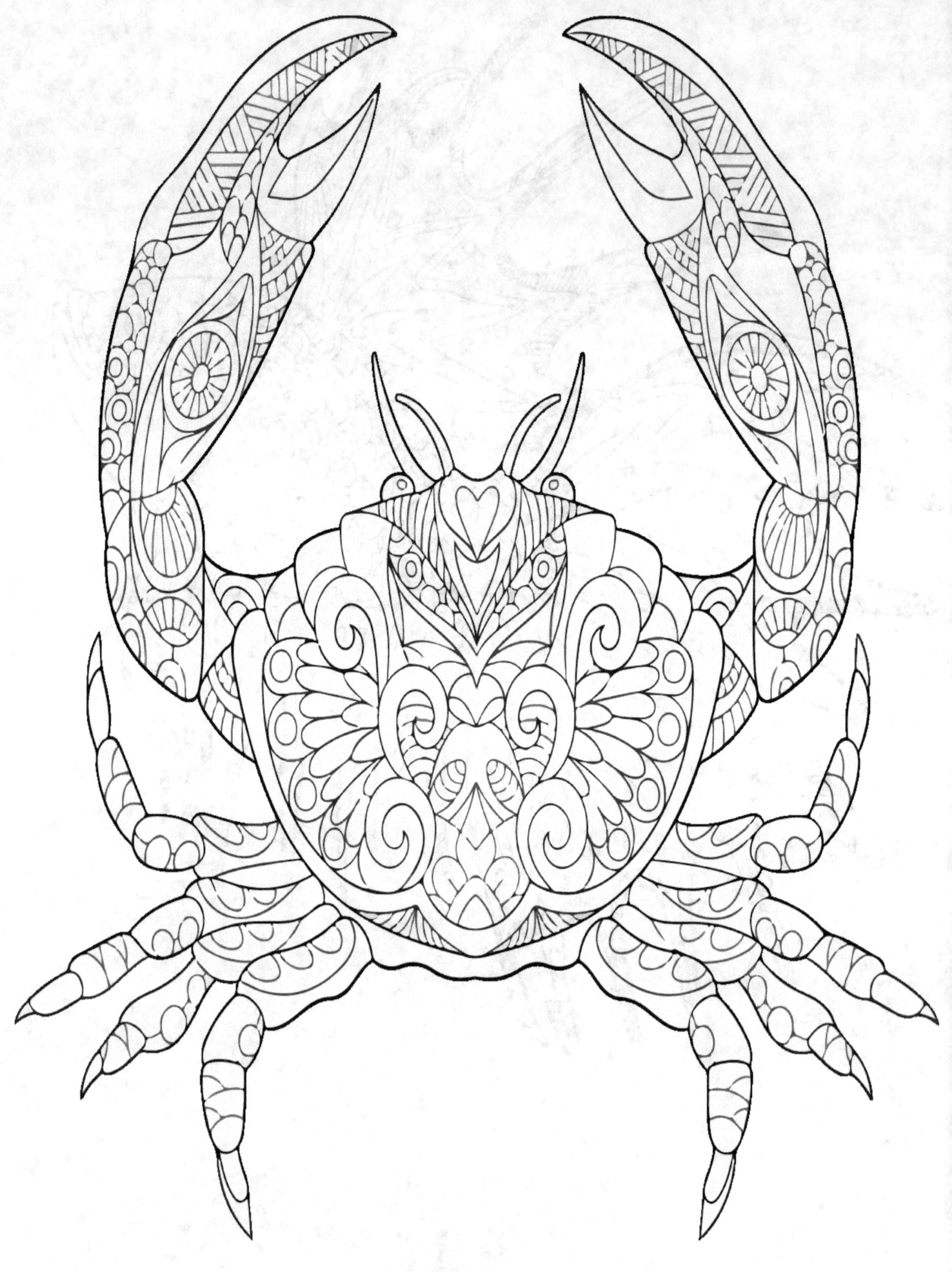

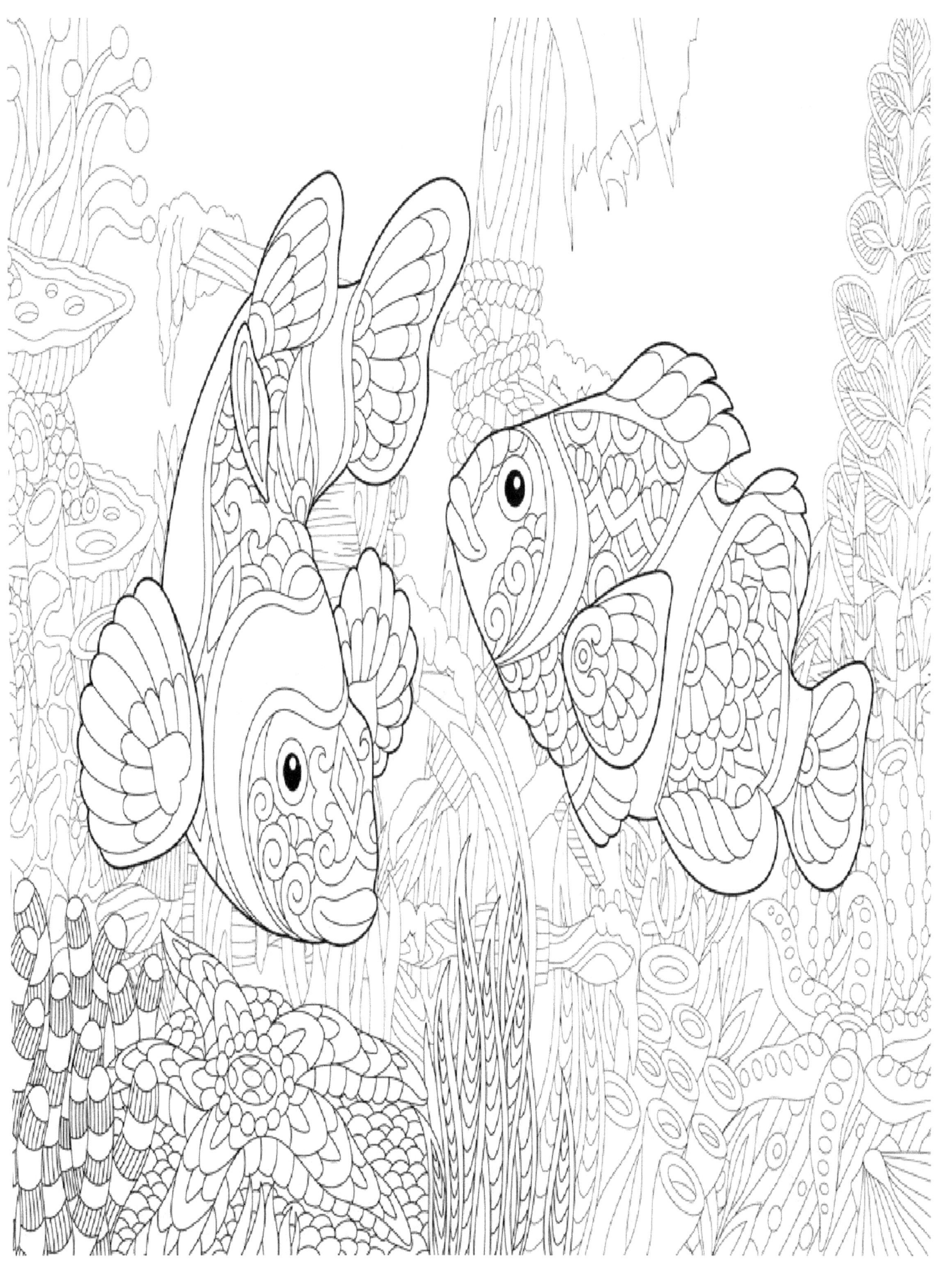

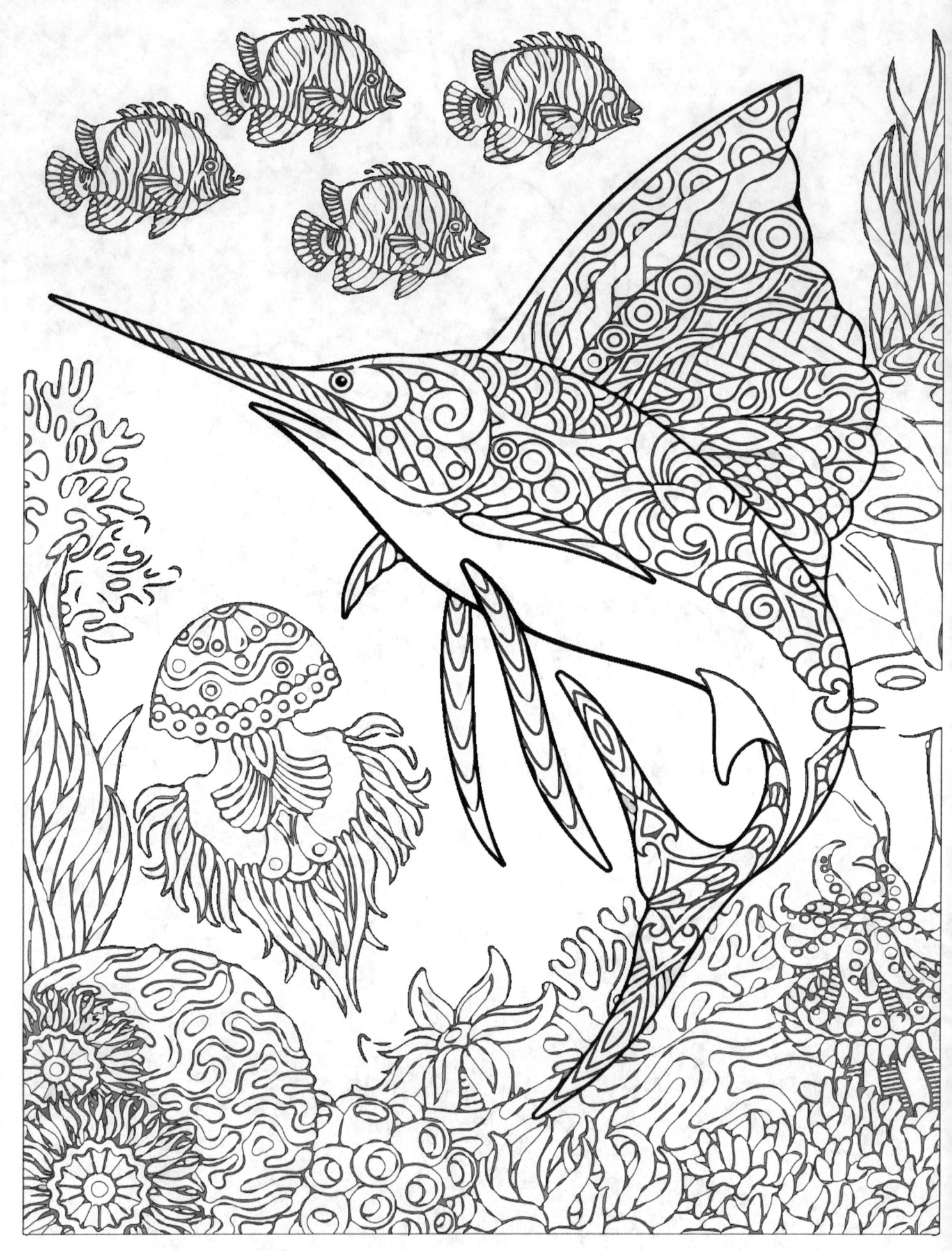

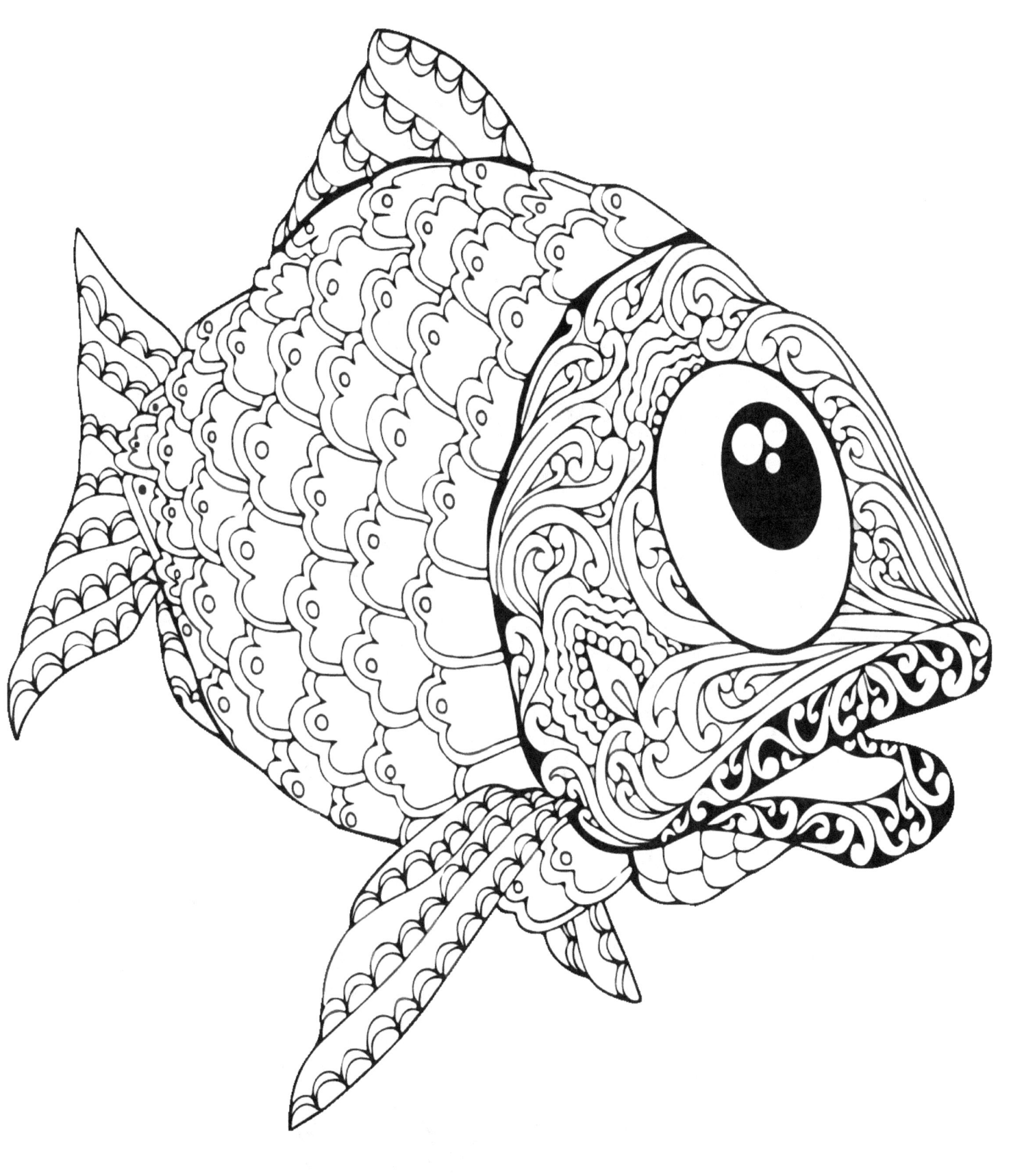

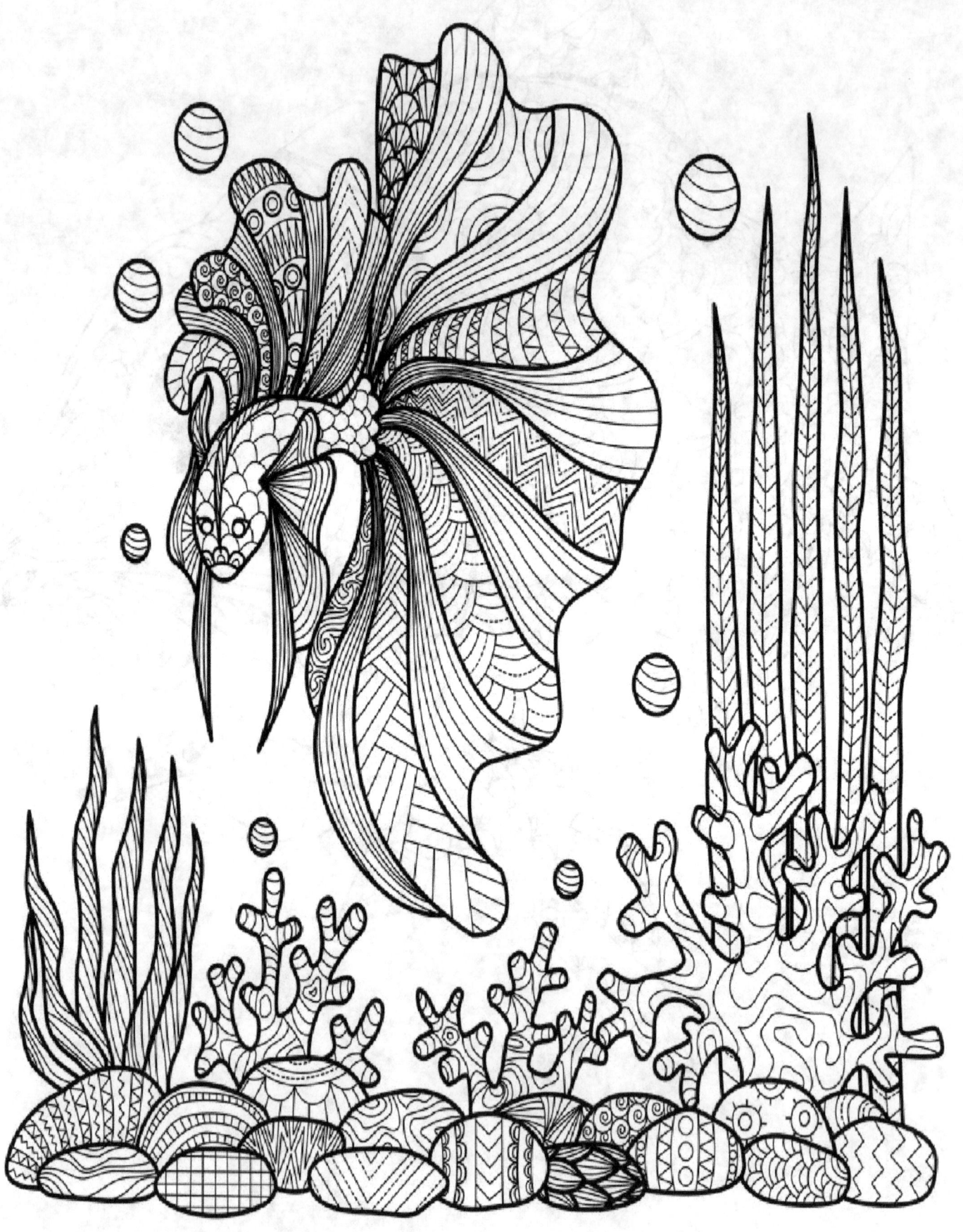

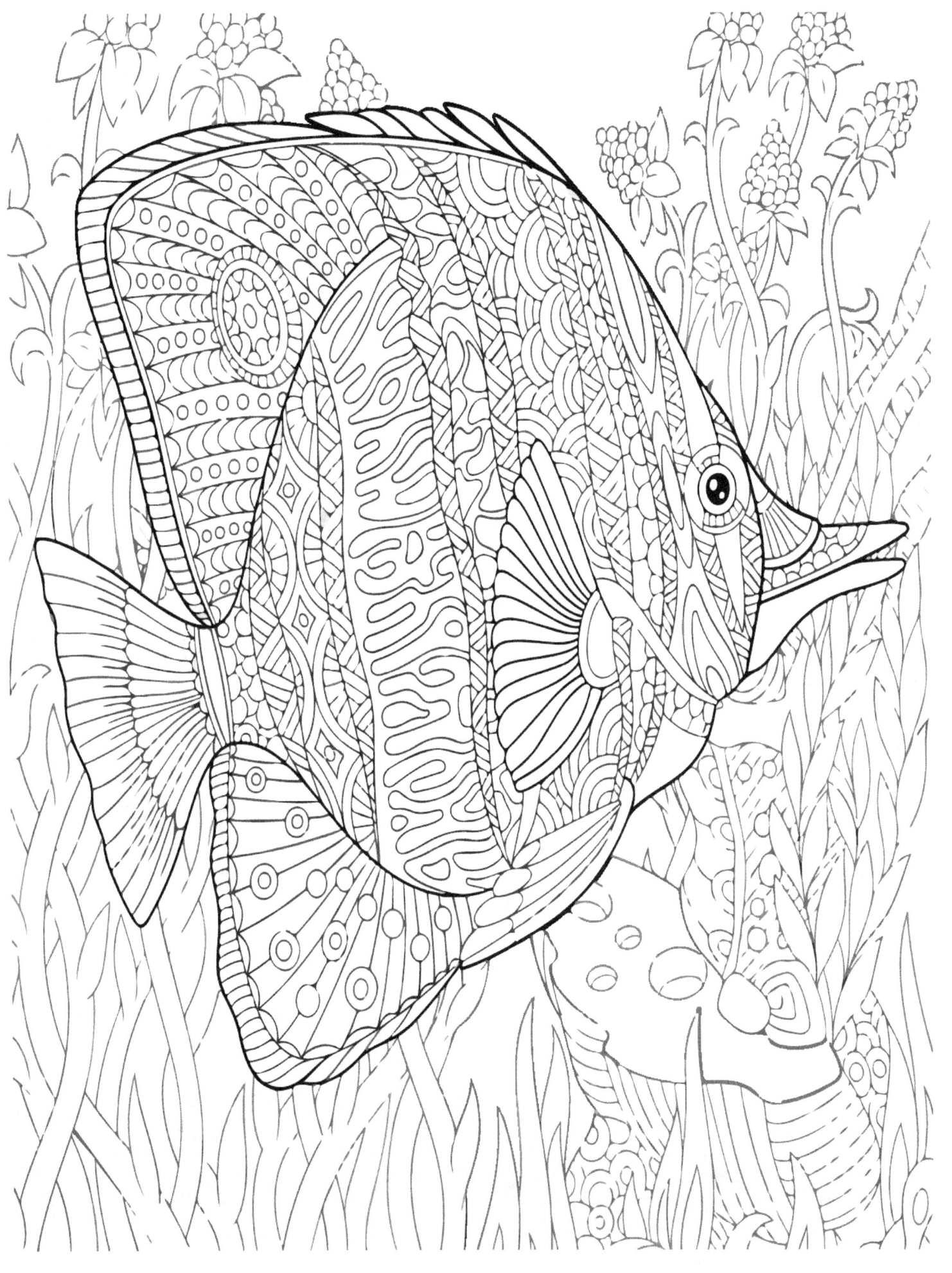

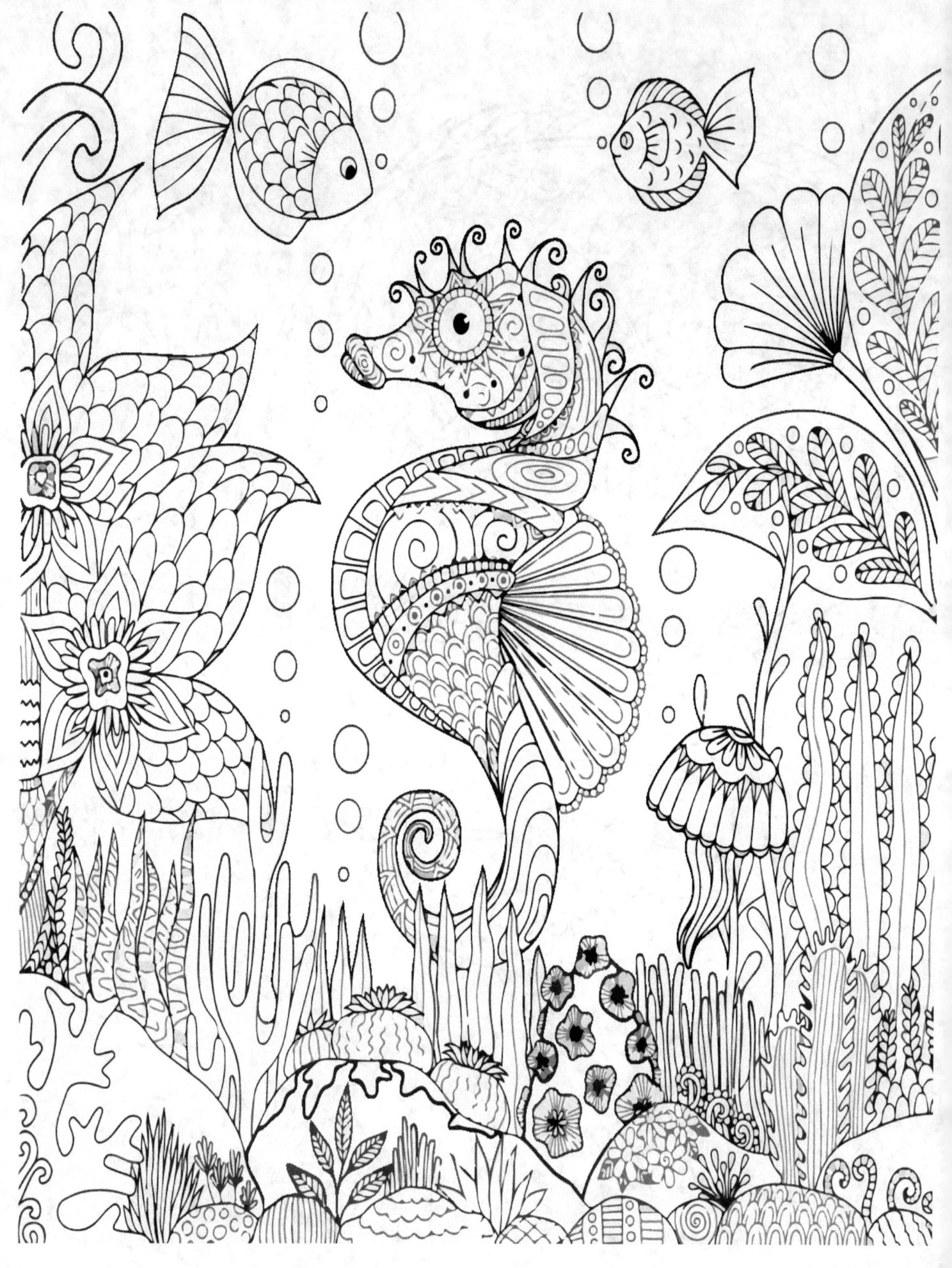

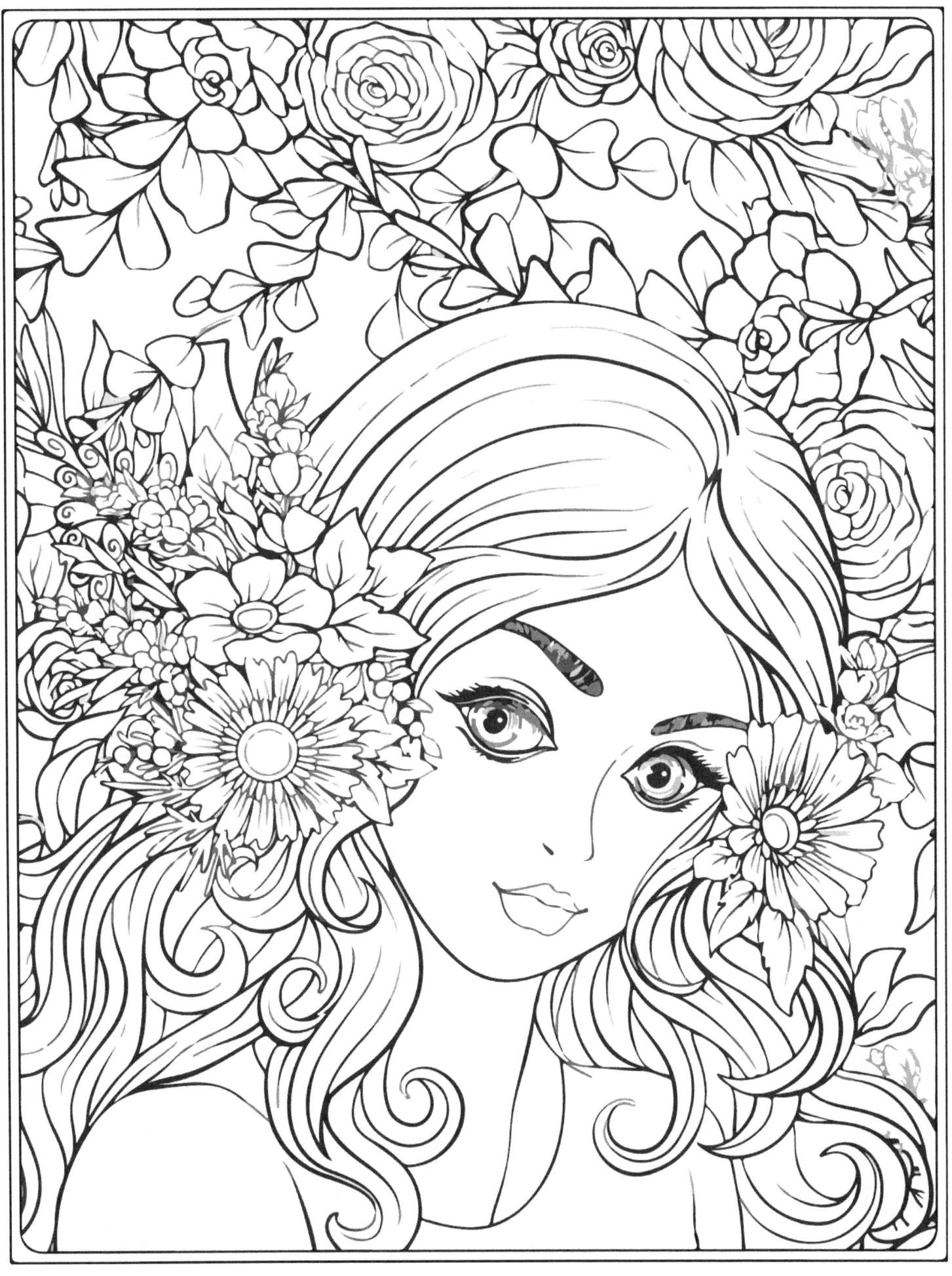

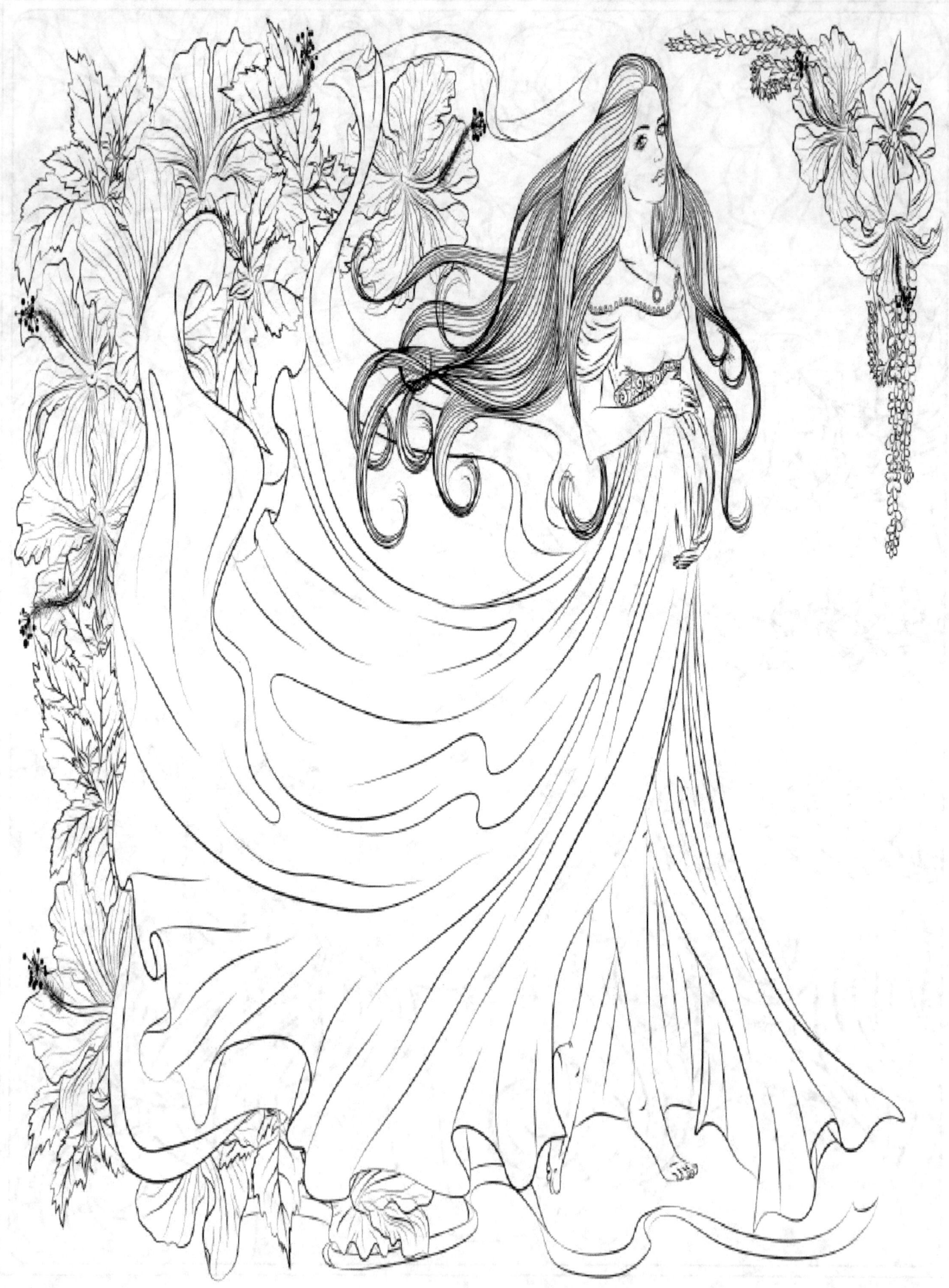

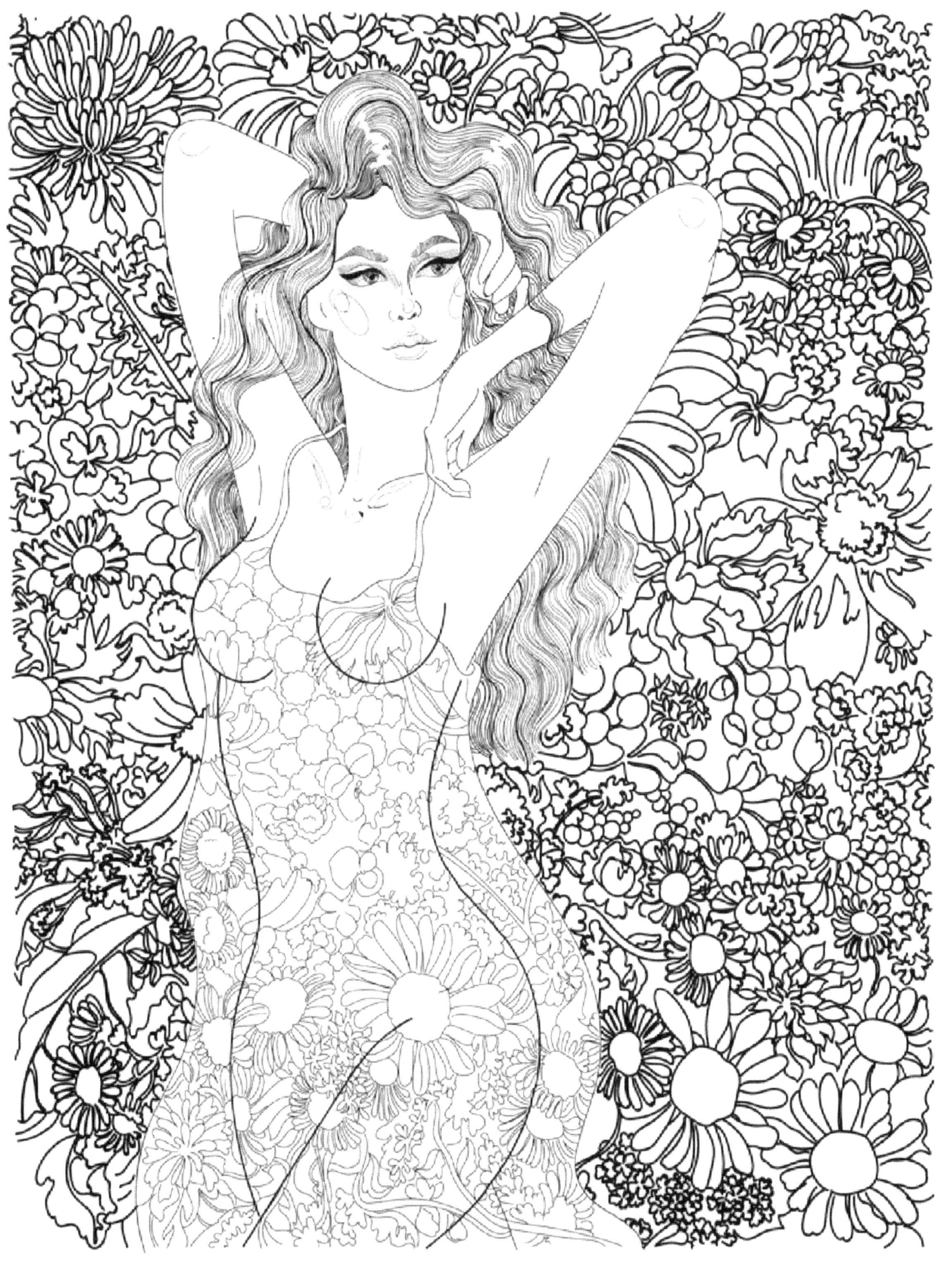

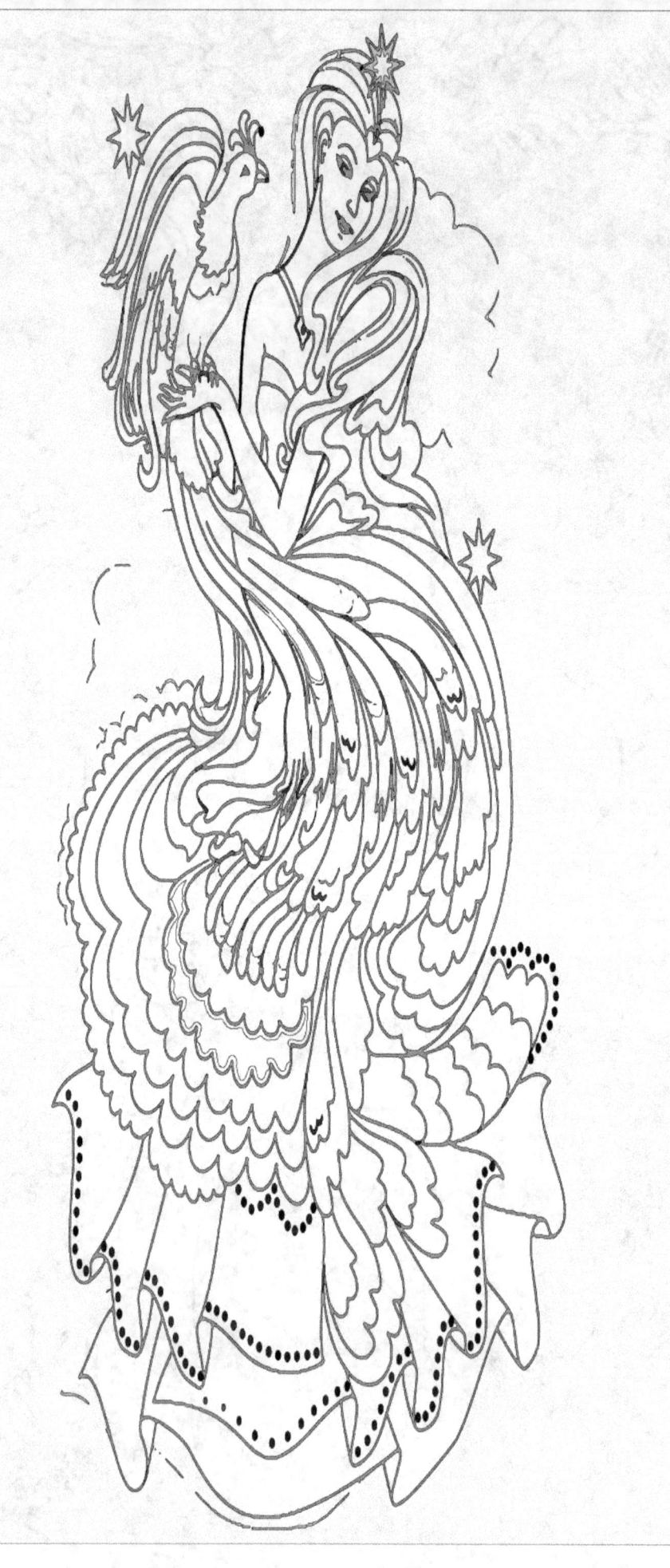

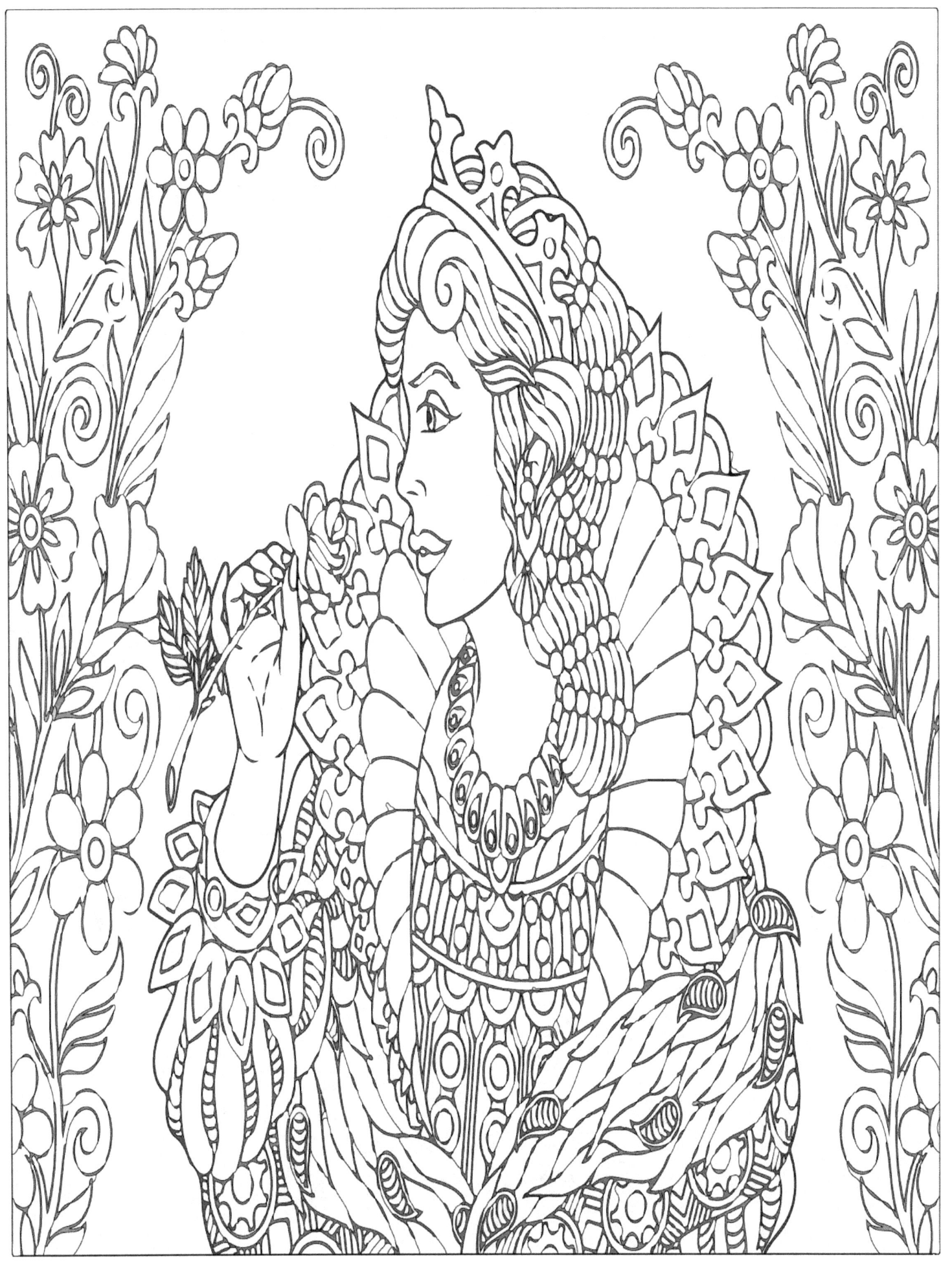

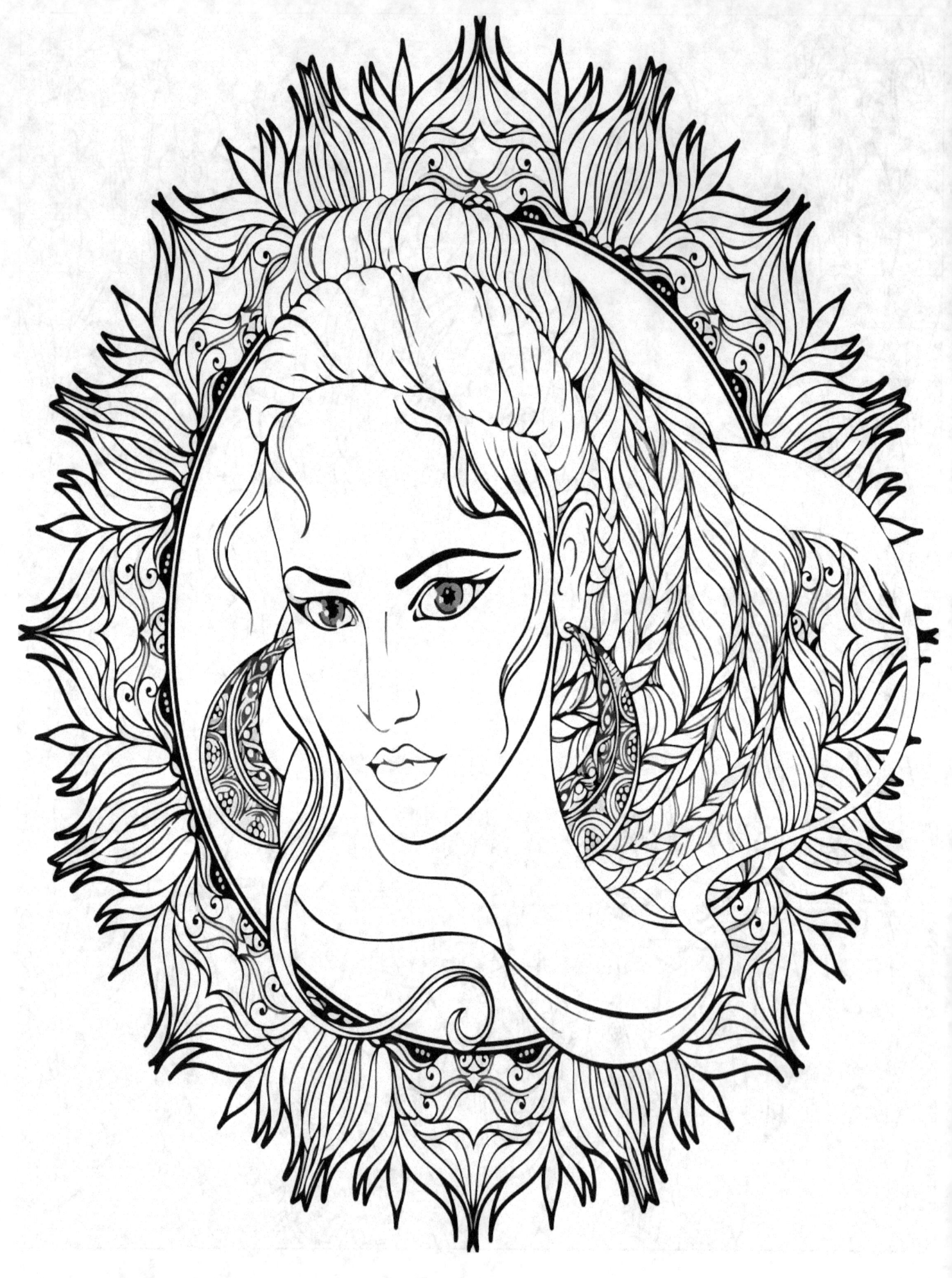

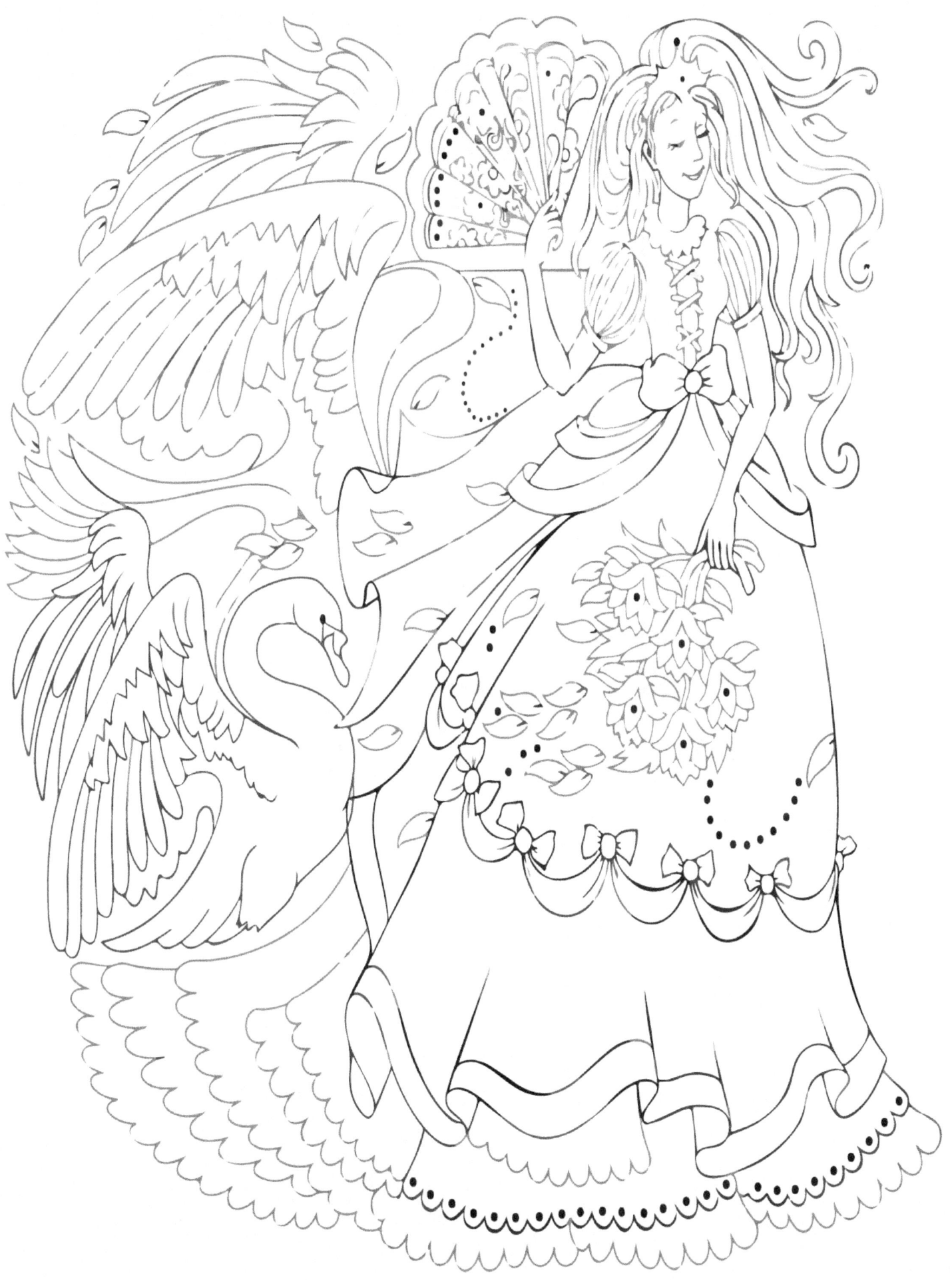

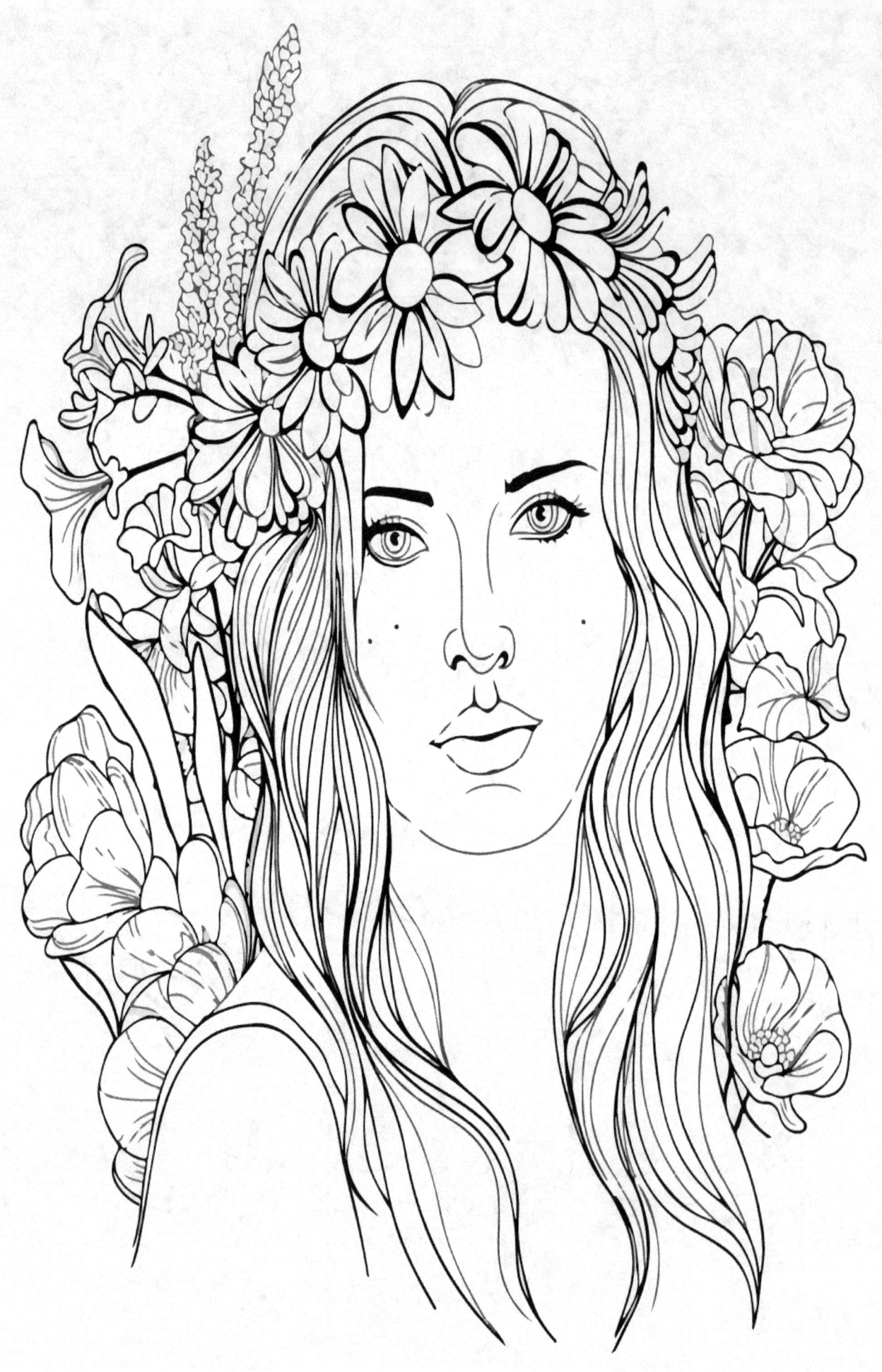

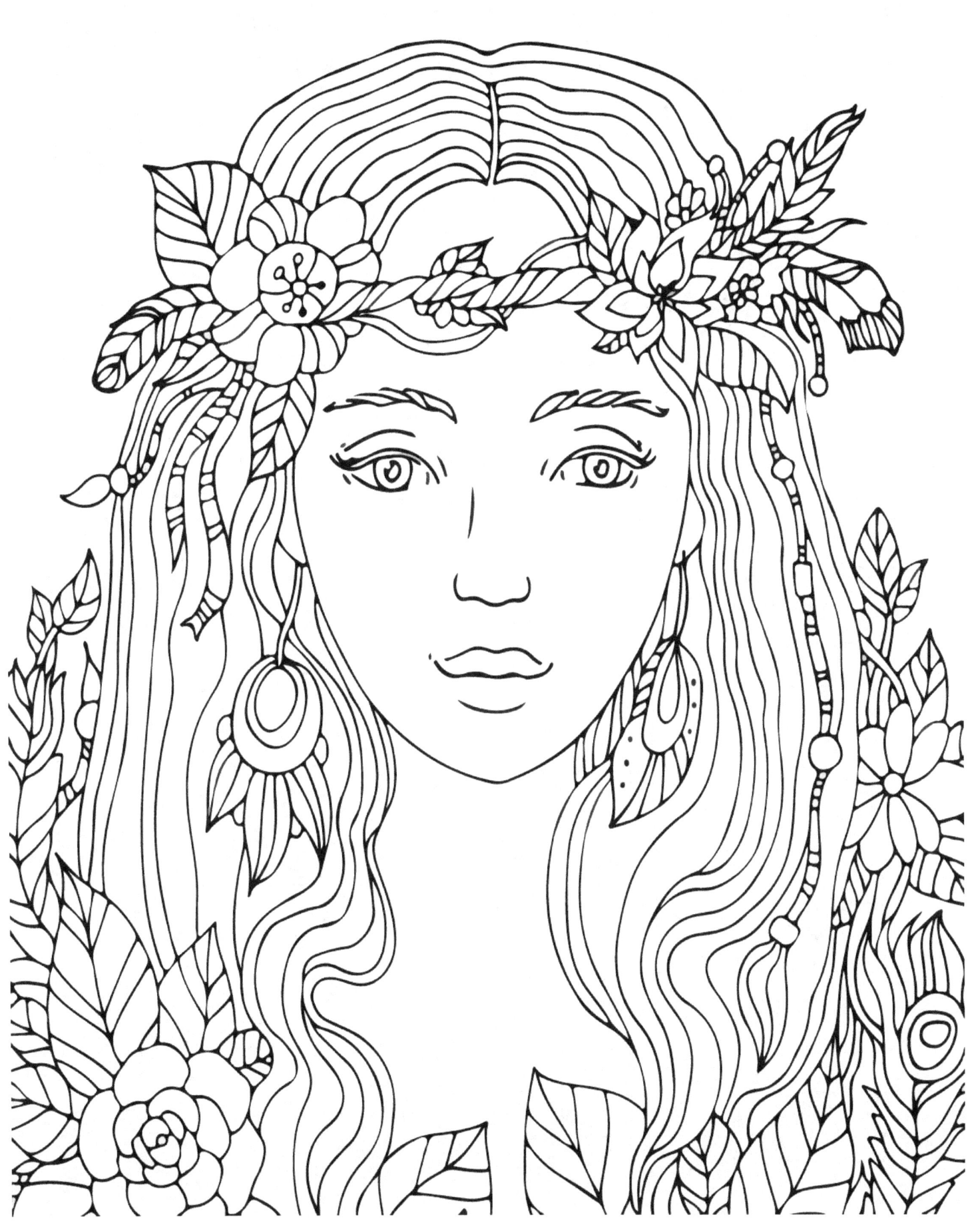

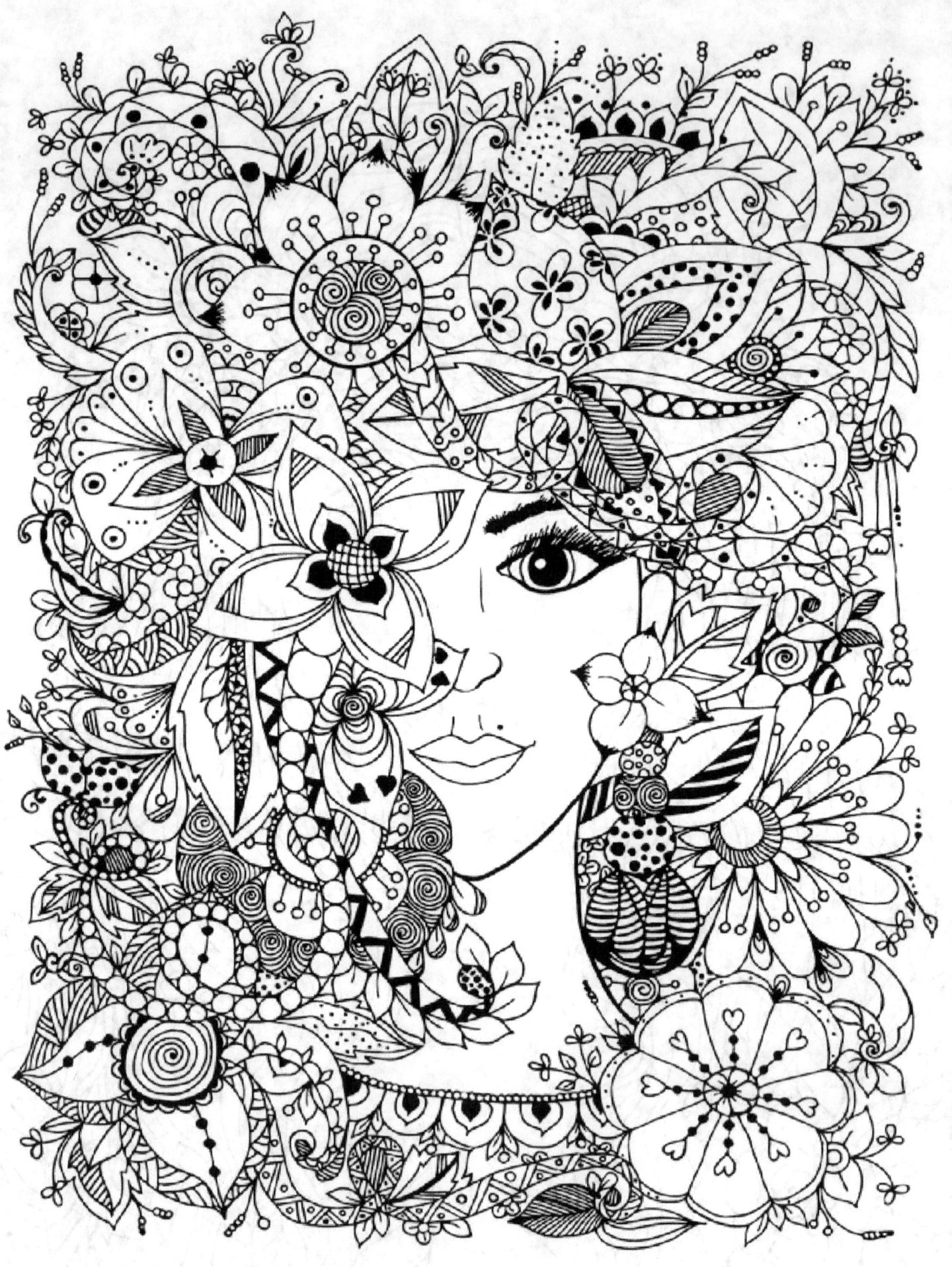

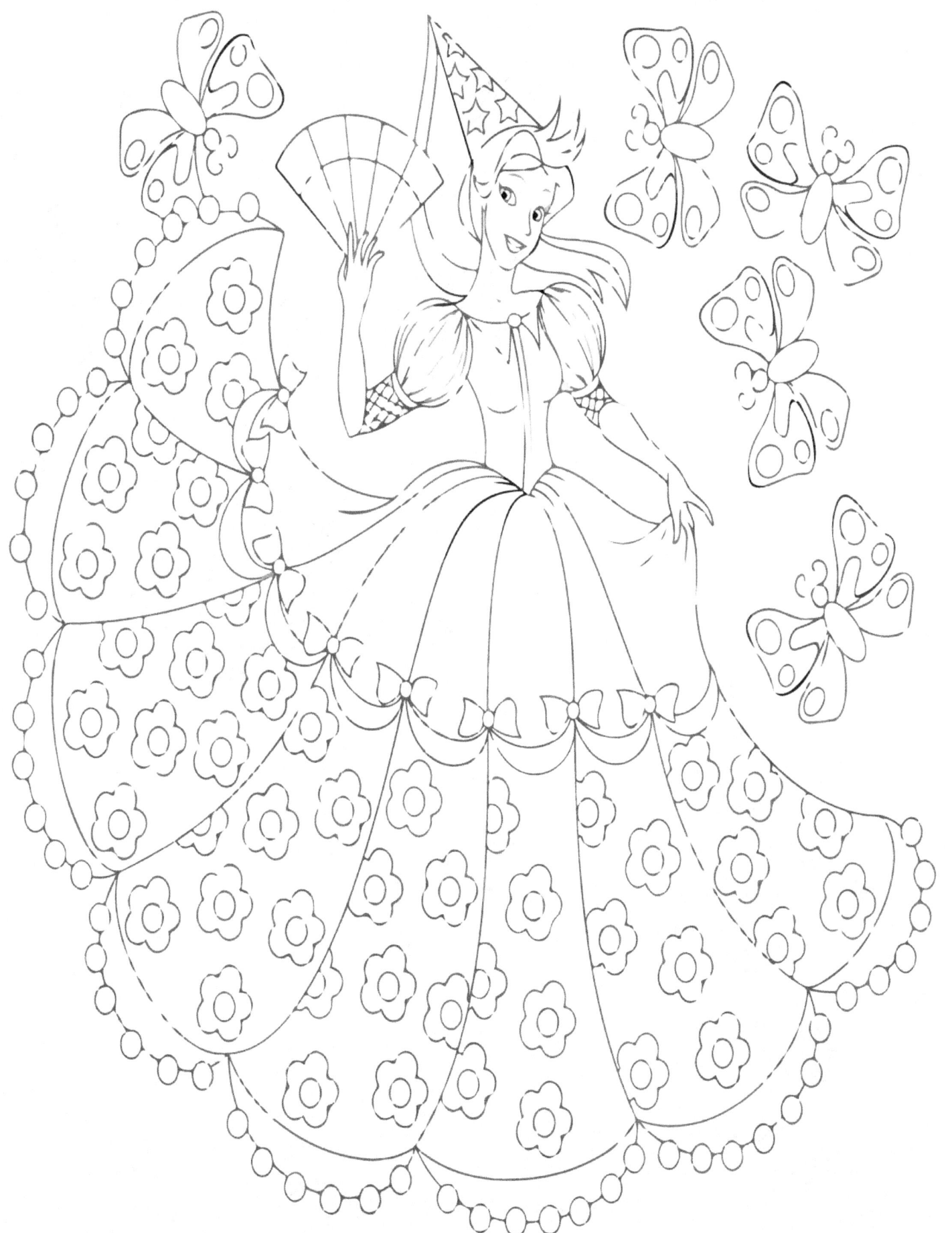

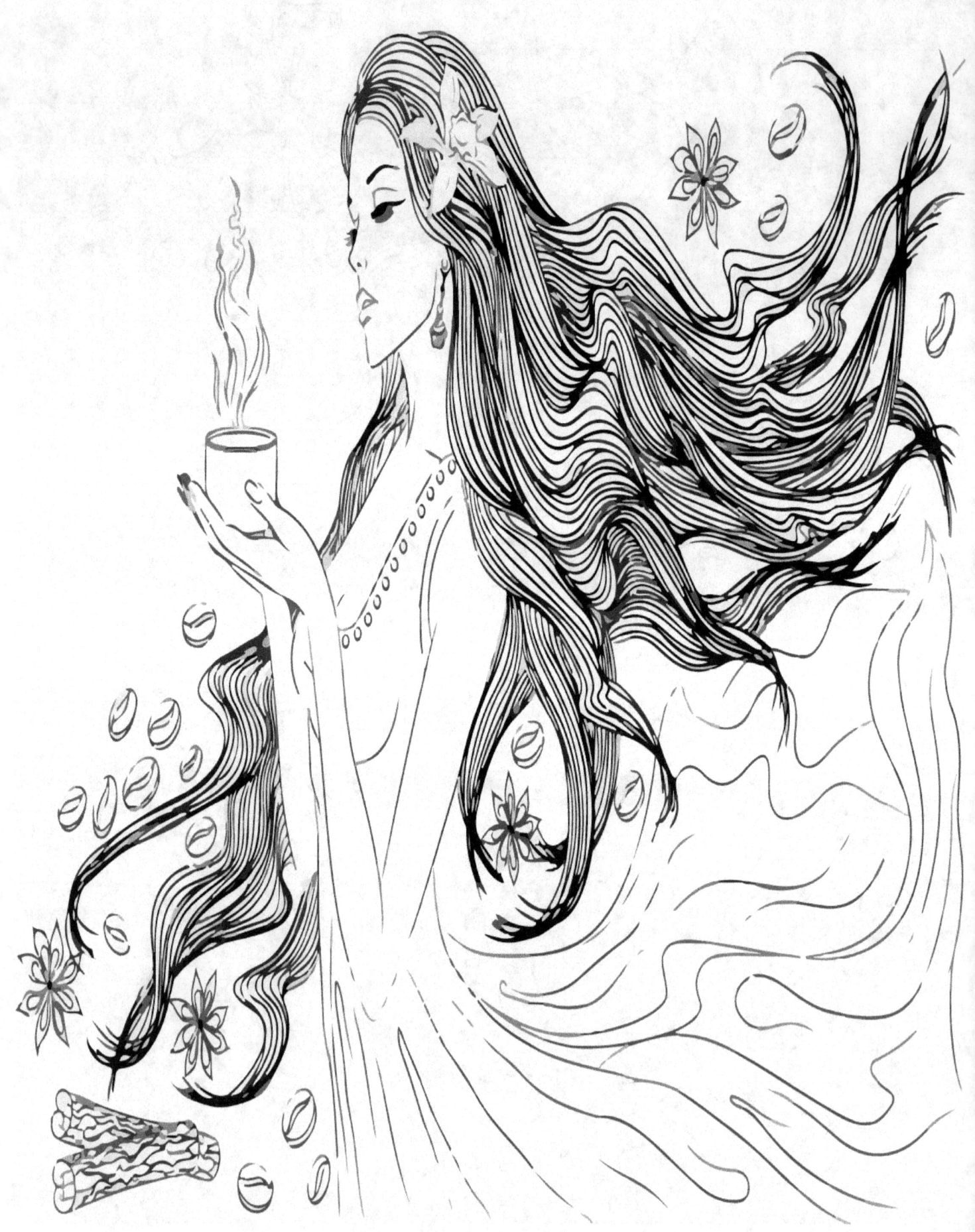

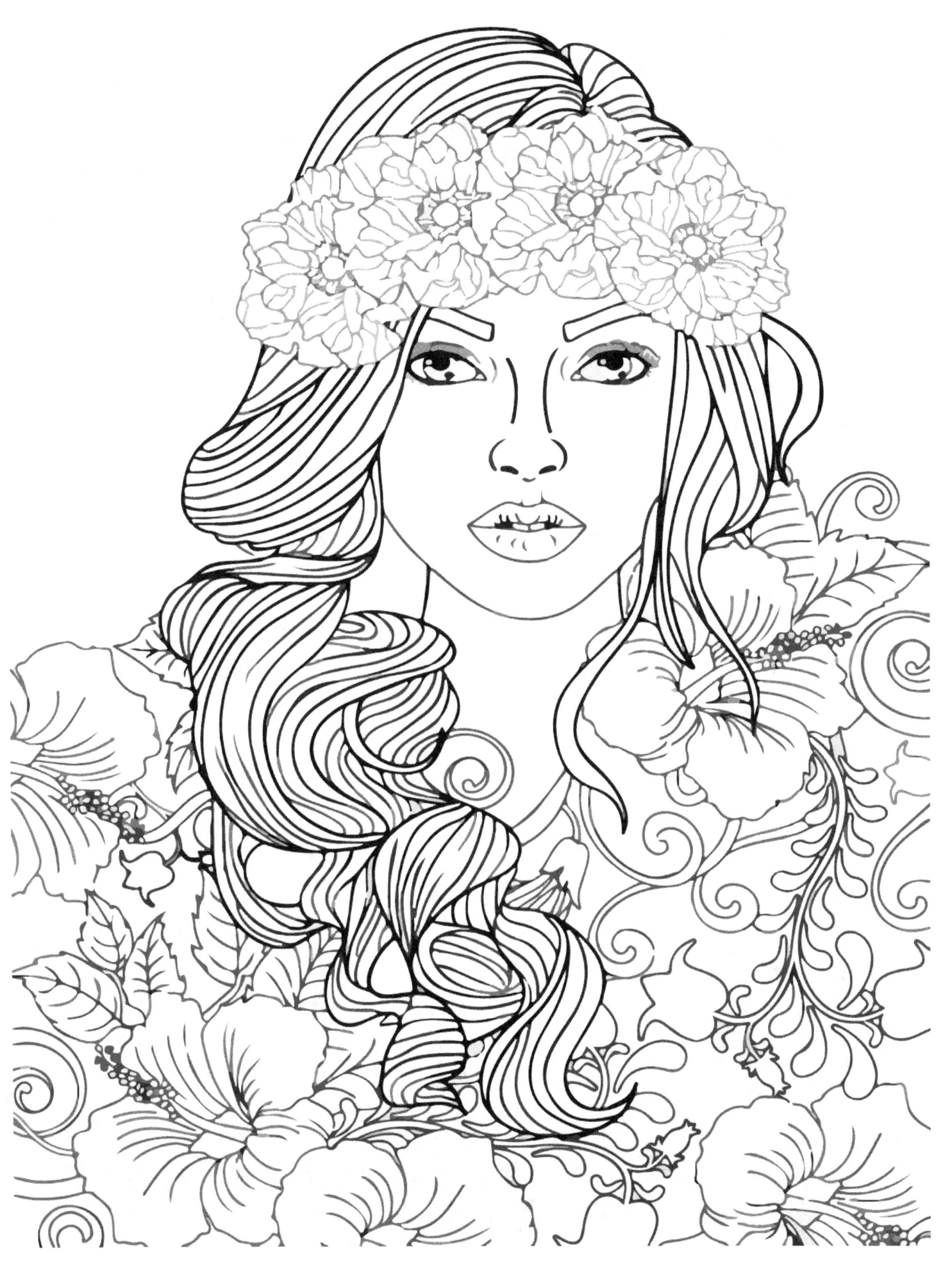

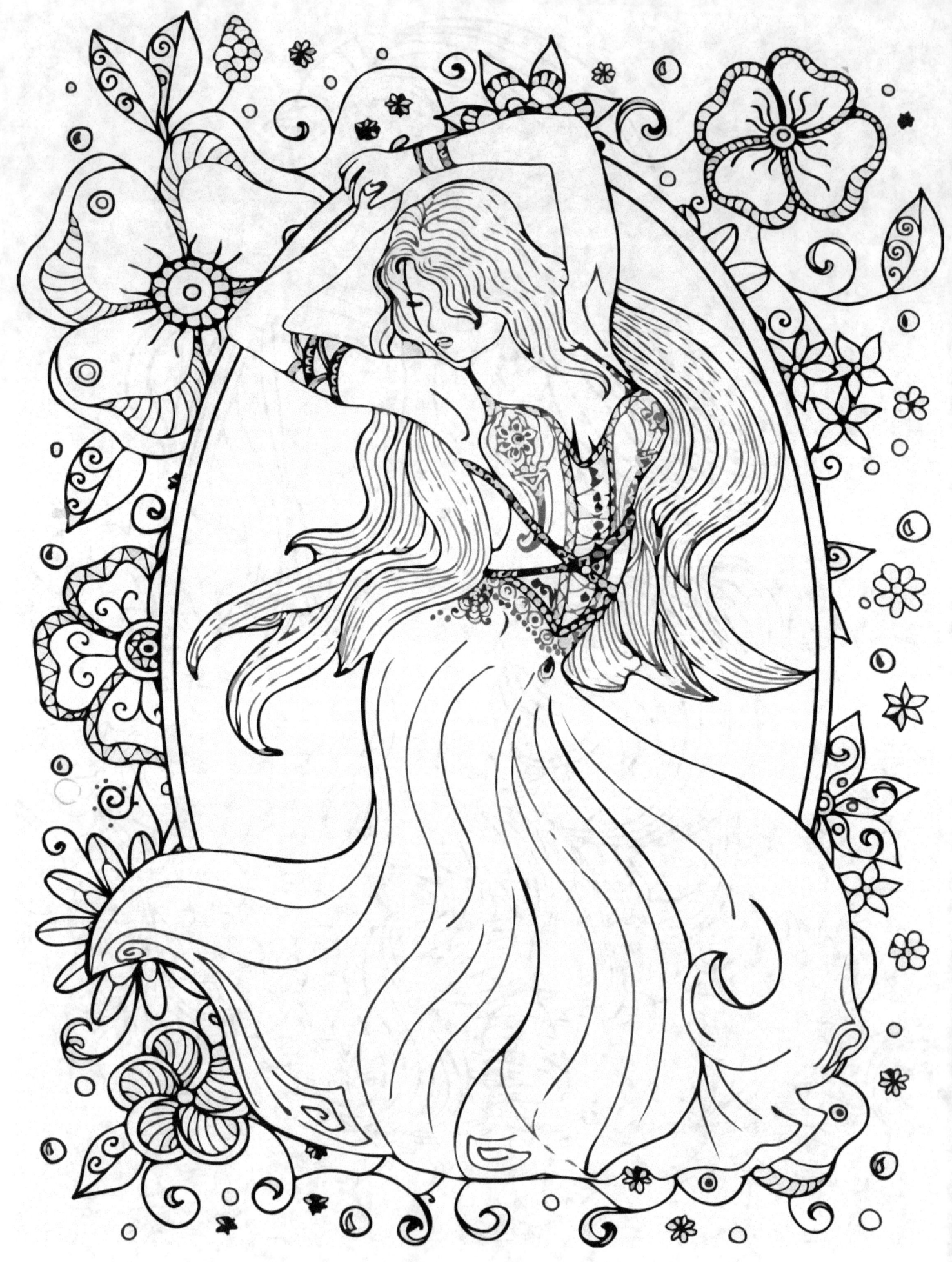

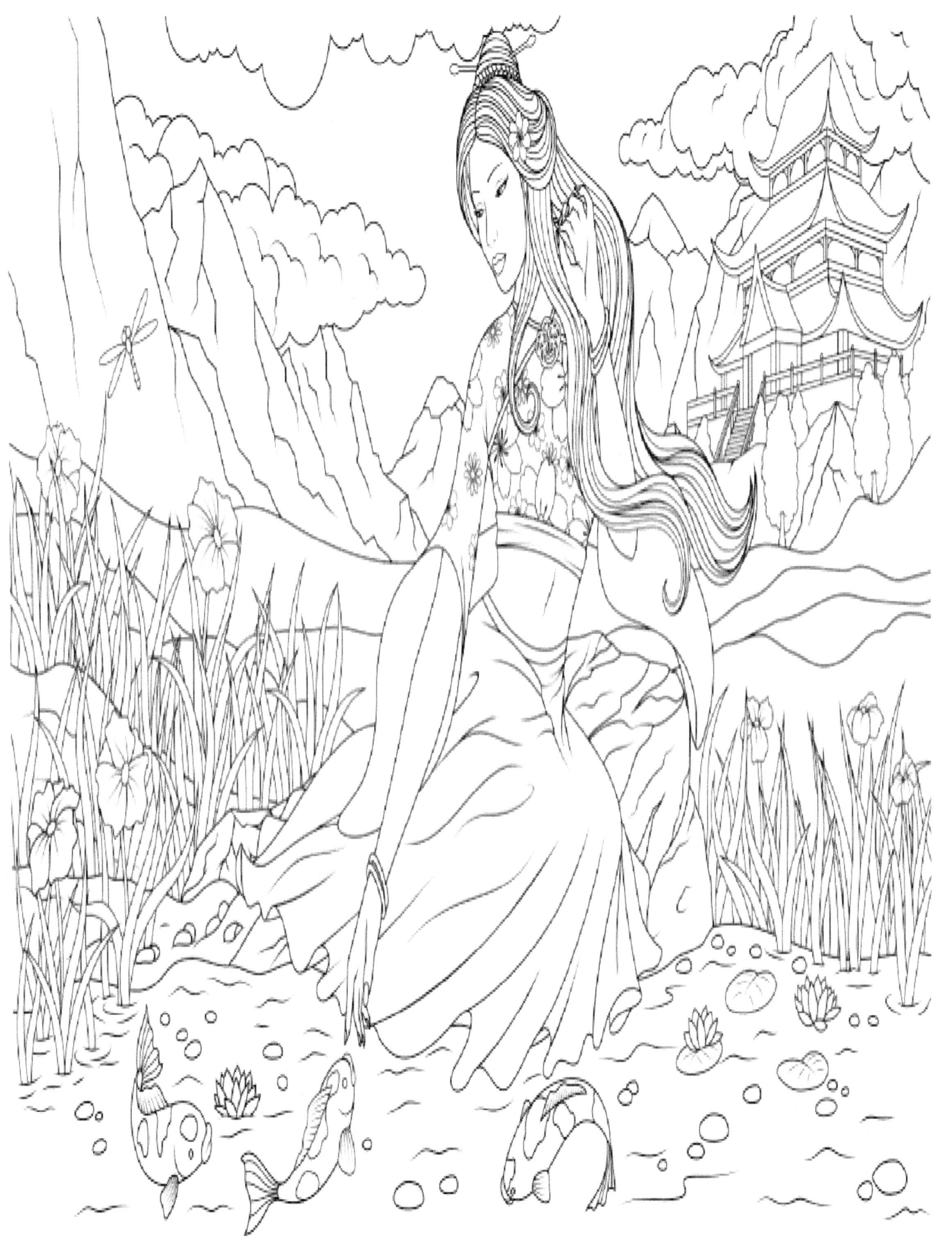

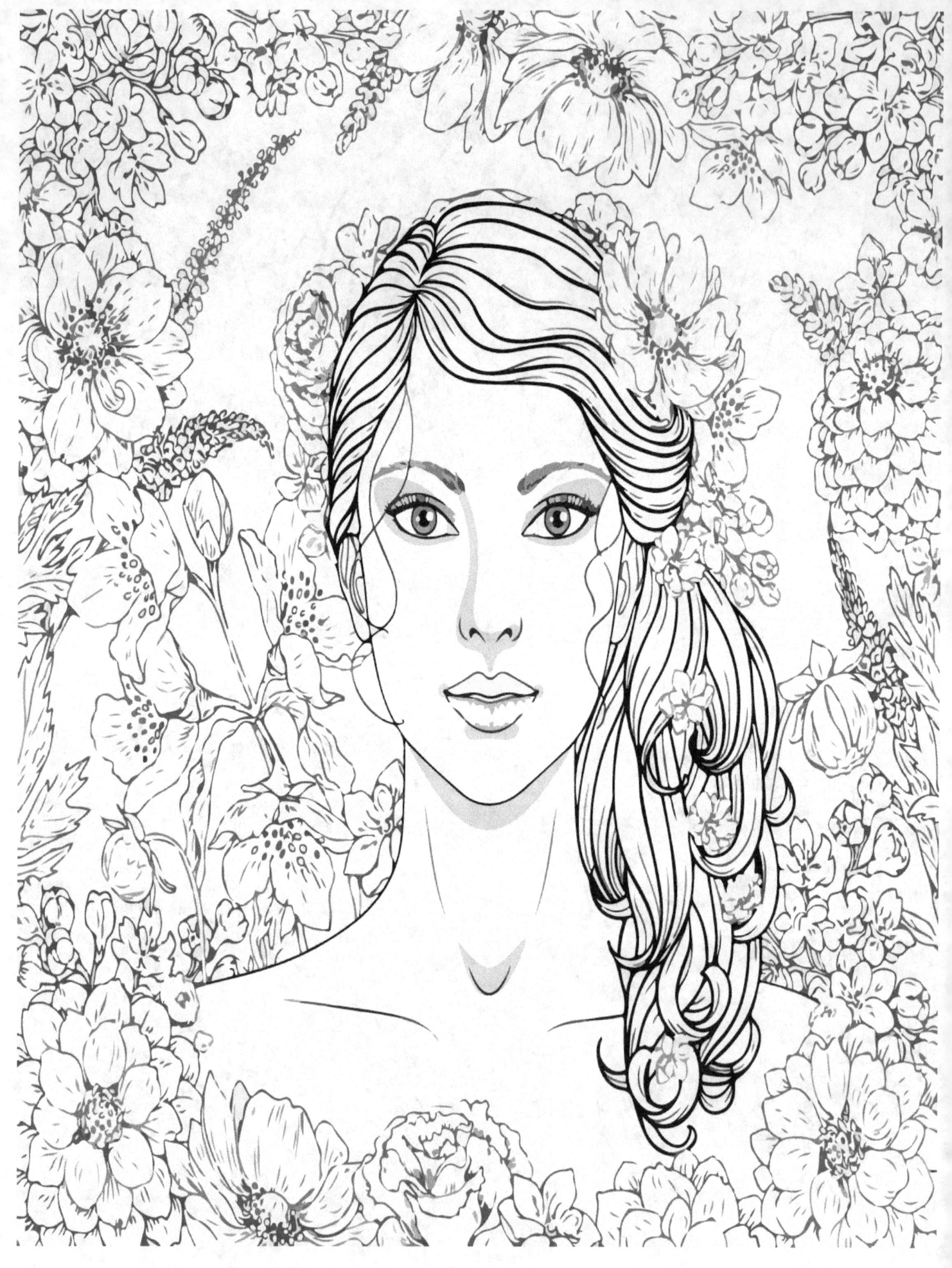

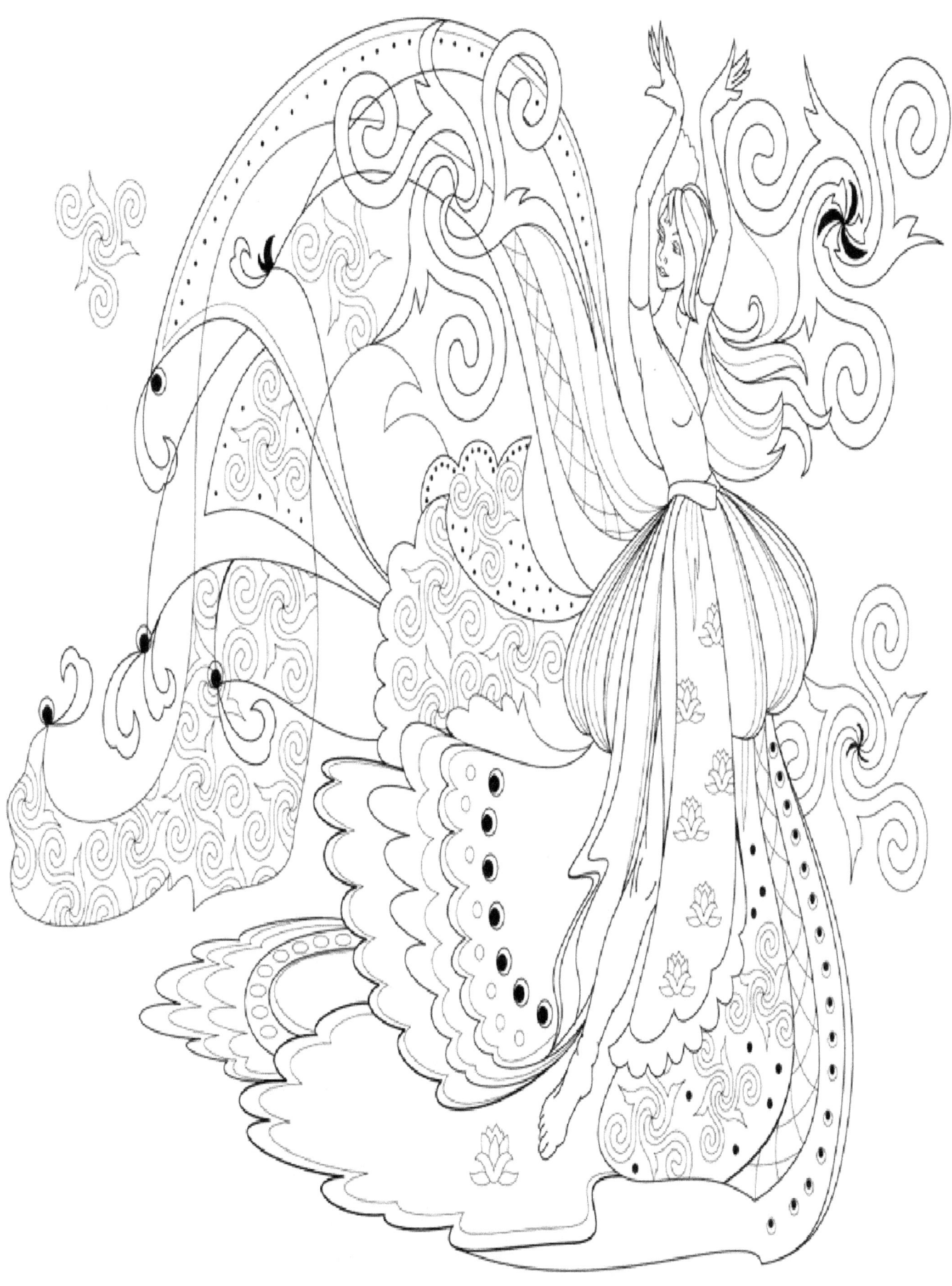

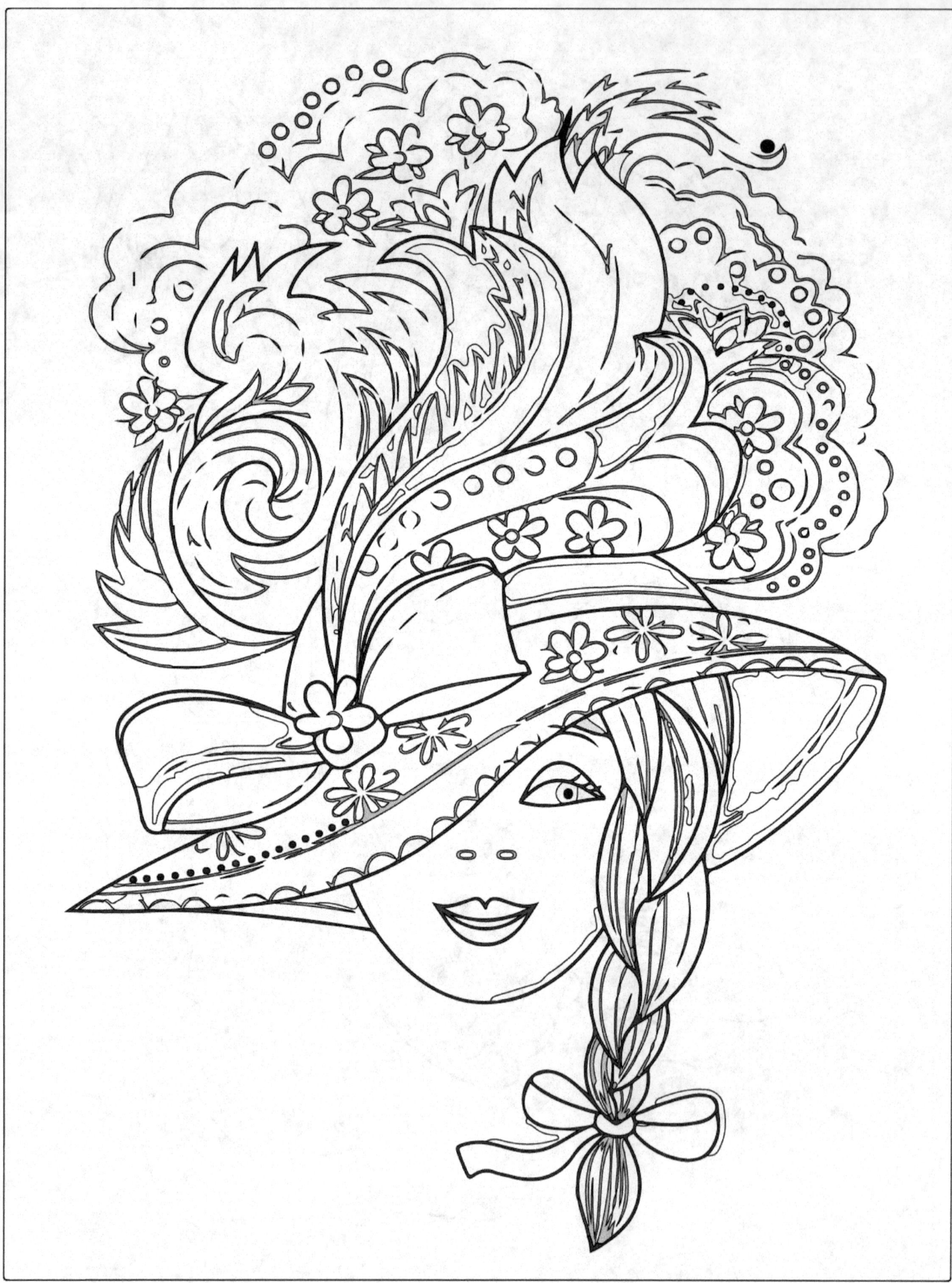

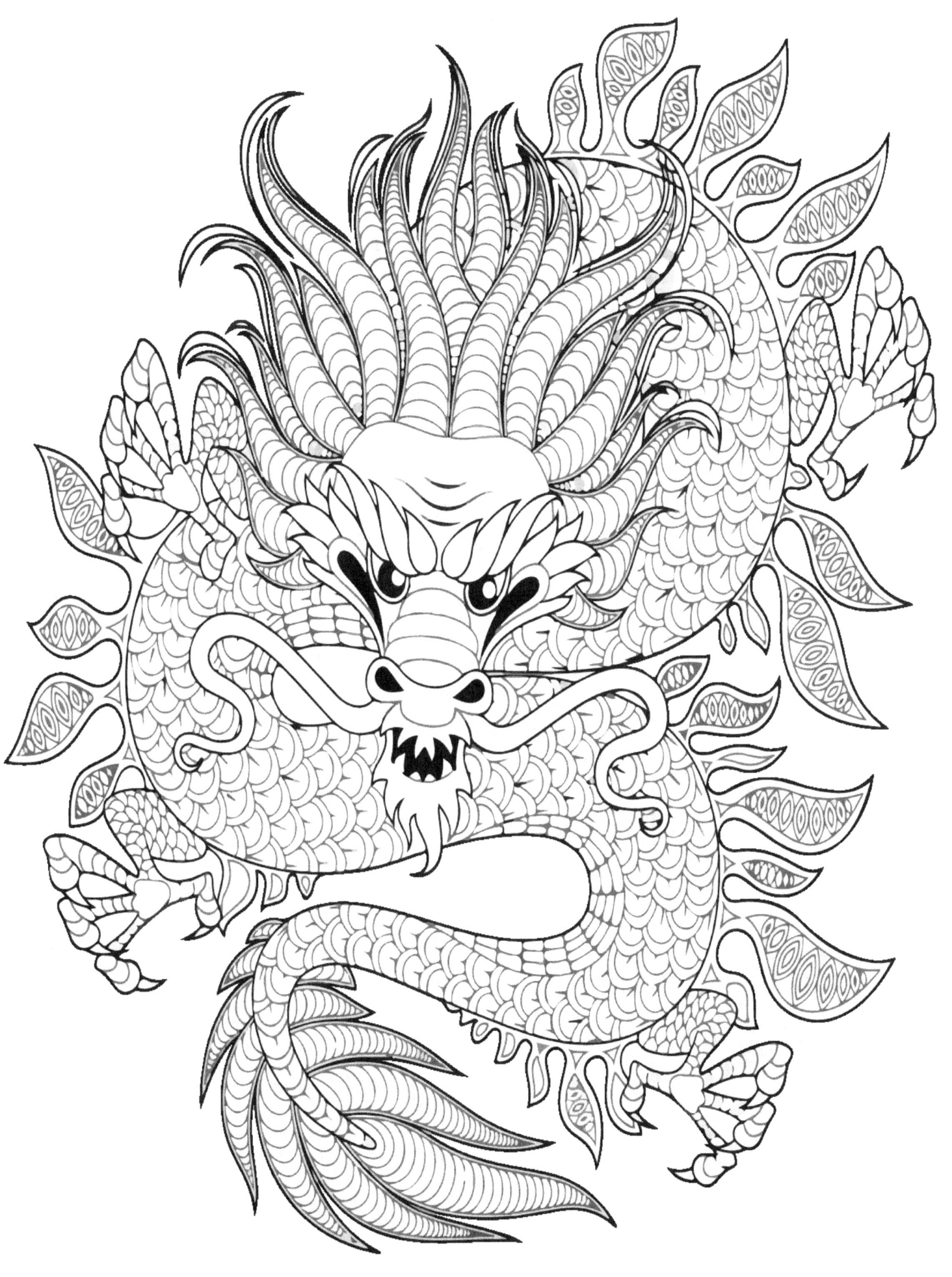

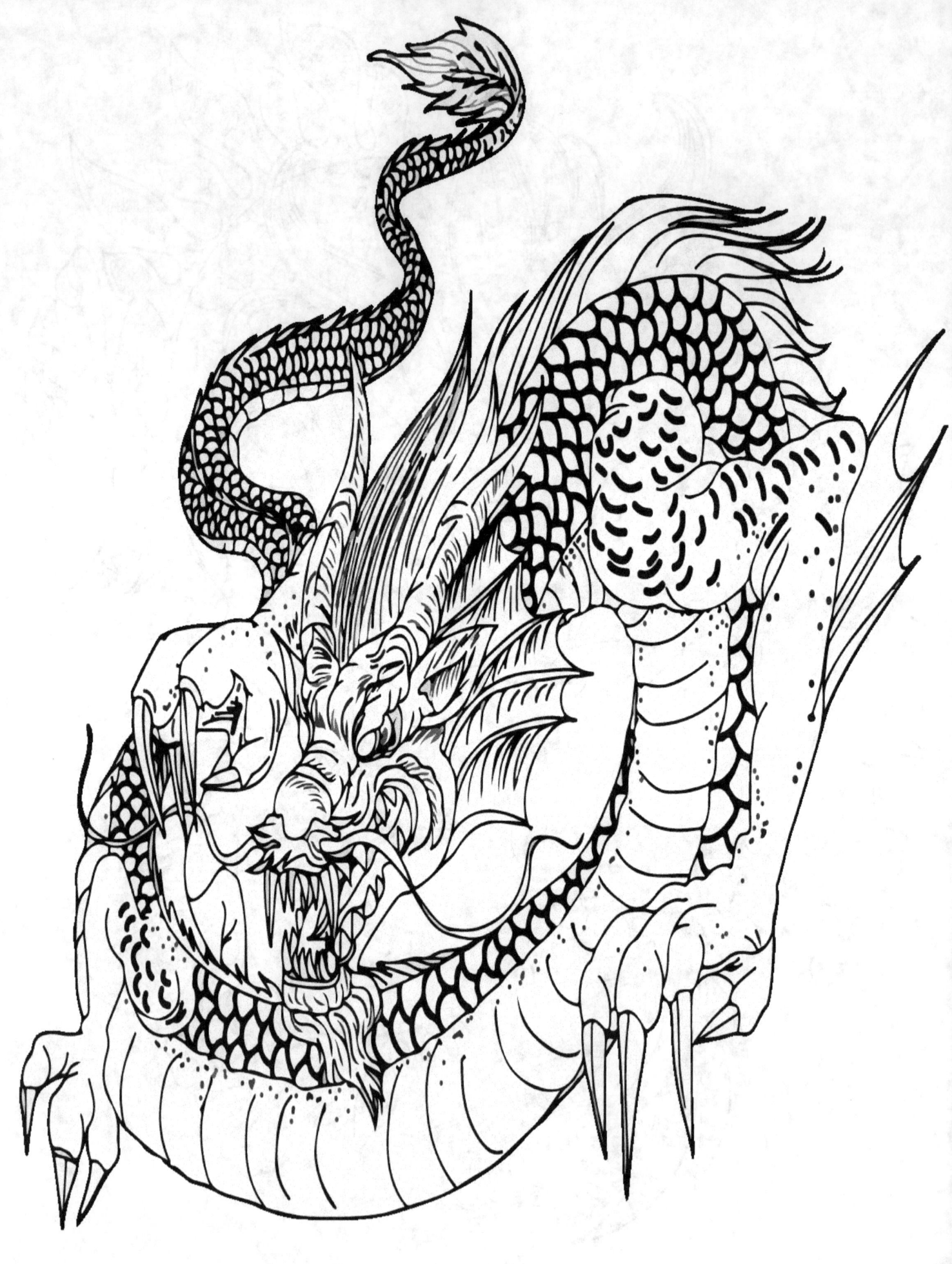

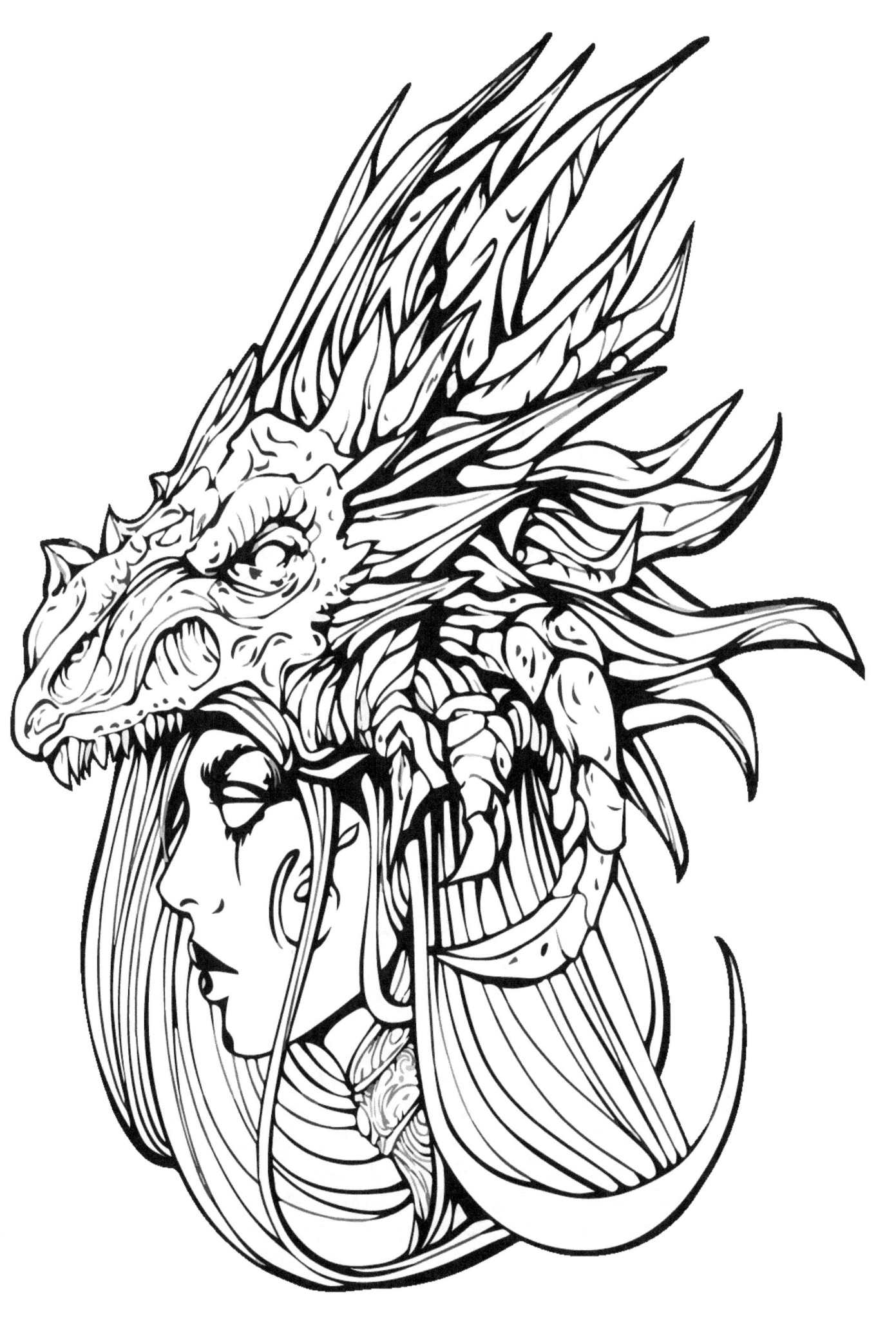

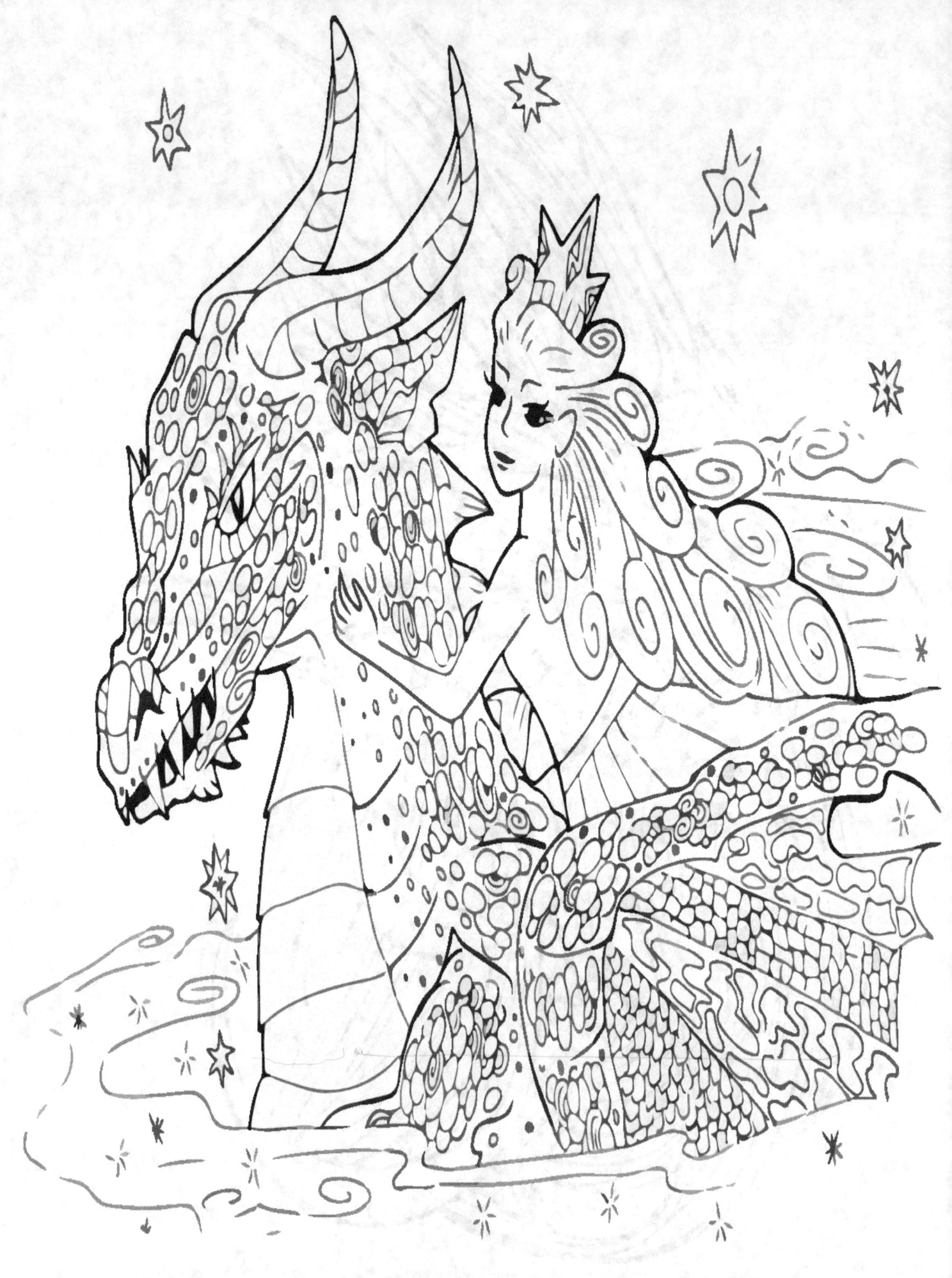

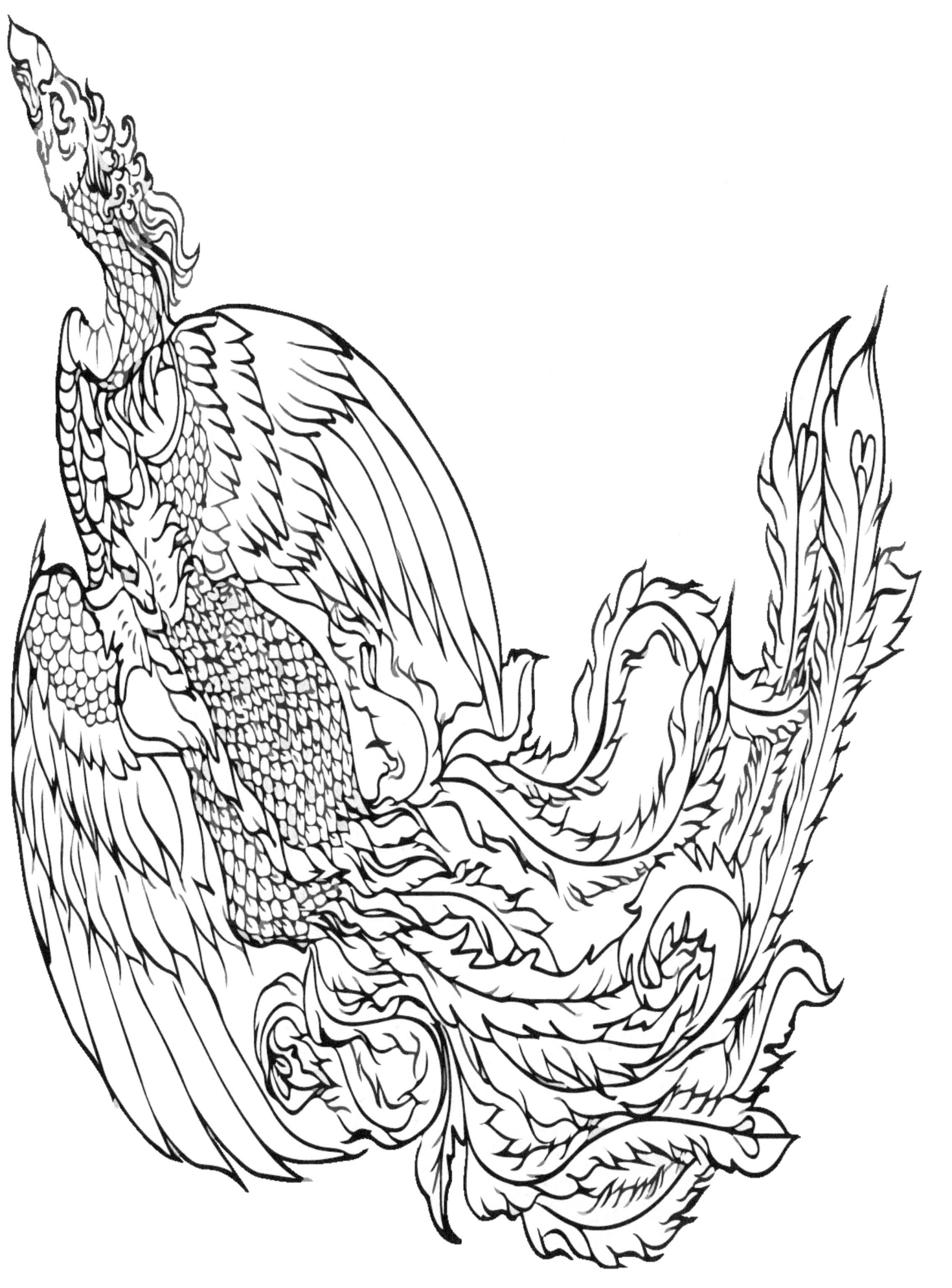

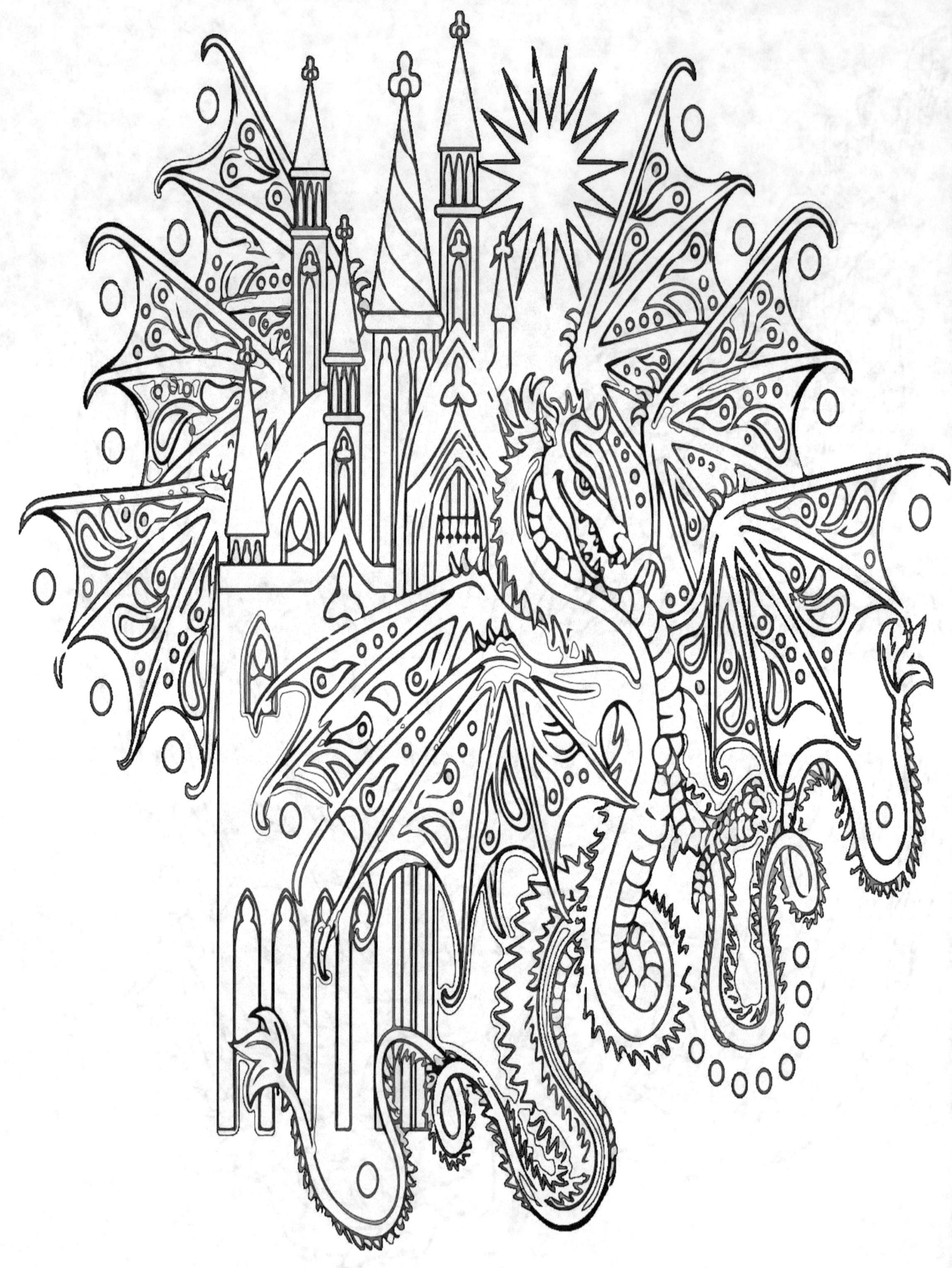

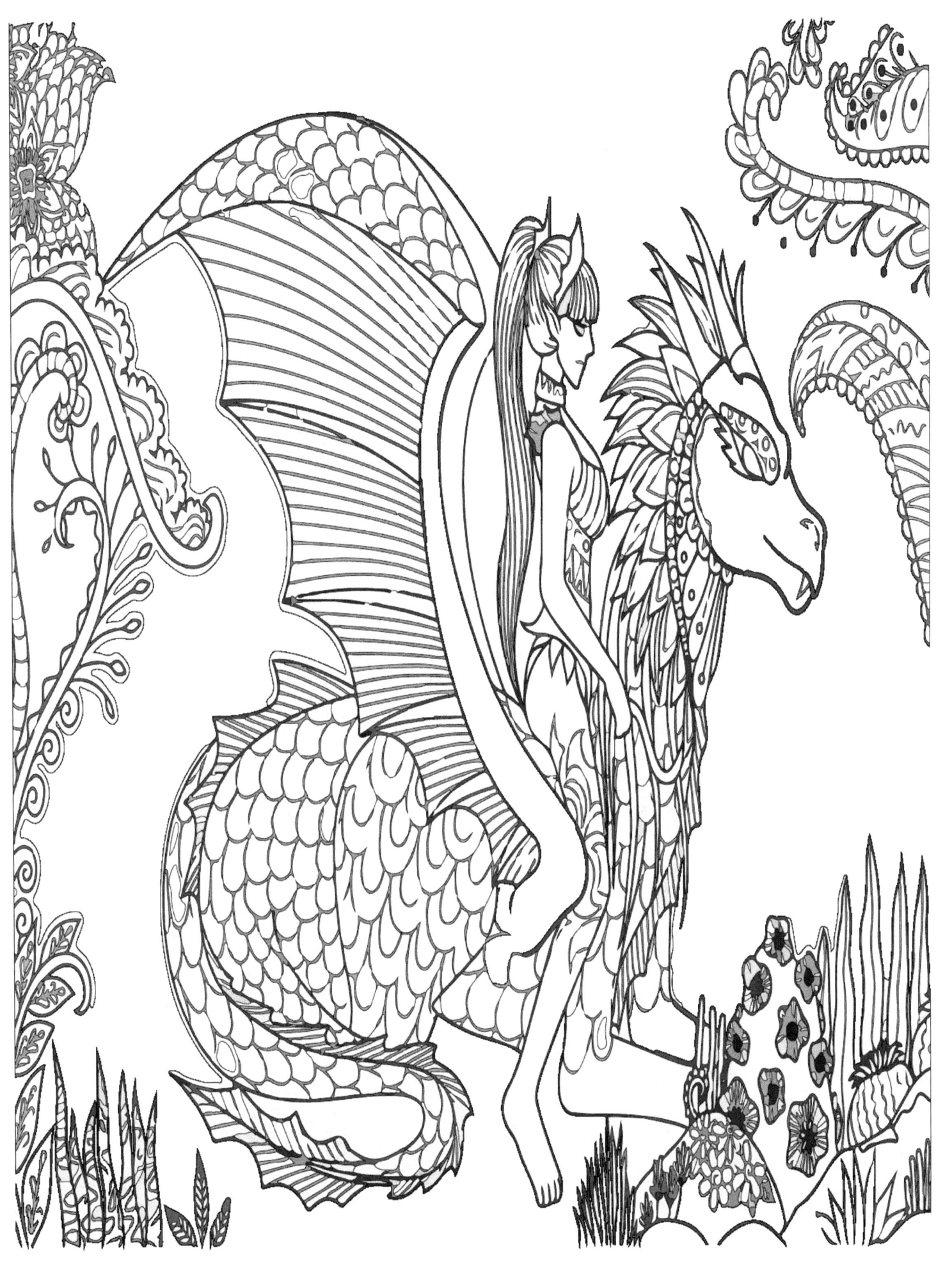

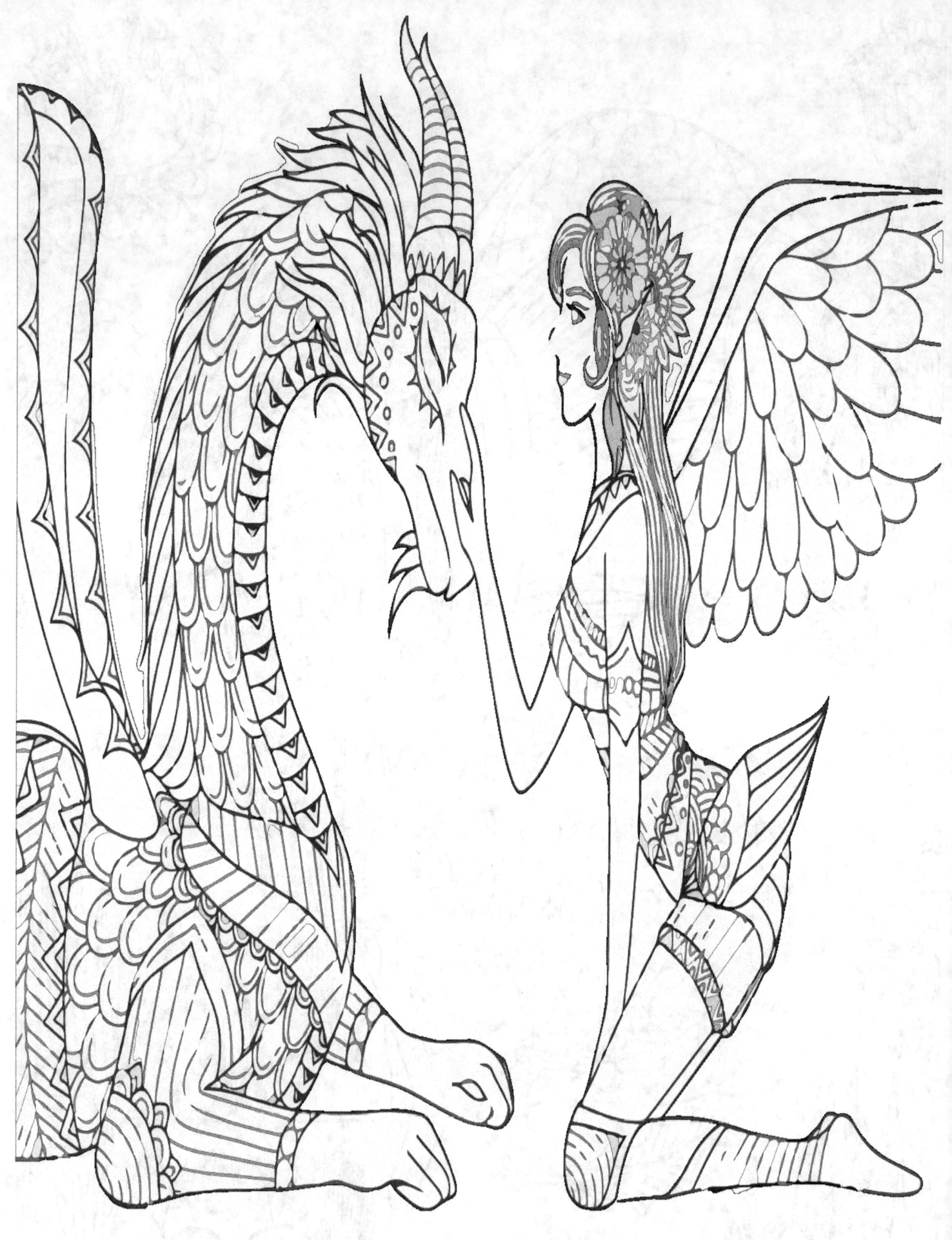

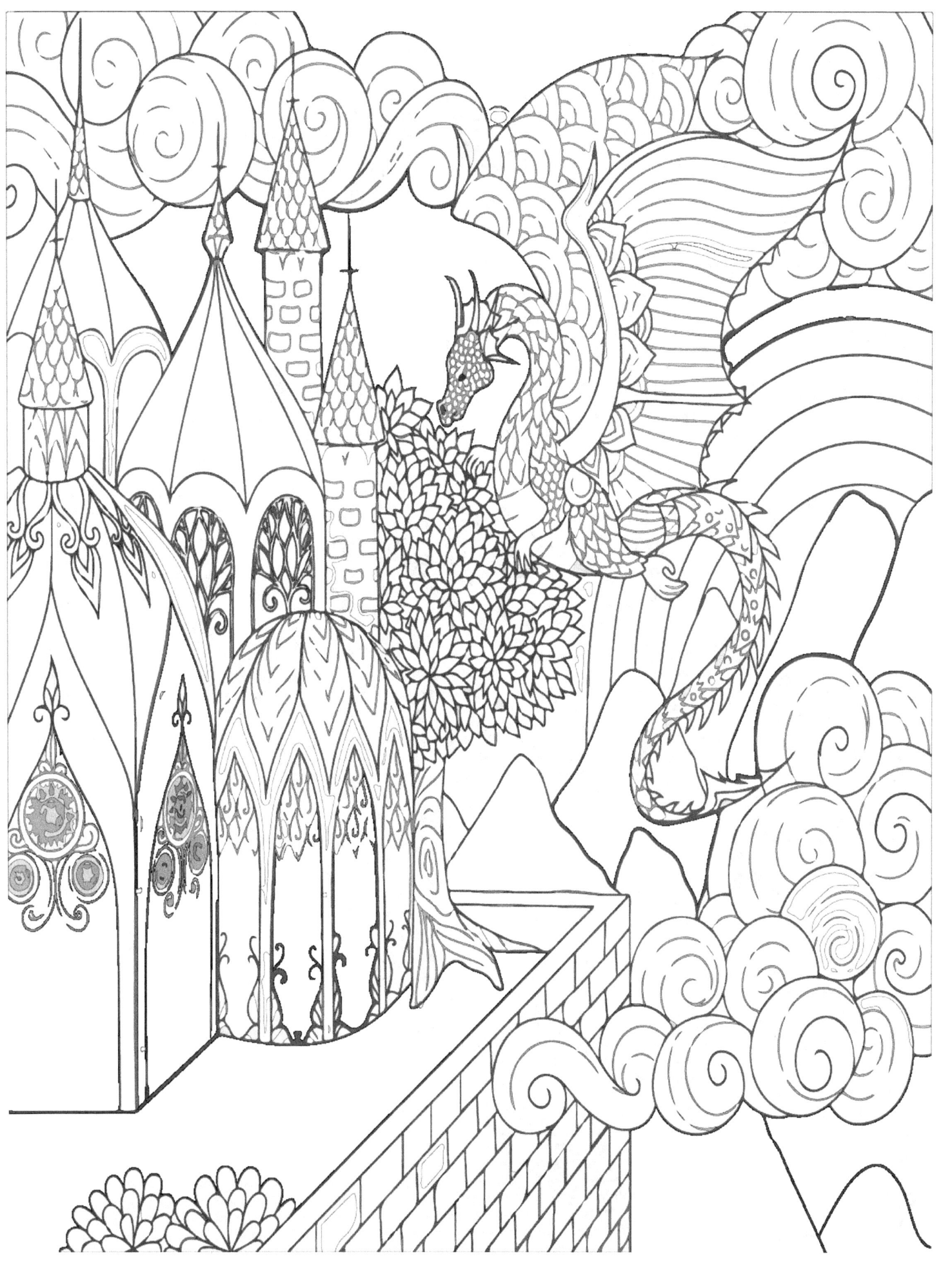

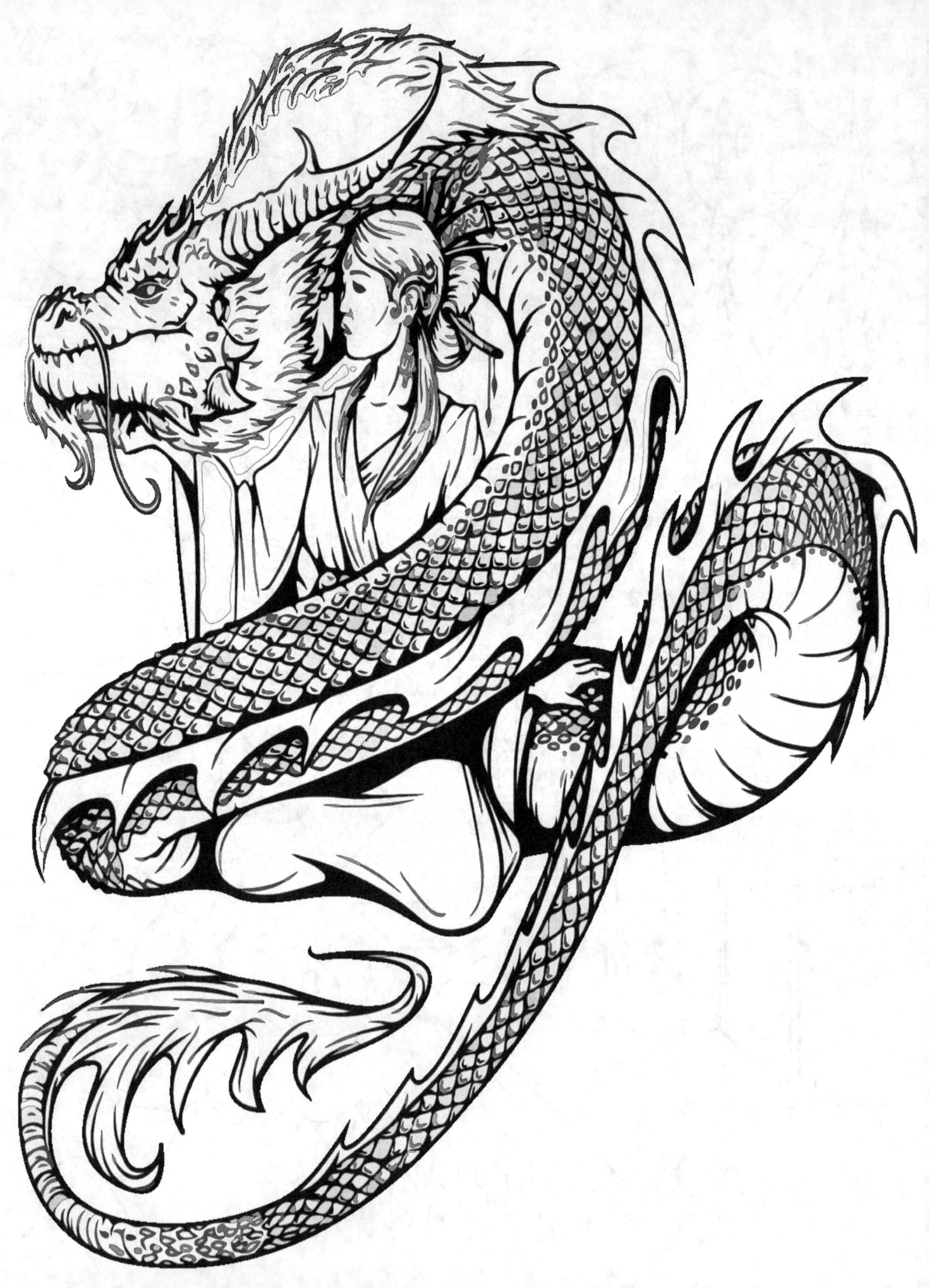

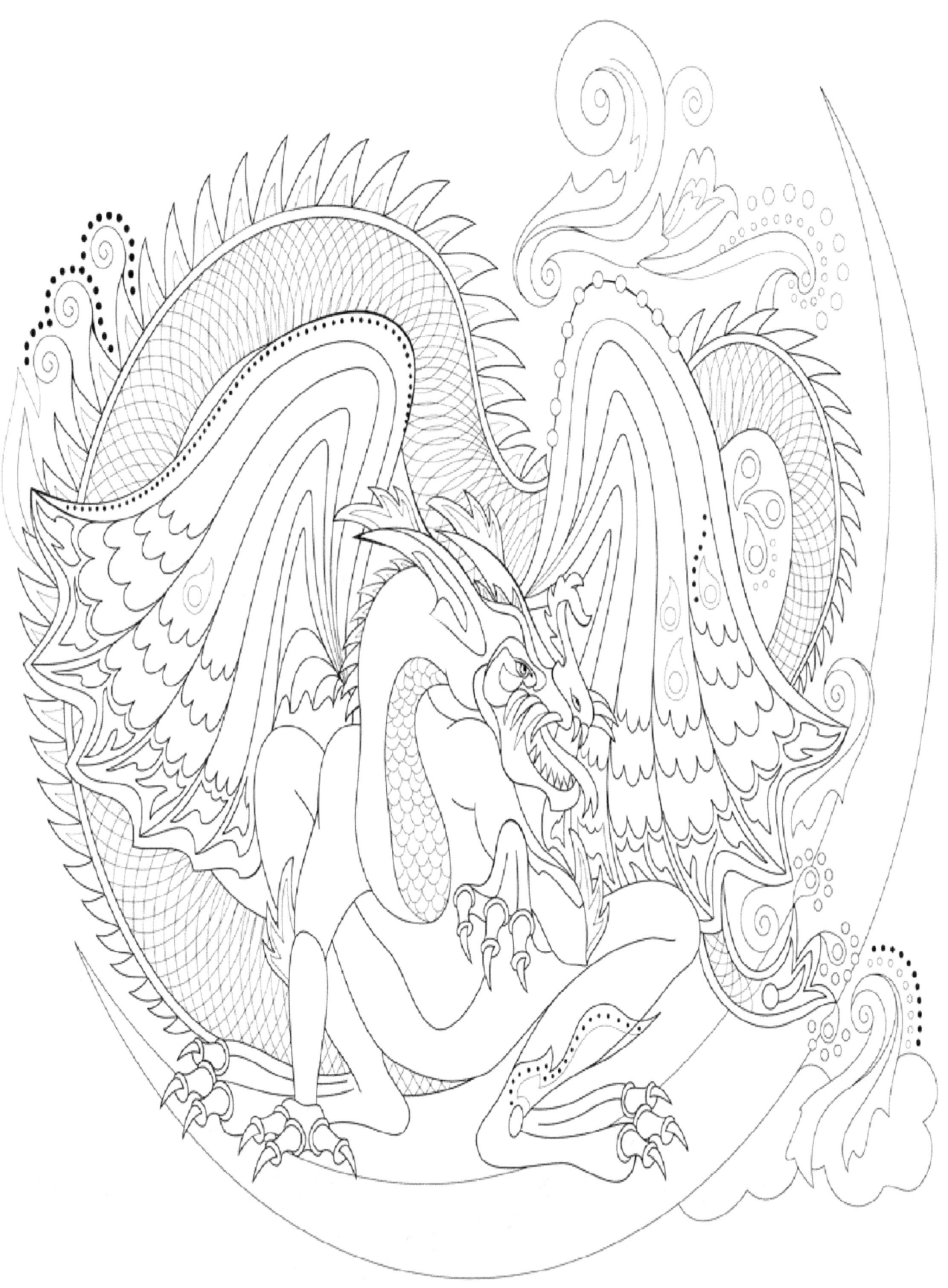

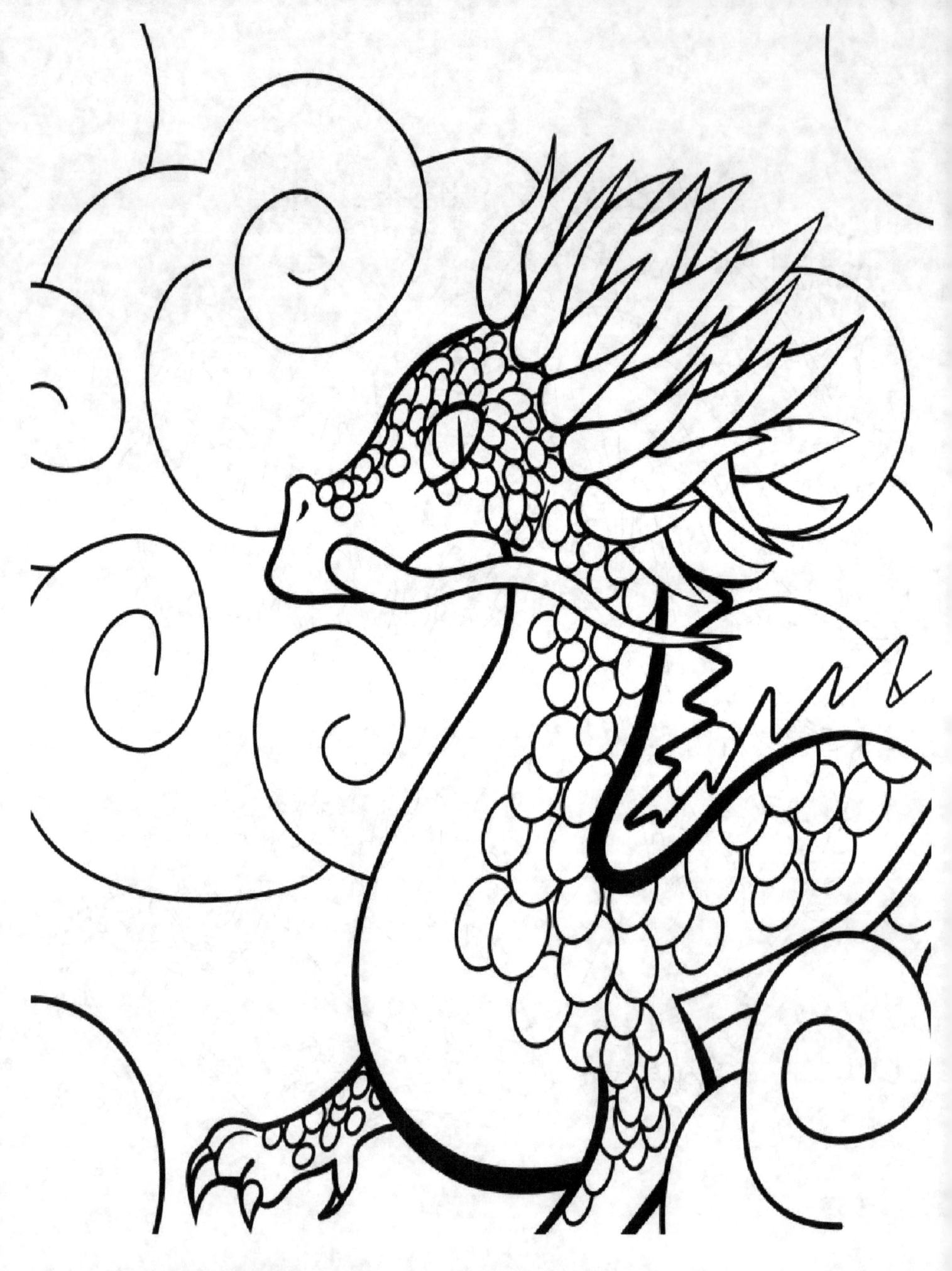

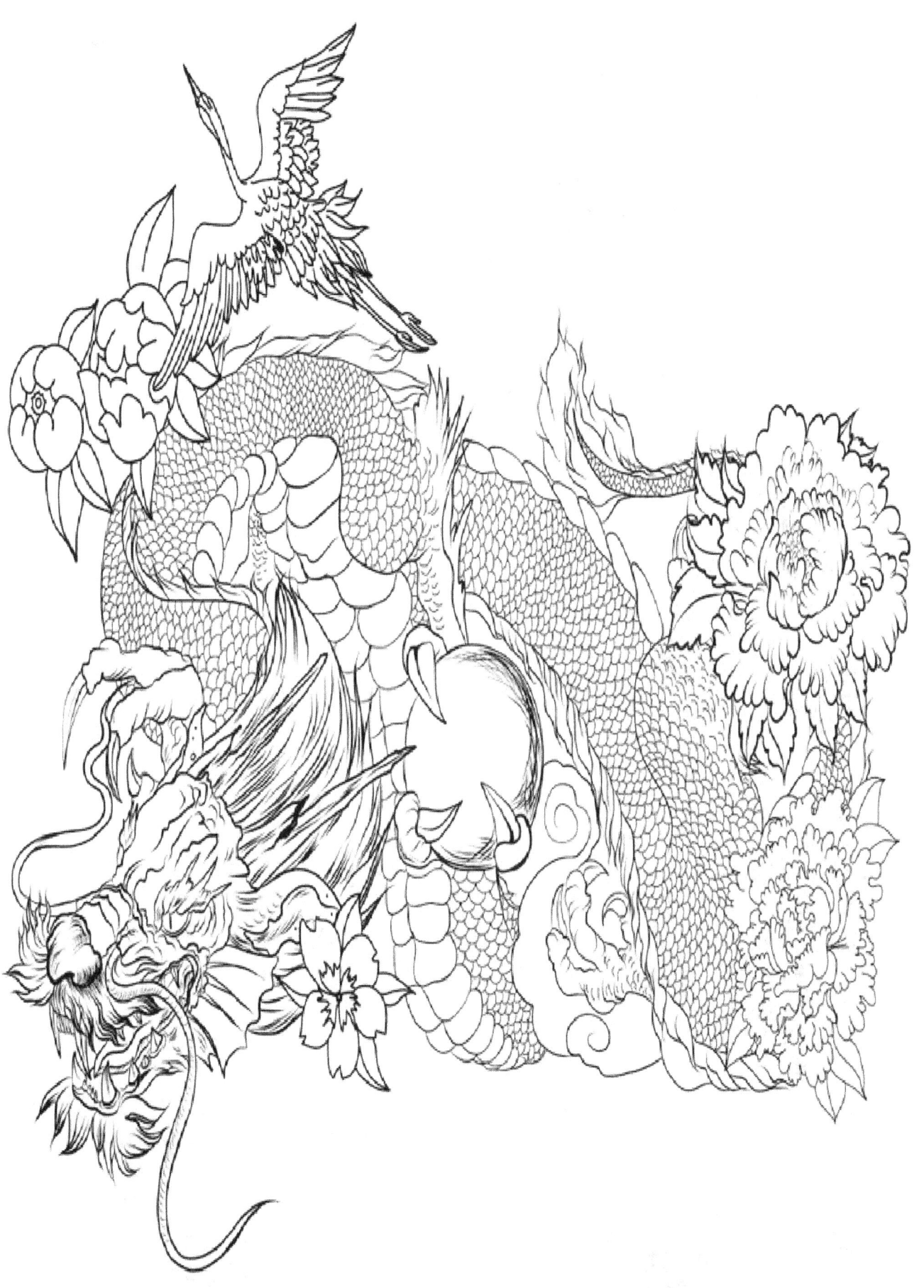

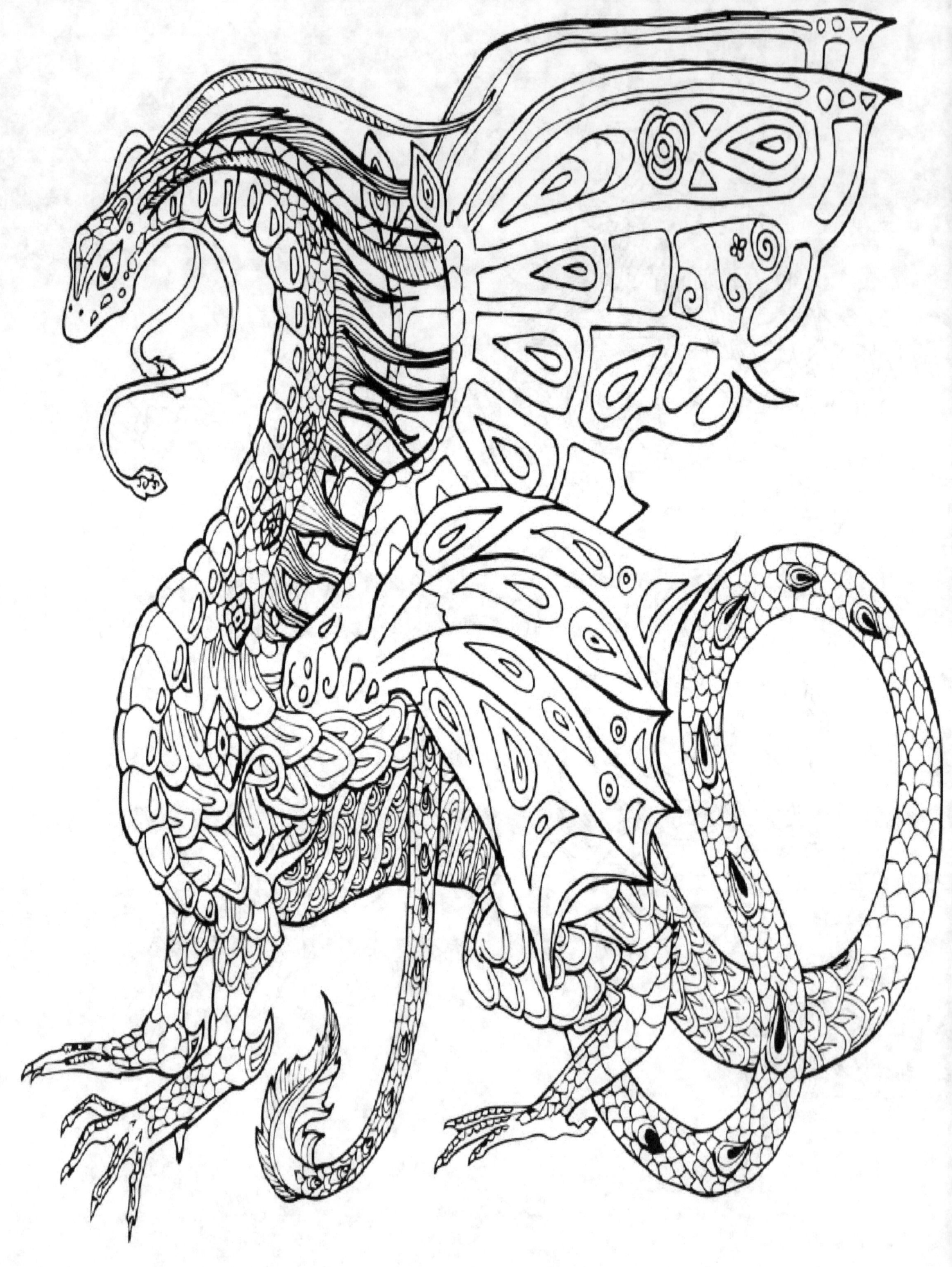

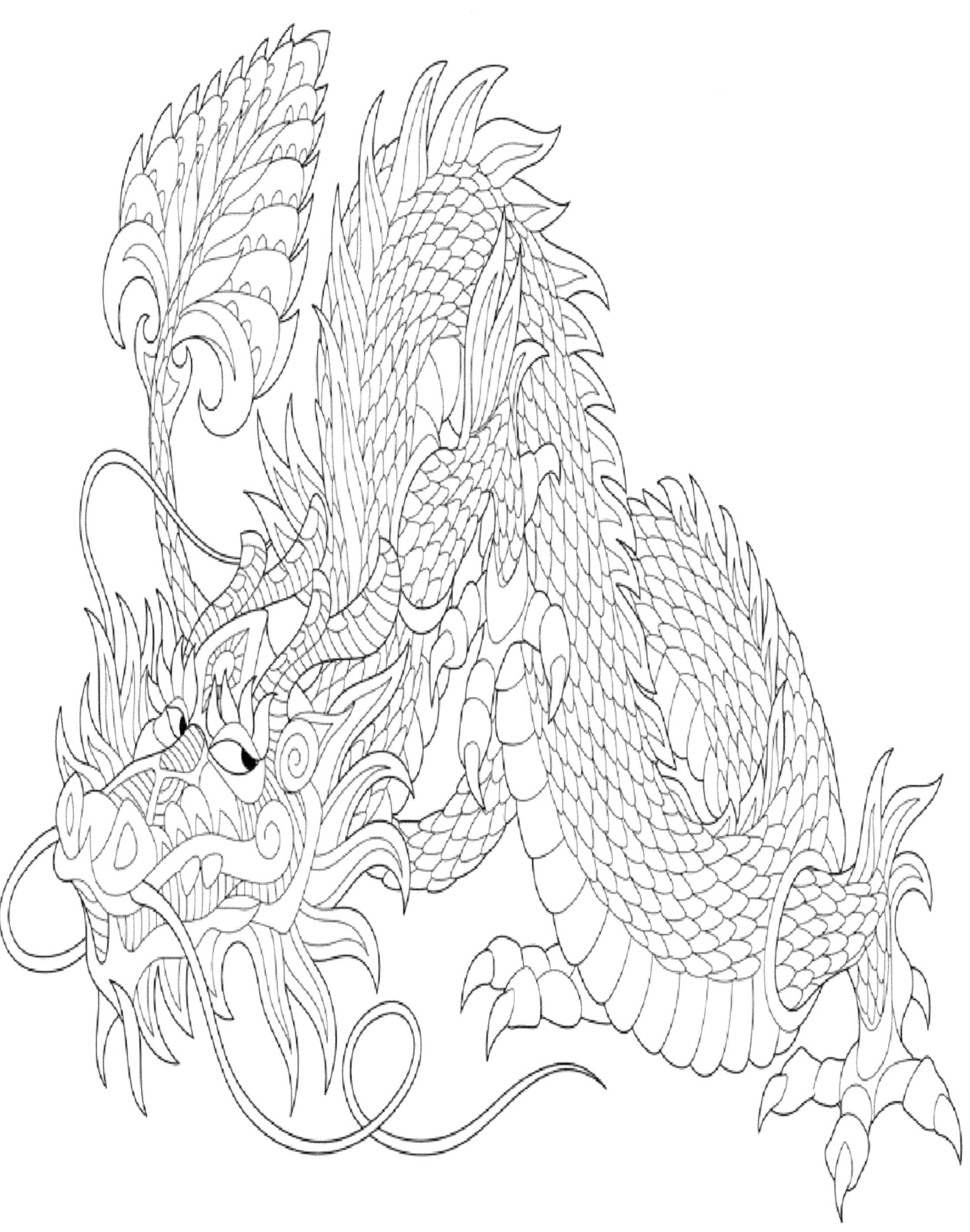

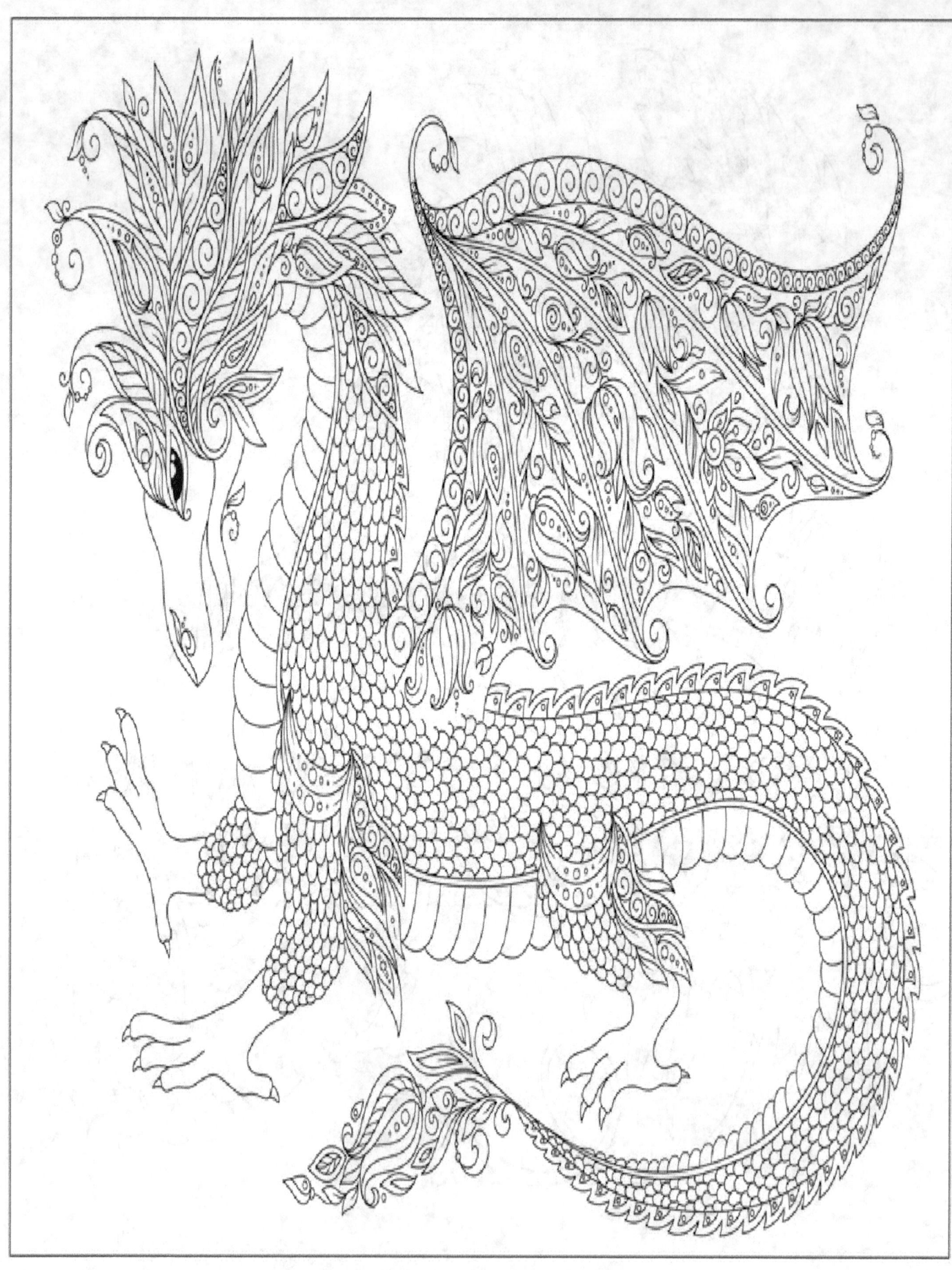

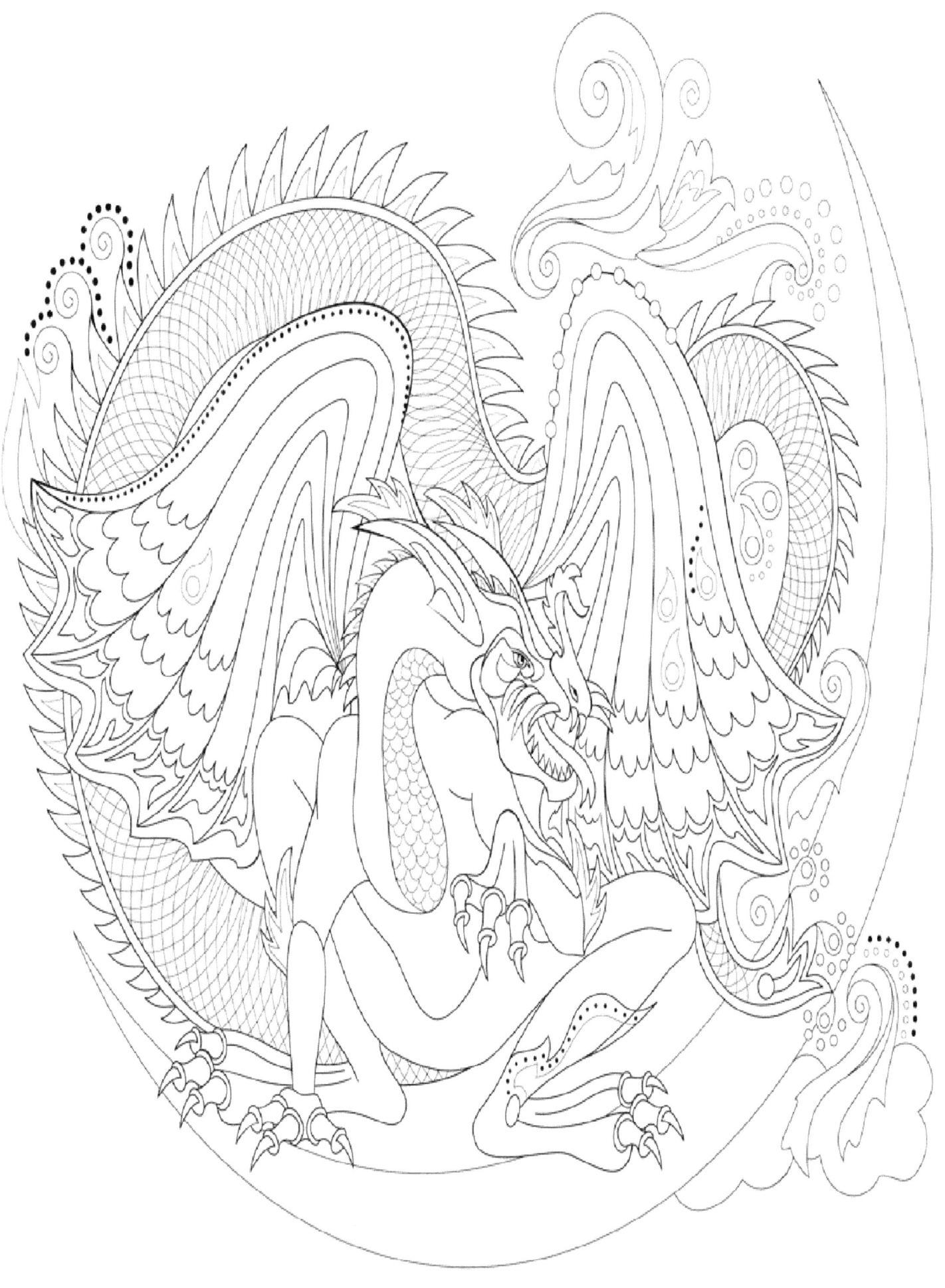

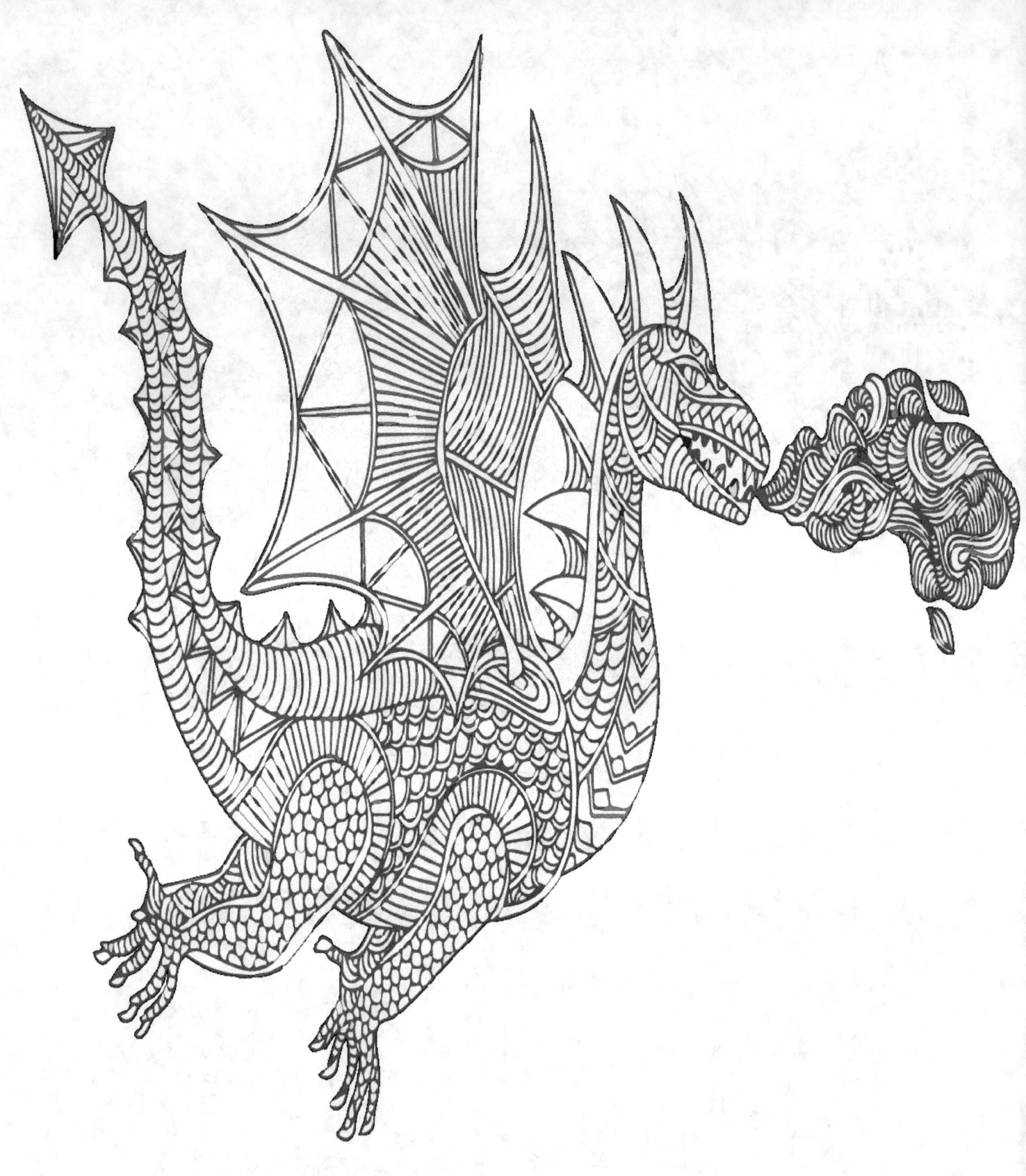

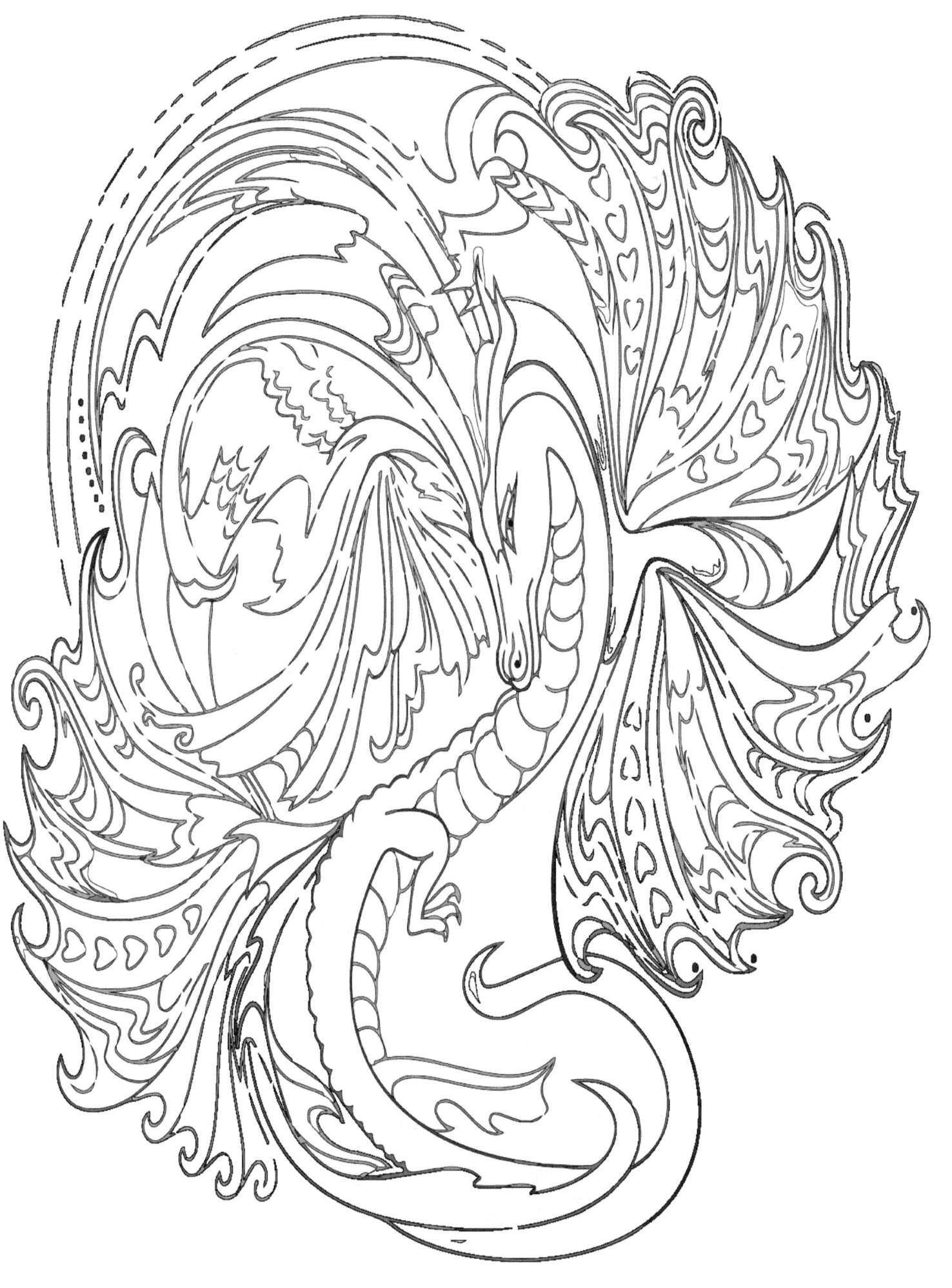

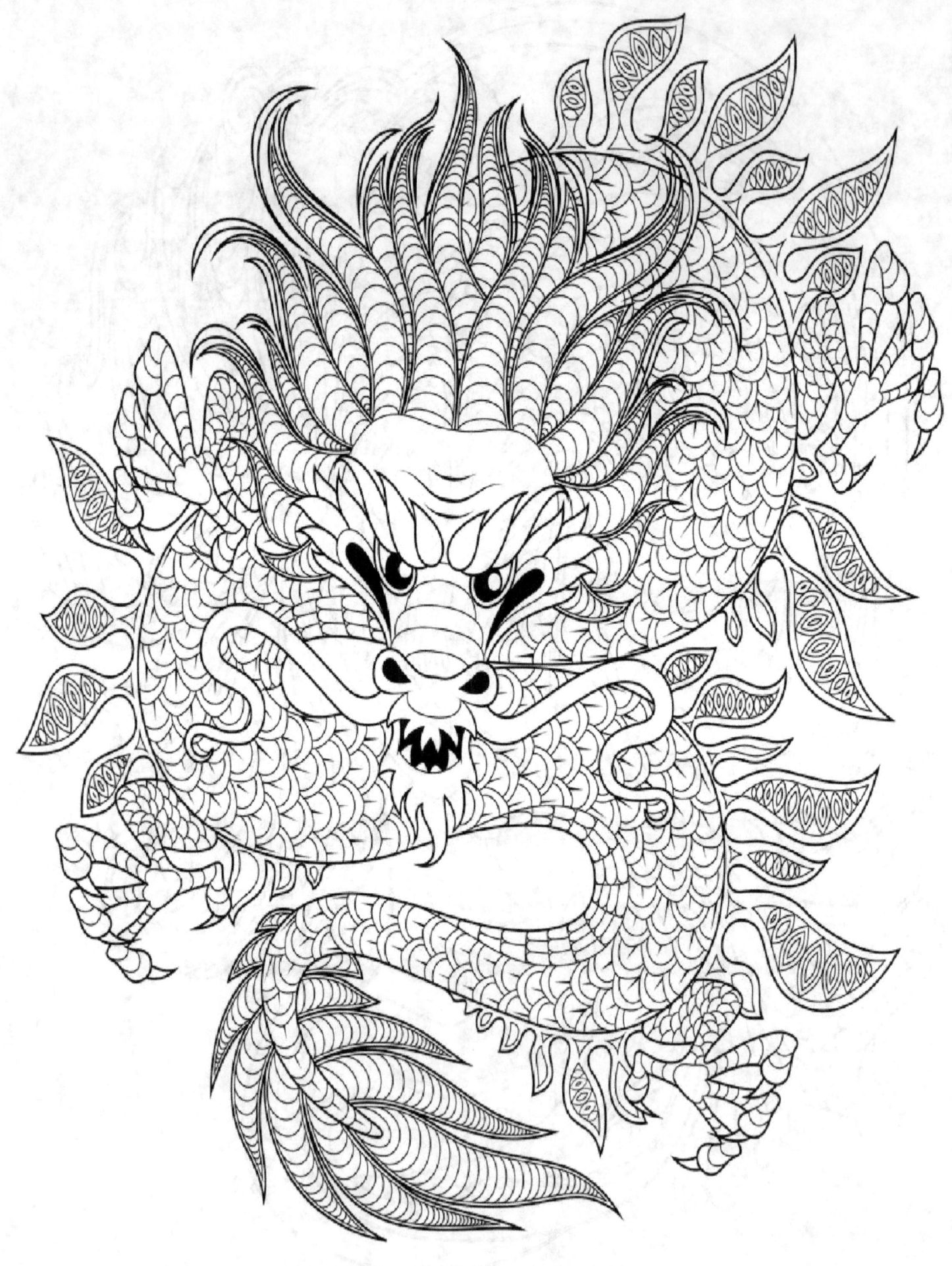

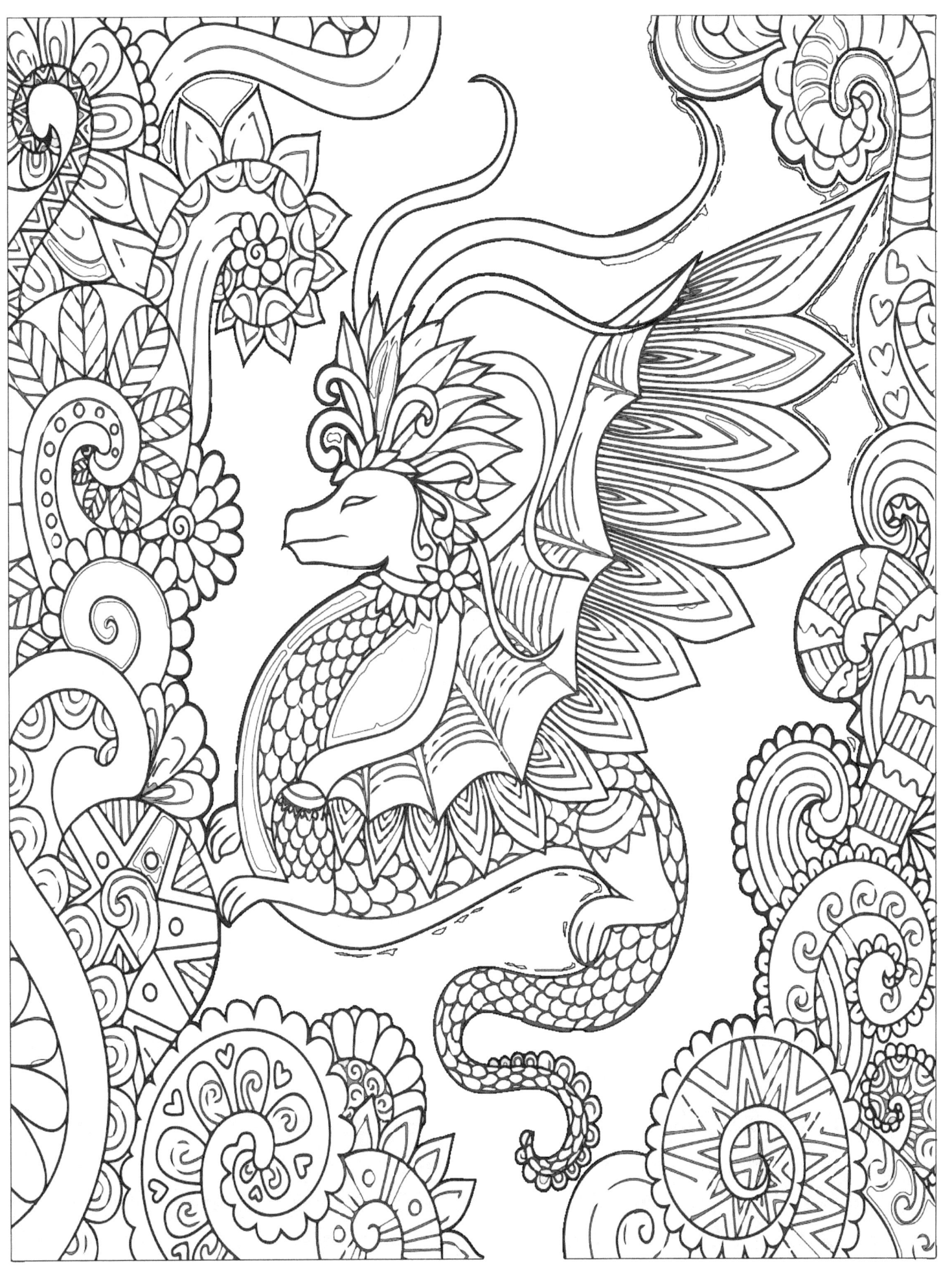

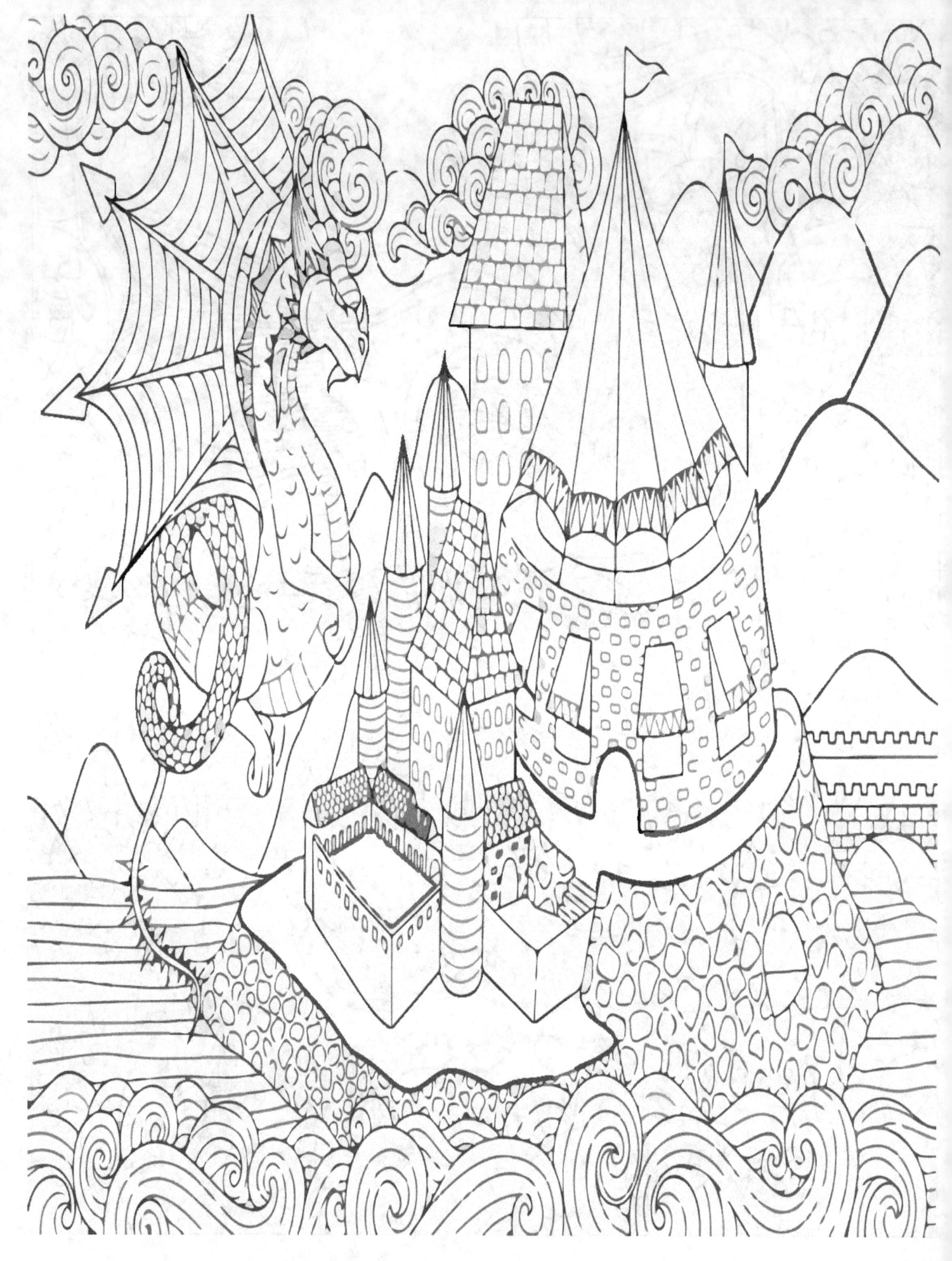

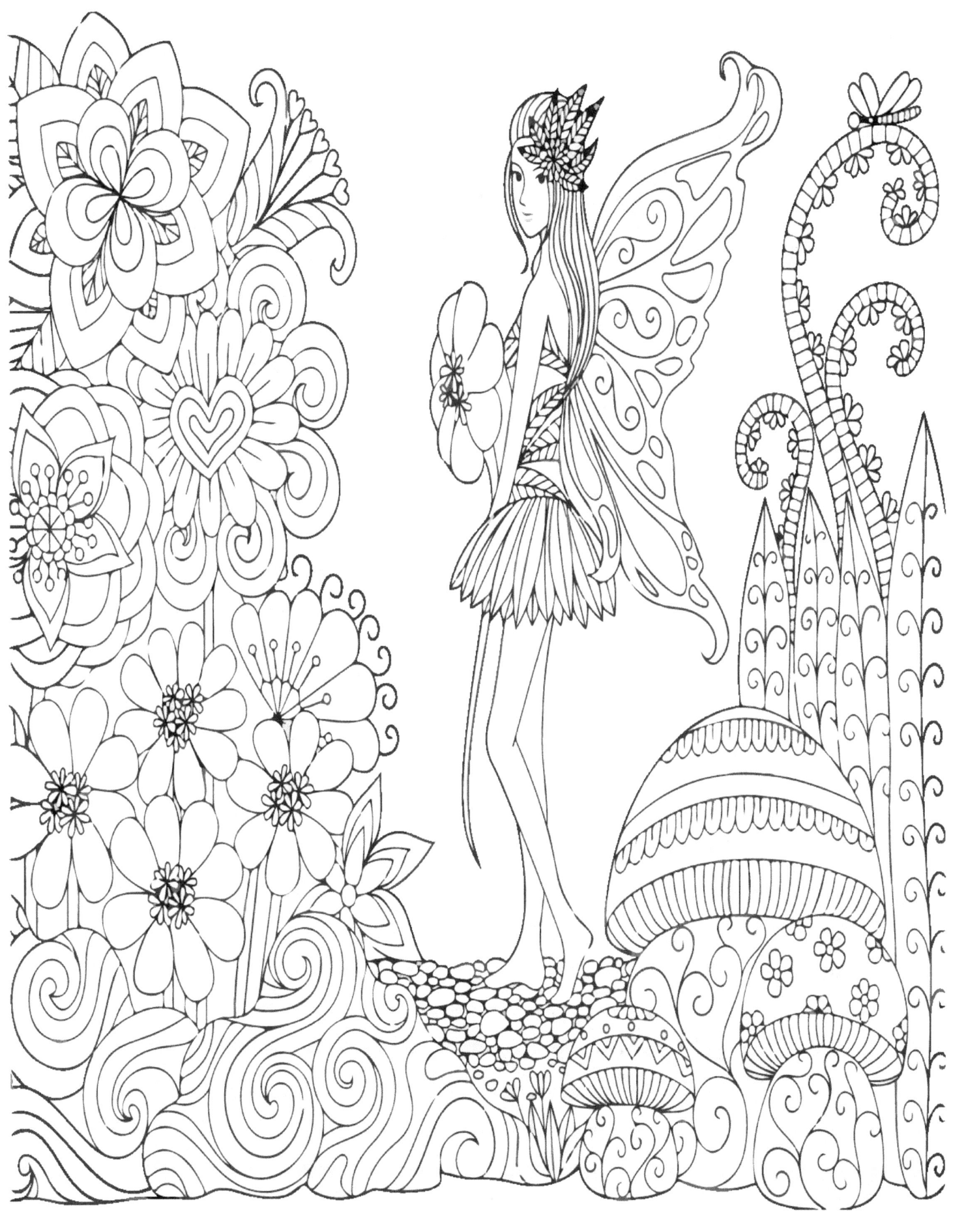

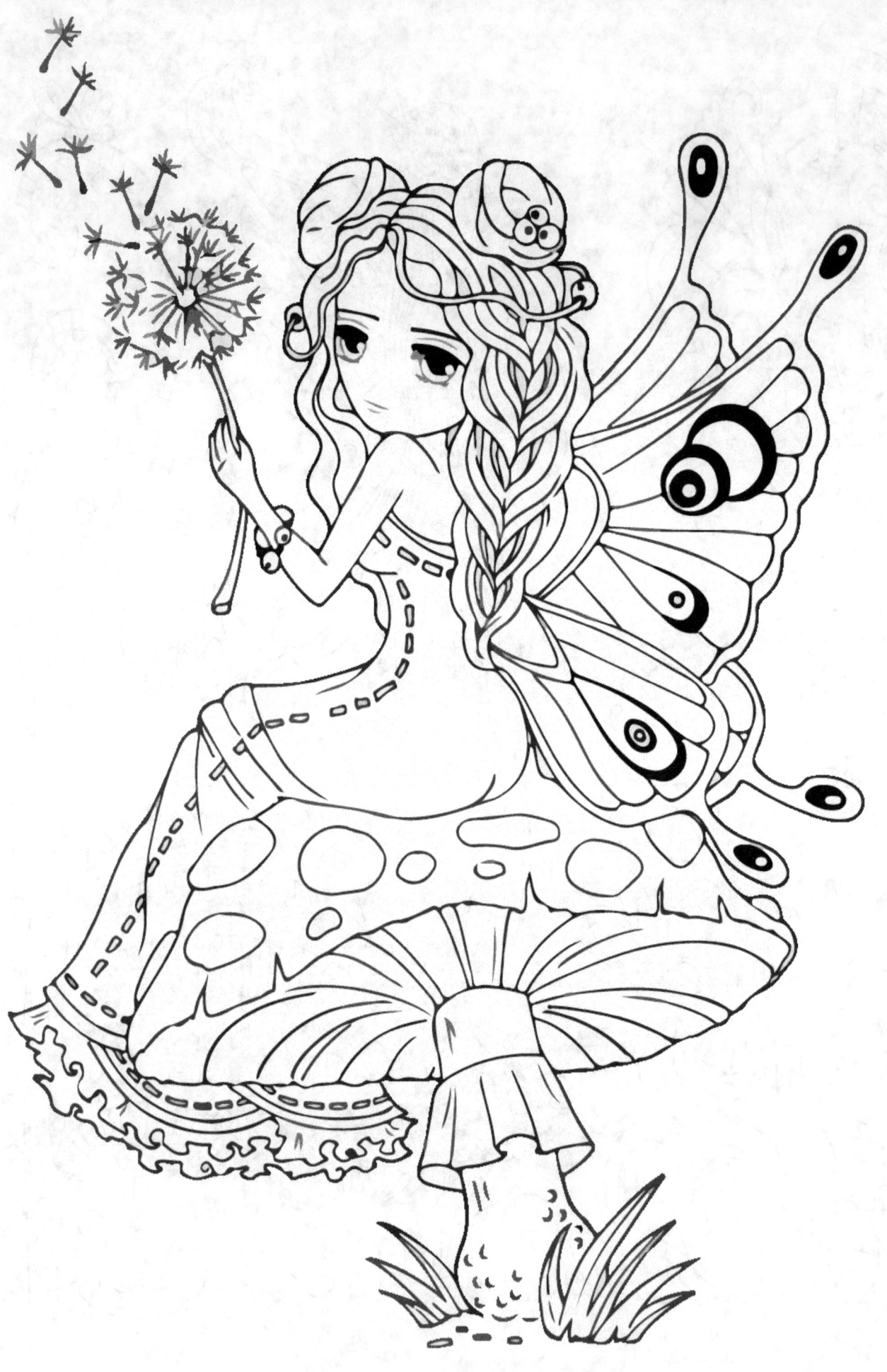

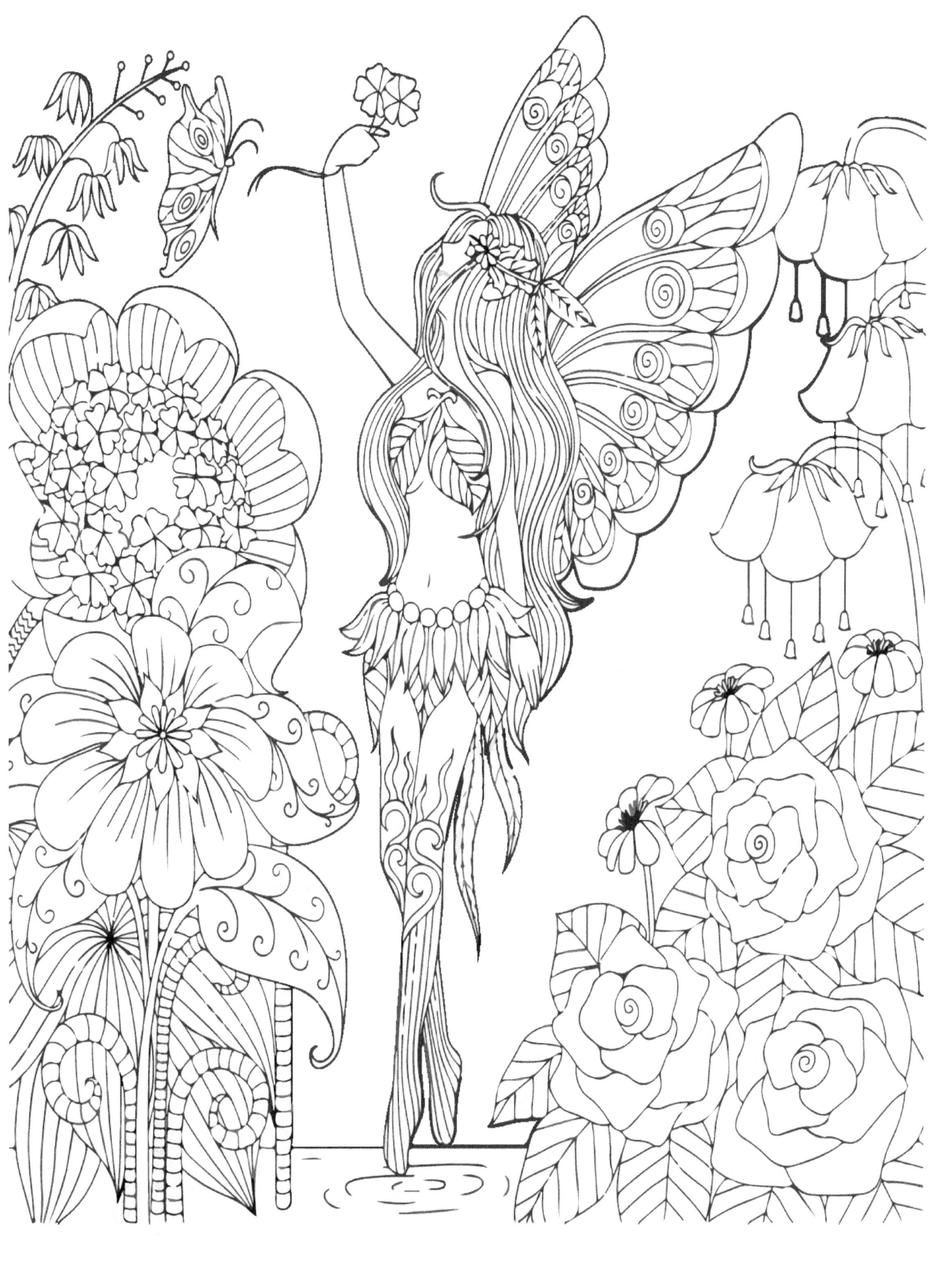

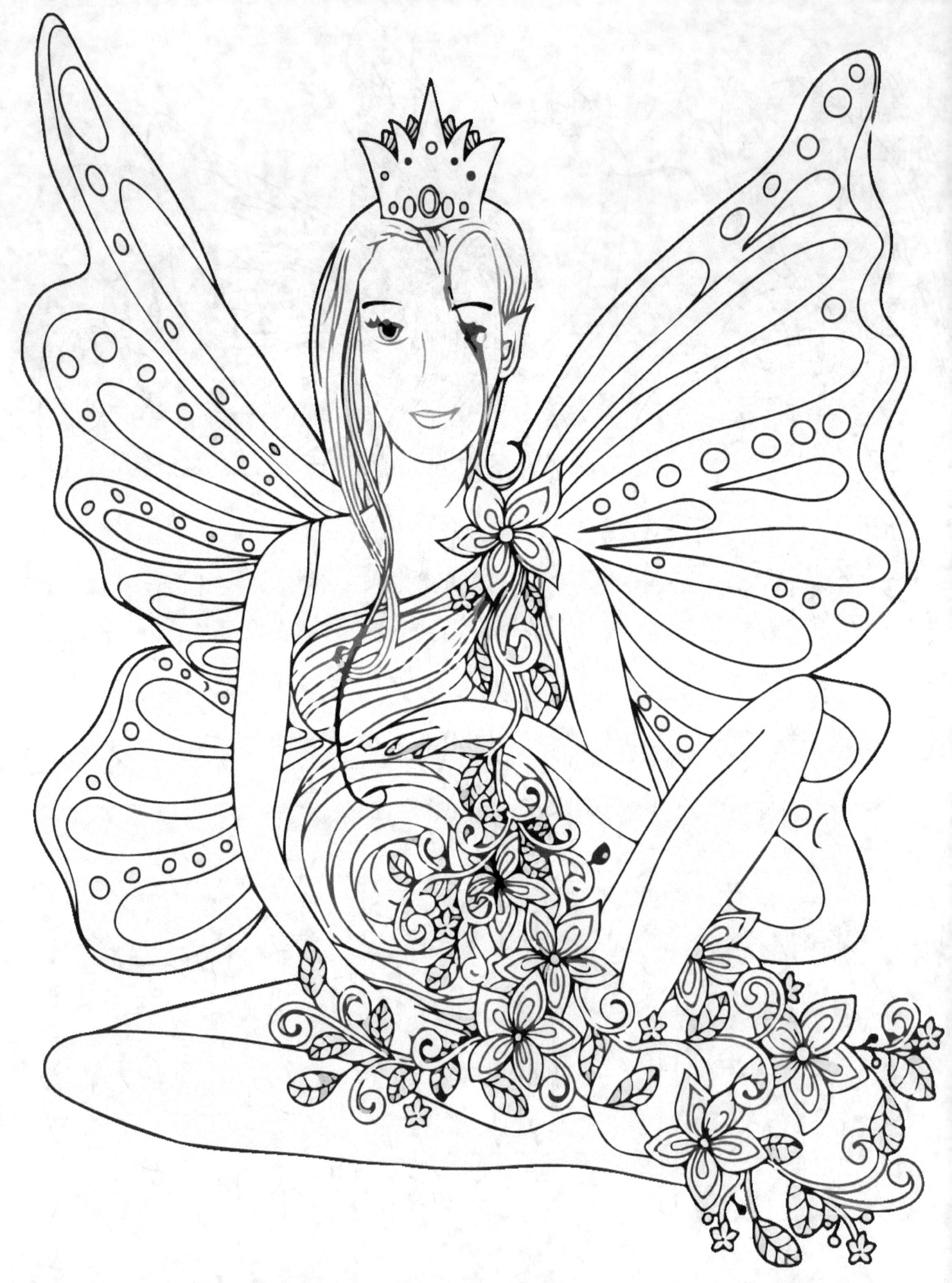

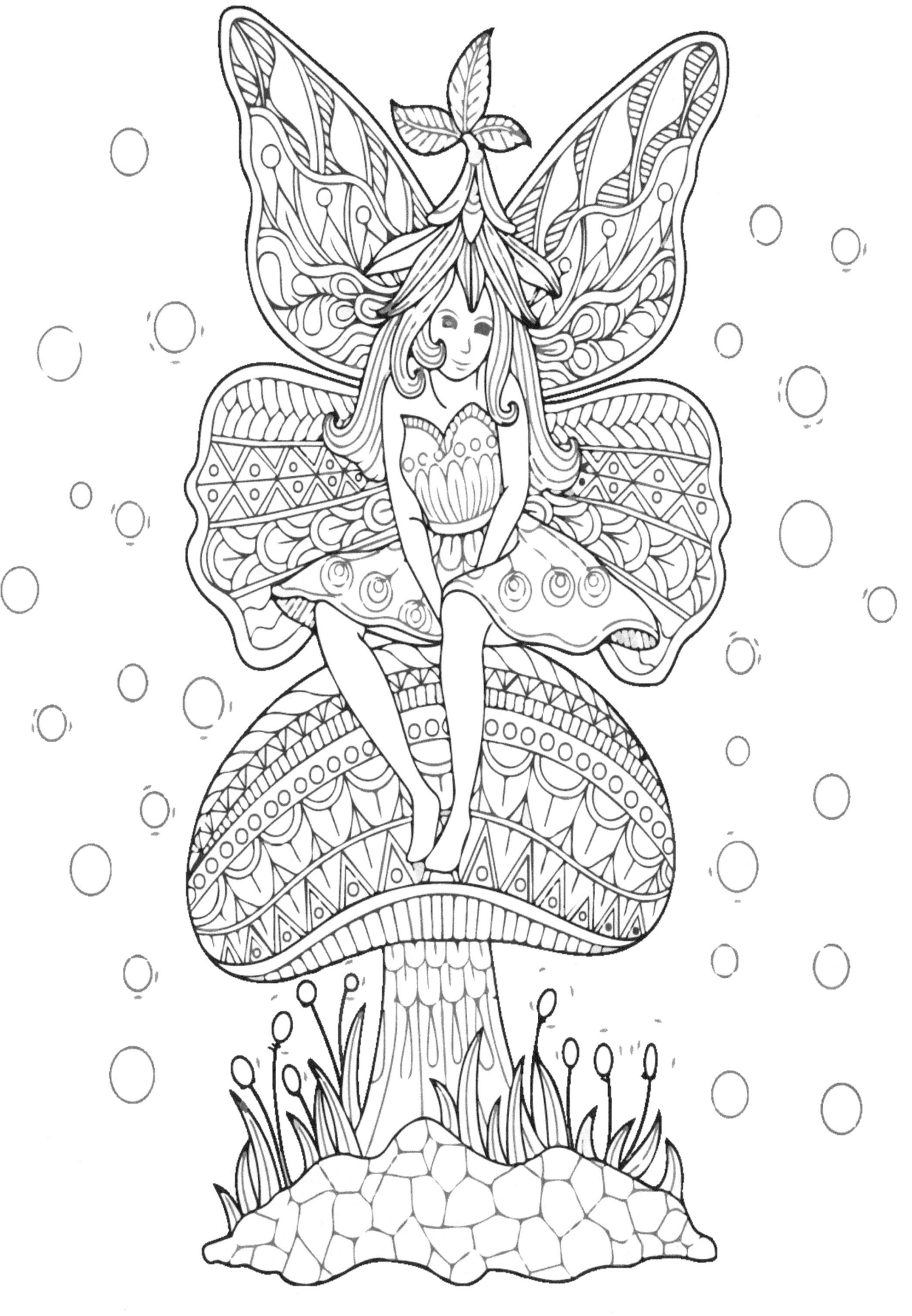

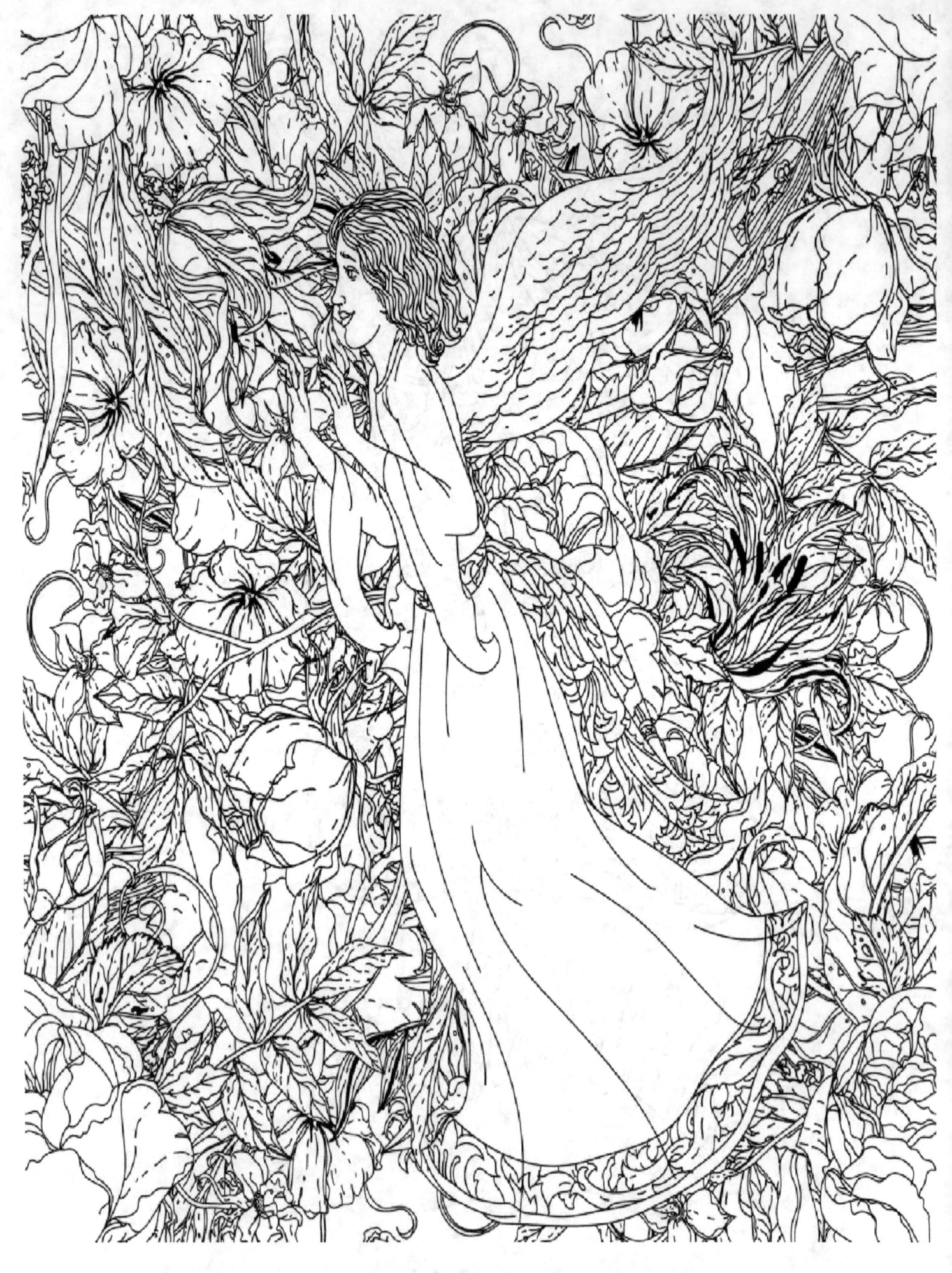

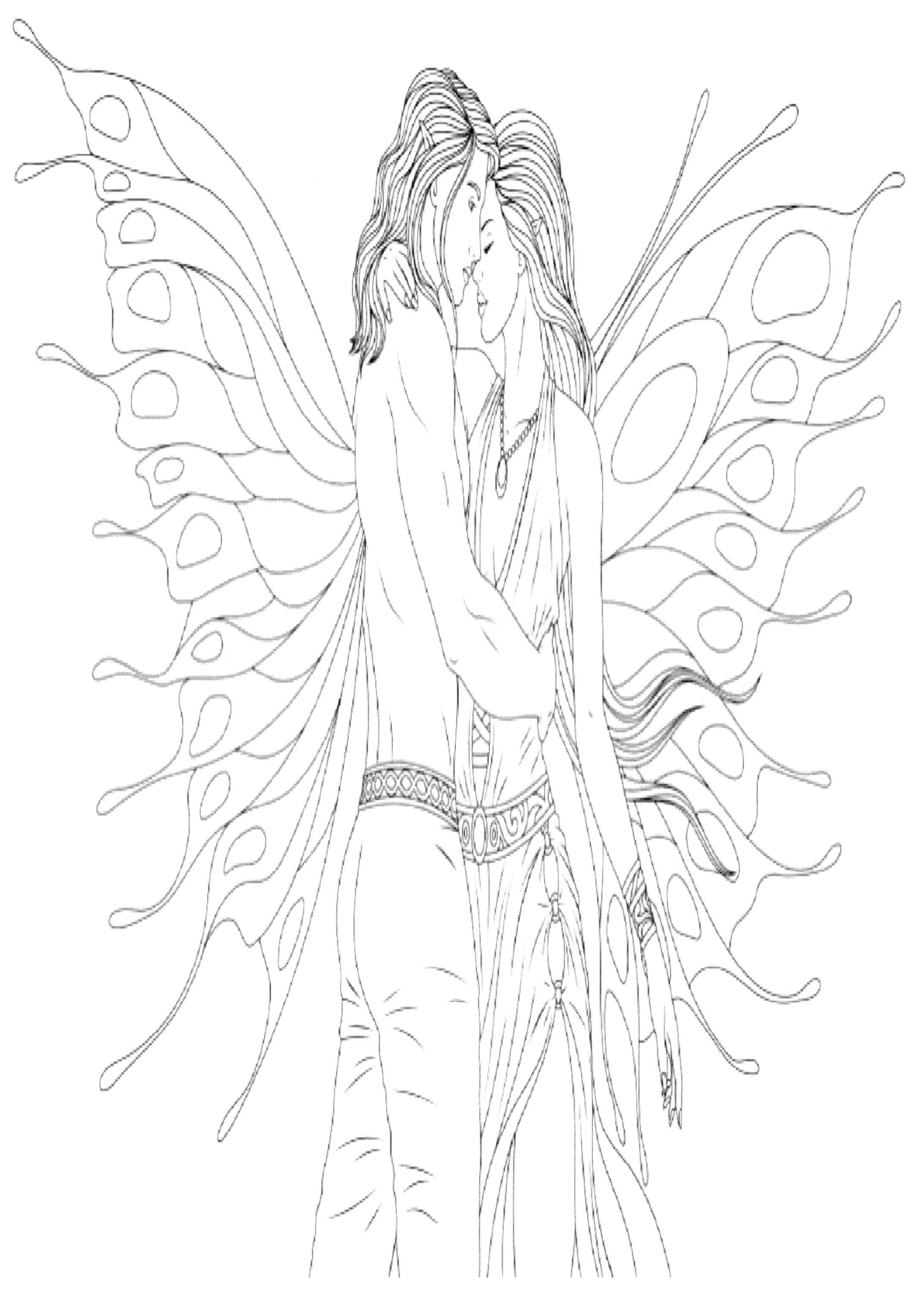

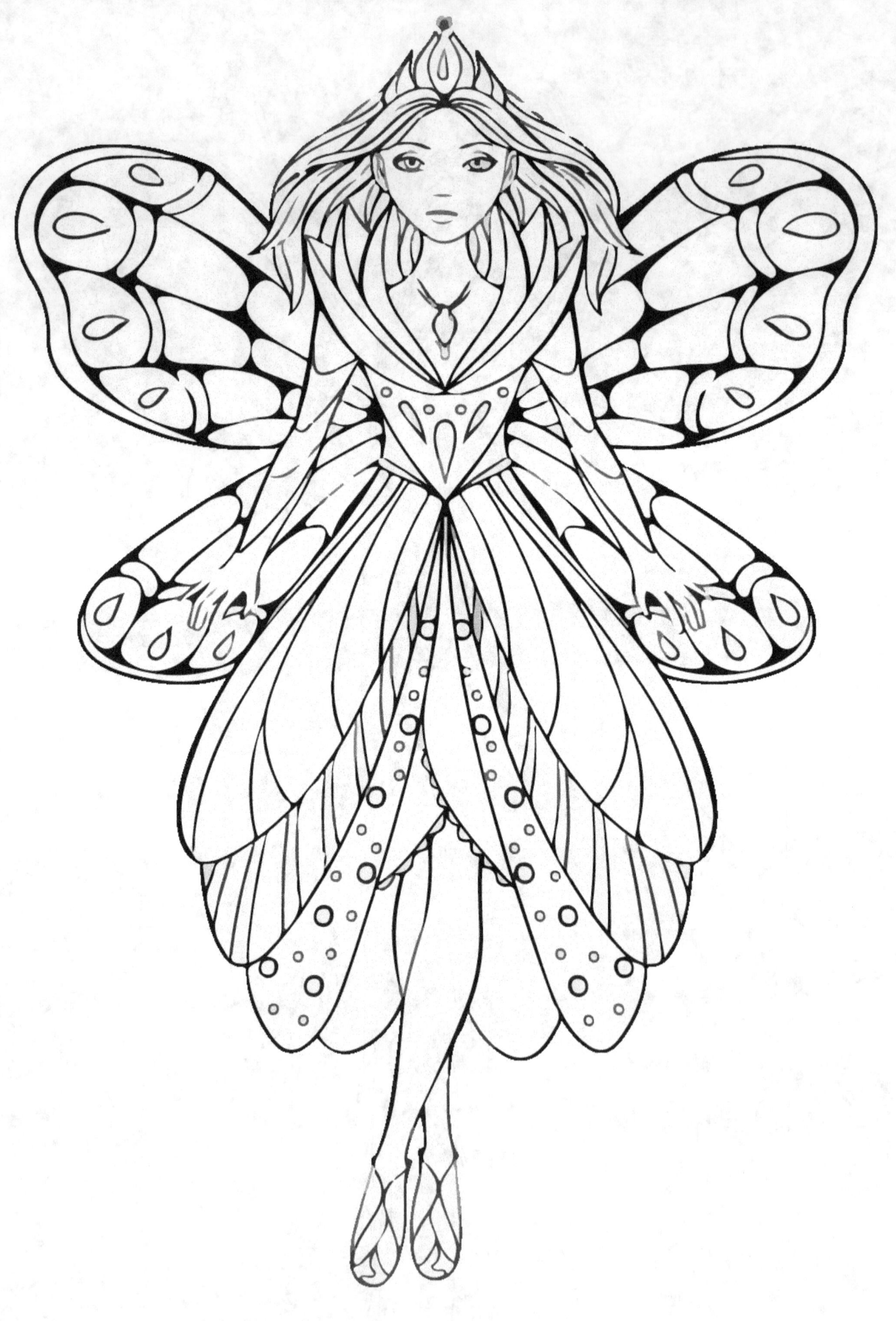

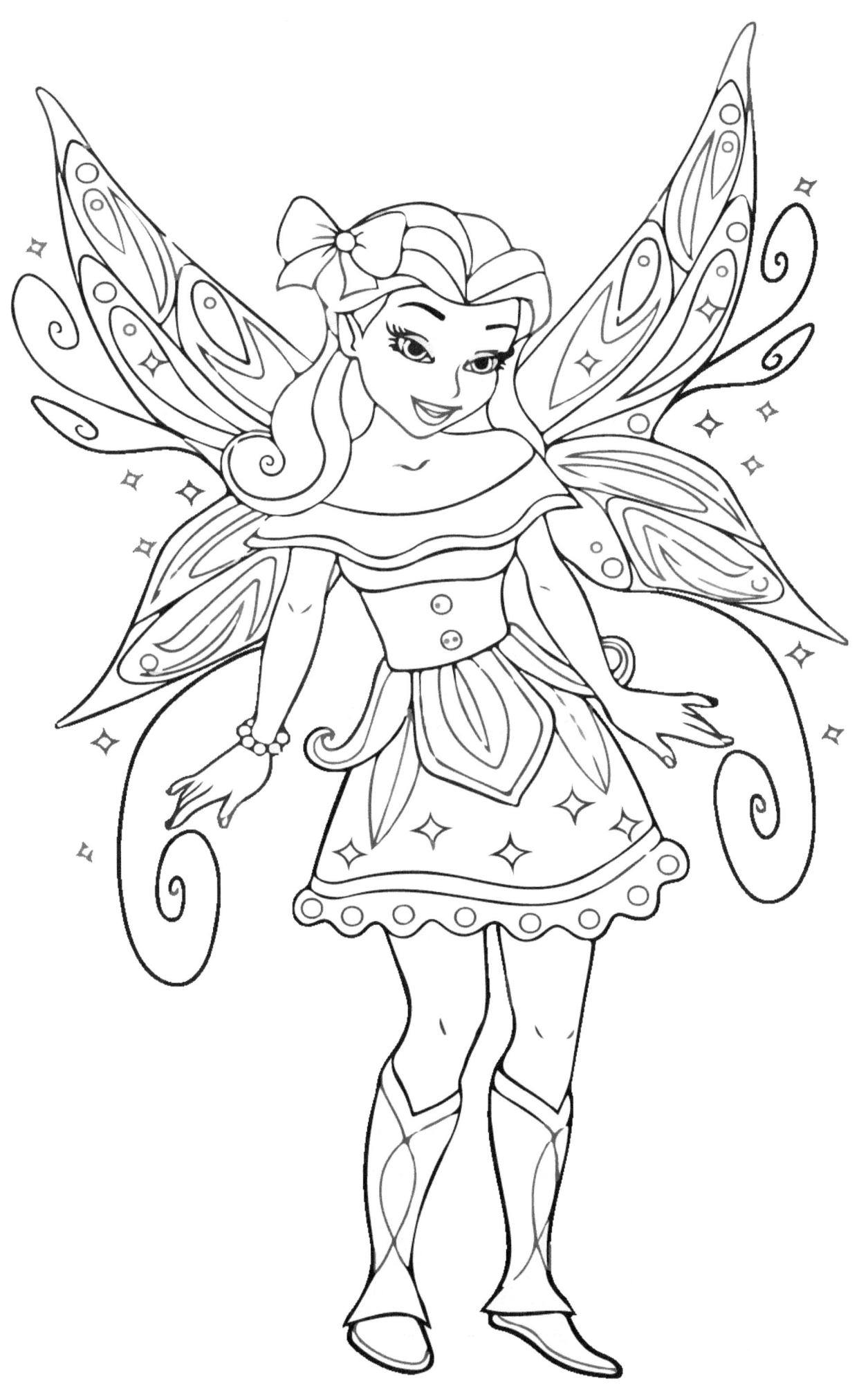

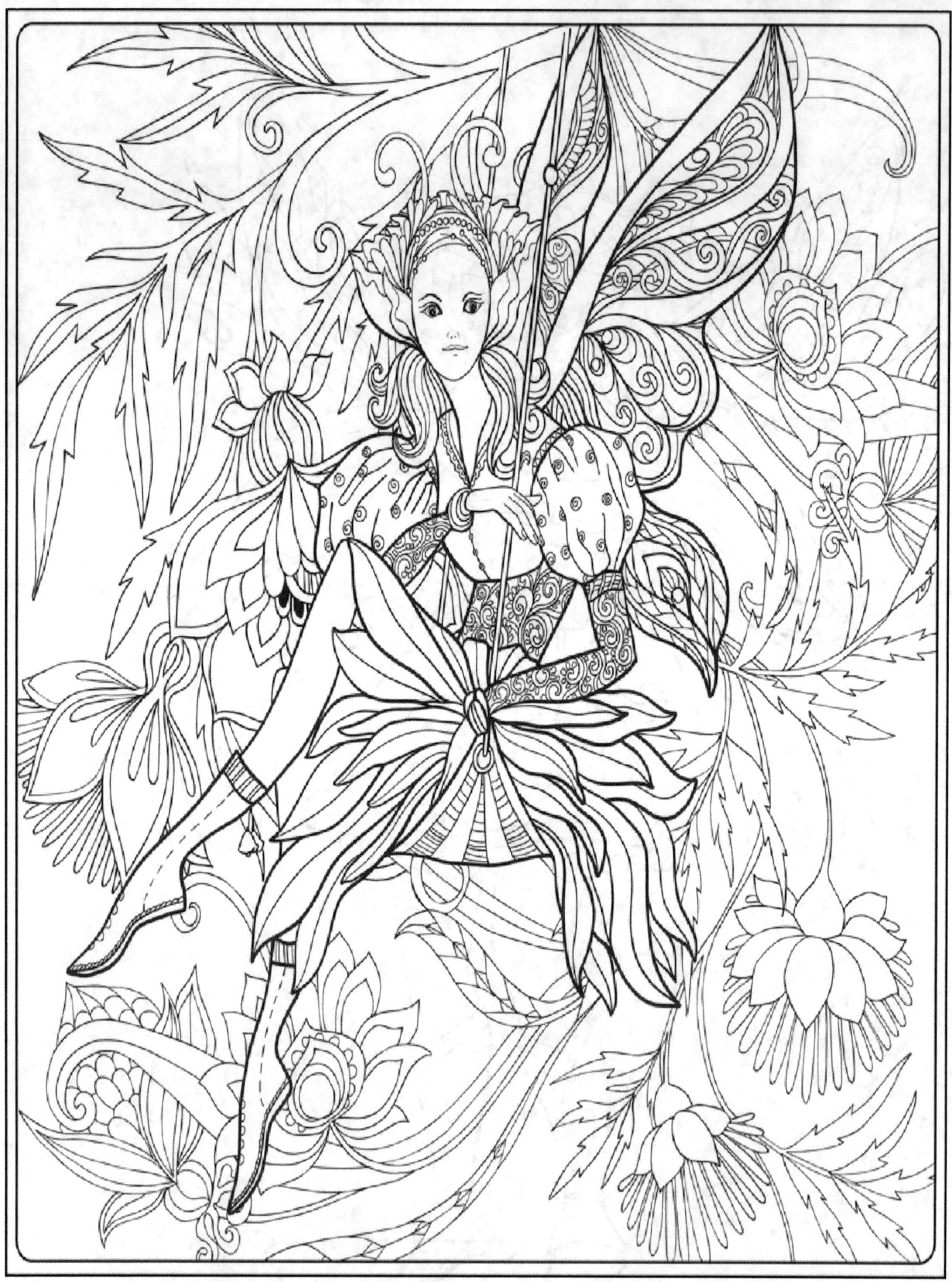

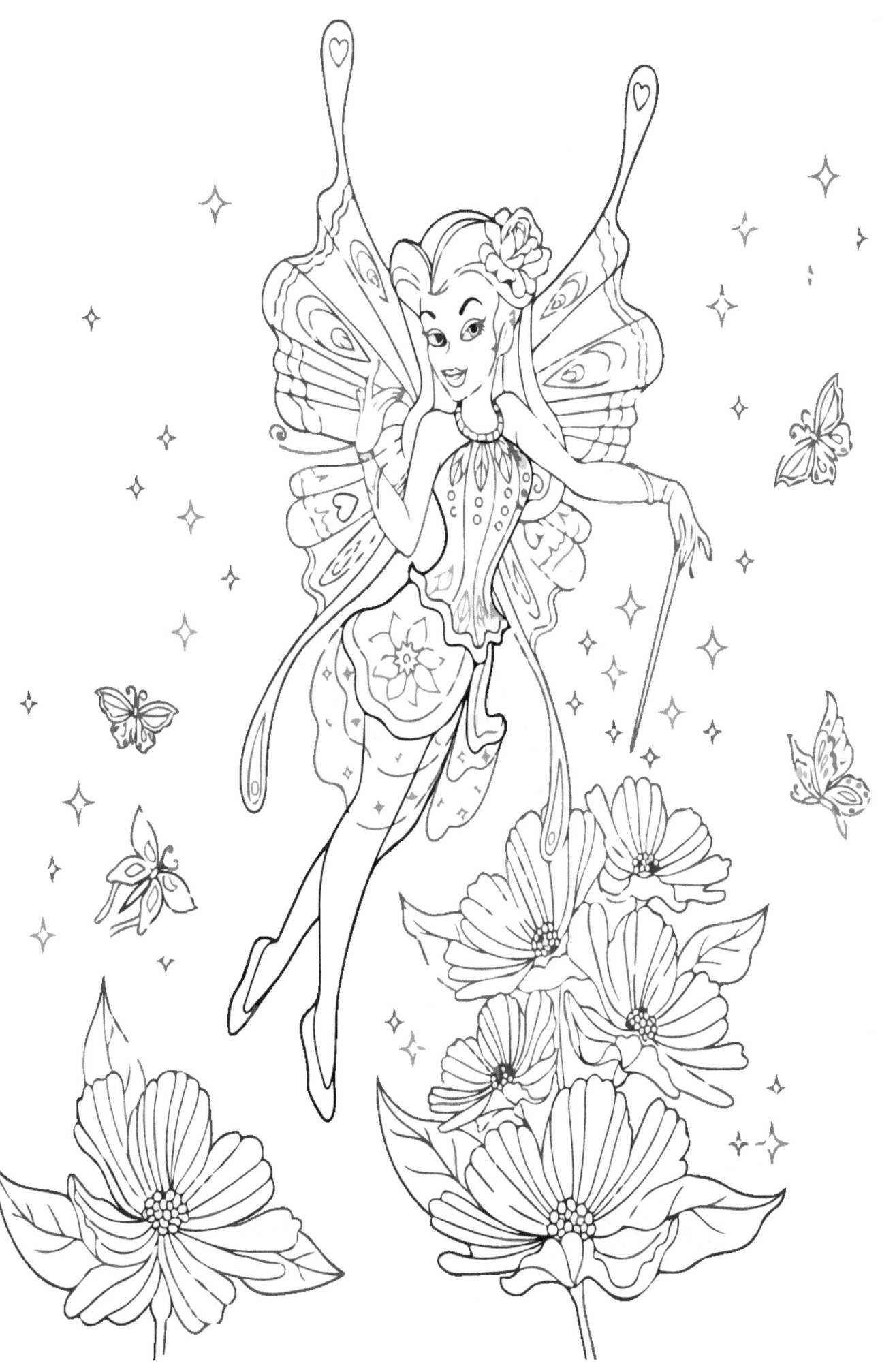

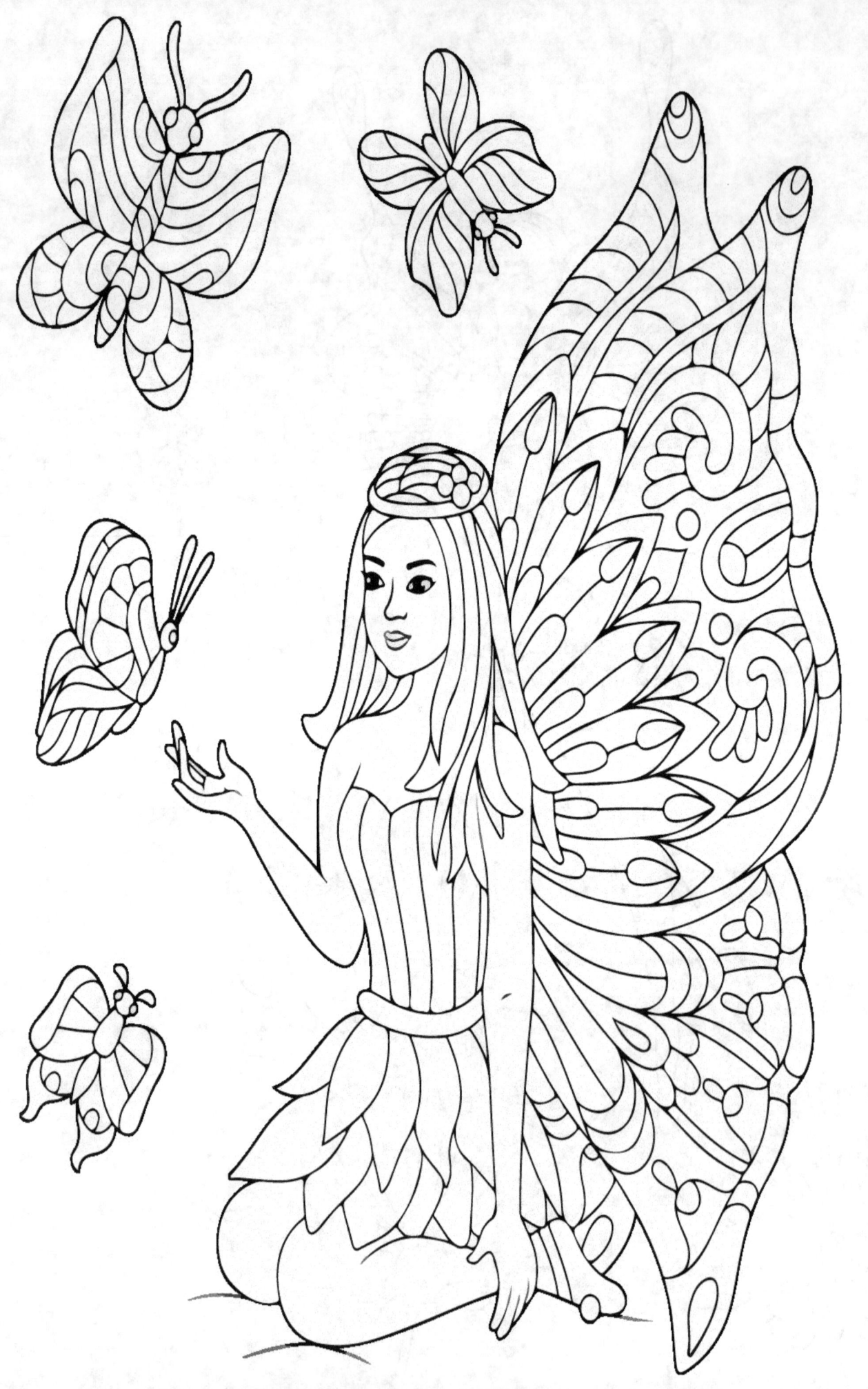

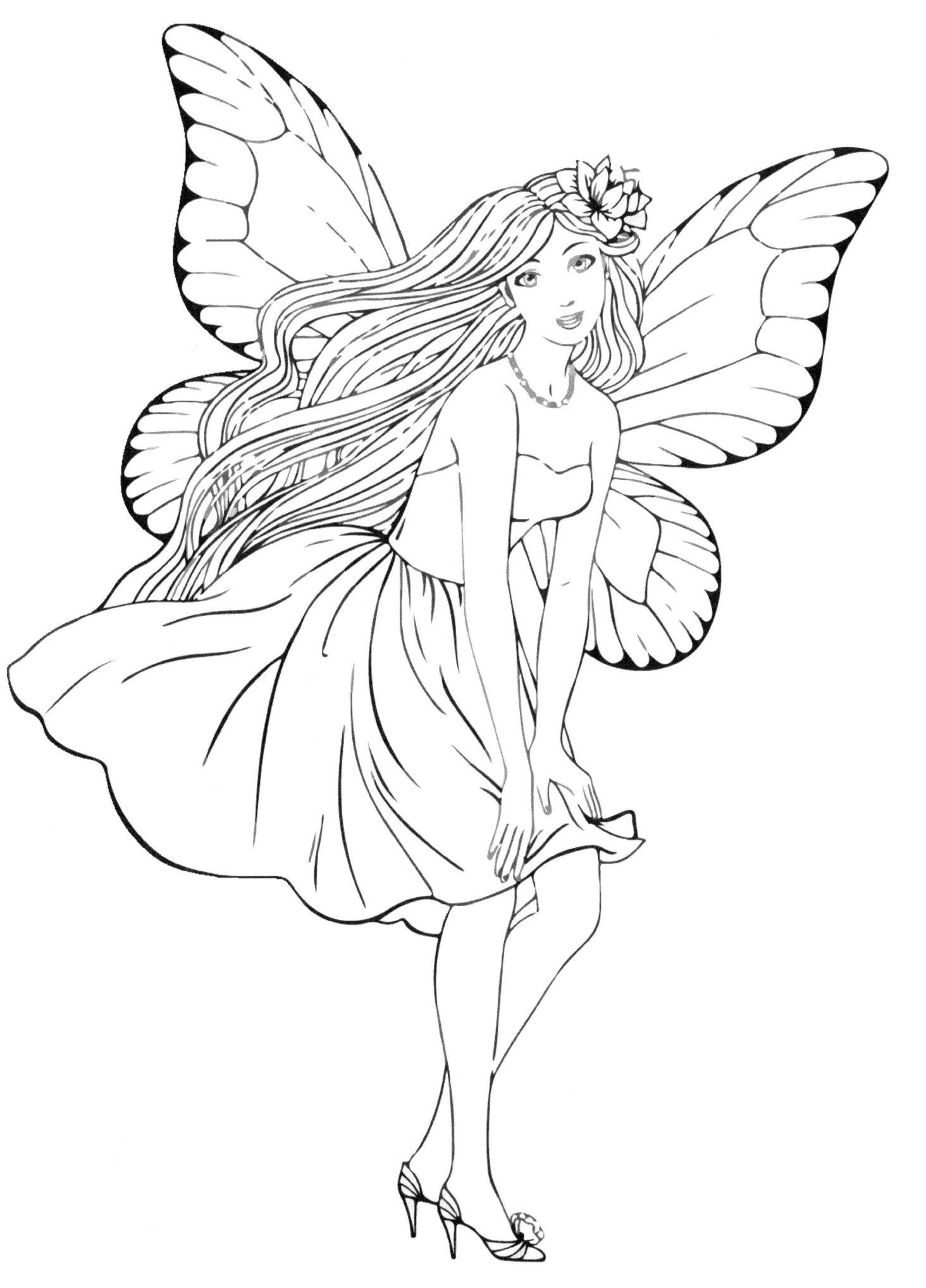

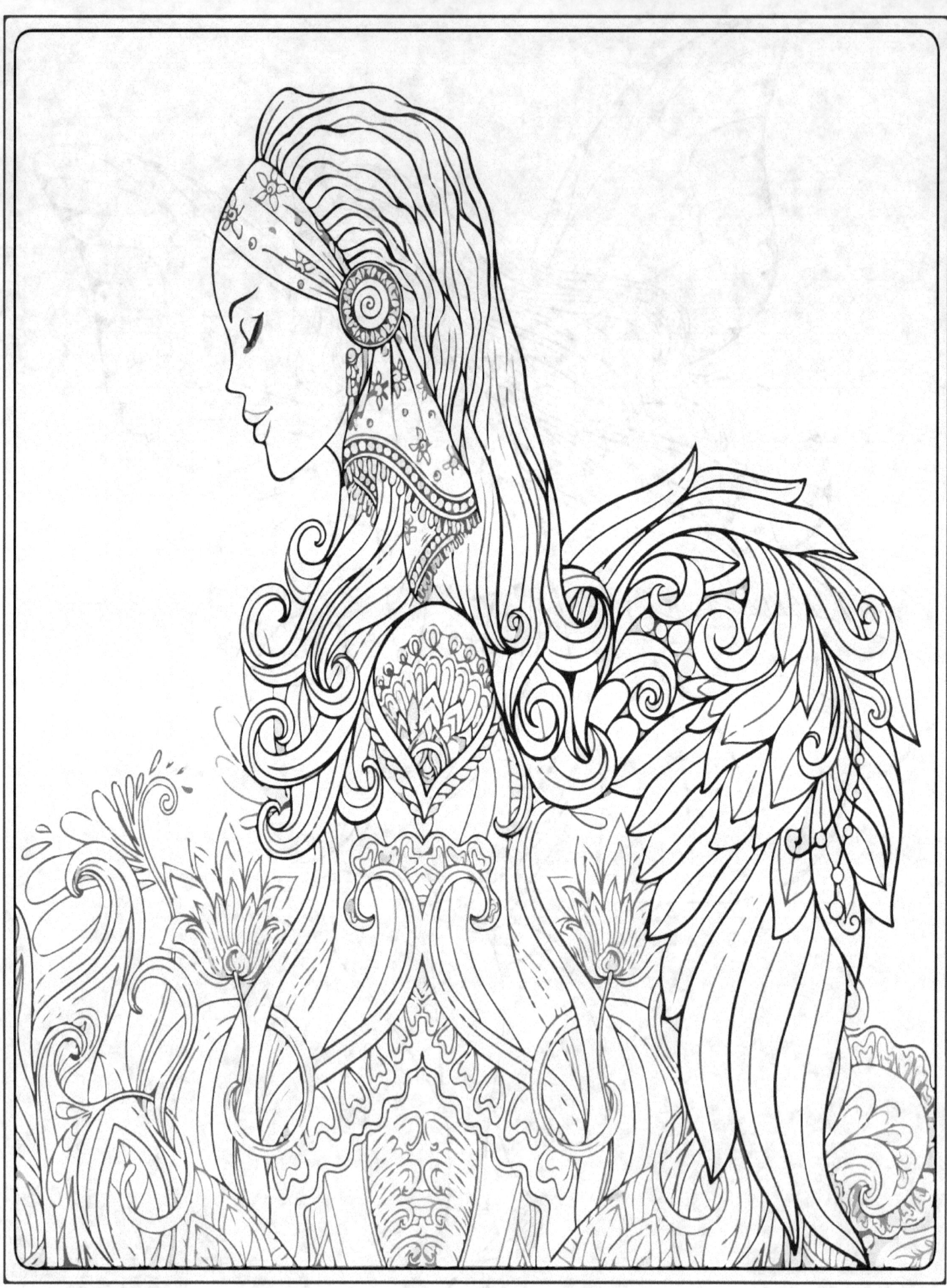

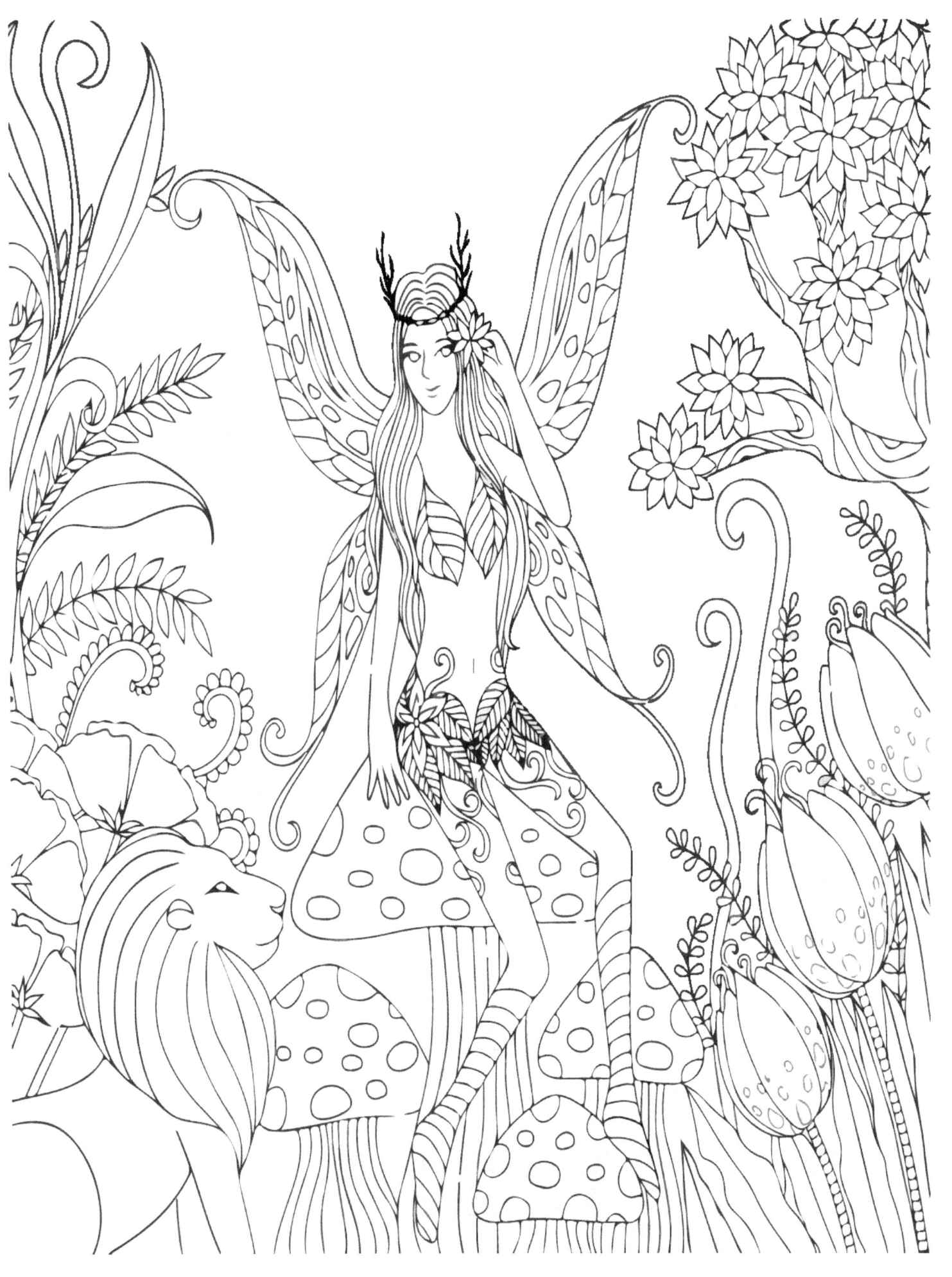

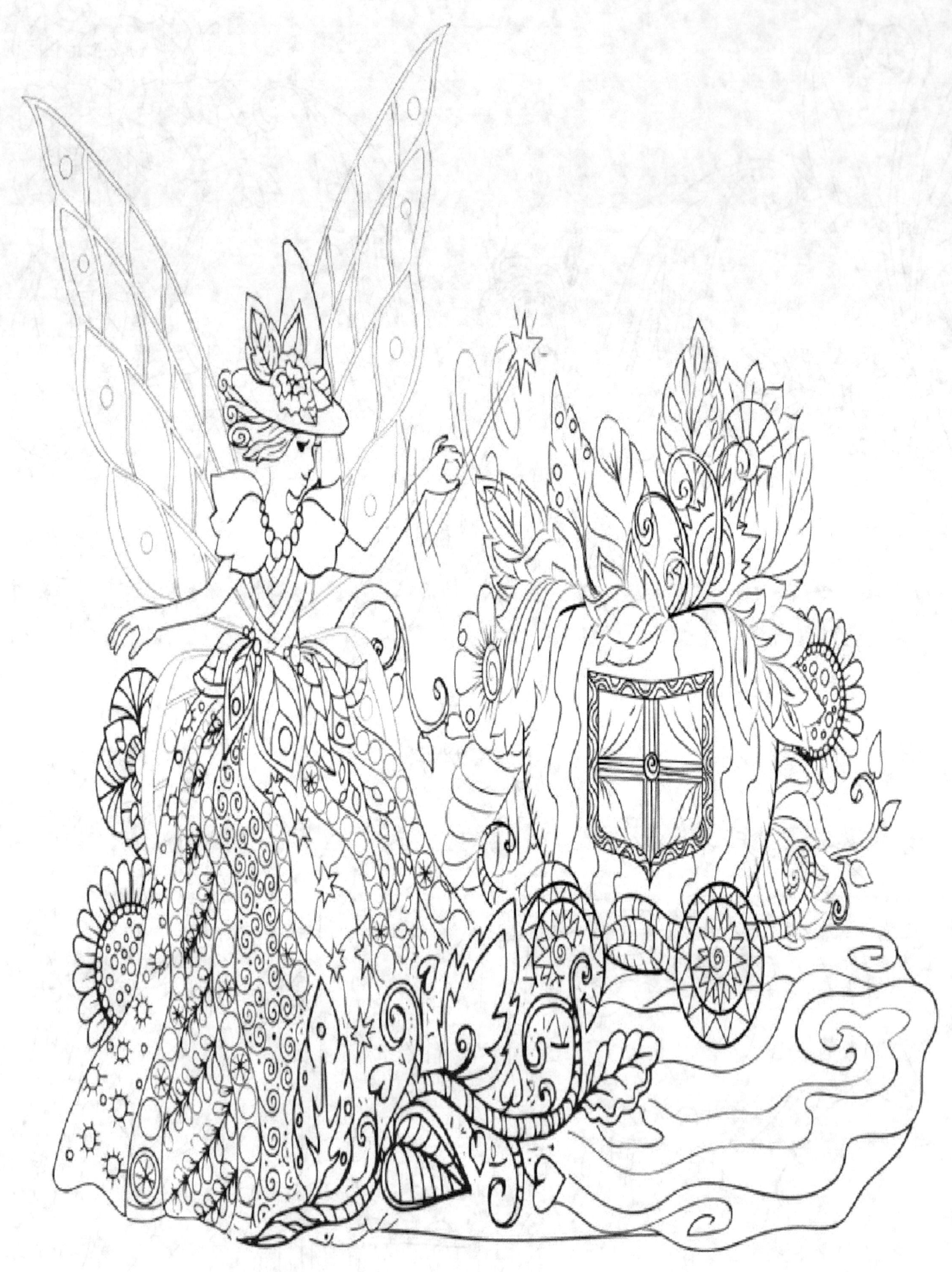

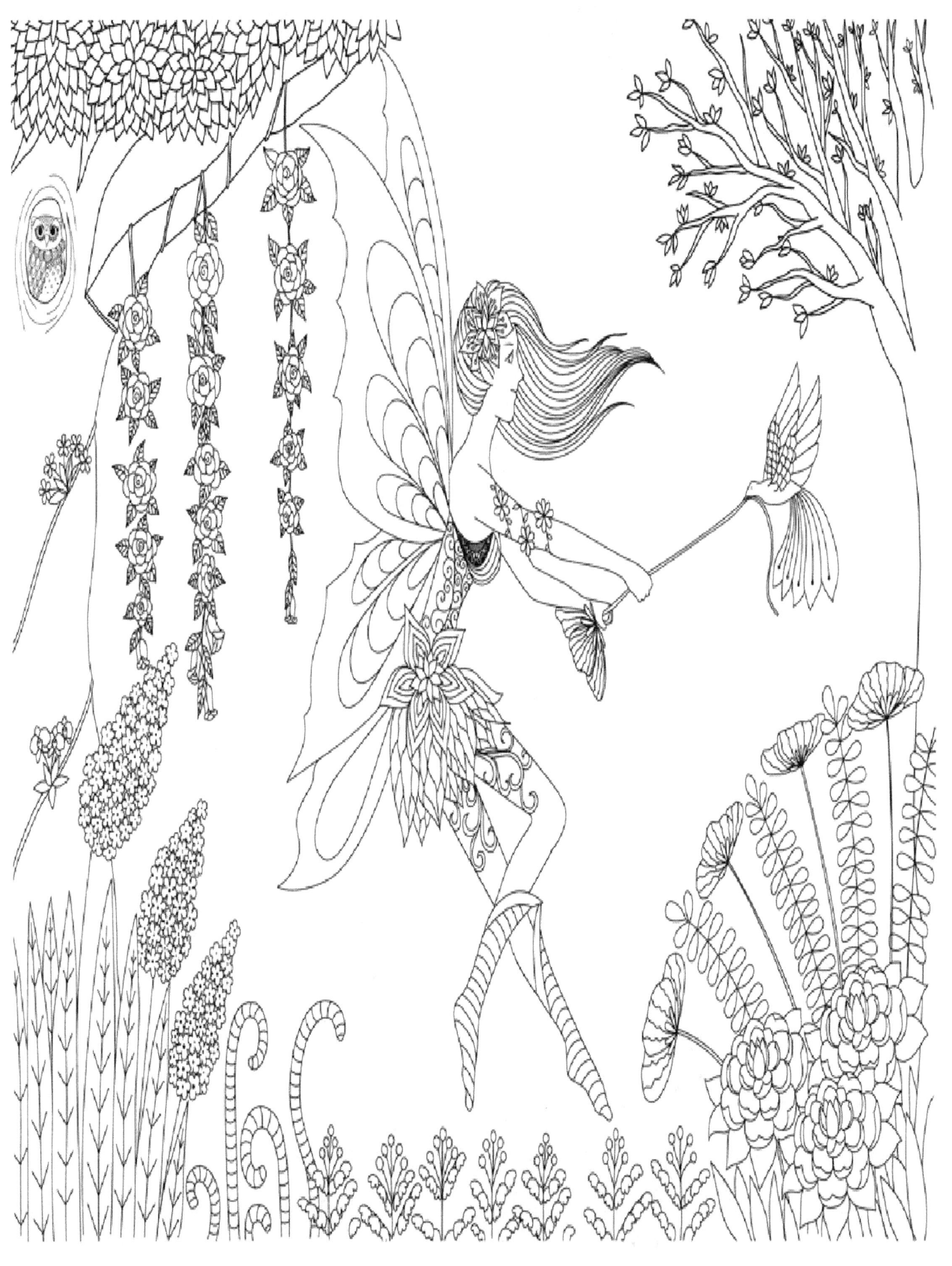

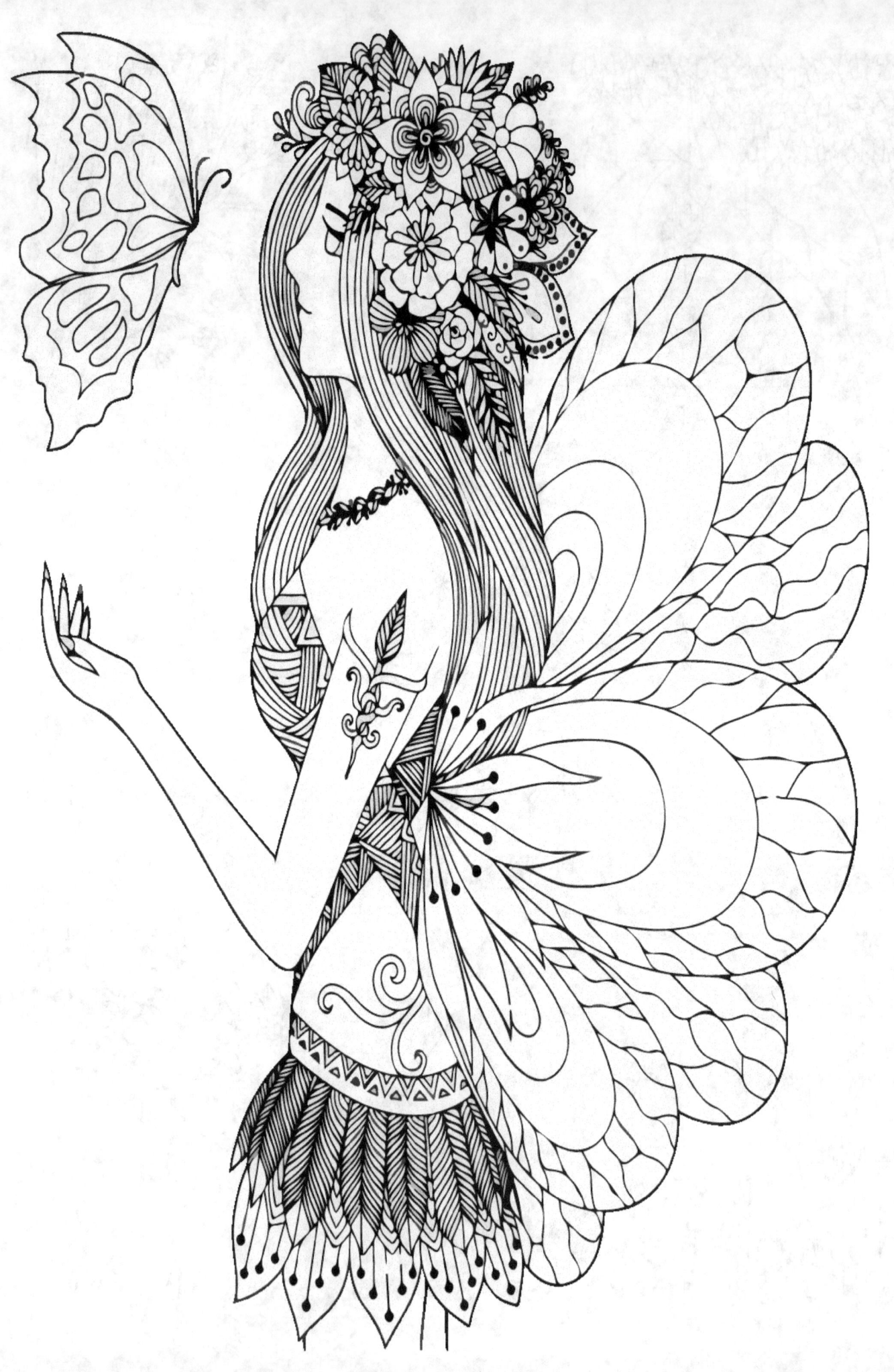

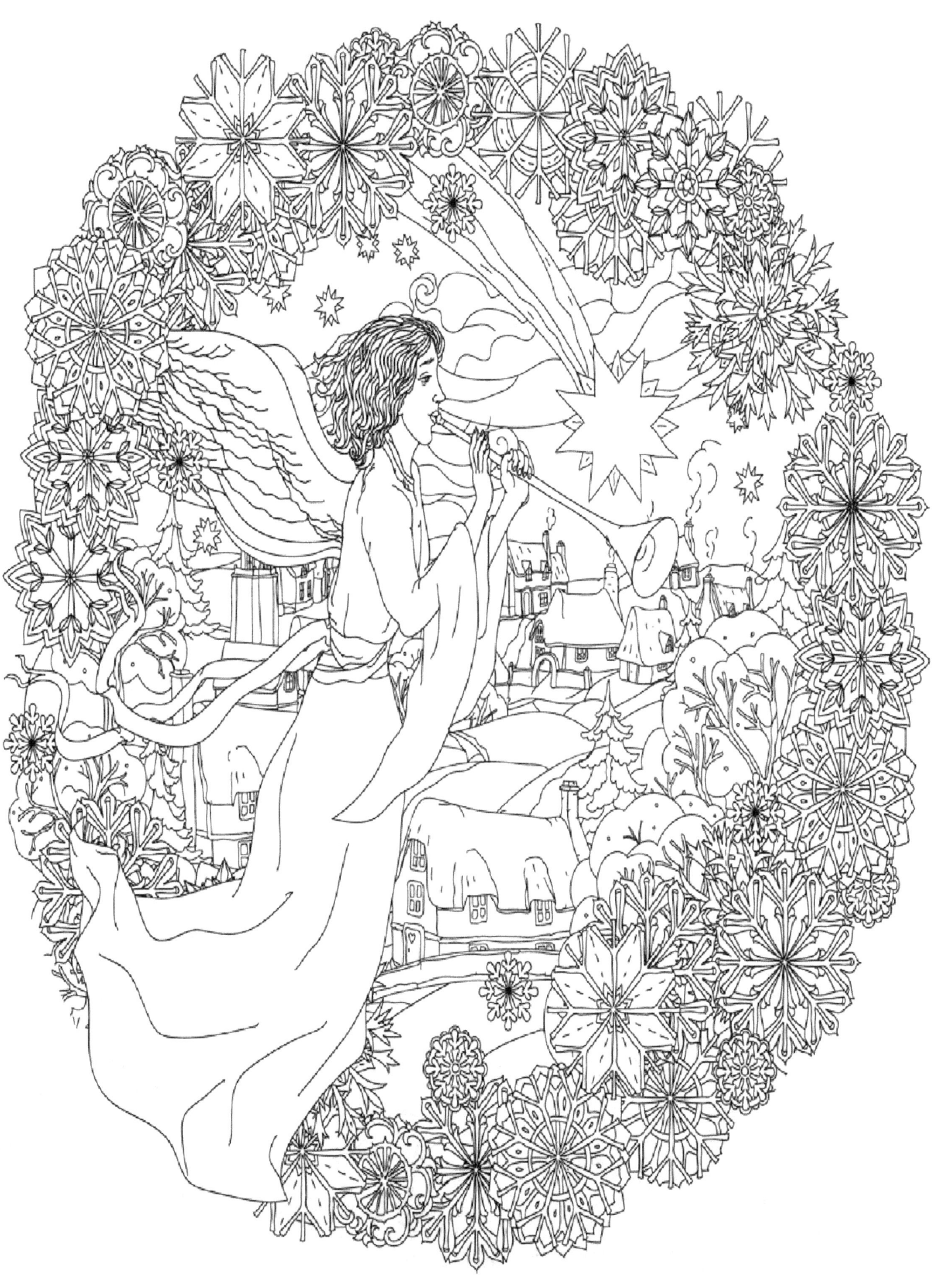

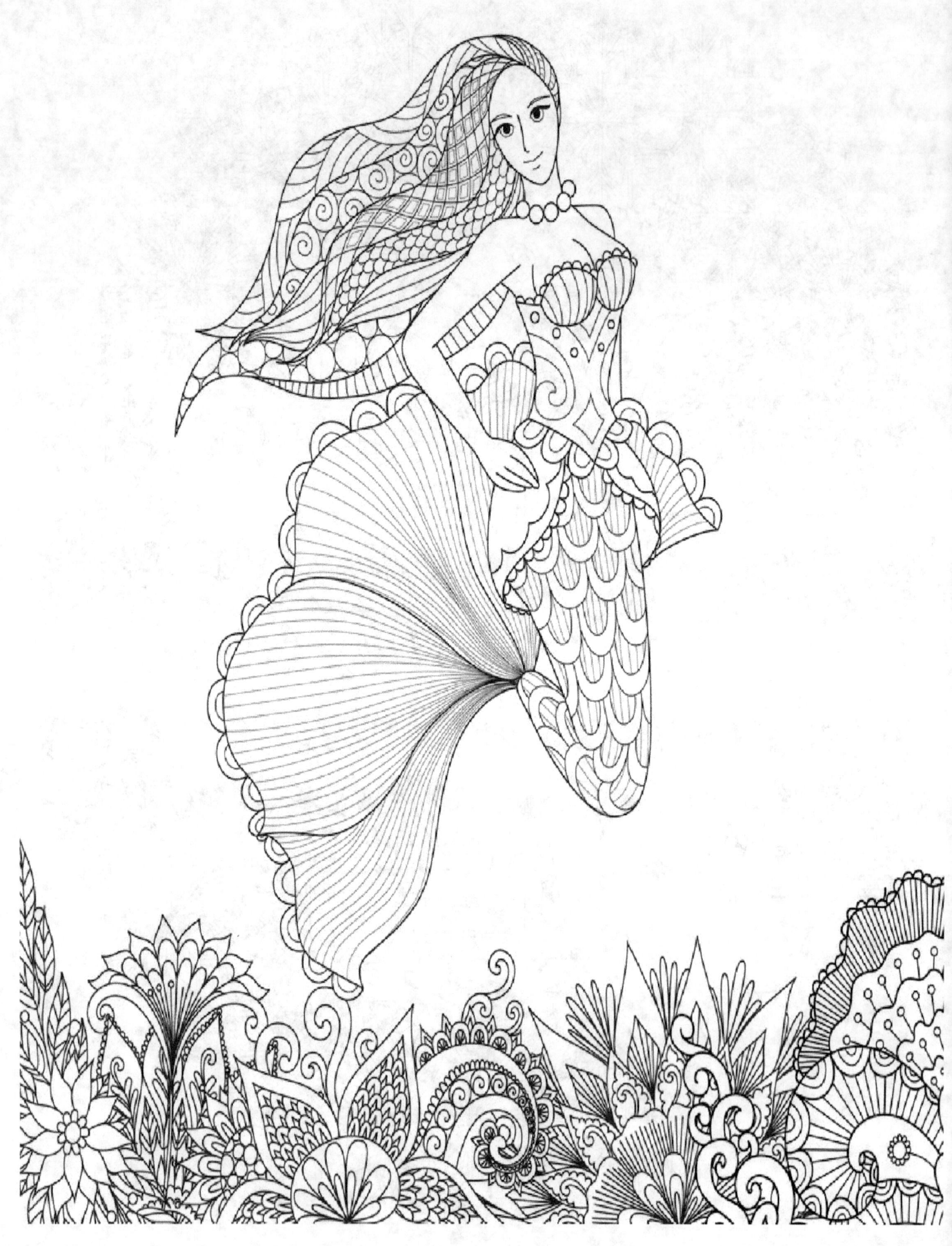

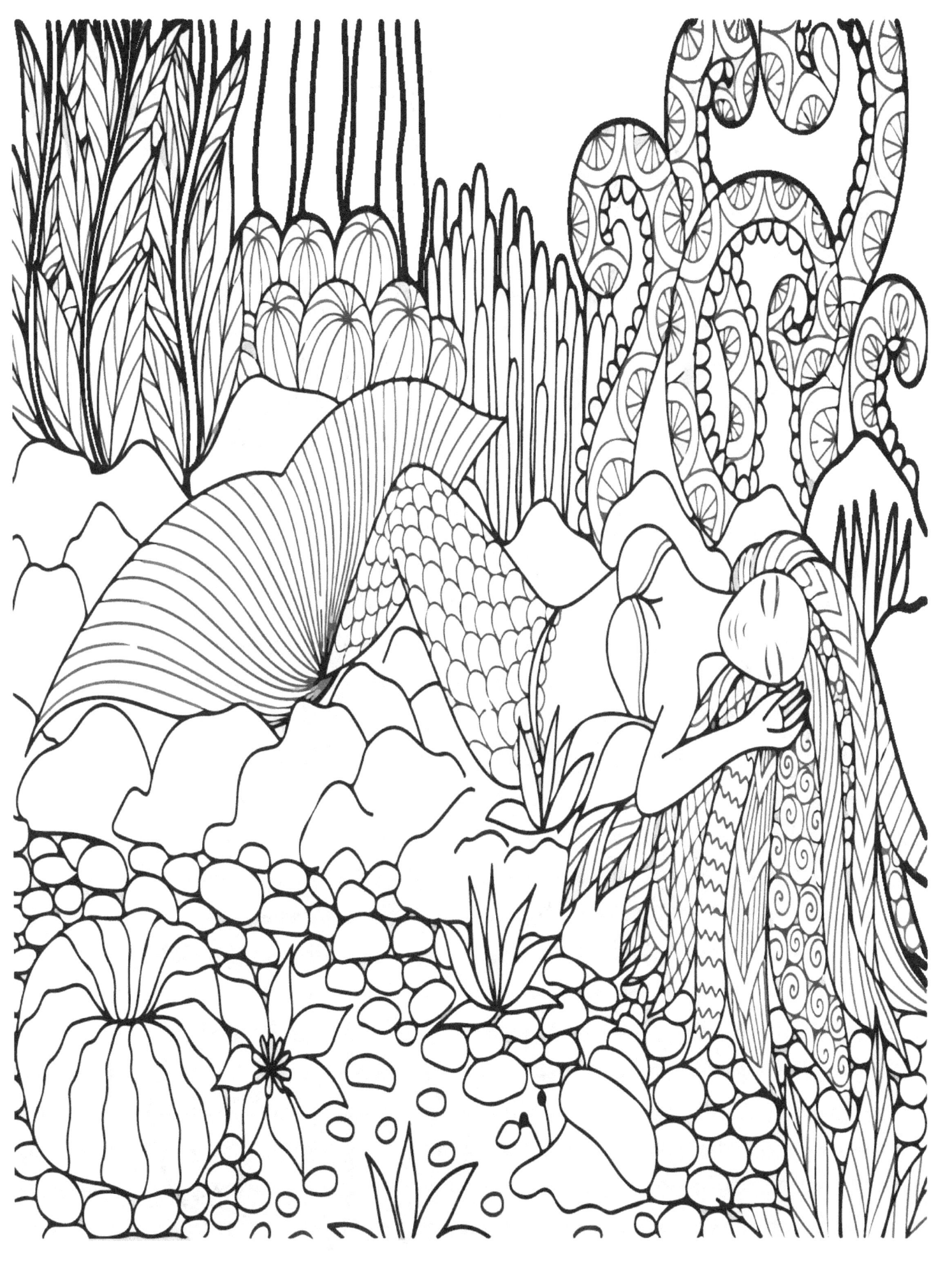

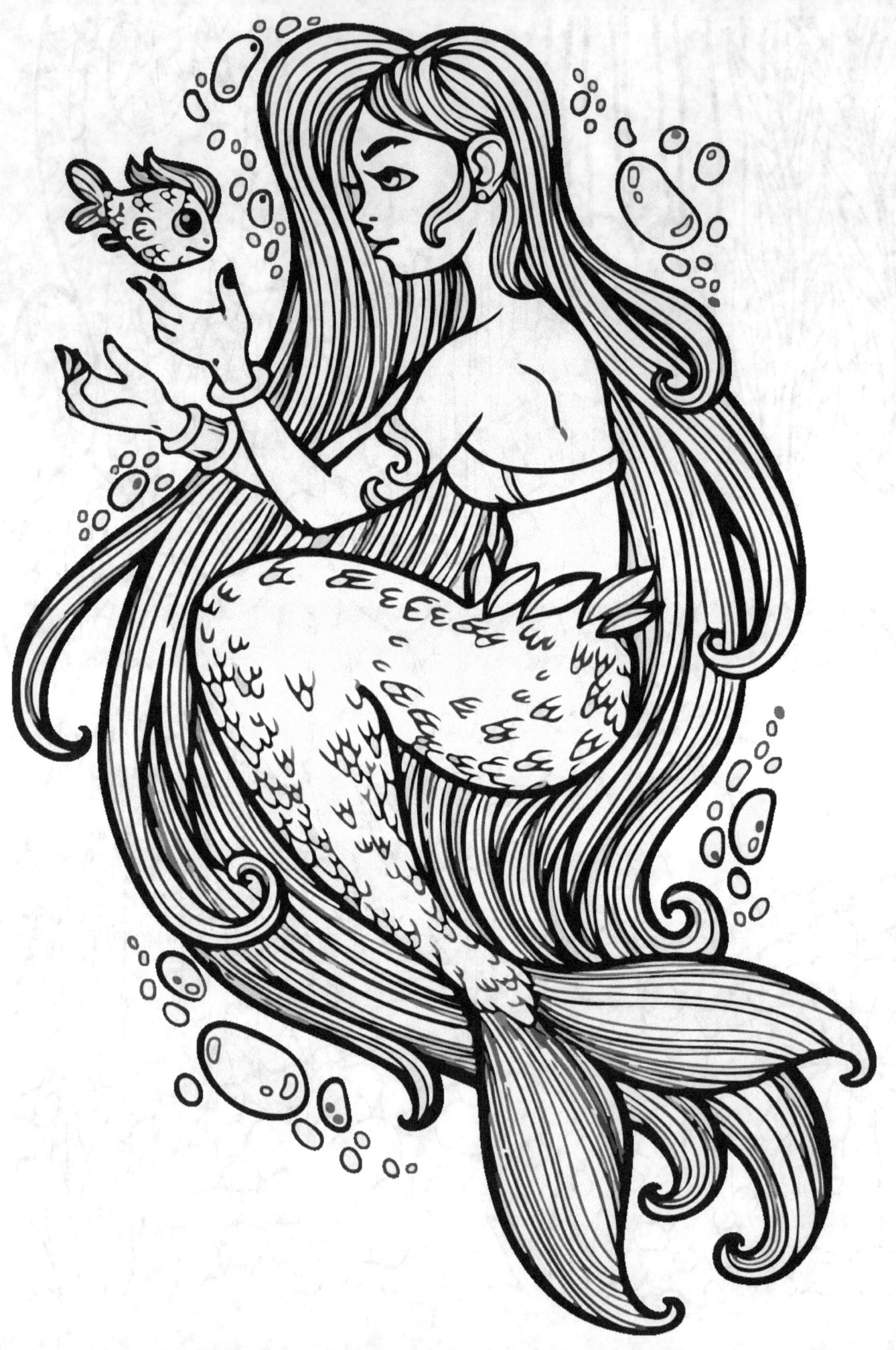

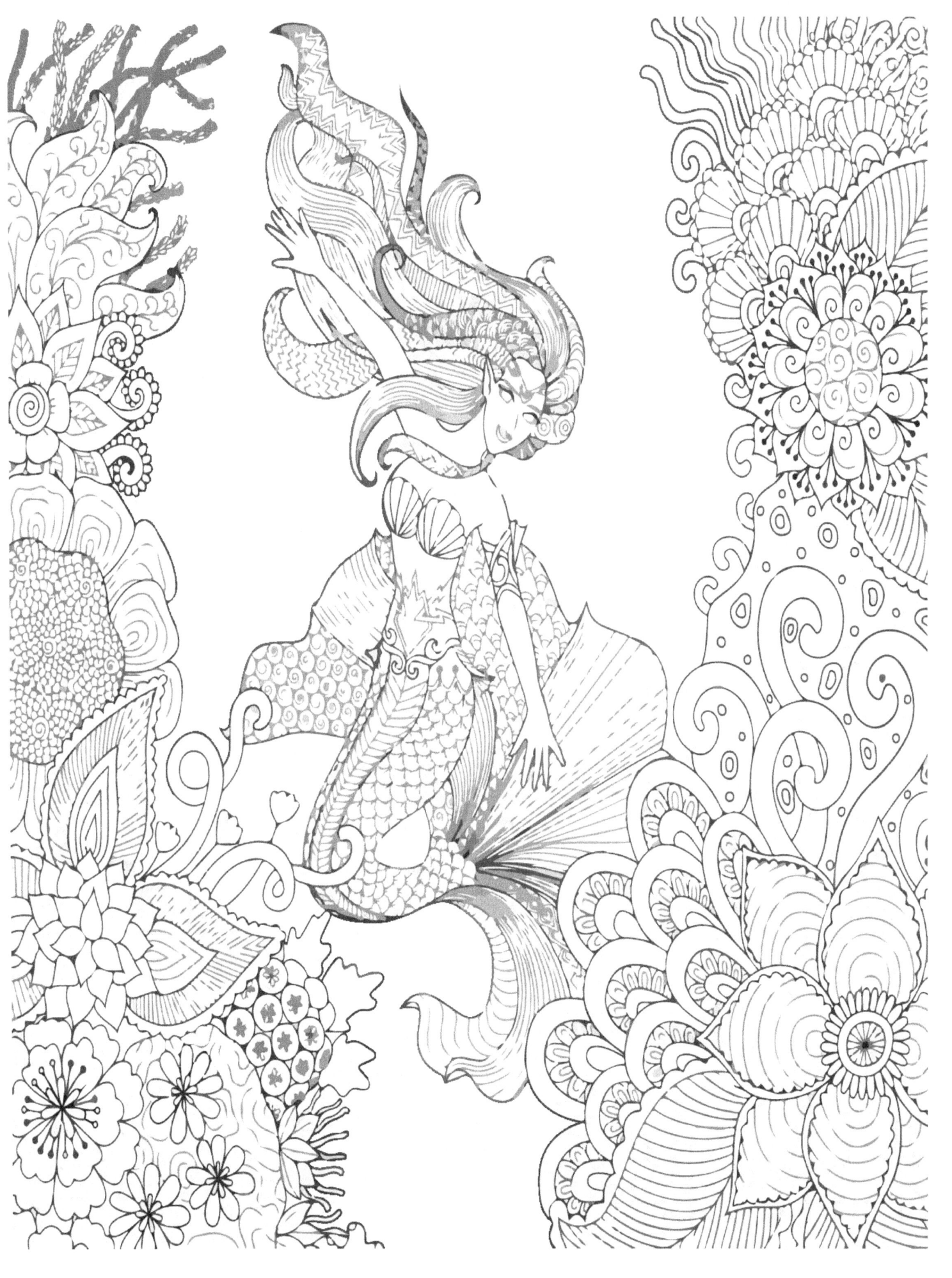

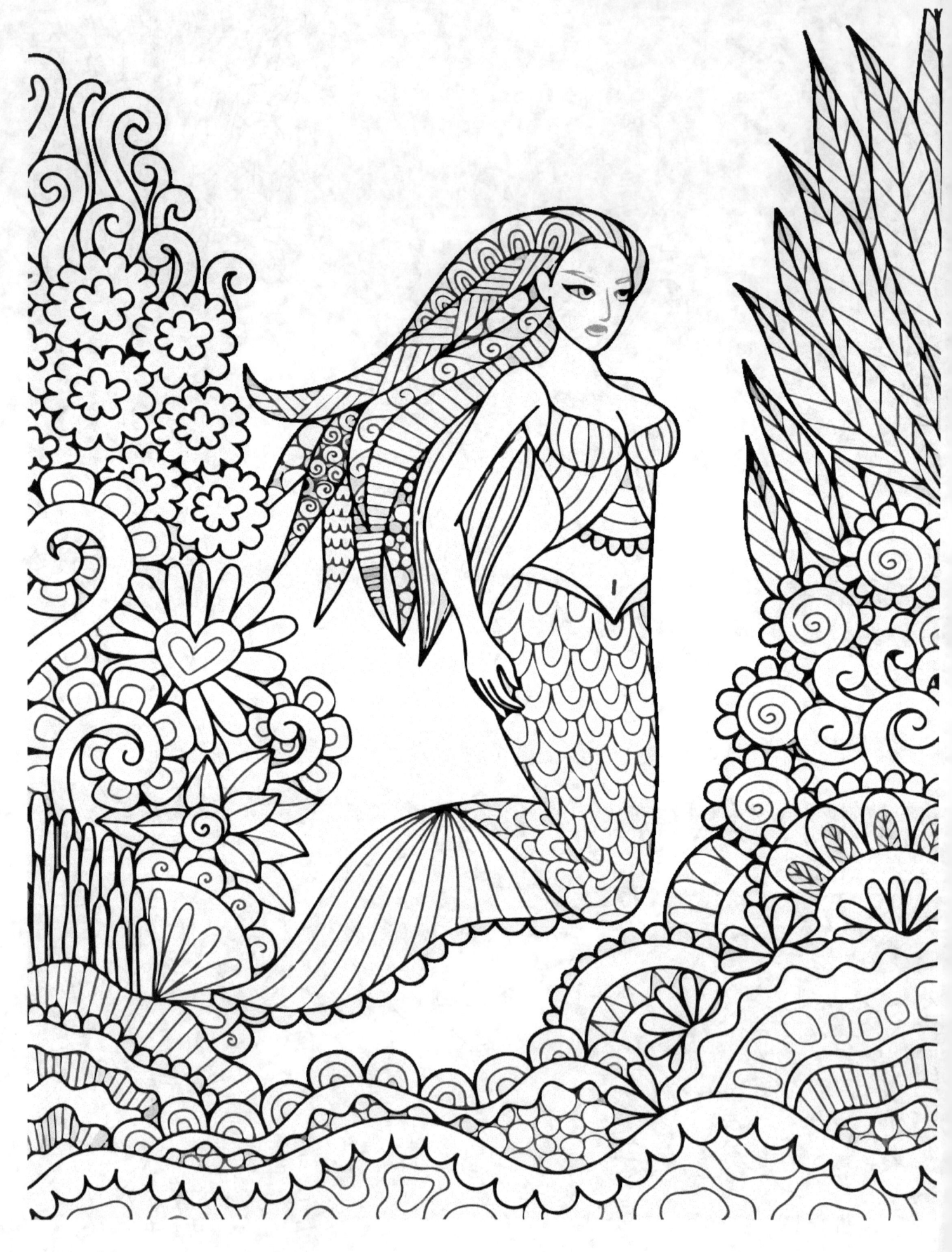

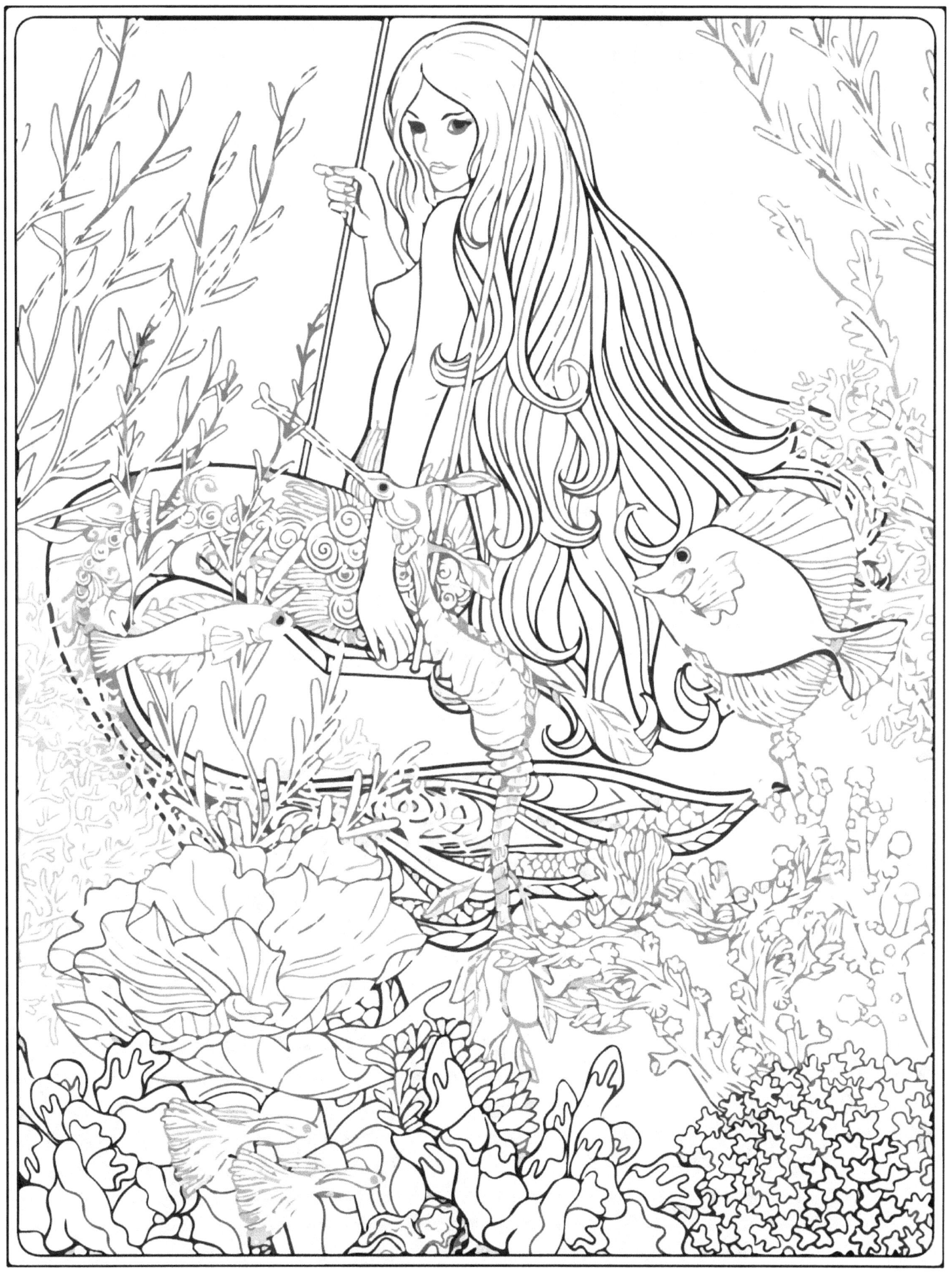

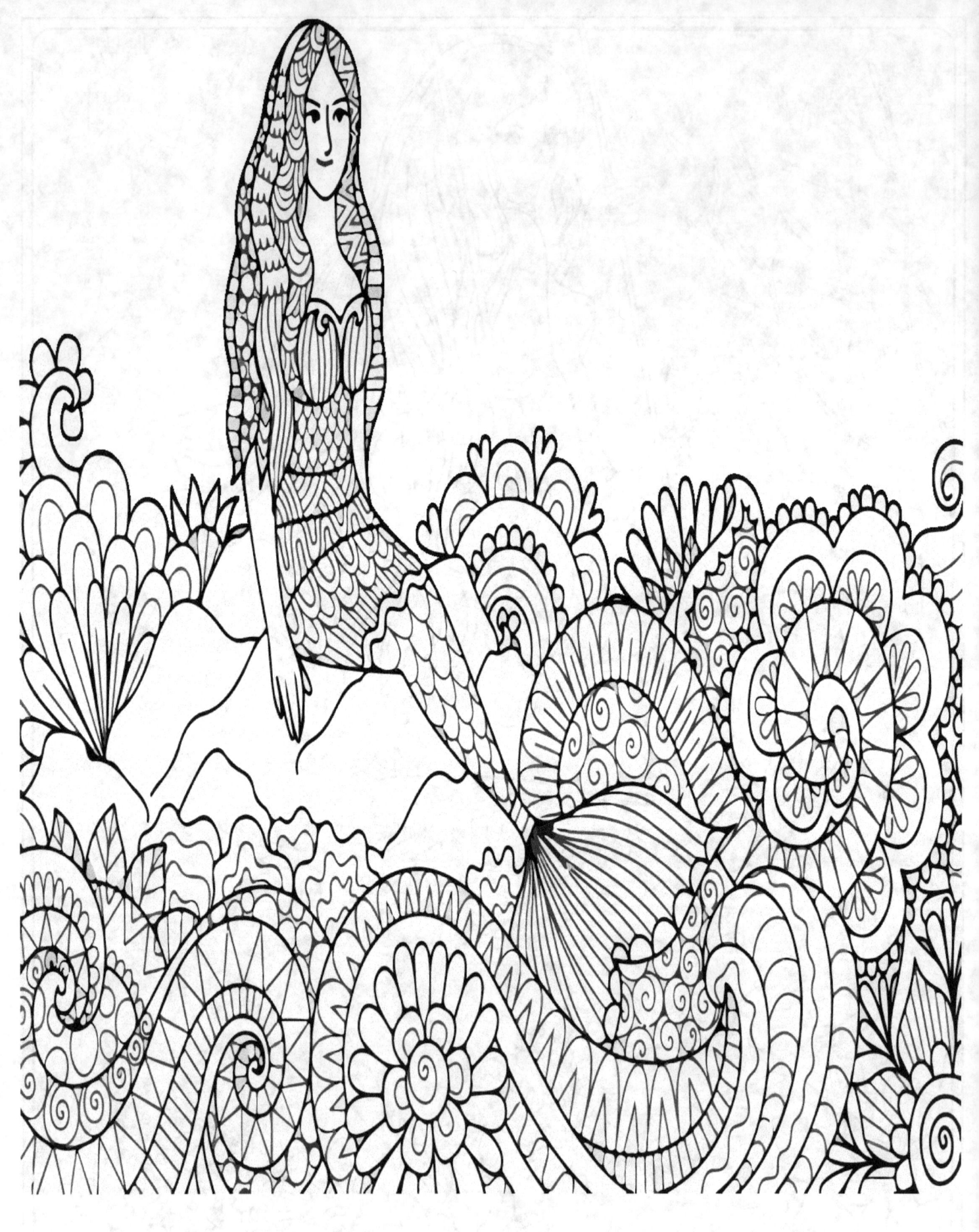

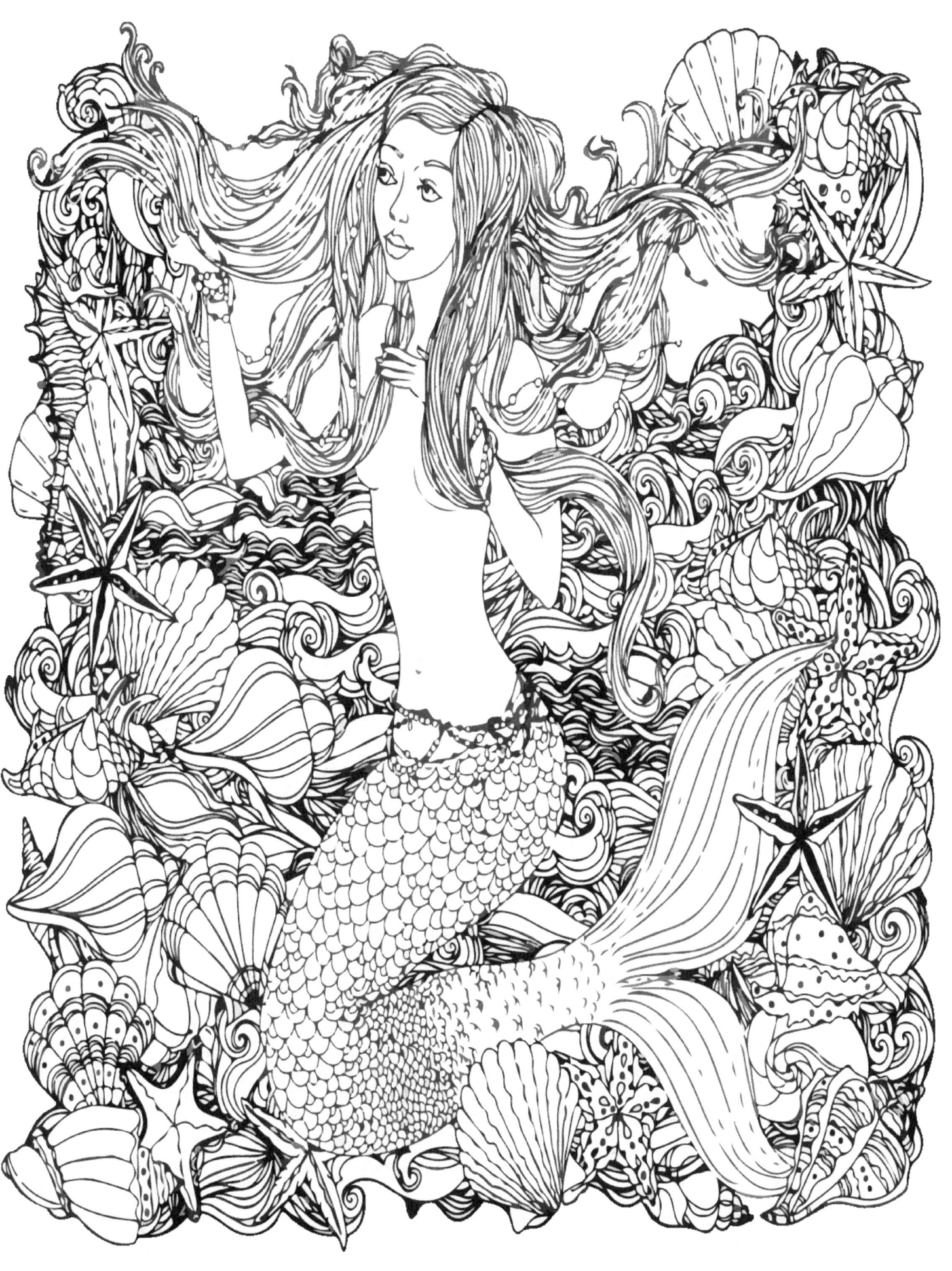

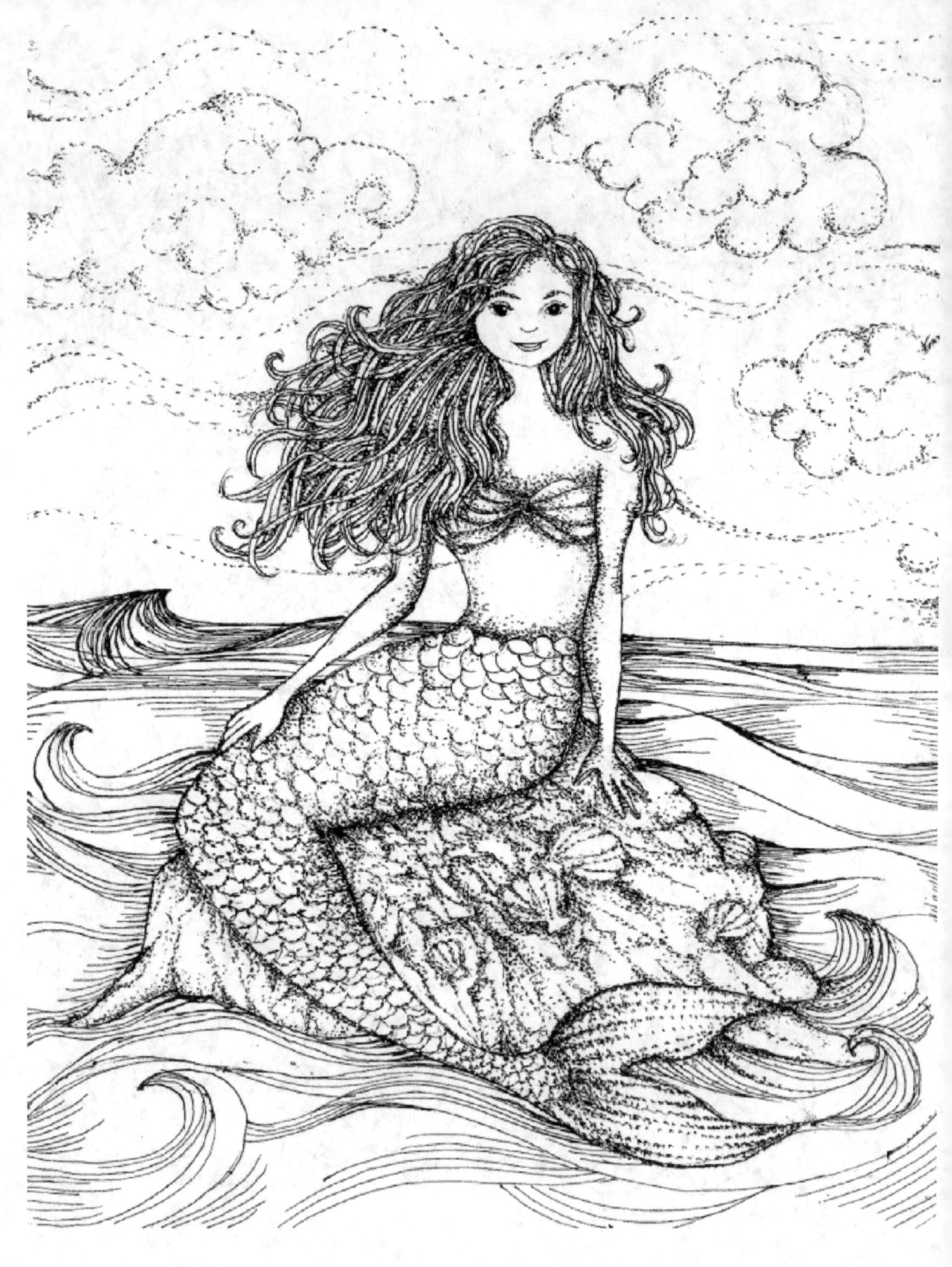

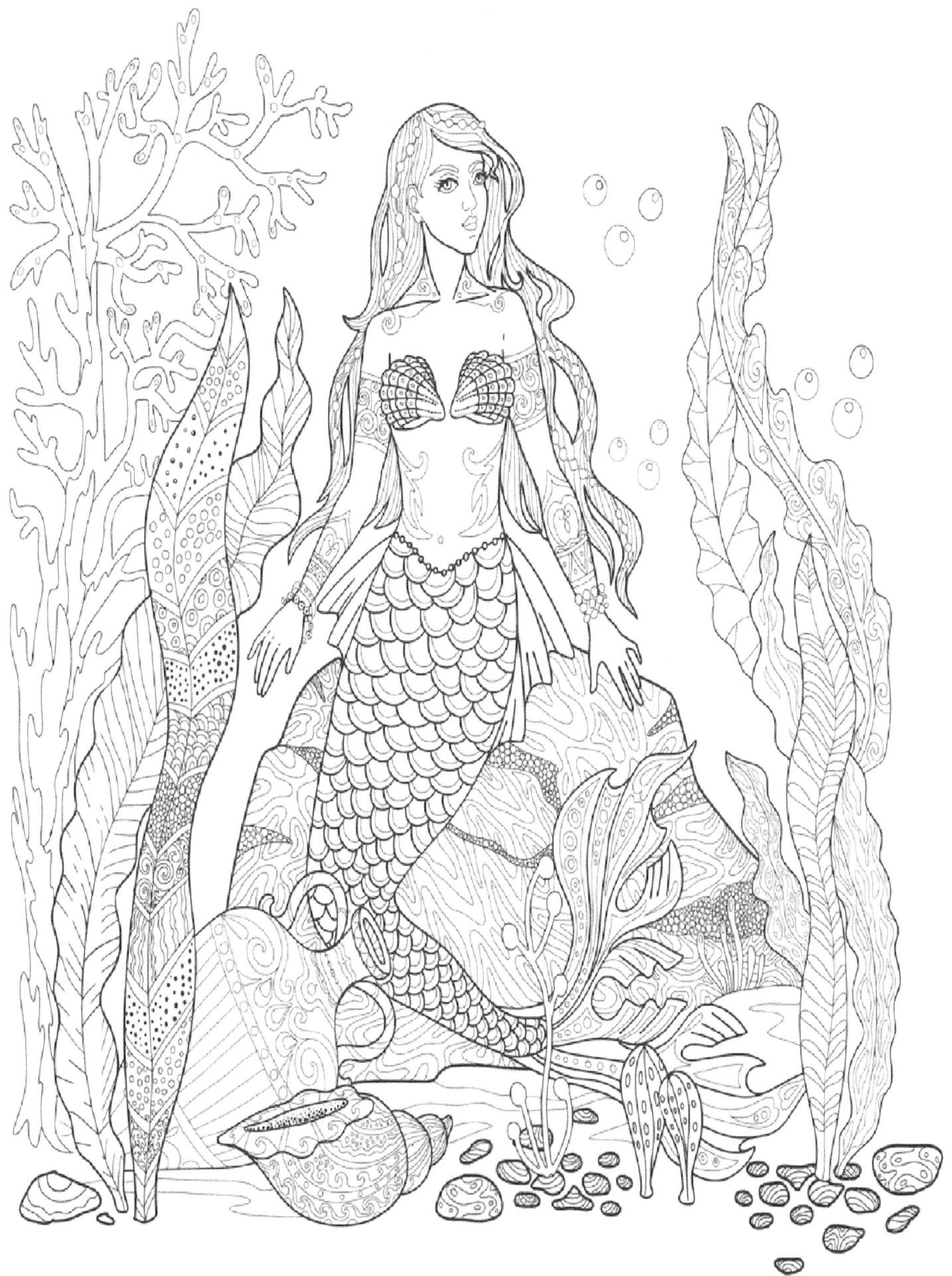

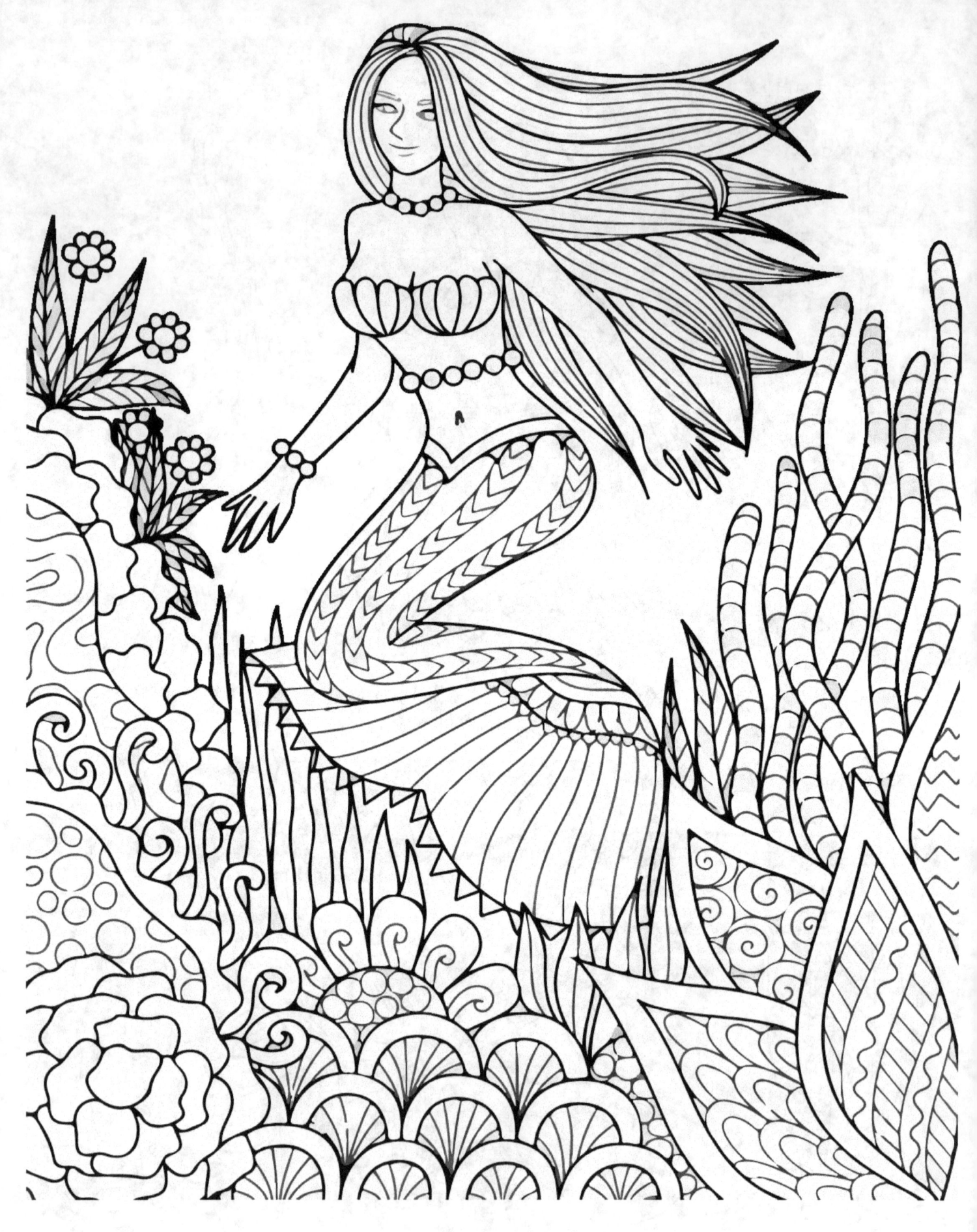

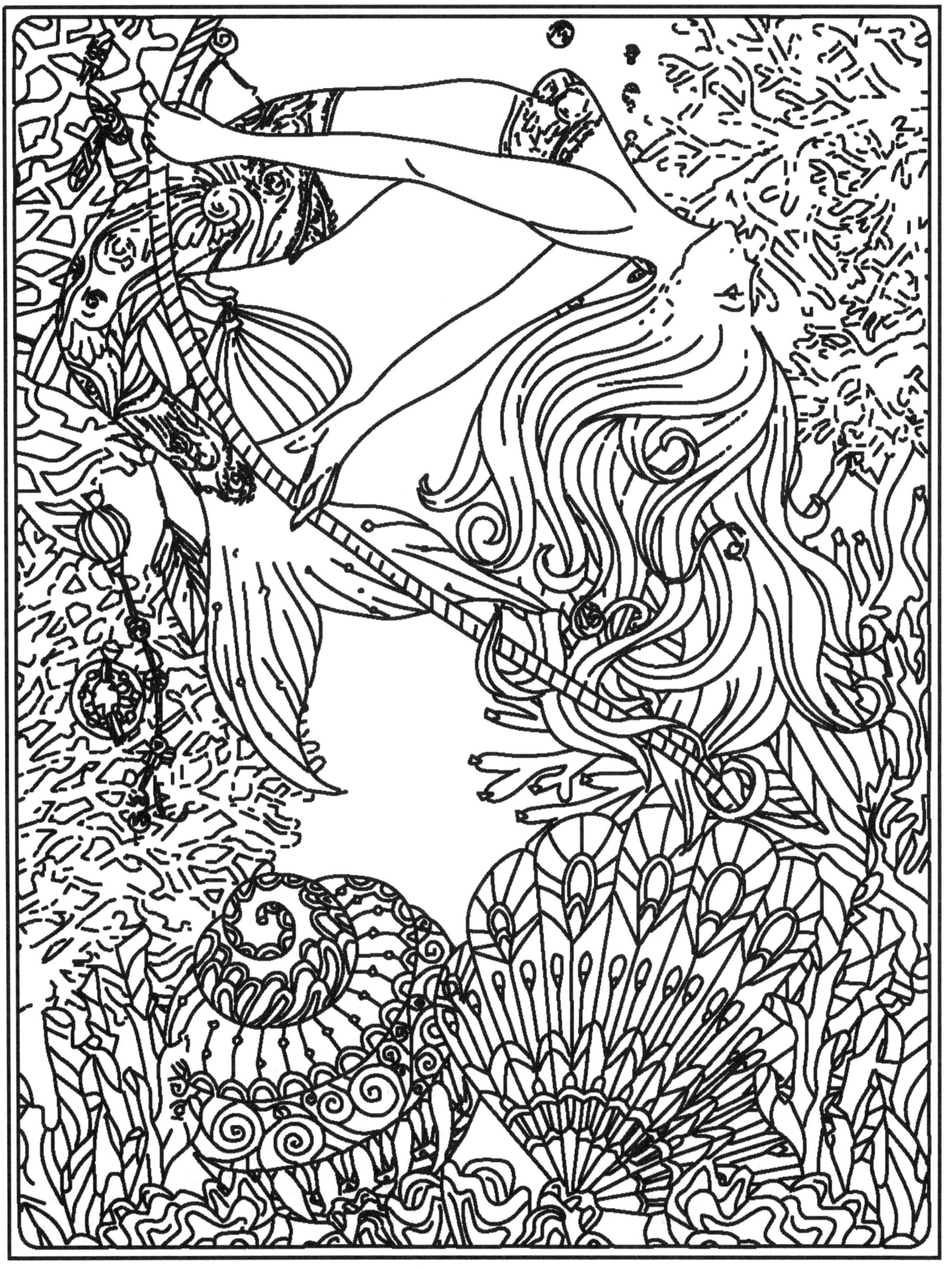

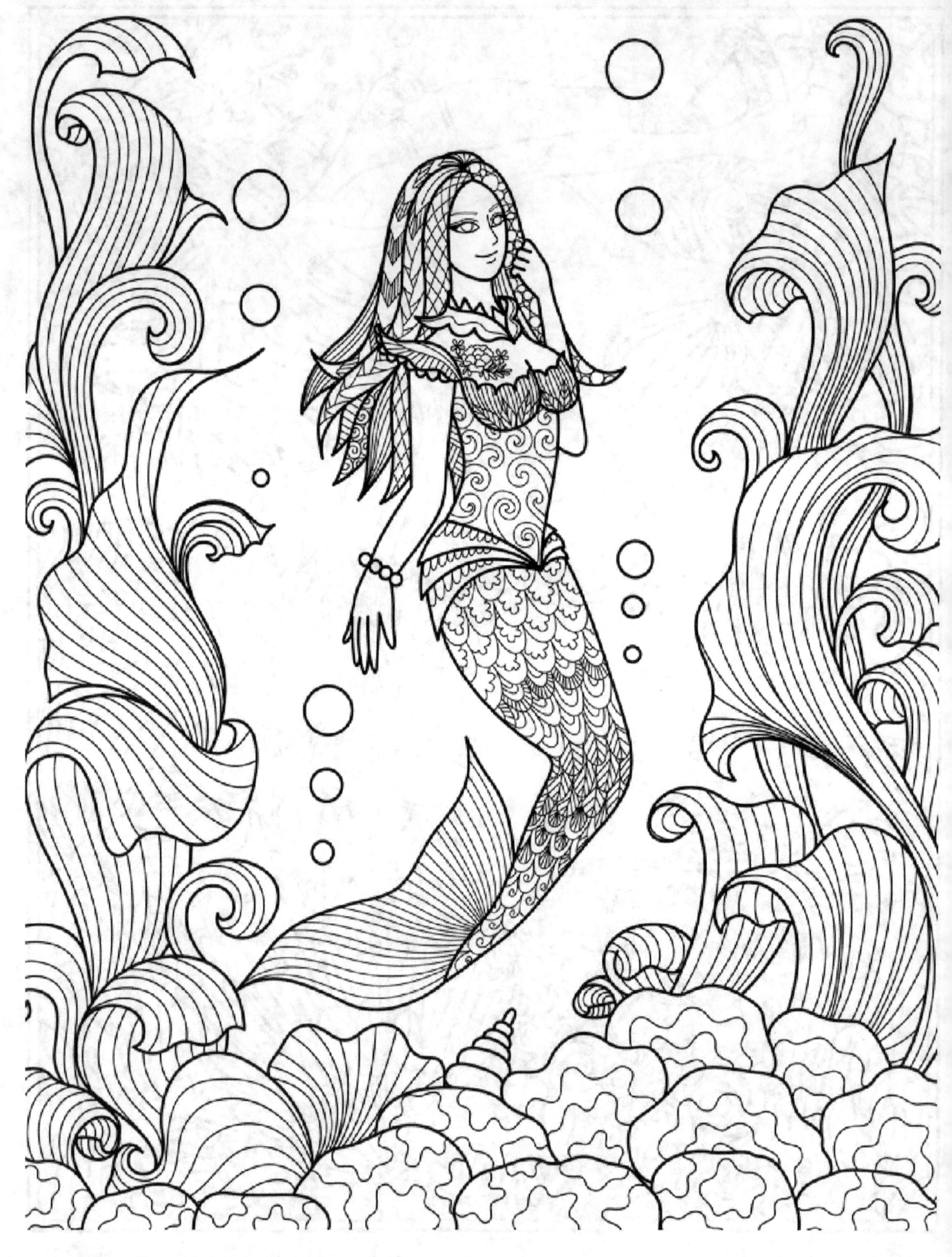

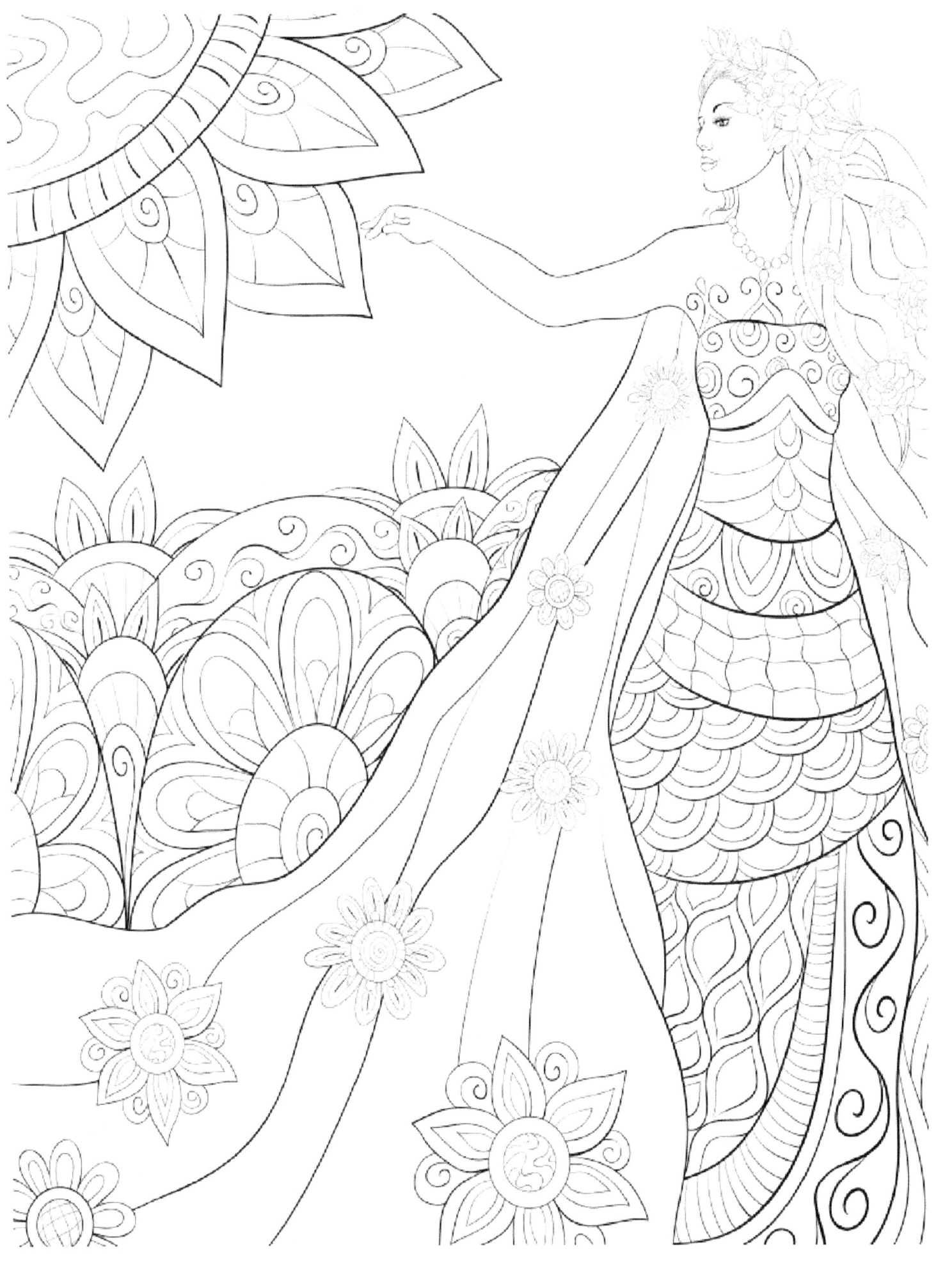

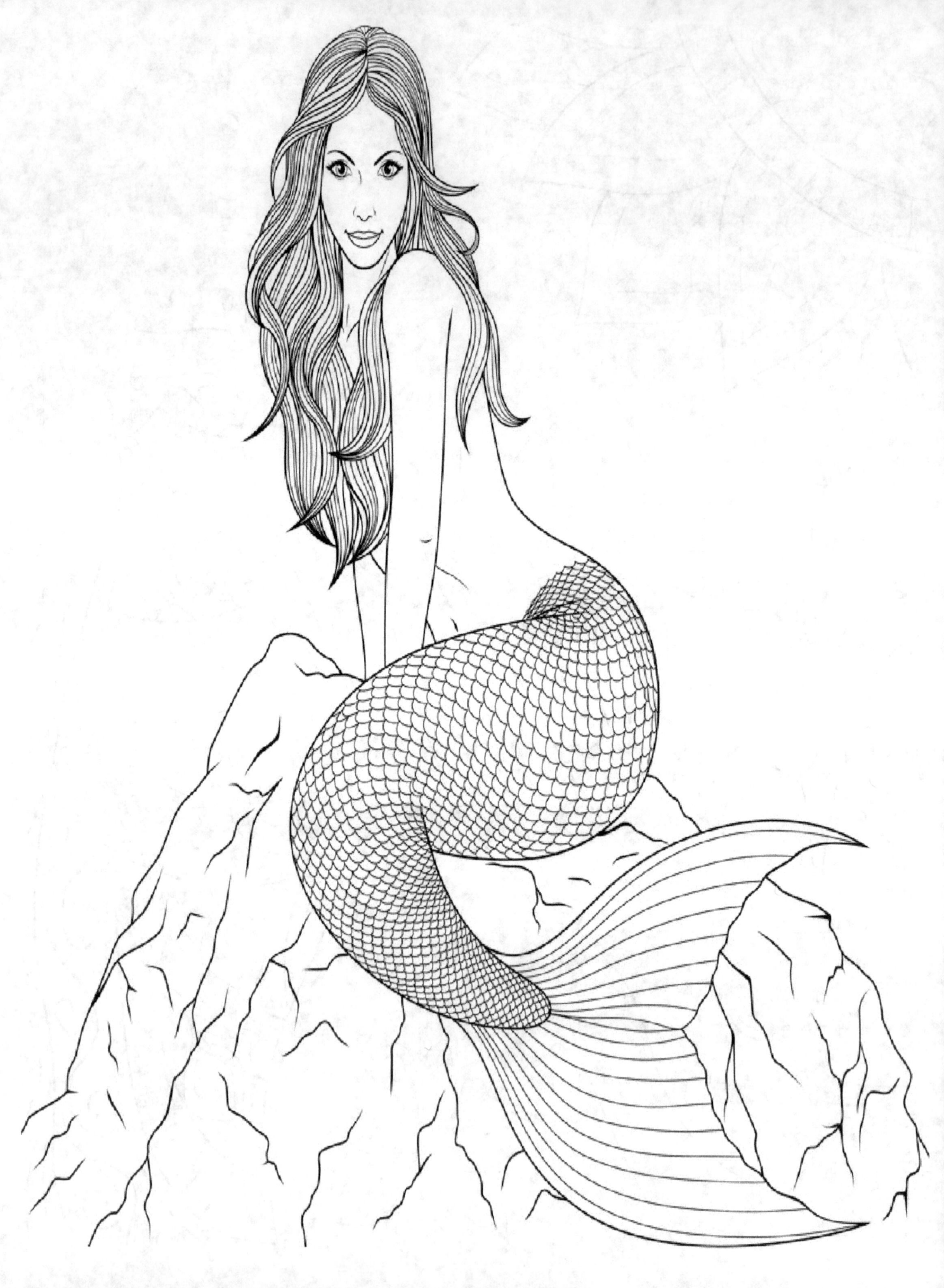

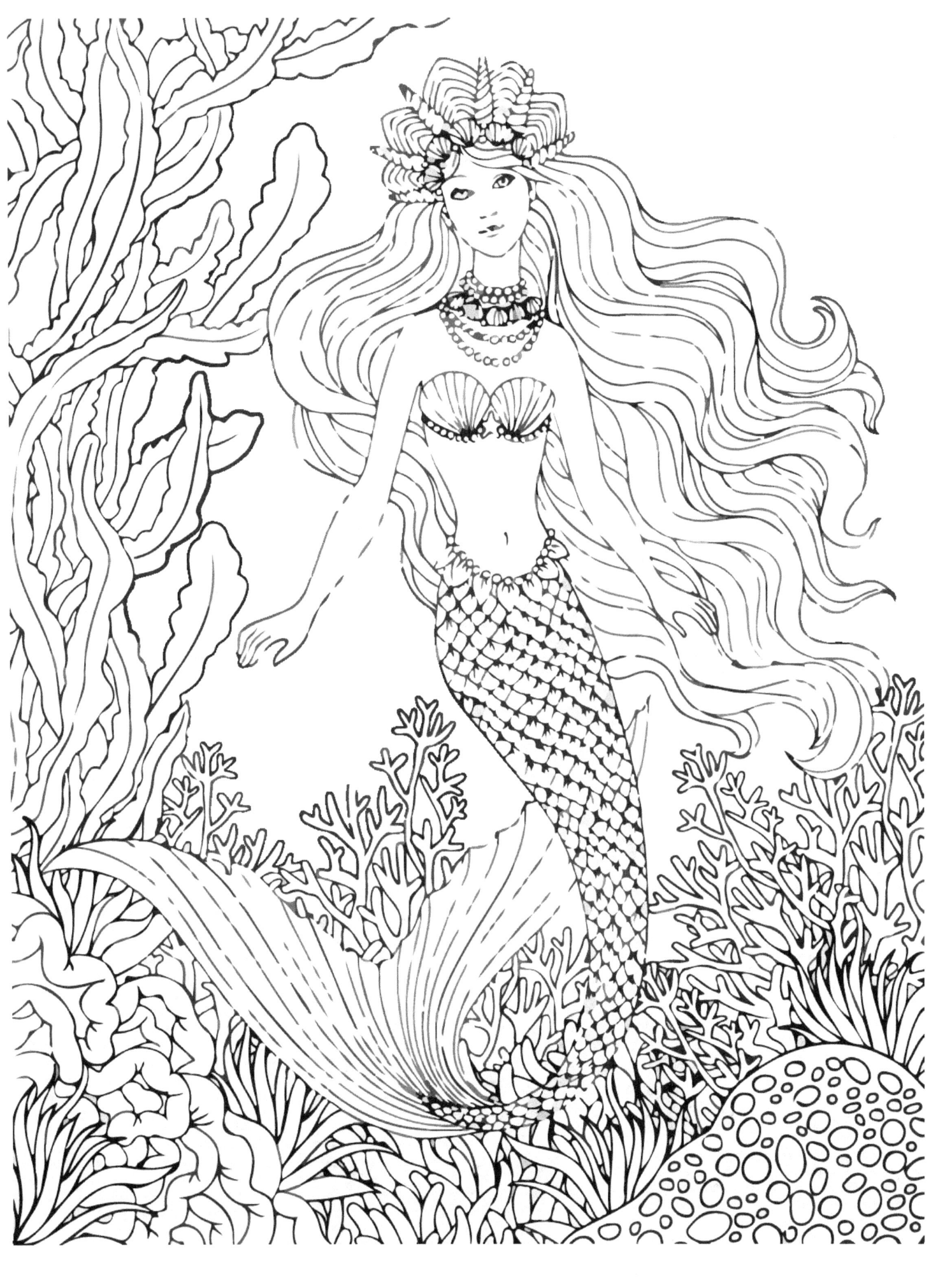

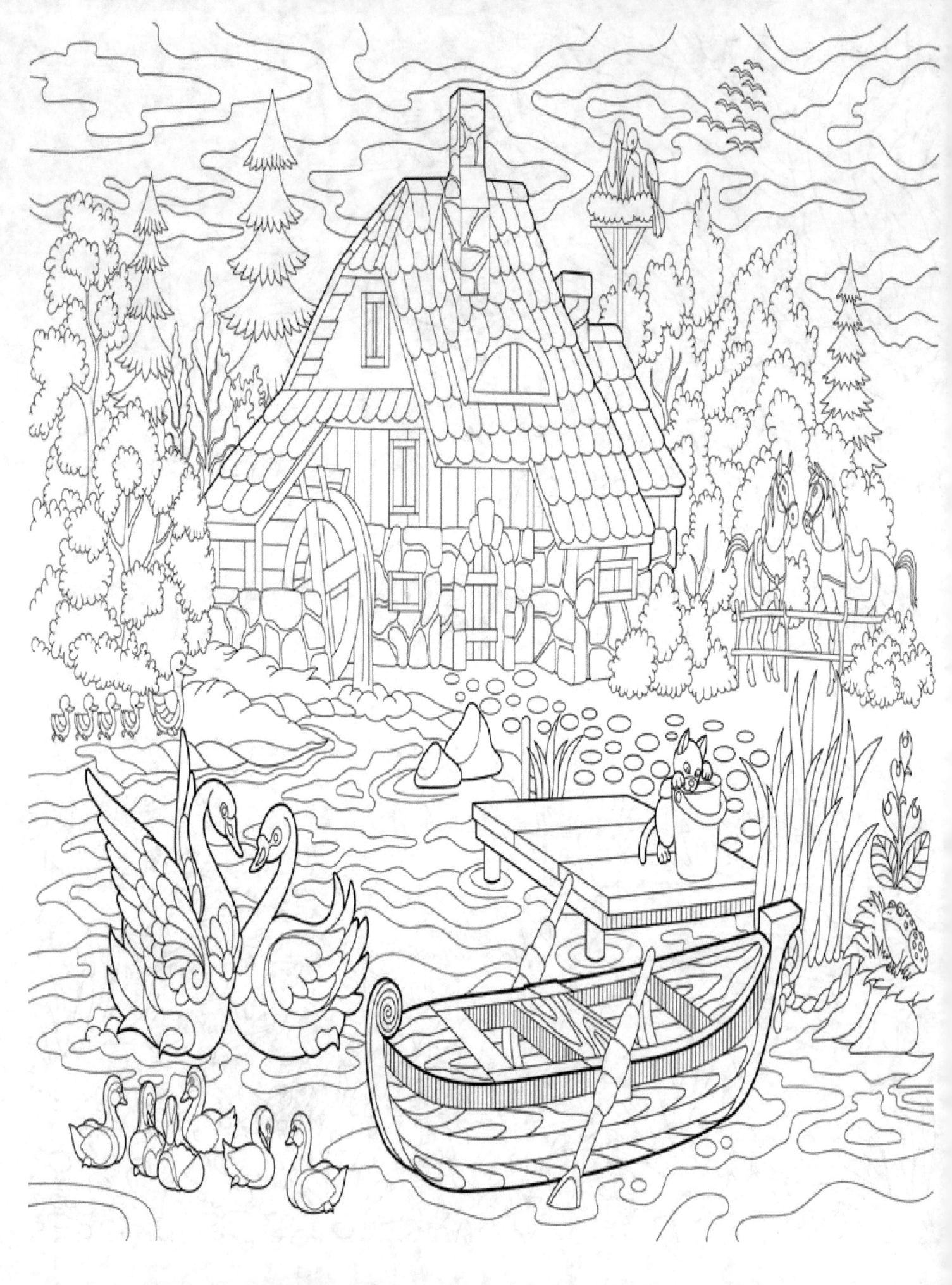

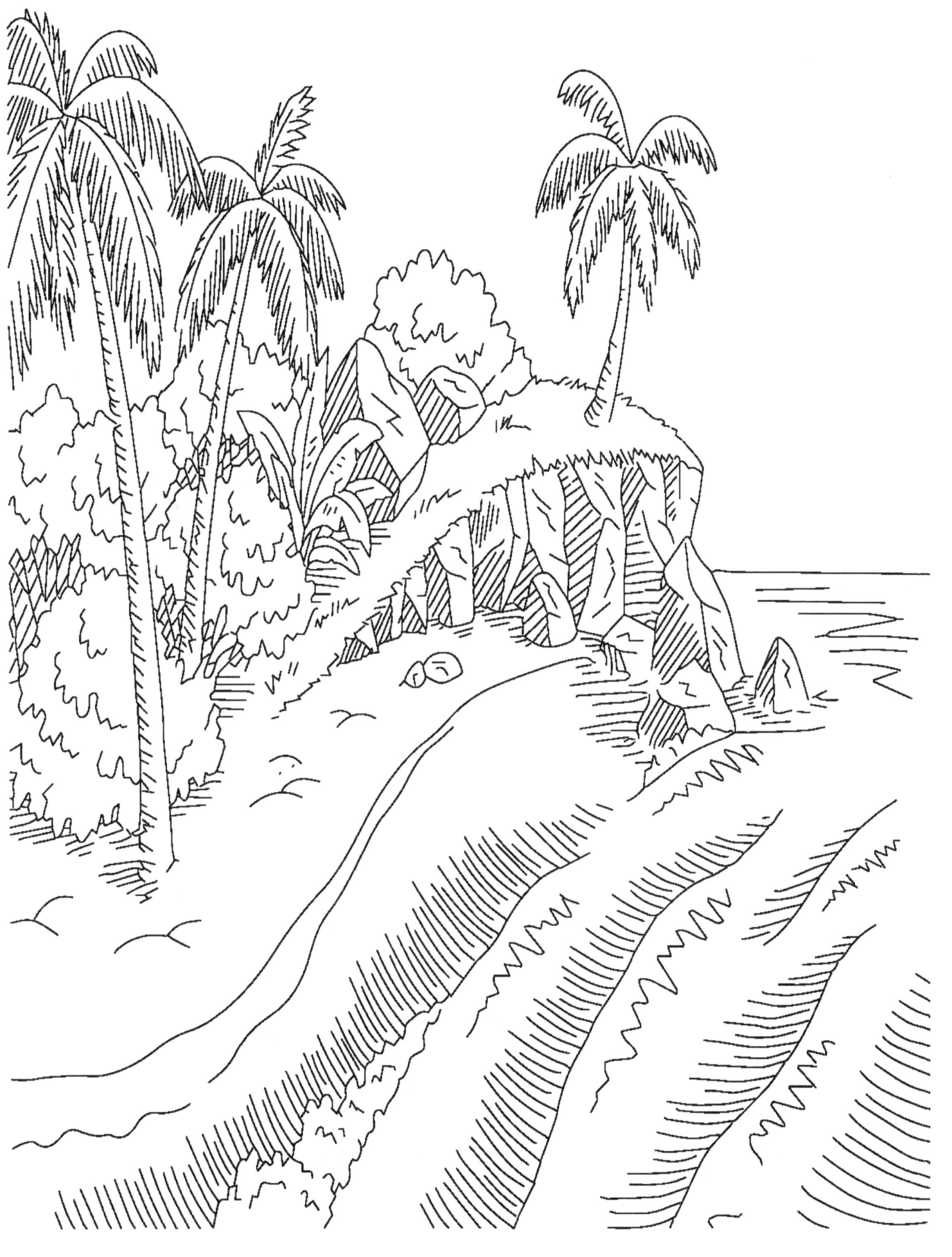

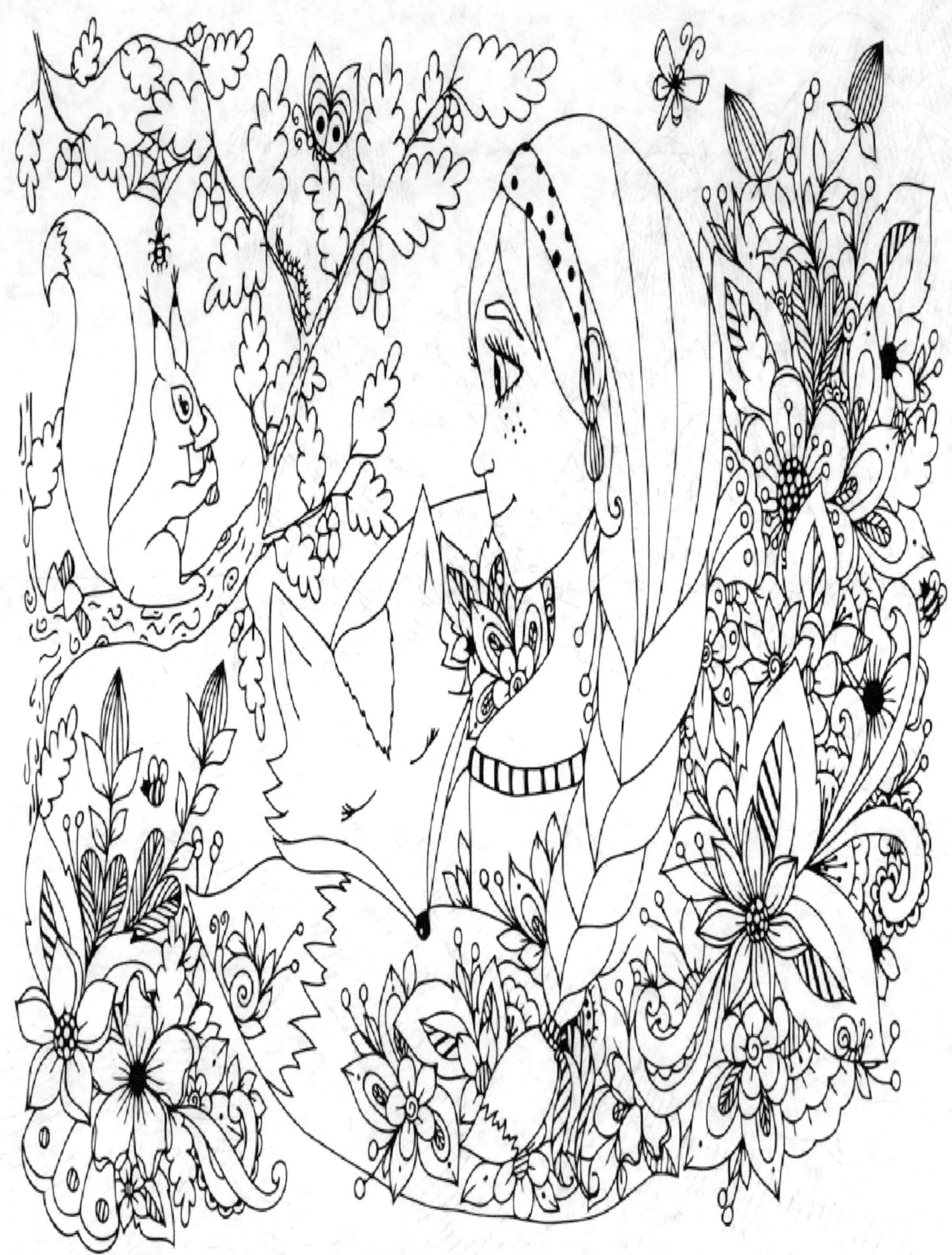

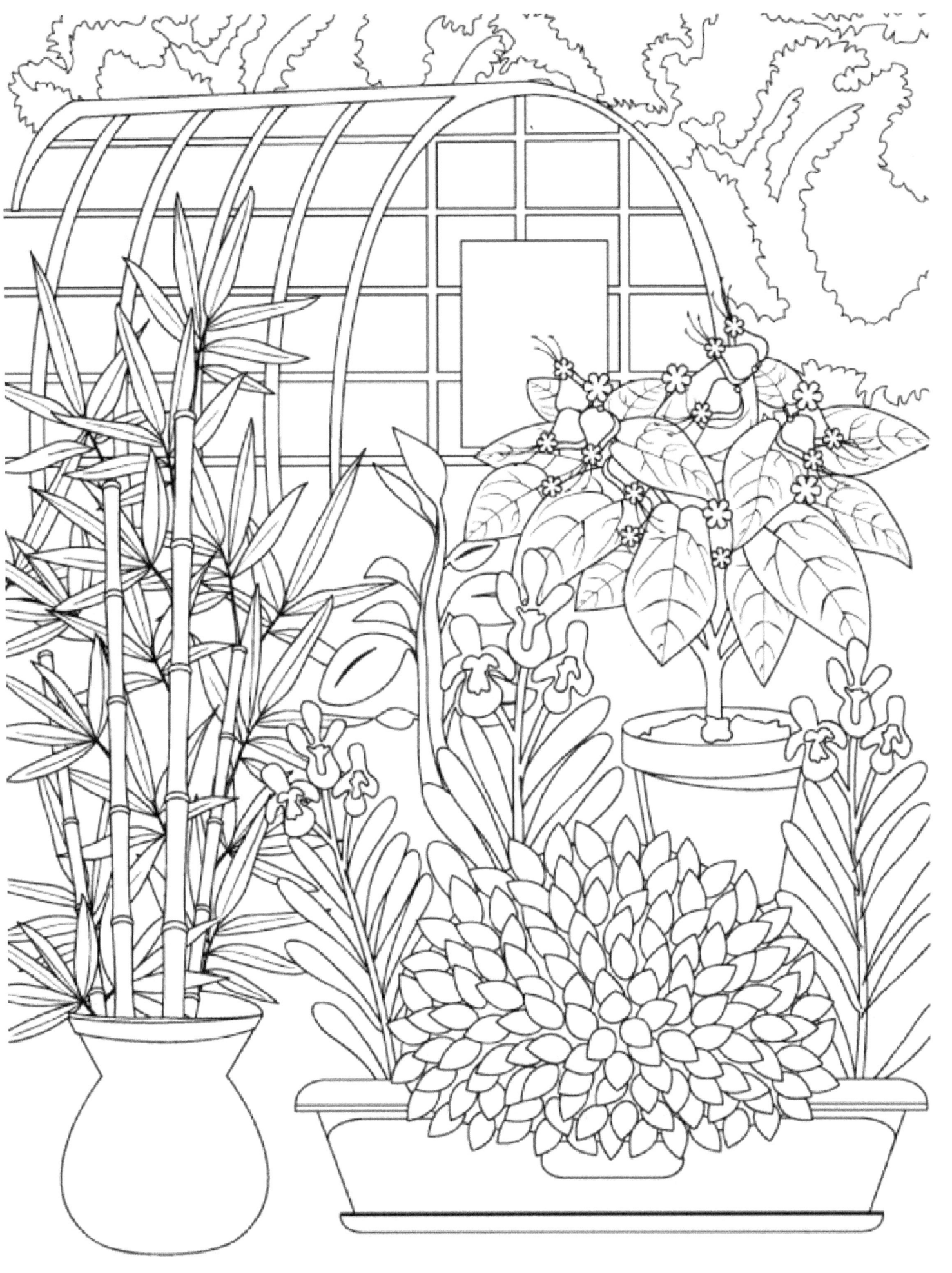

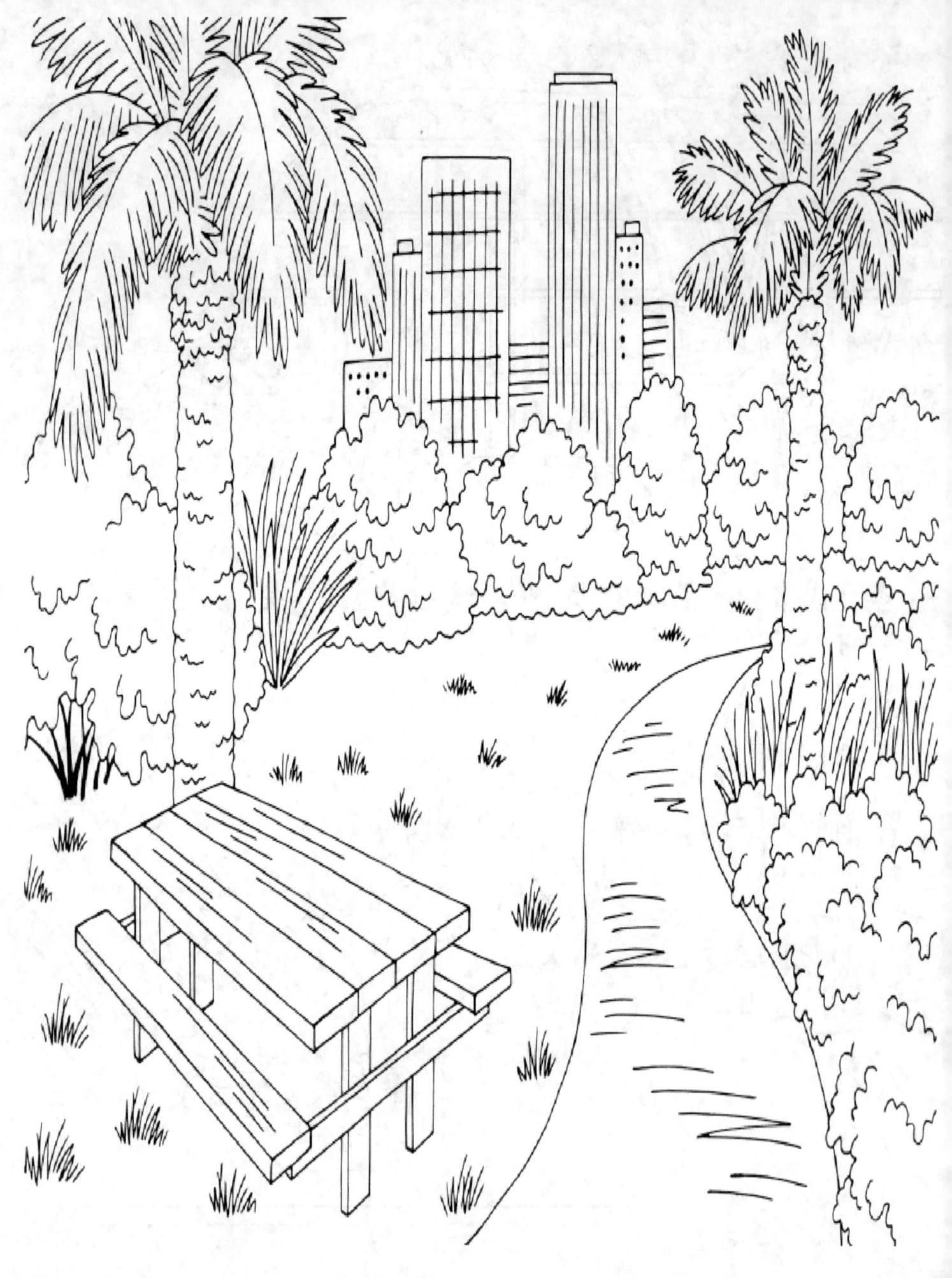

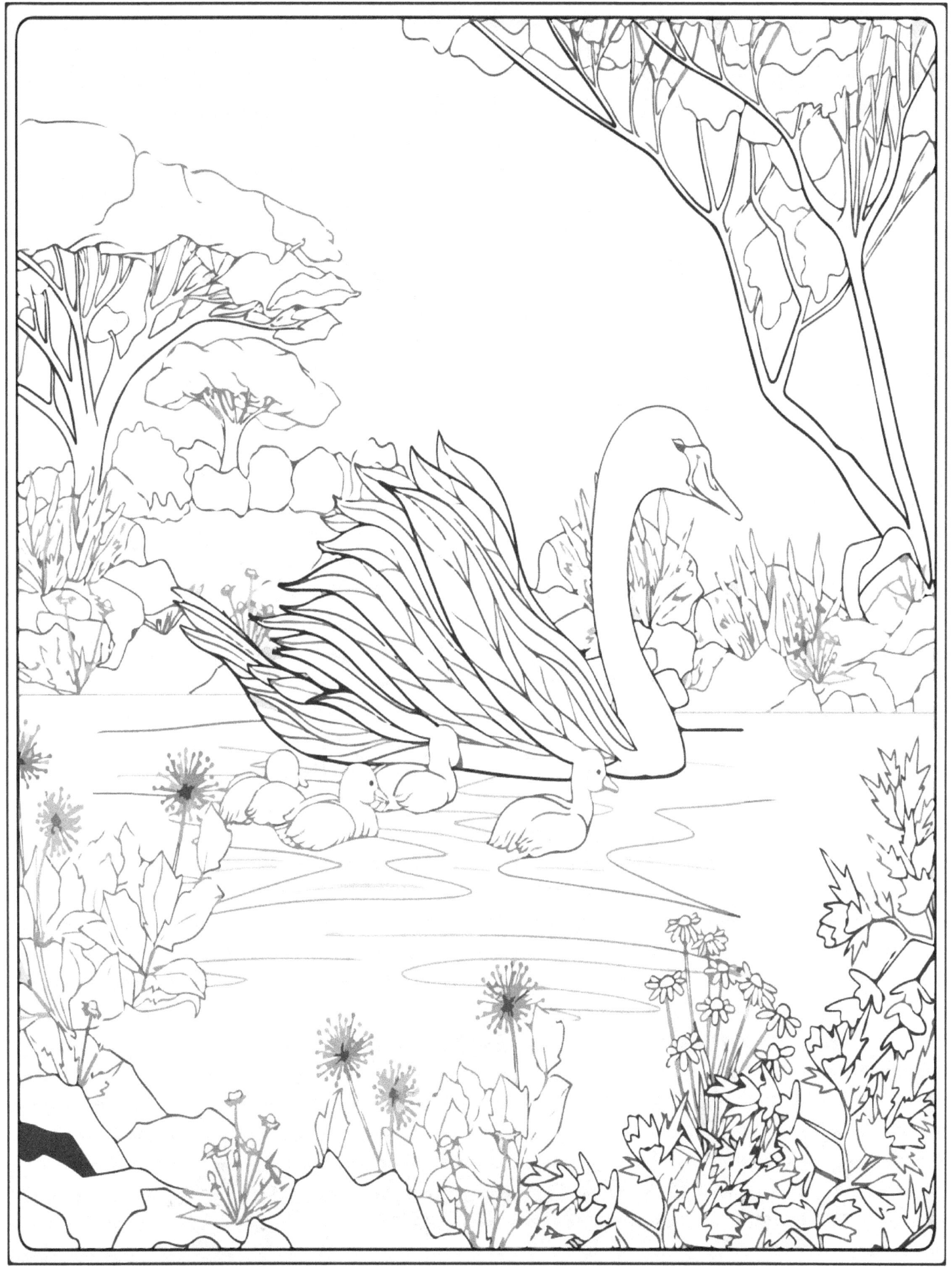

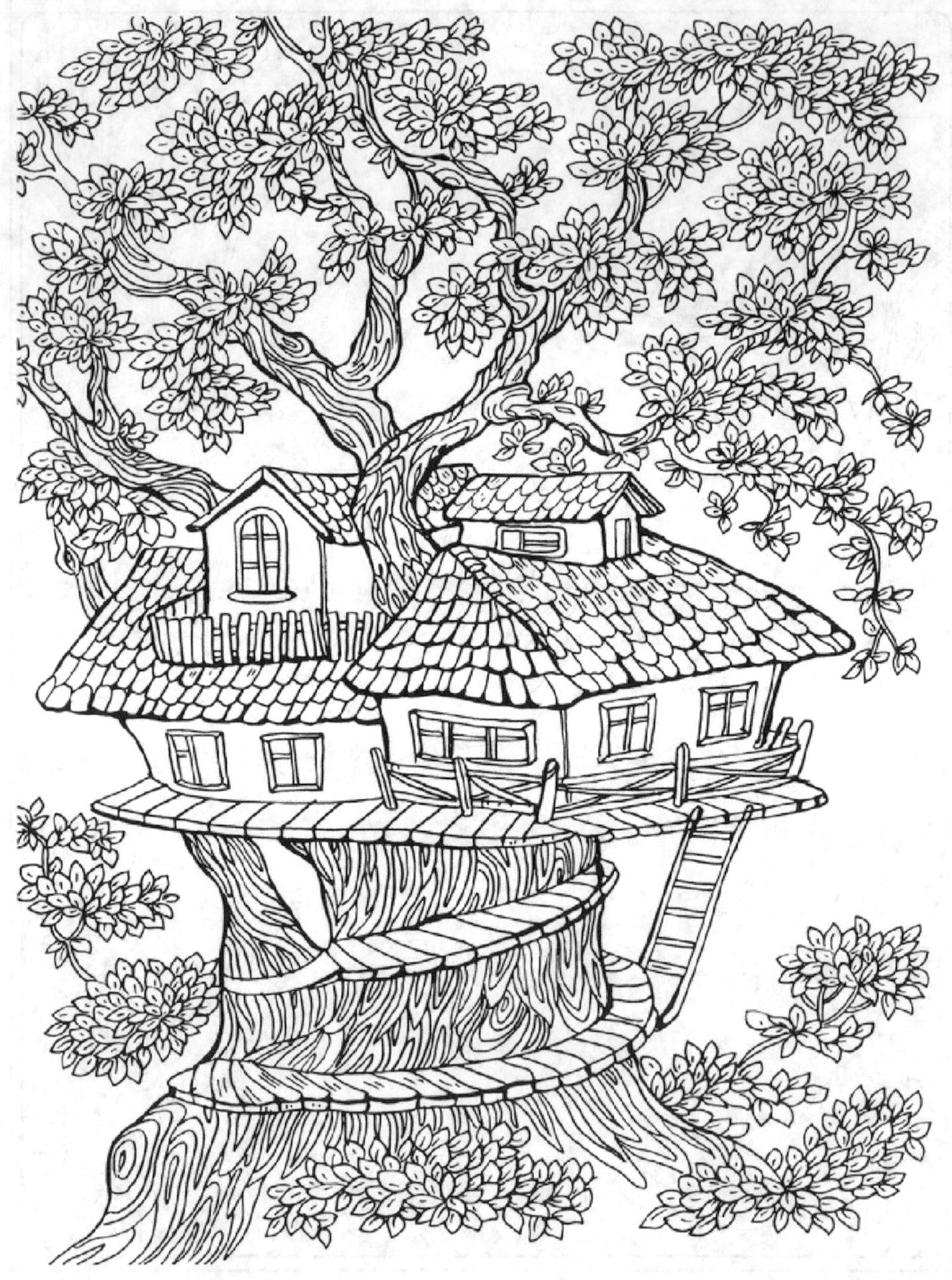

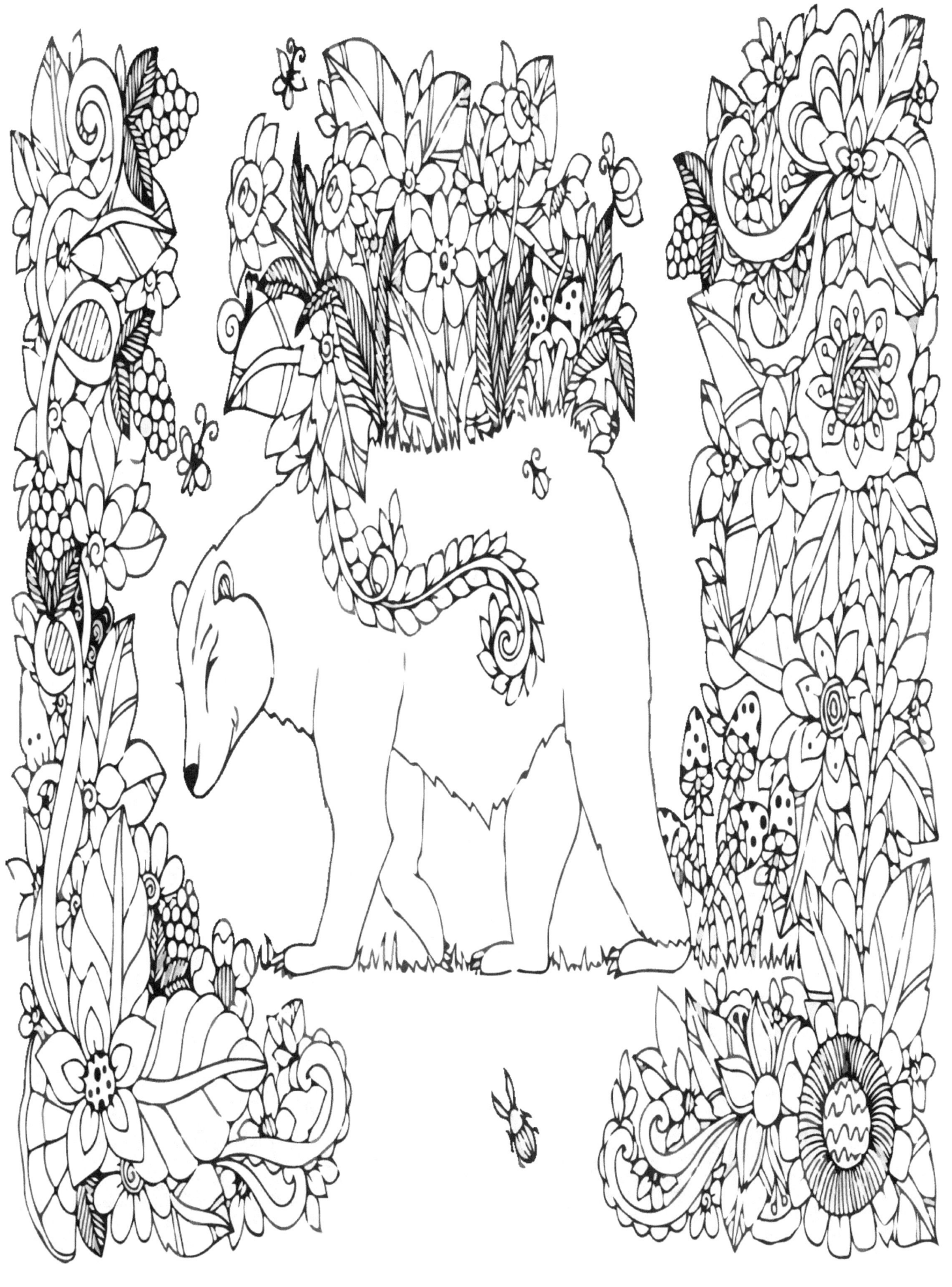

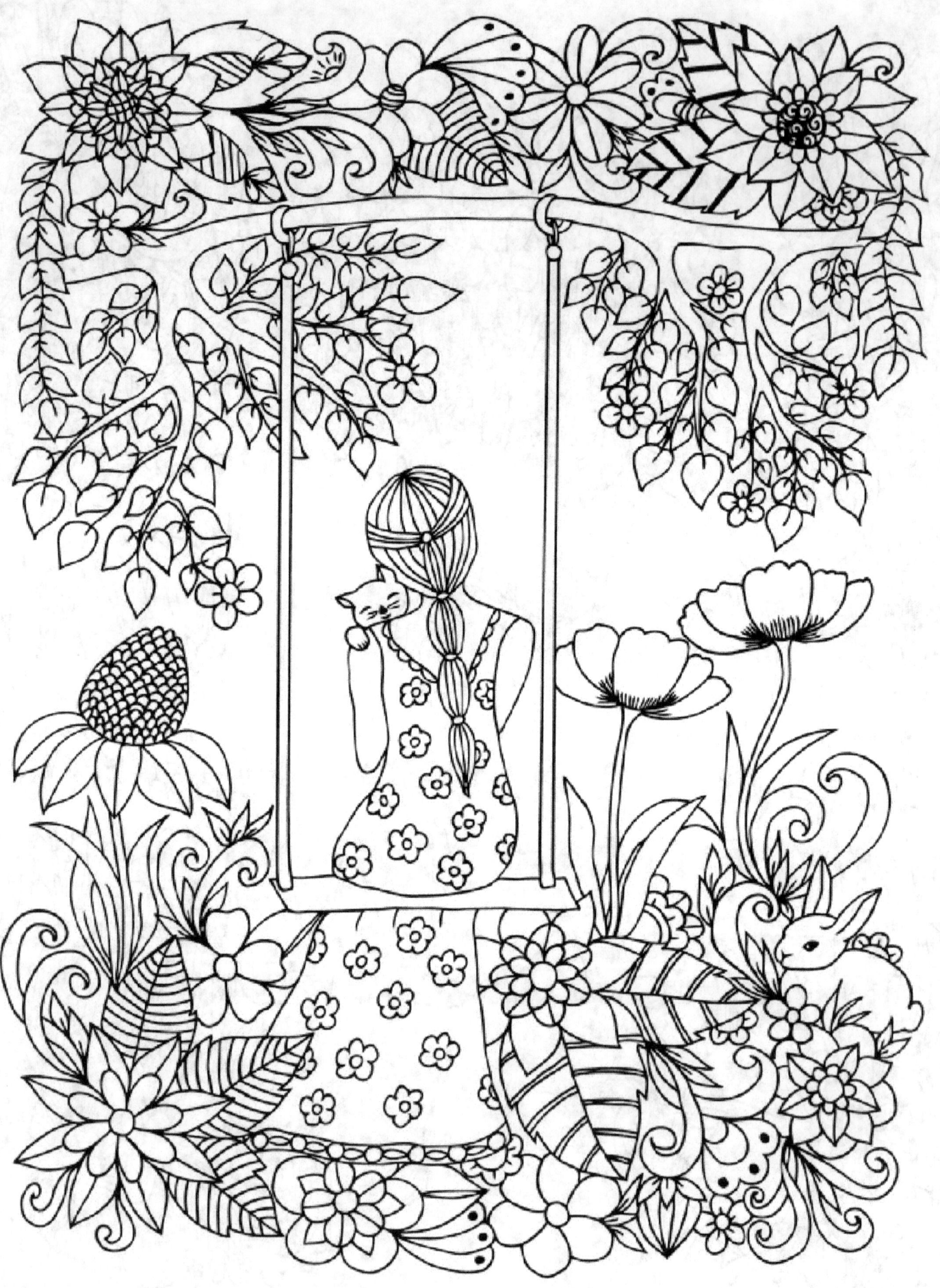

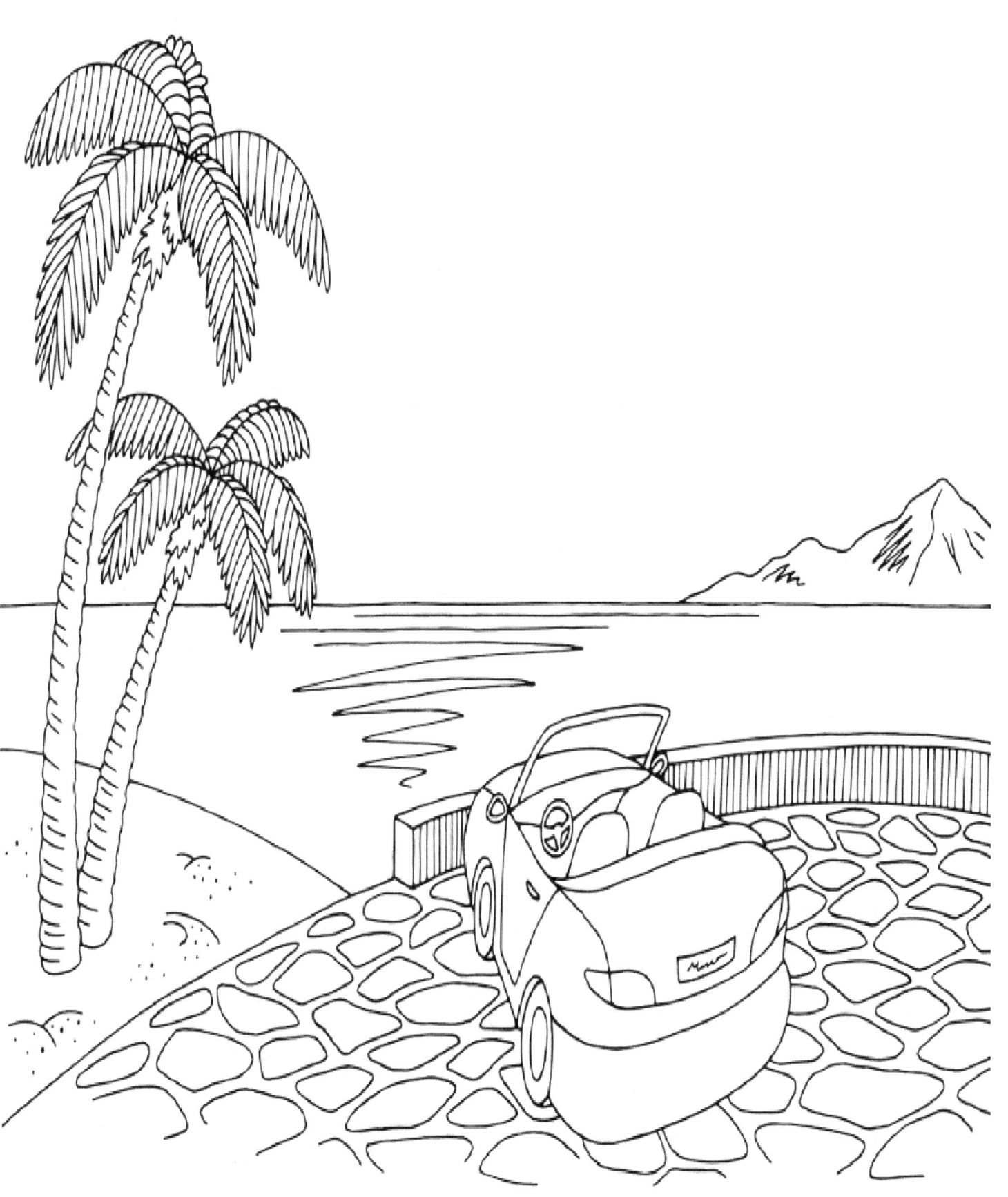

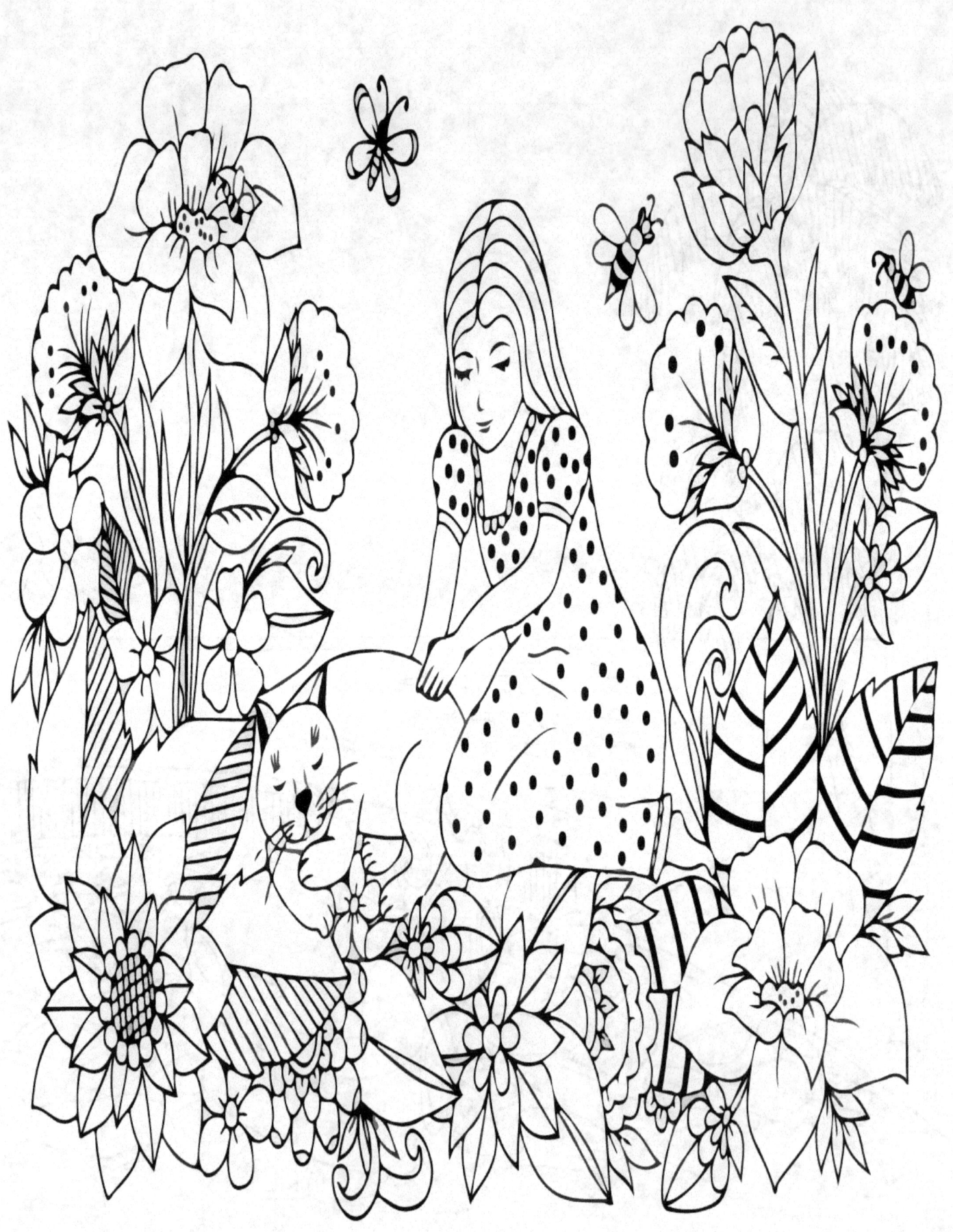

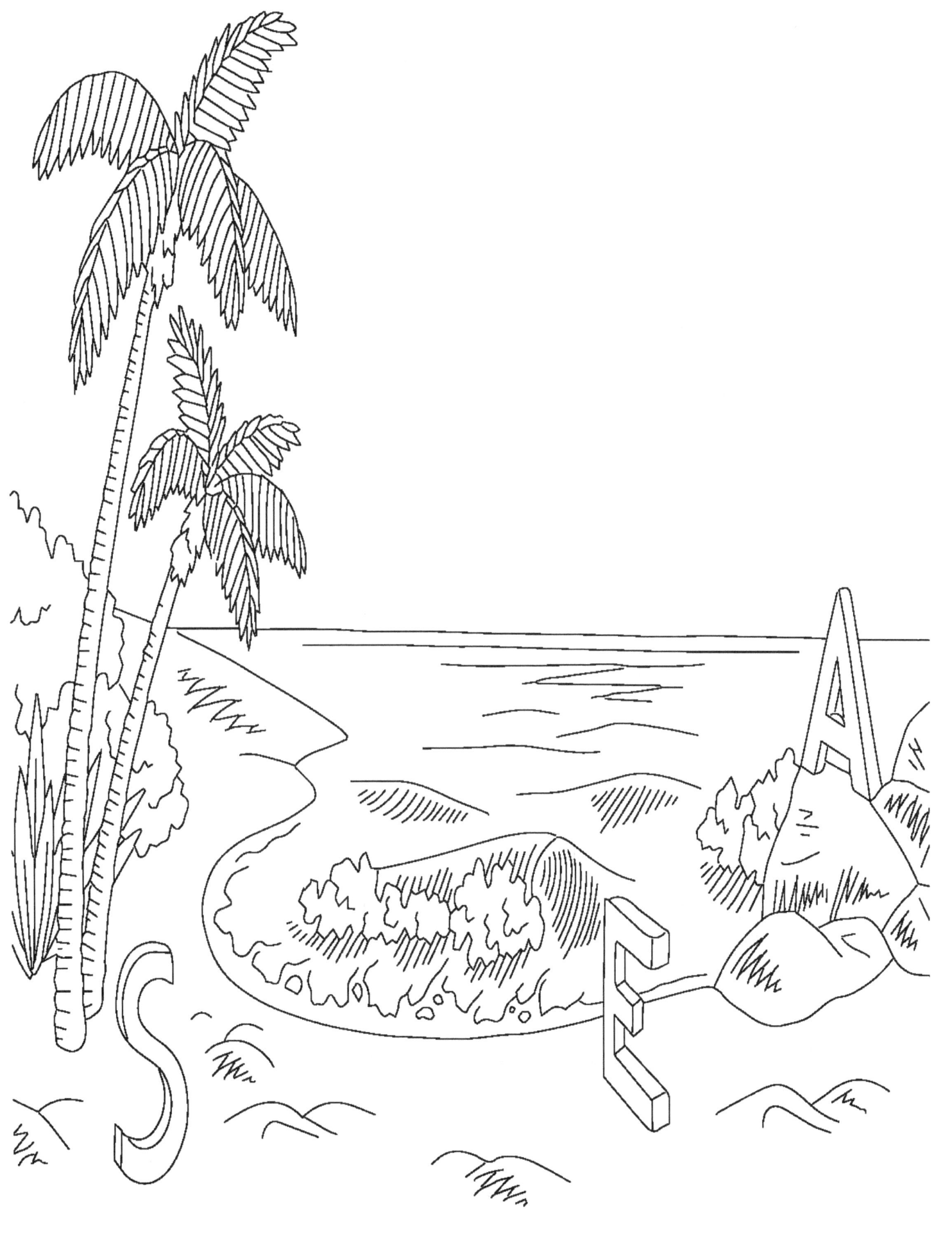

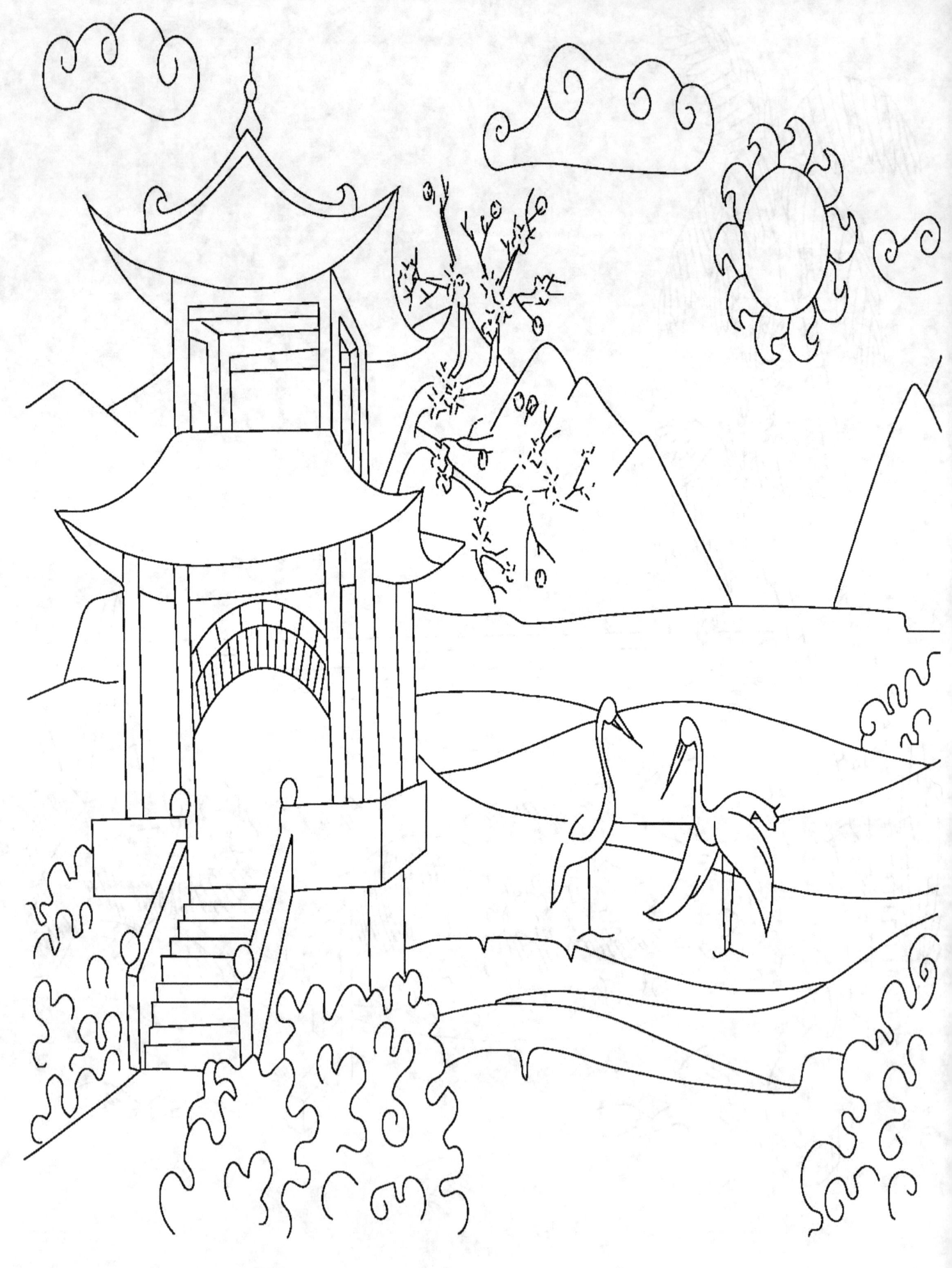

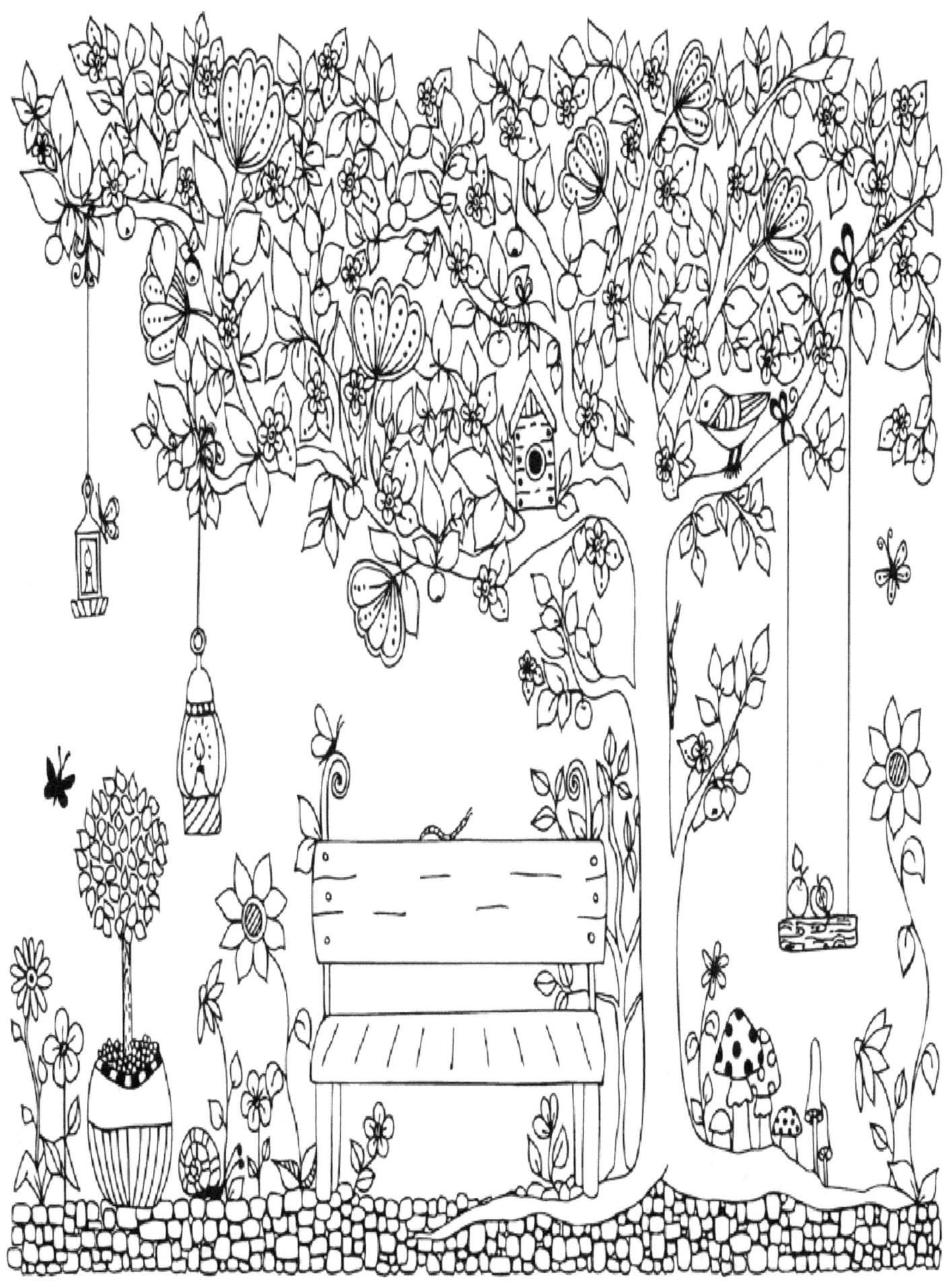

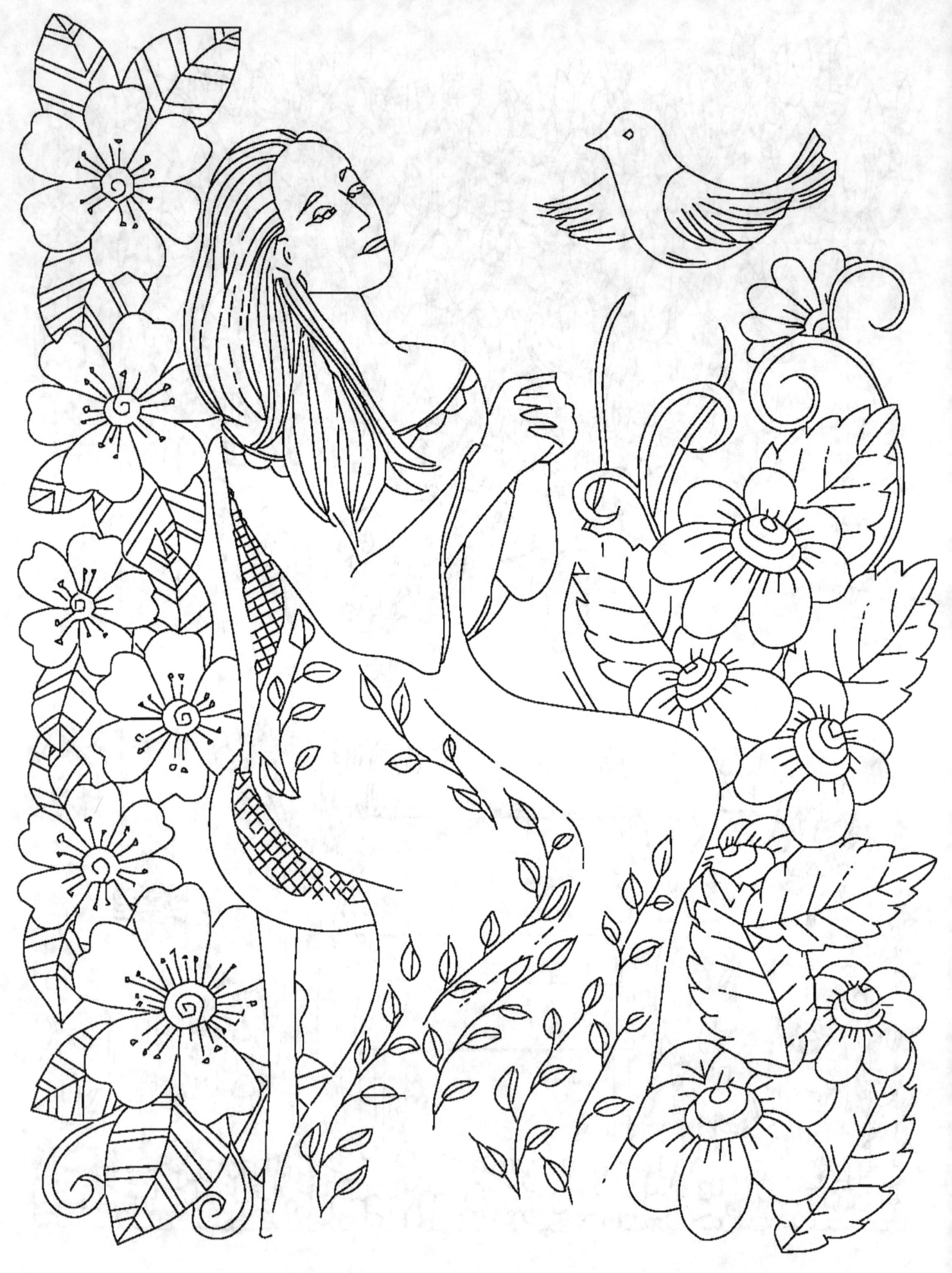

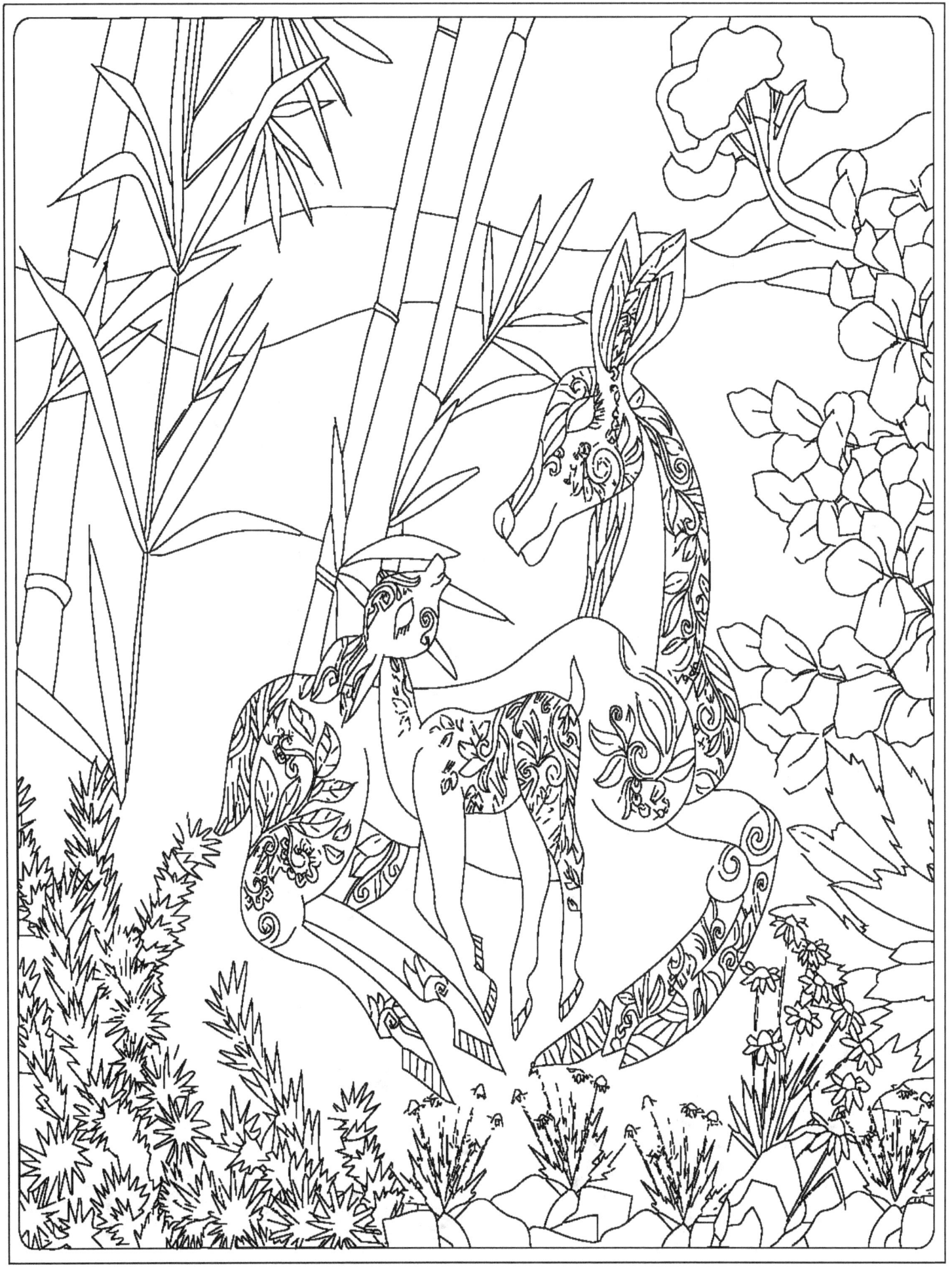

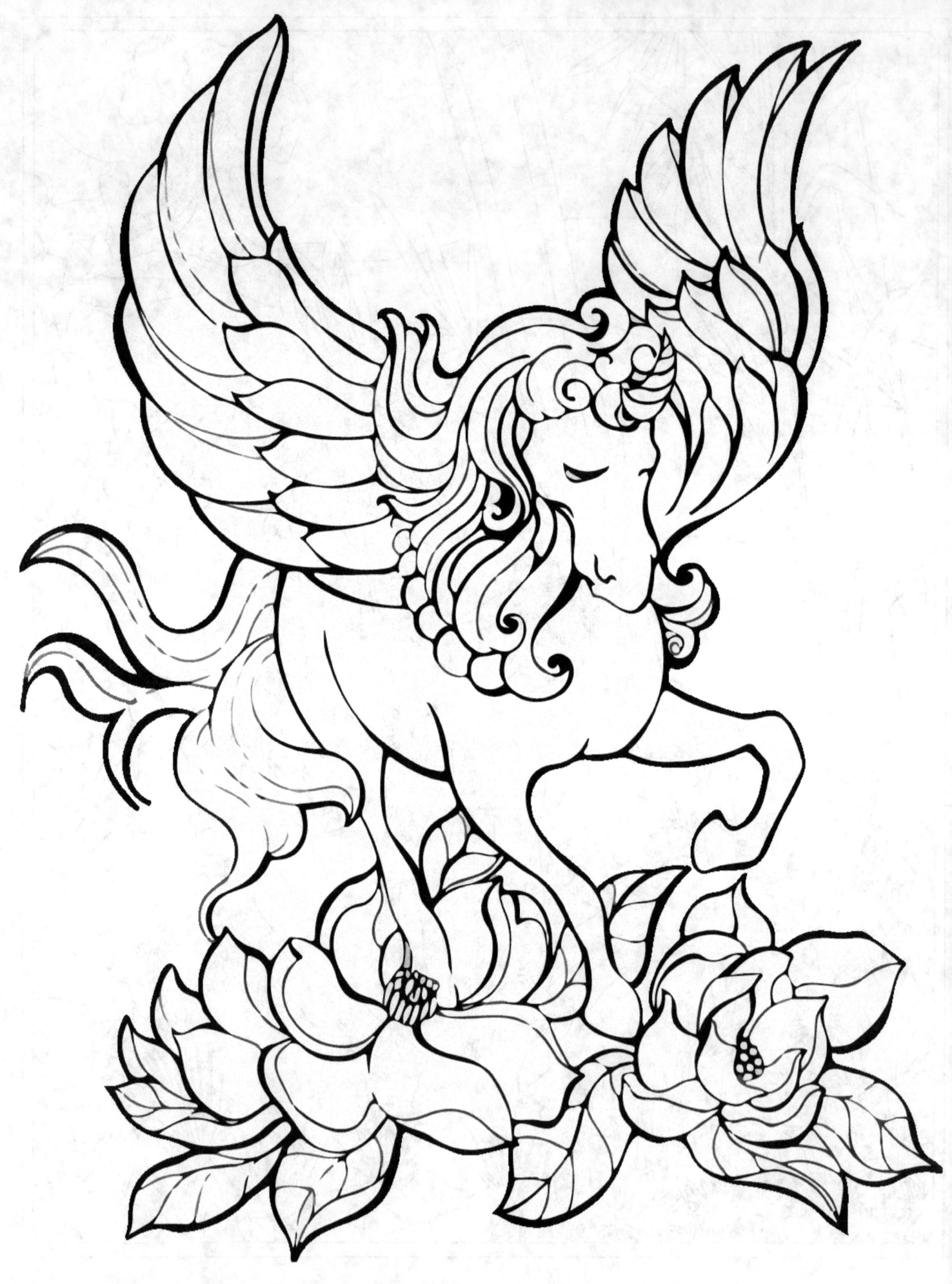

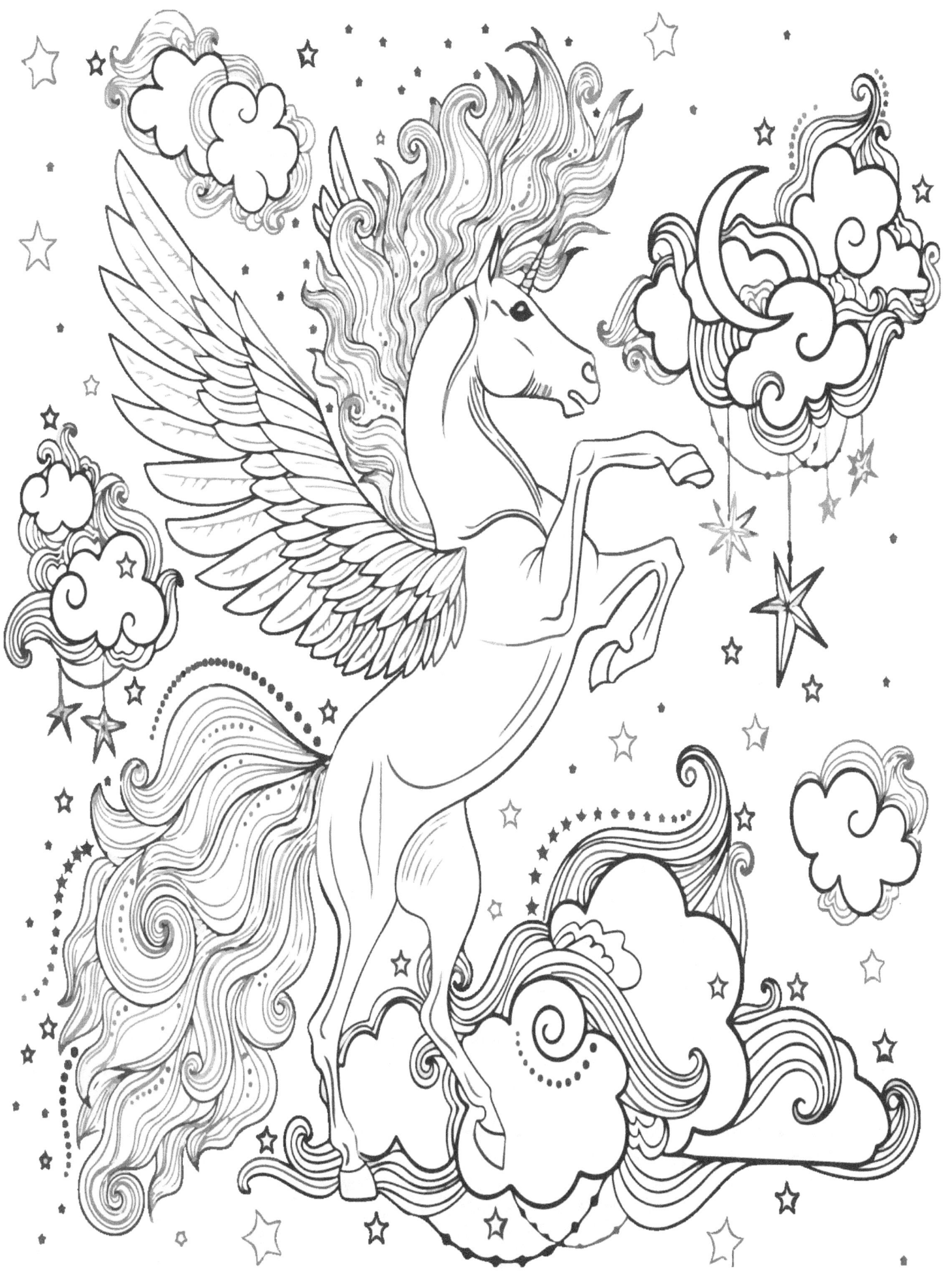

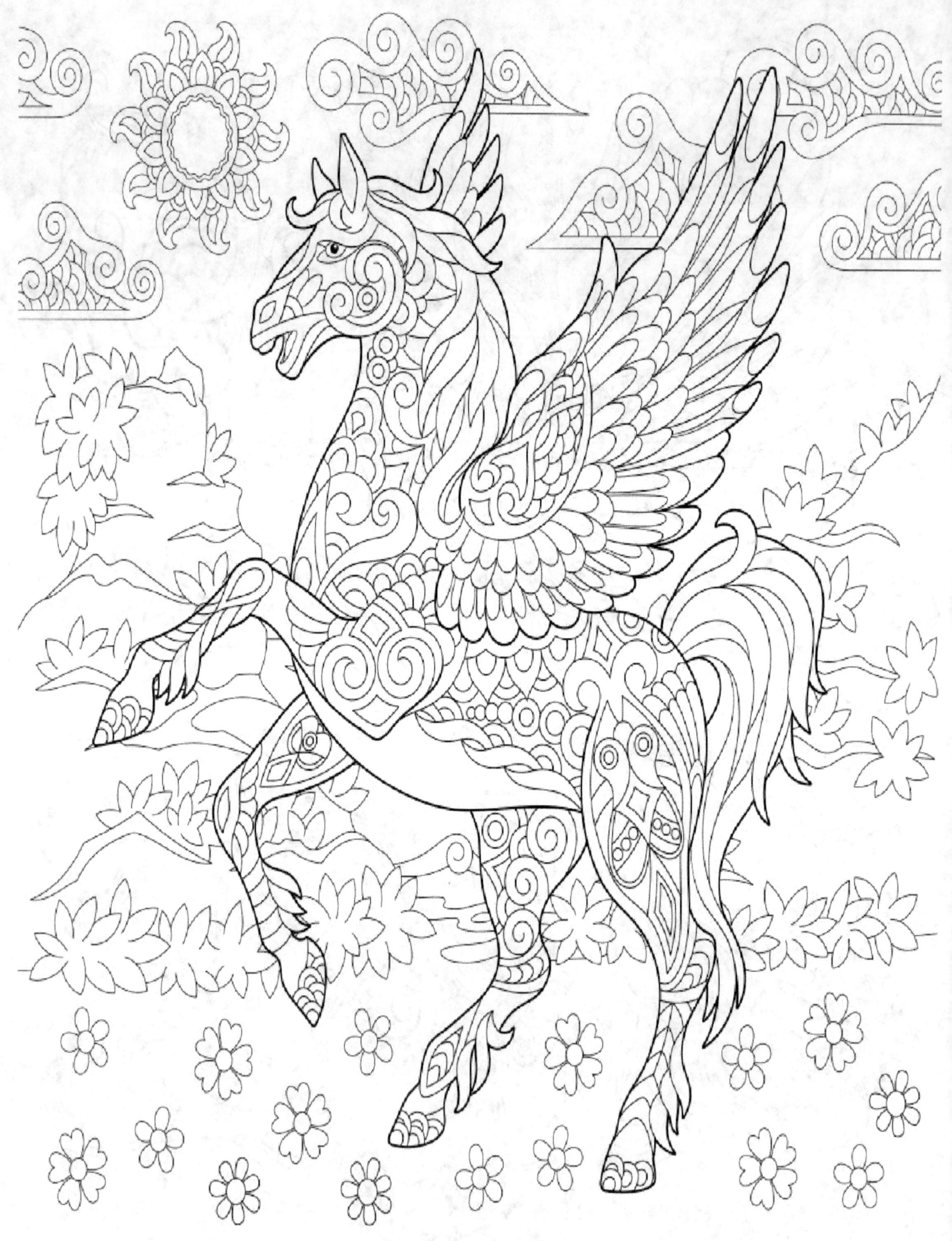

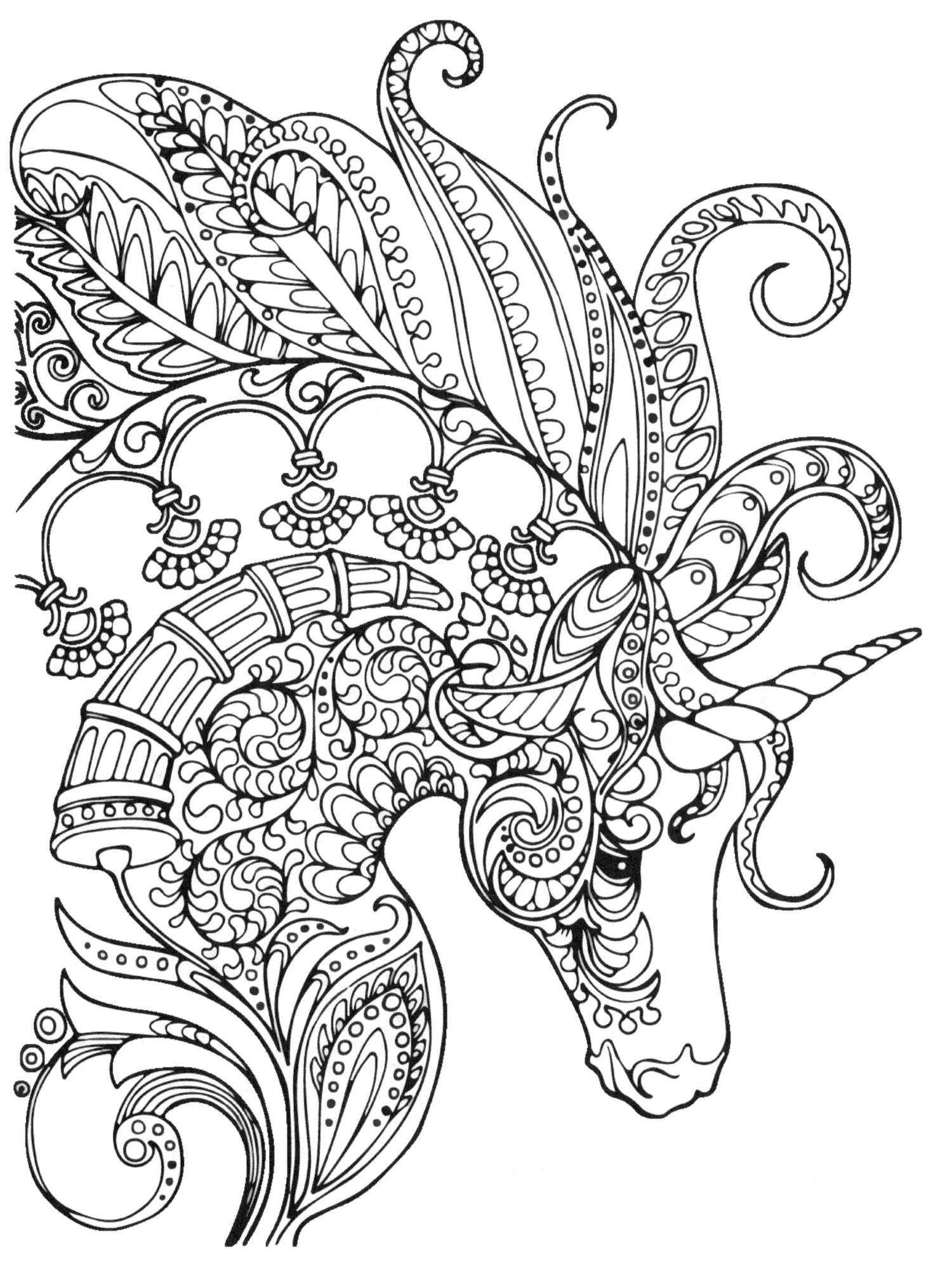

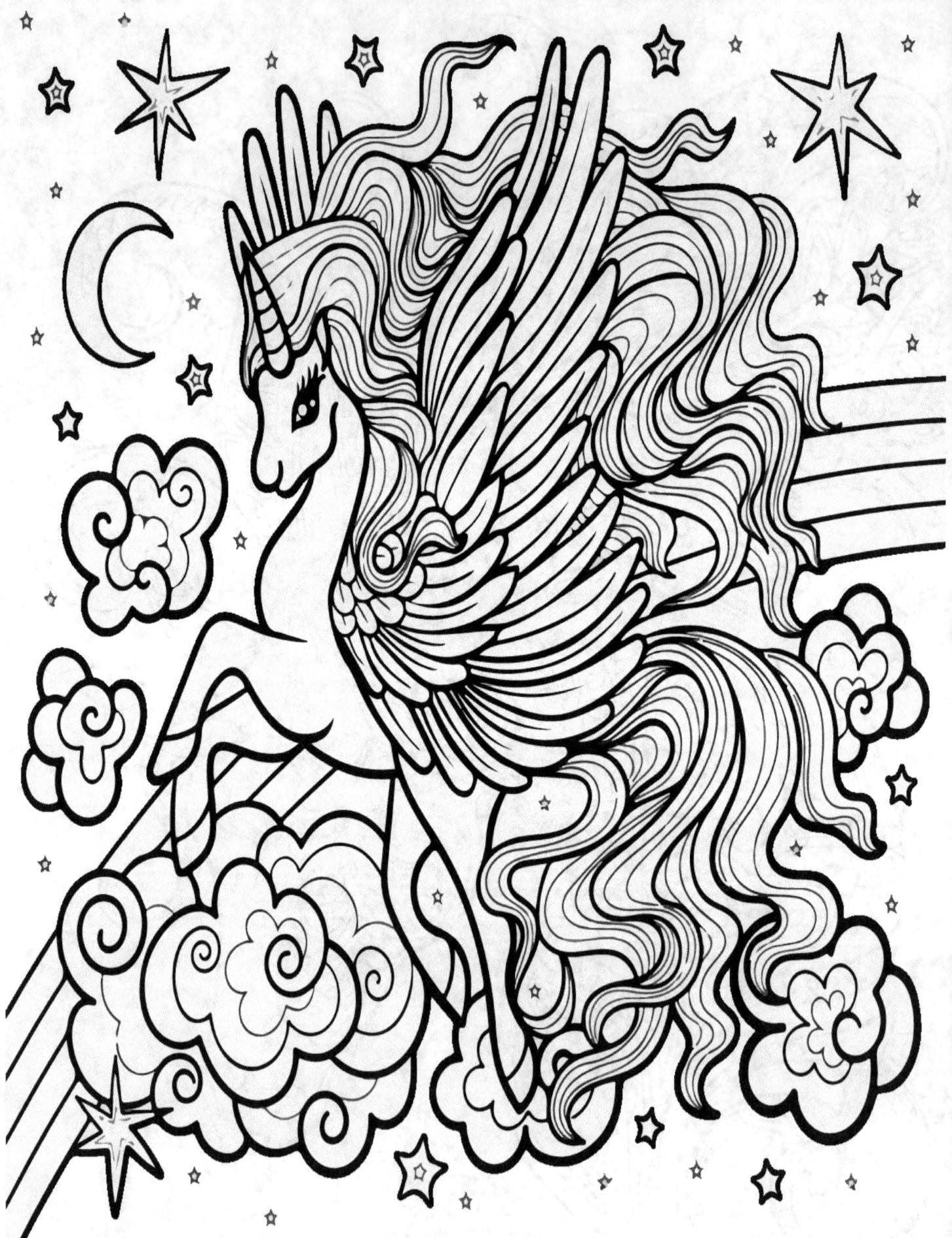

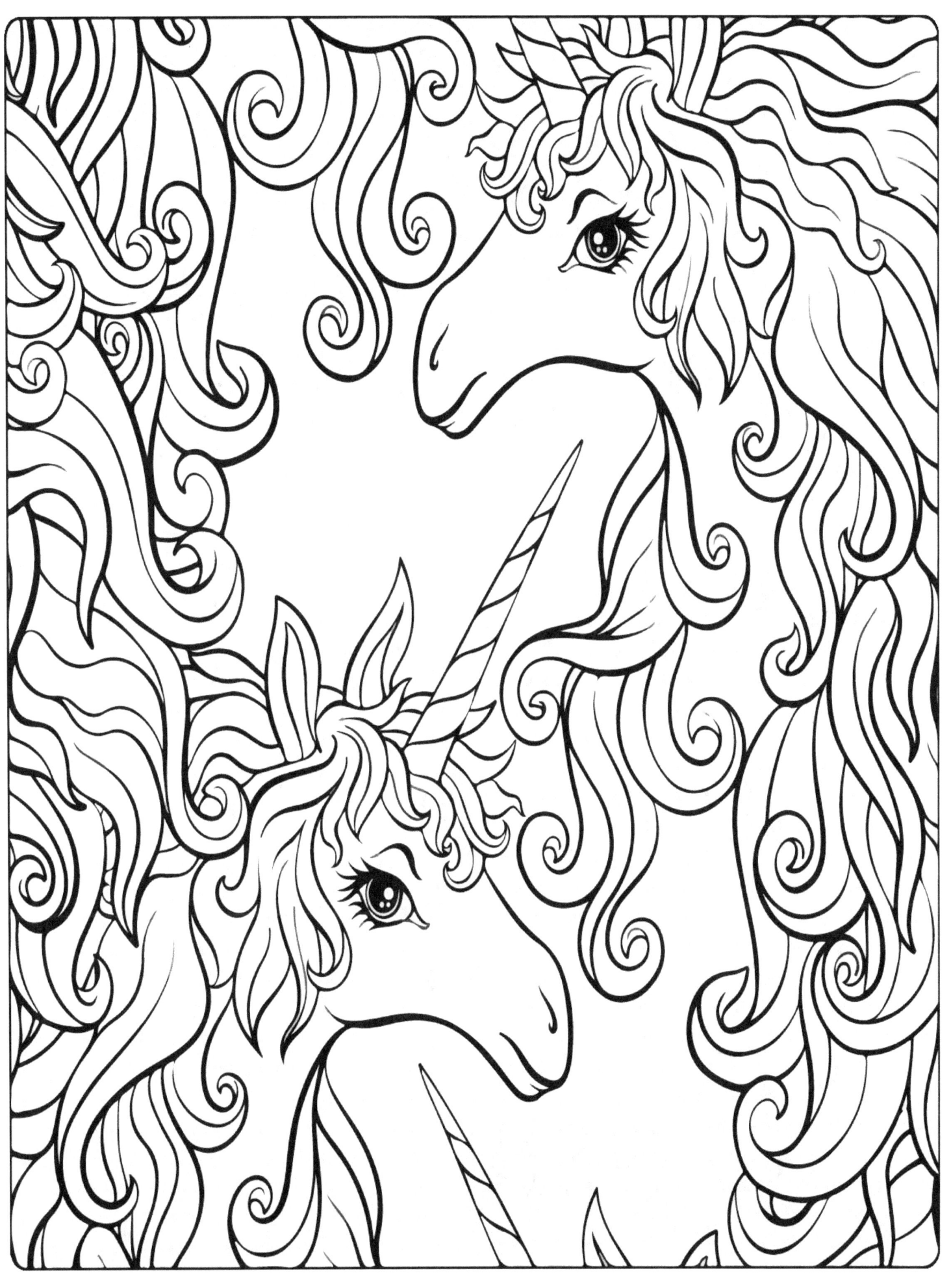

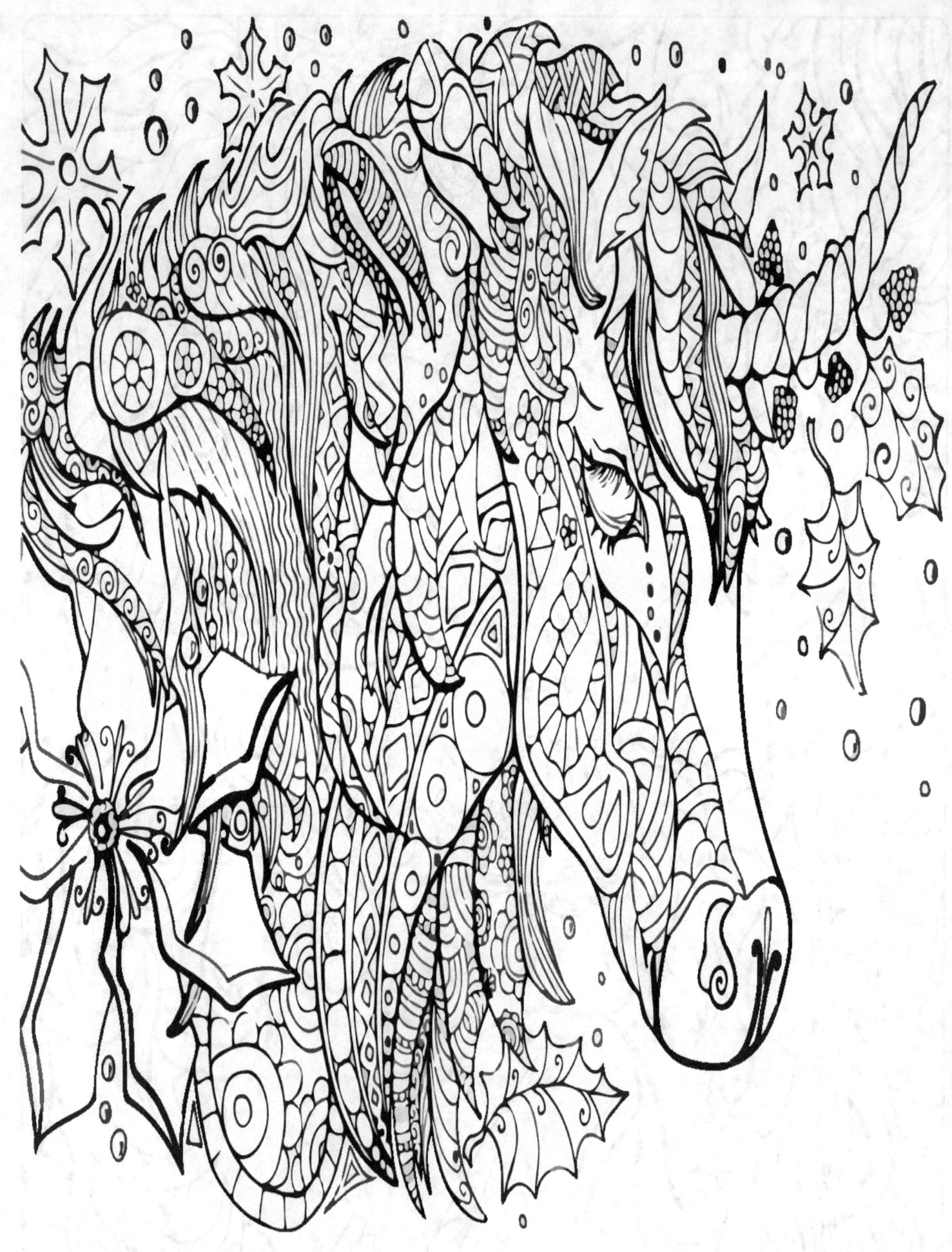

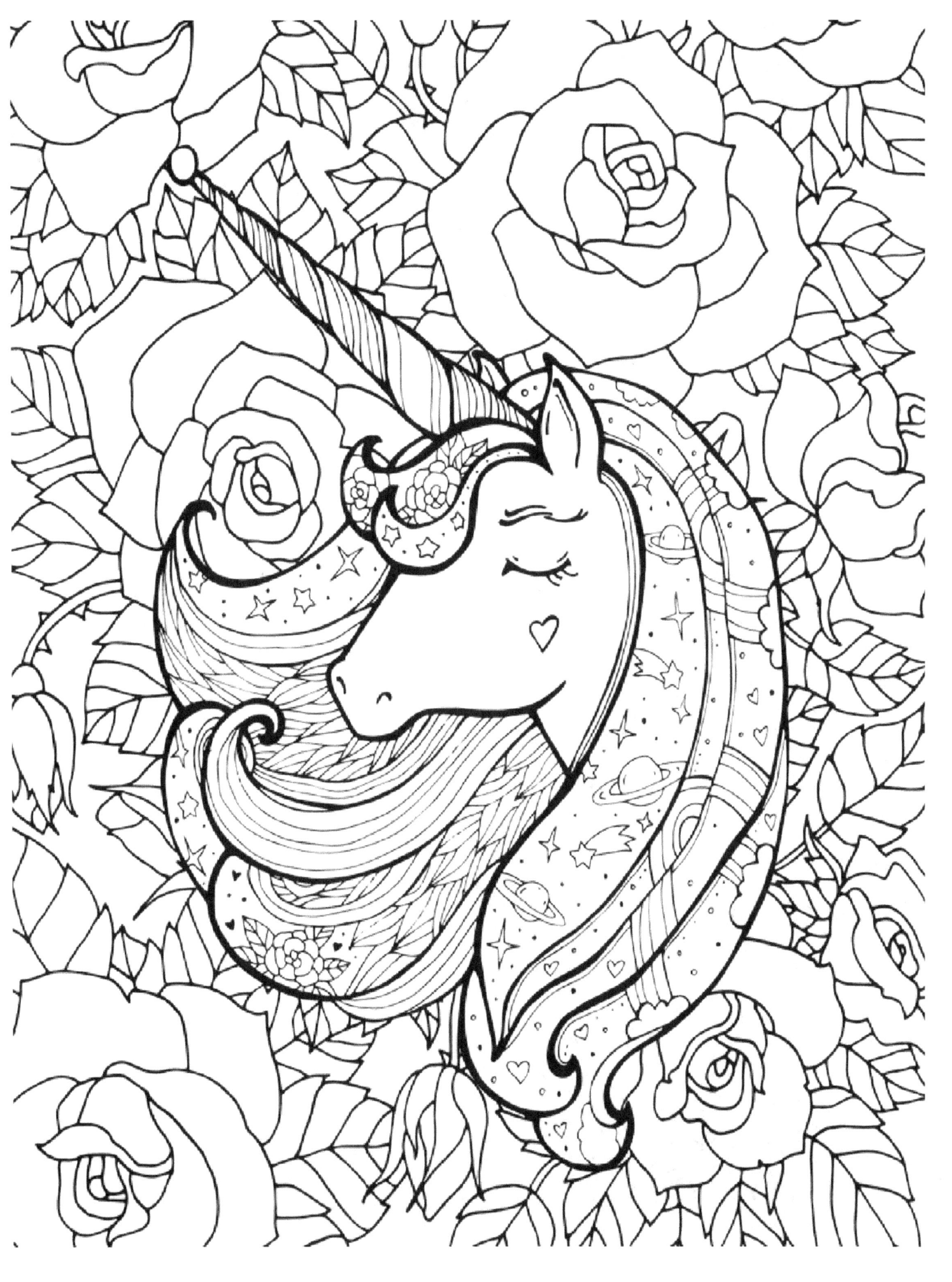

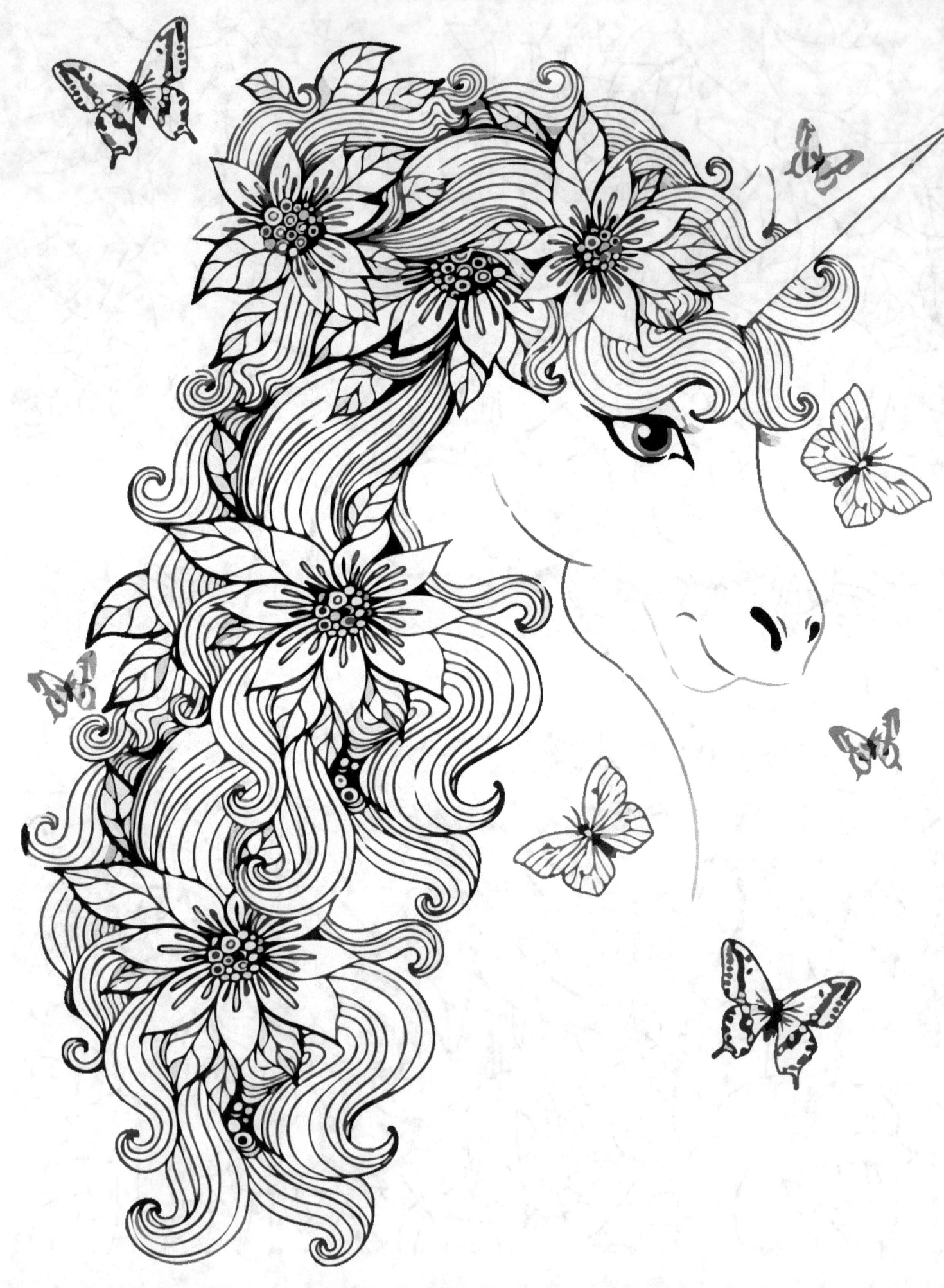

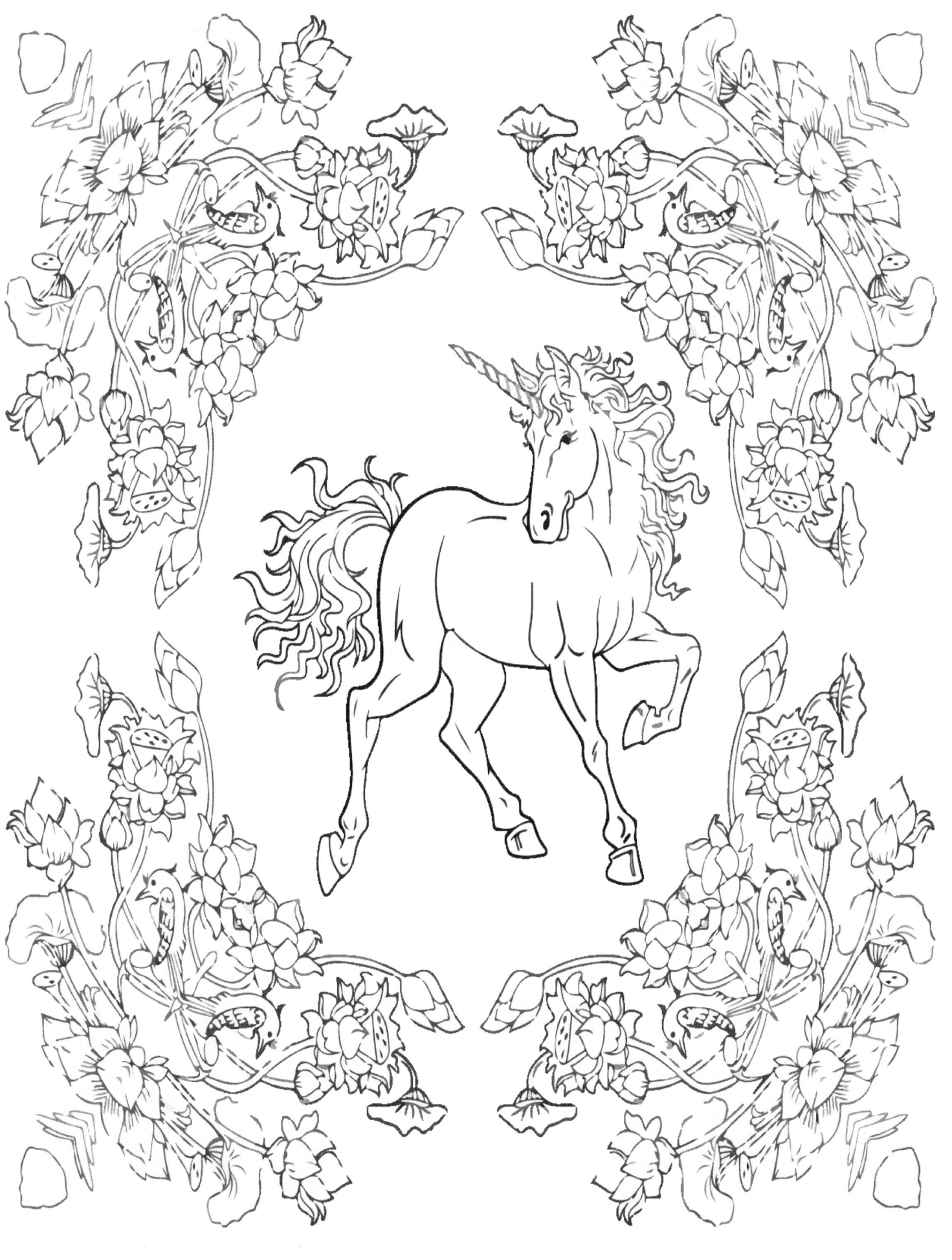

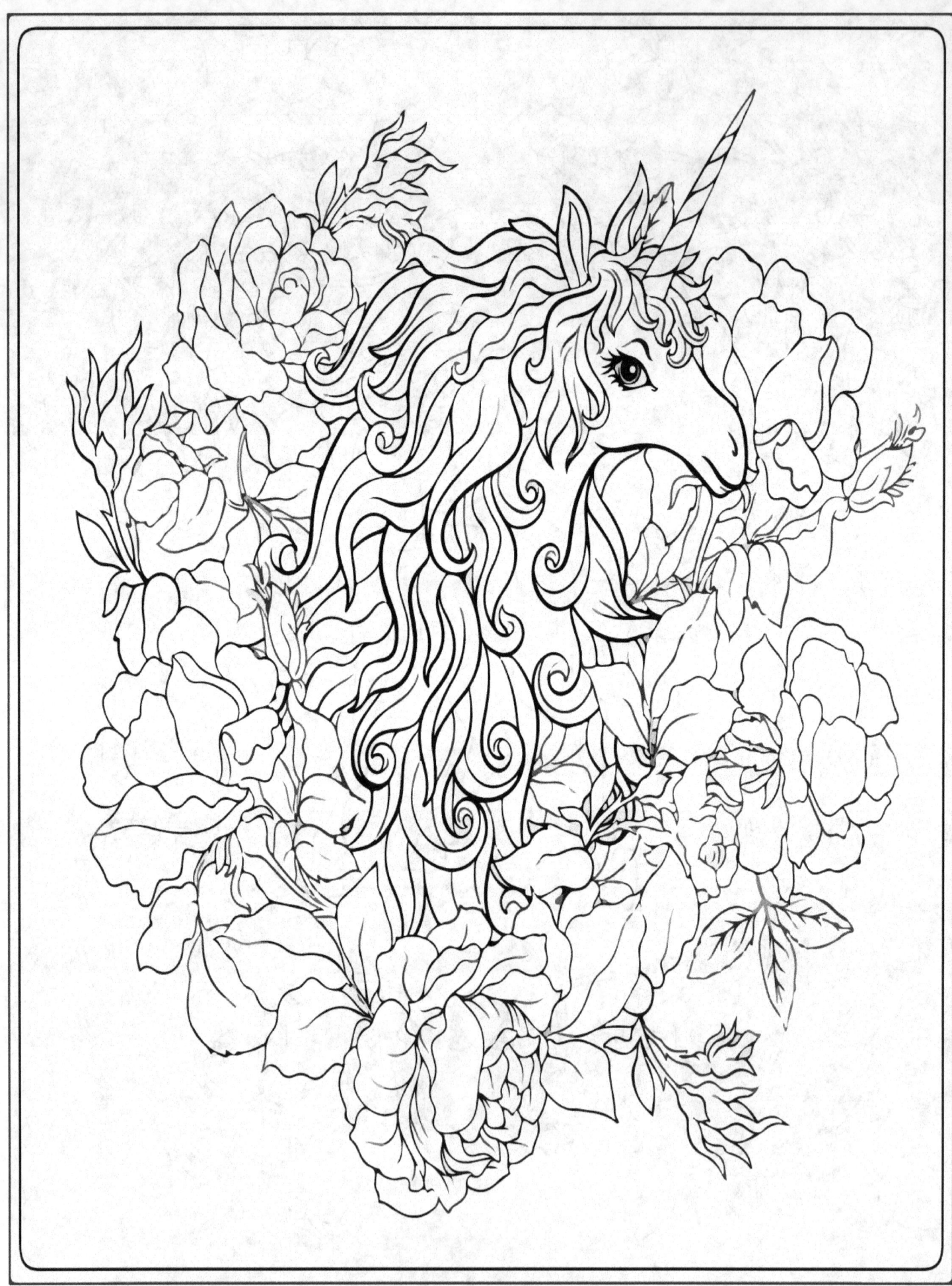

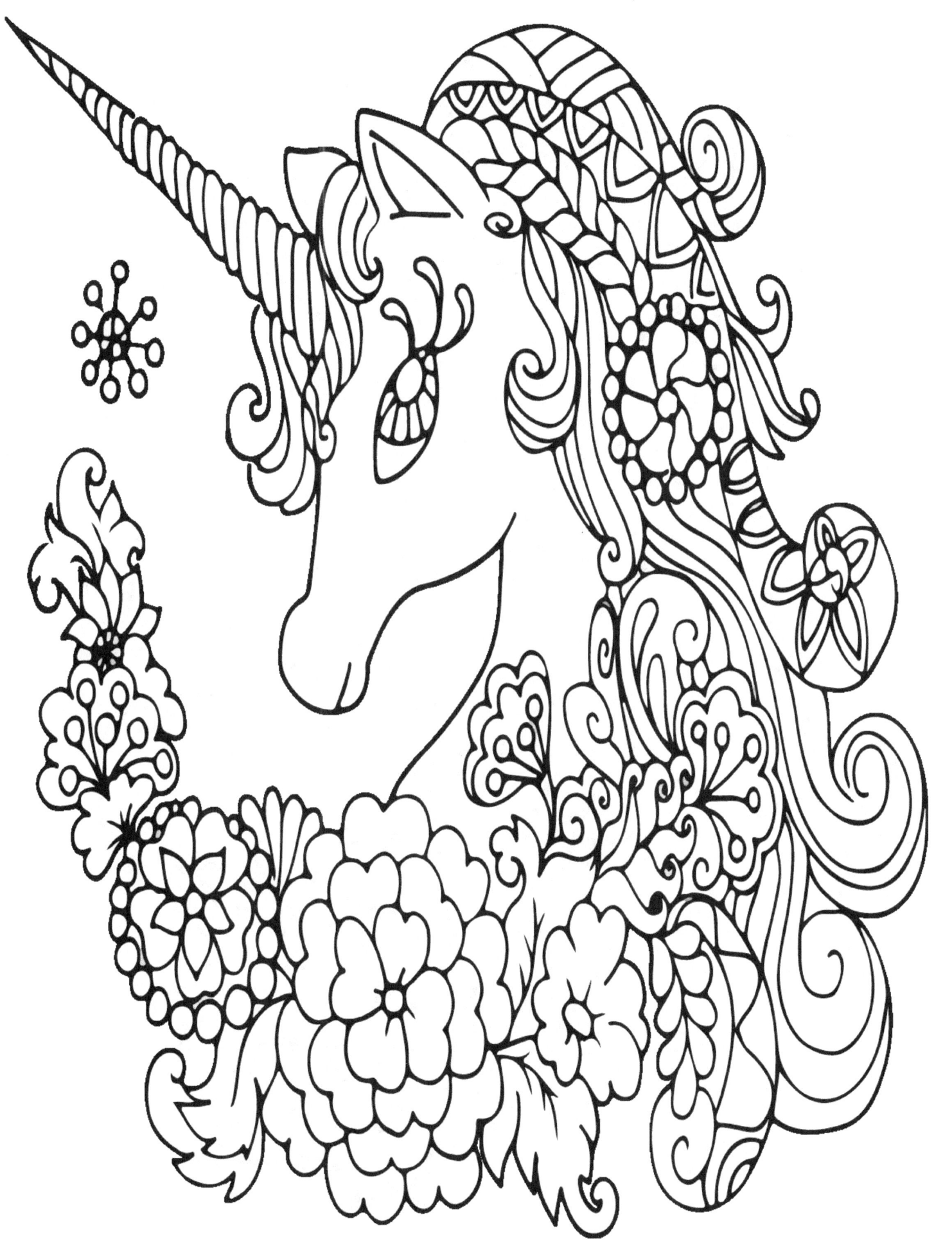

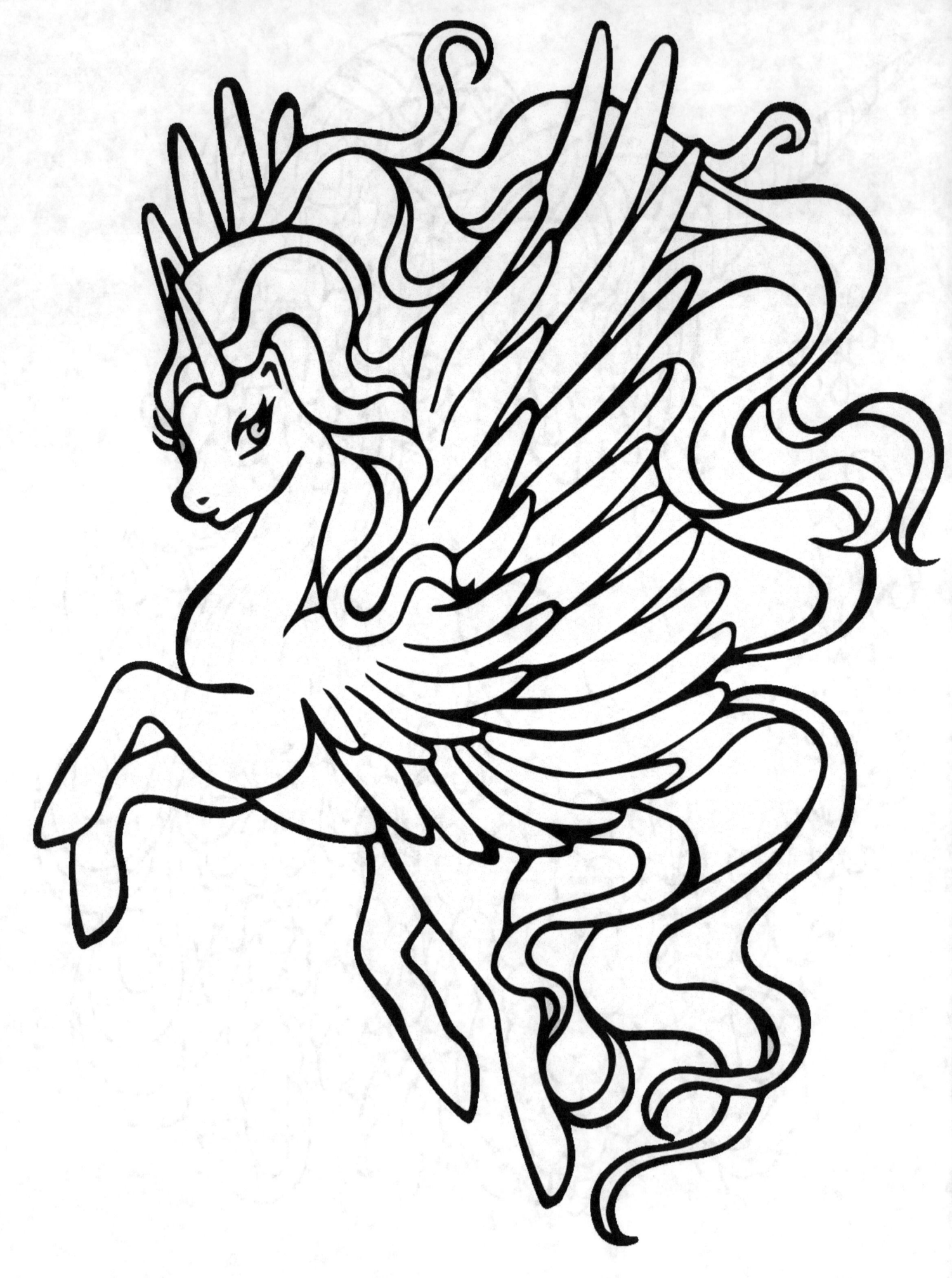

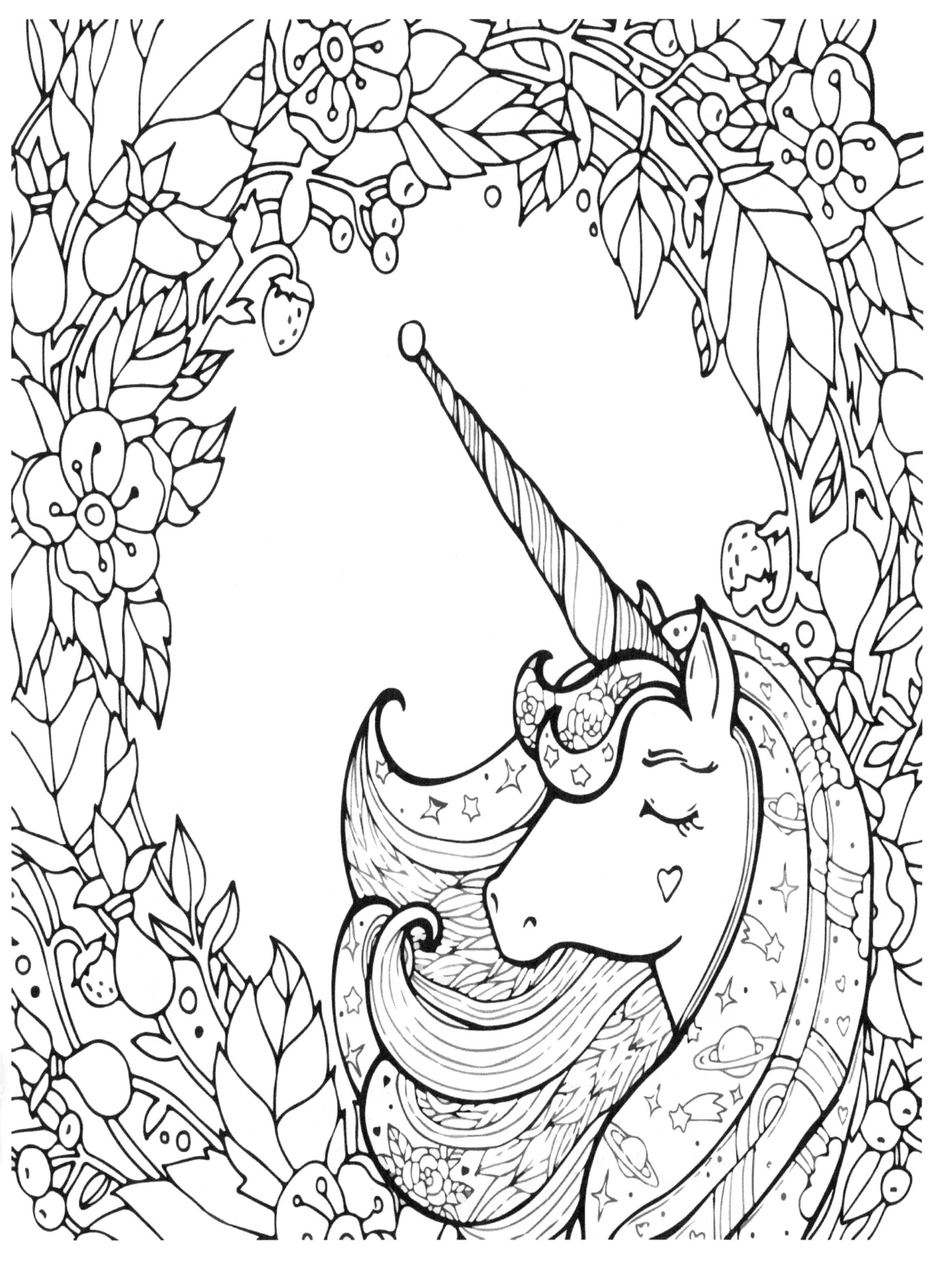

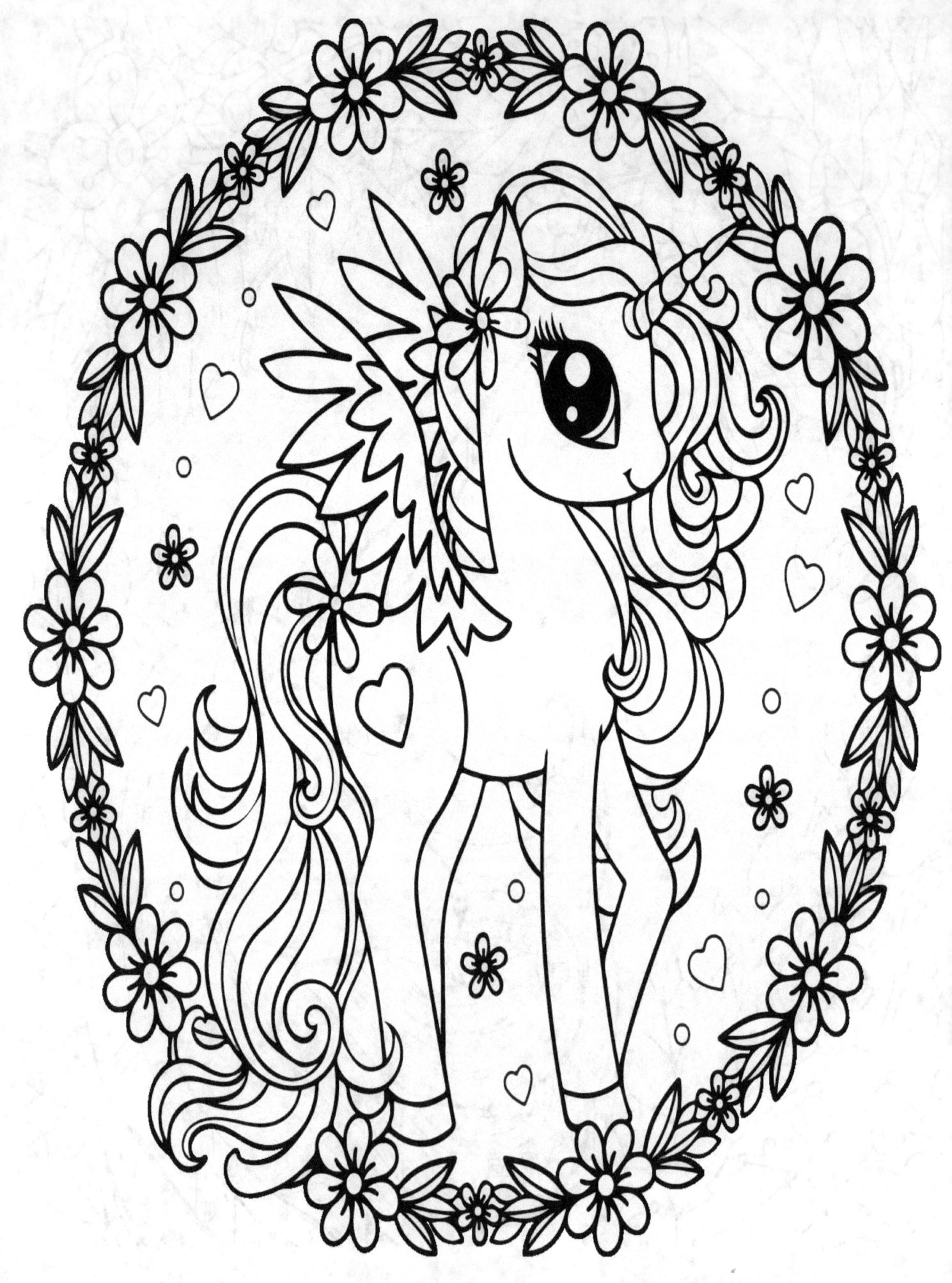

www.ingramcontent.com/pod-product-compliance
Lightning Source LLC
Chambersburg PA
CBHW060412220526
45465CB00008B/2852